Simon Heffer was born in 1960 and educated at King Edward VI School, Chelmsford, and Corpus Christi College, Cambridge, where he read English. After a spell as a medical journalist and leader writer for *The Times*, he joined the *Daily Telegraph* in 1986. In 1991 he became deputy editor and political correspondent of the *Spectator* also writing a column for the *Evening Standard* and then the *Daily Mail*. From June 1994 until October 1995 he was deputy editor of the *Daily Telegraph* and the paper's political columnist. Since 1995 he has been a columnist for the *Daily Mail* and a prolific contributor to other newspapers and periodicals. His life of Enoch Powell, *Like the Roman*, was published to widespread acclaim in 1998. He is married with two sons and lives in Essex.

POWER AND PLACE

The Political Consequences
of King Edward VII

Simon Heffer

A PHOENIX GIANT PAPERBACK

First published in Great Britain
by Weidenfeld & Nicolson in 1998
This paperback edition published in 1999
by Phoenix, an imprint of Orion Books Ltd,
Orion House, 5 Upper St Martin's Lane,
London WC2H 9EA

A CIP catalogue record for this book
is available from the British Library.

ISBN: 0 75380 750 5

Printed and bound in Great Britain by
Butler & Tanner Ltd, Frome and London

To Fred and Johnnie

I had long learnt that history was not an account of what actually had happened, but what people generally thought had happened.

Sir Frederick Ponsonby, *Recollections of Three Reigns*

CONTENTS

ILLUSTRATIONS

Between pages 182 and 183

Sources

[1] National Portrait Gallery
[2] Hulton Getty

ACKNOWLEDGMENTS

I have been greatly assisted by a number of people and institutions in assembling the material for this book, and wish to thank them sincerely. Material from the Royal Archives is reproduced by the gracious permission of Her Majesty the Queen. Her Majesty's Private Secretary, Sir Robert Fellowes, generously gave help, advice, encouragement and support, and I have a special debt to him. Mr Oliver Everett, Her Majesty's Librarian, provided me with help and hospitality, and made some exceptionally helpful comments on the manuscript. The Registrar of the Royal Archives, Lady de Bellaigue, made tireless endeavours on my behalf and extended warm hospitality to me at Windsor. Her detailed comments on my manuscript were indispensable and, thanks to the benefit of her immense expertise in this area, I have avoided several embarrassing errors. The Marquess of Salisbury kindly allowed me access to the papers of his great-grandfather, the 3rd Marquess. I am also grateful to Lord Salisbury's librarian, Mr Robin Harcourt-Williams. The British Library provided me with access to the papers of the 1st Earl of Balfour and Sir Henry Campbell-Bannerman. The Librarian of Churchill College, Cambridge, allowed me to see the papers of the 2nd Viscount Esher. The Cambridge University Library gave me access to the papers of the 1st Baron Hardinge of Penshurst.

My parents-in-law, Mr and Mrs Peter Clee, provided a life-support system during my visits to Windsor, without which the task of writing this book would have been greatly complicated and made far less pleasurable. I thank them profoundly. Lord Patten helped me with research material, and I sincerely acknowledge his friendship. Mr

Andrew Roberts opened a very important door for me, and gave me great companionship on some of my researches. Mr Matthew d'Ancona gave me great assistance in formulating constitutional theory. Miss Sally Chatterton, with great efficiency and initiative, kindly performed many vital tasks for me in assembling material. Miss Venetia Turner of G. Heywood Hill quickly found many necessary books for me.

Mr Ion Trewin sowed the seed that produced this book. I am indebted to him, and to my publisher, Mr Anthony Cheetham, for their close and stimulating interest in this project. My agent, Miss Georgina Capel, has as usual been wonderful.

Finally and fundamentally I am deeply grateful to my wife, Diana, without whose very special inspiration and support this book could not have been written. In dedicating it to our beloved sons, I trust she will recognise it as a compliment to her.

Simon Heffer
Great Leighs
4 February 1998

INTRODUCTION

T his is a book about the relations between a king and his ministers at a turning-point in the modern history of Great Britain: at the moment when the remnants of feudalism and hereditary power finally yielded to power that had been democratically elected, breaching the constitutional dam that had been Queen Victoria. It is an intimate portrait of those relations, characterised as much by the humanity, prejudices and foibles of those involved as by the necessities of constitutional practice in a changing world. It serves as a constitutional history, but it also describes how a man born to be head of state in what he and his contemporaries defined as a constitutional monarchy trained for, perceived and discharged his political duties. Above all, it seeks to discover what results for the politics of the time, and for the future of the British constitution, King Edward VII's conduct of monarchy had.

We are not used to thinking of King Edward VII as a political figure. For all his prerogative powers as head of state, he is generally established in popular historical memory in a less serious context. First and foremost, he has a popular reputation as a playboy. This goes beyond his various affairs with celebrated women of his time to embrace his love of overseas travel, of the turf and of gambling: without him the Tranby Croft baccarat scandal of 1891 would have had little of its lustre. He was no intellect. The best that can usually be said of him is that he provided a golden epilogue to the reign of his mother, Queen Victoria; and his reign will ever be associated with that metaphorically permanent summer that preceded the Great War.

Yet there was another, more profound dimension to King Edward, which caused him to leave a definite legacy to his country and the world. He deserves his own distinct place in British constitutional history, but it is one hitherto not well defined. During his reign, the notion of the powers of monarchy changed and developed. The battle between the elected forces of government and the hereditary ones reached its crisis. Queen Victoria is assumed to have been the last unconstitutional monarch, by which it is meant that she routinely disregarded the advice of her ministers, and forced them at times to do what she wanted. Her son is credited with being the first constitutional one, by which it is meant that he inevitably did as his ministers told him. Neither assumption is wholly true, the second perhaps less so than the first.

During the nine and a quarter years King Edward reigned he fought constant, sometimes attritional, battles with those ministers who had the misfortune to preside over departments in whose affairs he took a special interest, notably the Foreign Office and the War Office, but also the Admiralty. He was not inevitably compliant, either, with the wishes of the four men who served him as Prime Minister – Salisbury, Balfour, Campbell-Bannerman and Asquith. Towards the end of his reign he became a bulwark against the total democratisation of the British government. Finally, he was absorbed in what still remains the most bitter constitutional crisis of the twentieth century, the fight between the Lords and the Commons about the retention of the Upper House's veto on legislation. The extent of his power and influence can be measured by the speed with which, after his death, elected politicians saw to it that his son and heir allowed great changes to be made to the prerogative powers of the throne.

King Edward's main achievement was the initiation of the process that brought about the *entente cordiale* with France, and, later, the triple entente with France and Russia. The other great consequence of his conduct of his reign was the distance he put between himself and his highly antagonistic nephew, Kaiser Wilhelm II of Germany. In different ways, both became factors that helped stoke up the tensions between Britain and Germany that led to the Great War. They alone made King Edward a figure in modern political and diplomatic history whose actions require analysis and consideration, but they were far from being the extent of his political activity or its consequences. One or two of his ministers seem to have recognised his significance, and therefore (as politicians do) to have sought to play it down, the more to build up their own place in history. To dismiss the King as a *flaneur* who dabbled in politics only so far as he had to by convention – as one of his Prime Ministers did – is a travesty; and this book hopes to prove it.

PRINCE

VICTIM OF HIS UPBRINGING

Albert Edward, Prince of Wales, eldest son of Queen Victoria of Great Britain and Ireland and Prince Albert of Saxe-Coburg-Gotha, had in many respects the ideal temperament and upbringing for one destined to take an active interest in politics. Like many aristocratic children of his time, he grew up in a family that was involved in political life and through whose domestic circle politicians frequently moved. Unlike most other aristocratic children, however, he grew up partly under the influence of foreigners, and in a family hardly any of whose members could in the literal sense be said to be English. It was scarcely surprising, therefore, that he should so naturally take an interest in foreign affairs. He was not, like many politicians of his time and since, a gifted intellectual; but, again like many politicians of his time and since, he had a sufficient interest in human nature and the 'game' of politics to grasp its basic points, and to understand that it was, to use a twentieth-century phrase, about 'people'.

His bizarre breeding for the public service by his parents reflected more than anything the fact that at the time of his birth in November 1841 his mother and father were both just twenty-two years old, and (for all the training they had had for their respective stations in life) somewhat inexperienced. Prince Albert, a good Christian man of learning and true Carlylean earnestness, was devoted to his children and had a pleasant sense of fun, but was in other respects one of the worst sort of humourless Teutons. In bringing up the heir to the English throne, Albert relied heavily on the advice of his own mentor, Baron Stockmar, a former doctor and royal private secretary. Albert

4

Edward's role in childhood and youth was, it seems, to be an almost incessant disappointment to his parents. His shortcomings, as perceived by the Queen and the Prince Consort, were widely known at court and, inevitably, subtly disseminated therefrom. On the occasion of the Prince's eighteenth birthday, on 9 November 1859, Delane, the editor of *The Times*, acting apparently on a court briefing about the character and attainments of the Prince, patronisingly observed that 'he may be great without the possession of extraordinary talents': an observation that, according to the Prince's first official biographer, Sir Sidney Lee, 'echoed the disappointing conviction cherished [at court] that the heir-apparent, now come of age, showed no signs of commanding ability'.[1]

This assessment seems to have been formed largely because the boy was not as high-minded, or, to put it another way, as boot-faced, as his parents. That he was no intellectual should not have counted against him, as it was a condition apparently *de rigueur* in most of his family. Yet he had certain attainments and serious interests. He was fully bilingual in his parents' languages, though it seems to have been an exaggeration that he spoke with a German burr; the guttural 'r' he affected appears to have been just that – an affectation. He acquired faultless French too, highly useful as the diplomatic language of the civilised world. Lee claims that six-year-old Bertie was alert enough to grasp the threats to other European thrones of the events of 1848. That seems somewhat far-fetched. However, if true, it might indicate that the ultra-careful regard the Prince had for monarchy went deeper into the soul than simple self-interest ever could. He gave a mature indication of this after the murders of King Alexander and Queen Draga of Serbia in 1904, when explaining his refusal to recognise the new regime until the officers who had carried out the murders of these two unpleasant and hated royals had been removed from their posts. '*Mon métier à moi est d'être Roi....* I cannot be indifferent to the assassination of a member of my profession or, if you like, a member of my guild. We should be obliged to shut up our businesses if we, the kings, were to consider the assassinations of kings as of no consequence at all.'[2]

A visit to France with his parents in 1855 is credited by most biographers as having sealed the Prince's love of that country, a love that was to form the centrepiece of his main diplomatic activity once he had ascended the throne. But it is more certain that the Prince, by nature a gregarious youth seeking to shrug off and escape from the

5

rigidities of his Teutonic upbringing without schoolfellows – except his own brother, Prince Alfred – and at the hands of Stockmar and a series of devoted professional gentlemen, found at last the scope to express these feelings on his first great overseas trip, to North America in 1860.

While Lord Palmerston, the Prime Minister at the time of the Prince's coming-of-age, sought to educate the youth about 'how greatly the welfare of this great nation may be influenced by the course which you may pursue', there were to be few chances for Albert Edward to put such theory into commission.[3] His father's death from typhoid at the early age of forty-two, in December 1861, should have been the opportunity for him to take a heavy share of his mother's responsibilities, not least because she herself signalled that, devastated by her bereavement as she was, she had no intention of fulfilling much of a public role in future. However, the Prince Consort's timing defeated his son's ambitions. His father had had a dim view of his frivolous and unintellectual nature, which had only partly been improved by good reports of the Prince's conduct and demeanour on his first few overseas excursions. However, a couple of months before the Prince Consort's death he and the Queen had been scandalised by reports of goings-on in Dublin, during a brief spell their son passed at the military camp at the Curragh, and which had included one of the Prince's first (and, regrettably for him, most publicised) forays into carnal pleasure. On her husband's death, the Queen was determined to keep everything as he would have wished it, which included the ossification of the Prince Consort's views on people and policies. Although Albert had forgiven his son for his loose conduct, he had died having settled with his wife that Albert Edward was simply feckless and untrustworthy; and so, despite her obvious deep maternal affection for him, he was to remain for years in the Queen's estimation, with no court of appeal open to him in the matter.

The Queen had taken the entirely unconstitutional view that her husband was the next most important personage in the realm to herself, and to try to enshrine this prejudice in law had asked Palmerston in 1857 to enact a statute according the Prince Consort a place in the order of precedence above that of the Prince of Wales. Pressure was put on the Queen through Stockmar to dispense with this notion, which she reluctantly did; but it meant that, when Albert died, she remained firmly of the view that their eldest son was quite unfit to take his father's place – a place as second to her that had no position in the constitution, but which existed, *de facto*, in the Queen's world view. This led her towards a serious perversion of the constitutional position. Because she viewed her husband as irreplaceable, and because to allow their son and her heir to take some royal responsibilities would be tantamount to replacing Albert, the Prince of Wales would have to go without those responsibilities. 'I am *also determined*', she wrote on 24 December 1861 to her uncle Leopold, 'that *no one* person, may *he* be ever so good, ever so devoted, among my servants – is to lead or guide or dictate *to me*.'[4] As a dutiful wife, she had accepted her husband's lead, guidance and possibly even dictation readily. She would not take such from her son; but, then, that is not at all what her son wanted. She would deal with Albert Edward, and the rest of her children, as the Prince Consort would have wished, and that view would not change for years. As a result, as Lee observes, 'from any share in her constitutional functions of rule, she to the last rigidly excluded him' – though it is hard to see how, within the rules, even the heir to the throne could carry out the constitutional functions of a monarch unless a regency were declared.[5] In 1862, not long after Albert's death, the venerable Lord Clarendon, once and future Foreign Secretary in Liberal governments, stayed with the Queen at Windsor and gave her 'much wholesome advice' on the future of the Prince of Wales, saying that she should bring him on 'by showing him correspondence and consulting him on matters of home and foreign policy, instead of treating him like a child'.[6] But a child, in that respect, was what he was destined to remain until he was well advanced into middle age.

POLITICAL INSTINCTS

Sir Sidney Lee notes that 'amid the multifarious calls of the Prince's busy life the observation, discussion and criticism of politics knew no interruption at any period of his adult career. If foreign affairs chiefly arrested his attention, he followed home affairs with unceasing zest – especially the changing fortunes of parties and the personal vicissitudes of party leaders.'[7] He adds that the Prince constantly met the leading political players when out in society and would question them 'without reserve on pending crises'. Nor, he says, 'was he backward in sending them written expressions of his views on those political themes which strongly excited his interest, and in freely offering them recommendations for the distribution of honours and appointments'.

Lee claims that 'the main political opinions to which the Prince was faithful through life reflected Lord Palmerston's creed, of which the chief articles were the maintenance of England's dominant influence on the world, the dissemination through Europe of the principles of constitutional government and of constitutional liberty, the protection of subject races from oppression, confidence in the value of religious toleration, and a suspicion of abrupt change in the established institutions at home'.[8] He adds that the Prince had a 'conviction that constitutional monarchy was the best of all forms of government': a euphemistic way of saying that, also like Palmerston, the Prince was careful to support anything that entrenched the position of his own class, and to be on his guard against threats to his position or dignity. Lee does say that, unlike Palmerston, the Prince was not so enthusiastic about war, and contends he was as distrustful of autocracy as he was of militant republicanism – 'like Queen Victoria, the Prince showed every respect for the memory of the Stuarts, but it was the tragic fall of a royal family from its high estate and not King Charles I's method of Government that generated his sympathy'. This is reflected, too, in the Prince's open-minded attitude to the French republic, and to the two audiences he had of the Pope on undergraduate visits to Italy, despite protests from some more bigoted Protestants at home.

The Prince always showed, in his biographer's view, a 'correct indifference' to party programmes, 'yet in private talk he freely expressed his opinion of measures and policies, inclining now to one side, now to the other'.[9] Lee's conclusion is that 'despite his Whiggish leanings, some Tory elements mingled in his political sentiment'. Such sentiments often manifested themselves. For example, he wrote to Lord Beaconsfield (as Benjamin Disraeli had become that year) on 27 November 1876 observing that he had breached precedent by recommending a commoner for a place in an order of chivalry that that hitherto always been filled by a peer.[10] Although the Prince wanted a more democratic group around the court – not least because he longed to be surrounded by people who could amuse and excite him, a condition not regularly to be found among the established caste of courtier – he was less willing to see the logical extension of these ideas throughout society. He complained when the pro-reform demonstrations took place in 1866, and even the Queen took issue with

8

him for his reactionary views. He wrote to her, having been chided for this, that 'I did not mean that the really hard-working labouring classes were getting too much power, because they indeed deserve to be noticed when they attain a higher sphere of existence by their own merits and industry. But I alluded to the "mob", and what are known as "roughs", and they, to a much greater extent than people are aware of are getting a greater power.'[11]

There were opportunities provided for him to exercise some influence on public affairs, and therefore to help train his judgment and give him political experience of a sort. The reactionary stamp seemed quickly to pass, and he began to look like a proper coalition between Liberal and Tory. He sat, when a little older, on royal commissions into the provision of dwelling-houses for the working classes, and on provision for the needs of the aged poor. He was sympathetic to trades unionism, opening on 16 July 1870 a Workmen's International Exhibition in London. In his speech he said that the event 'cannot fail to meet with cordial approval of all who are interested in the growth and rise of manufacturers and wish to connect that growth with a corresponding increase of sympathy and friendly relations between employers and their workmen'.[12]

The political temper of his early household was Whig: Colonel Robert Kingscote, an extra equerry to the Prince, had been a Liberal MP. Major George Henry Grey, an equerry, was the son and father of Liberal statesmen. Lord Alfred Hervey, the second lord of the bedchamber, was a former Liberal MP too. General Sir William Knollys, a former president of the Council of Military Education, who was appointed treasurer and comptroller of the Prince's household in 1862, was a Liberal. So was his son Francis, who assisted him with his work and who in 1870, at the age of thirty-three, became the Prince's private secretary. Several of those prominent in the Prince's inner circle of friends were Liberals too, albeit of a rightward-leaning stamp: Lord Carrington; the Marquess of Hartington, heir to the dukedom of Devonshire; Earl Spencer; and the young Earl of Rosebery, to whom Francis Knollys wrote on behalf of the Prince in 1873 to ask whether he would mind letting the Prince and his younger brother, the Duke of Edinburgh, use his London home as a place for them to meet their 'actress friends' (Rosebery did mind).[13]

The Queen, when her favourite Disraeli was under attack in the

1870s, complained of the anti-Conservative activities of the 'Marlborough House set', which took its name from the Prince's London residence.[14] Sir Sidney Lee, however, does say the Prince was sometimes guilty of 'opportunism'. Once the Conservatives embraced the Liberal reform measures in 1867, he smothered his own doubts on the issue; he was often influenced to take a certain view on politics because that view was held by someone he liked or with whose views he strongly sympathised. Throughout Albert Edward's career as Prince and King, no consideration counted for so much as whether or not he liked somebody. Sheer talent aside from that was very much a secondary consideration.

The Prince took his seat in the Lords, as Duke of Cornwall, at the first opportunity, on 5 February 1863. He had come of age less than three months earlier, and Parliament had been in recess ever since. He took his seat after the reading of the Queen's Speech – read not by the Queen, who was still in retirement from public life after her bereavement, but by the Lord Chancellor – in which his own impending marriage to Princess Alexandra, daughter of the heir to the Danish throne, was formally announced. He sat on the cross benches and stayed until late in the evening to hear the debate on the address. His two main political mentors at this time, Palmerston and Lord Granville, the leader of the Liberal party in the House of Lords, both urged him to attend the Lords regularly, as what he would hear might prove instructive. His mother, though, disapproved, saying that he should attend only on important occasions if he happened to be in town. After a few years, however, the Prince began to ignore his mother's wishes, and from then until his accession he would be a regular attender, and occasional speaker, in Lords' debates, sitting on several uncontroversial select committees of the House (such as one to discuss whether the future supply of horses would match demand for them).

He would regularly sit in the Peers' gallery in the Commons, and from there heard Disraeli introducing the Tory Reform Bill on 25 February 1867. However, he was at the start better acquainted with and more sympathetic to Gladstone, having been a childhood friend of Gladstone's son William; and once he became Prime Minister in 1868 the Prince wrote him a fulsome letter of congratulation, and praised him for appointing his friend Earl Spencer as Lord Lieutenant of Ireland. When Disraeli won in 1874 the Prince was just as charming.

He wrote from Russia, where he was visiting, to congratulate Disraeli on becoming Prime Minister; and invited him and Gladstone to Marlborough House to dine shortly after the election.[15] However, Disraeli – who had been careful to ingratiate himself with the Prince at every opportunity, ever since first meeting him at Windsor as a sixteen-year-old boy – would usually take Queen Victoria's side against her son when the two of them disagreed.

There were strong views among certain Liberals that the Queen should, in light of her abhorrence of public life since her husband's death, abdicate in favour of her son; but she would not hear of it, and expected the people to show her their full sympathy in her bereavement. The Prince had no truck with notions about her abdicating. Although she stayed on the throne, her son became *de facto* the head of society, not just in Britain but, in time, throughout Europe. The Queen bowed to reality and, from the time when he was twenty-one, allowed her son to conduct levees, and to receive foreign heads of state on their visits to London. She viewed these as non-political activities; but meeting those diplomats and foreign crowned heads provided the Prince with an opportunity to conduct diplomatic business, and acquire high-quality information, unseen by the Queen. Also, because of the Prince's interest in politics, and because political life was becoming steadily more democratic and less the exclusive preserve of aristocratic families, he had a strong influence on breaking down the rigid class barriers that had hitherto prevented easy entry by newcomers into society.

Lee wrote that the Prince took an 'active interest from early manhood in the distribution of the Crown's patronage'.[16] Thanks to his 'familiar relations' with successive Prime Ministers he was able to importune them for honours for his friends 'incessantly'. Nor was he just concerned with high honours: humble placements in the diplomatic corps were just as likely to excite his attention. He was never without a view on who should be favoured when governments were being formed or reconstructed; and would let his mother, through her private secretary, know his views, and even, later on, Prime Ministers themselves, usually with the intention of furthering the career of close friends. He was not always successful. He interfered in appointments to embassies, in the Church and to the Privy Council. Nor was this a habit he felt able to break when, as king, he was weighed down by far more pressing cares of state.

FAMILY TIES

One of the main drawbacks of the Prince's involvement with
international diplomacy was that he was frequently perceived to be
taking sides at a time when British foreign policy was rooted in the
country's neutrality. Because of family ties it was hard for him to avoid
taking sides, though he was often indiscreet, bearing out his mother's
main reservation about him. Also, because it was members of his
extended family abroad, rather than democratically elected ministers,
who were often discharging policy, the Prince's relations with them
could have a more direct political effect than might otherwise have
been the case. However, he began well. Lord Augustus Loftus, the
British ambassador to Berlin, entertained the Prince as he passed
through on his way to Russia in the autumn of 1866, and reported back
to London that 'the golden opinions he was winning in every country
and every court in Europe had an "intrinsic value" in England's
international relations'.[17]

Ironically, given that the Prince's family were German, and that his
elder sister Vicky was the Crown Princess of Prussia, he was most
strongly perceived as being hostile to Prussia and Prussian expansionism – which, at the time, under the influence of Bismarck was the
state's principal policy. This problem first manifested itself in 1864,
when the combined armies of Prussia and Austria sought to wrest from
Denmark the two duchies of Schleswig and Holstein. Since the Prince's
father-in-law had, just a few months earlier, succeeded as King
Christian IX of Denmark, there was little question about which of the
combatants the heir to the British throne would favour. This was a
quite correct loyalty for him, but one he would have been better
advised to hold privately. He had already shown himself easily swayed
by romantic and emotional considerations in undertaking quasi-
diplomatic acts – he had, but weeks earlier and to his mother's horror,
rushed from his new country house at Sandringham in Norfolk to join
a party at the London home of his friend the Duke of Sutherland for
the buccaneering Italian unmaker of kings, Garibaldi.

At least in his support of the Danes the Prince was to an extent in
line with government policy – Palmerston upbraided Prussia for the
assault, but would not hear of any intervention by Britain. The Queen,
resorting to the ultimate authority in claiming that the late Prince
Consort 'would have at all hazards avoided a British conflict with
Prussia', endorsed this neutrality, and was embarrassed by her son's

pro-Danish sentiments.[18] He wrote, for example, to Mrs Bruce, the wife of his governor, on 17 February 1864 that the attack 'will be a stain for ever on Prussian history' and that 'it is very wrong of our government not to have interfered before now'.[19] He told Spencer on 5 May that 'if we had sent our fleet to the Baltic at the beginning, all this bloodshed might possibly have been avoided, and we should cut a much better figure in Europe than we do at present'.[20] Having failed to persuade the government to intervene militarily, the Prince then started on the Foreign Secretary, Earl Russell, to have him make some diplomatic interventions; but nothing came of that, save for a conference in London in April where the parties to the conflict met to discuss the terms of the Danish humiliation.

The Prussian ambassador, Count von Bernstorff – the only representative of a European power in London with whom the assiduous Prince was not on congenial social terms – started to complain of the Prince's interference. The Queen told Sir William Knollys to order her son to restrain himself, but that proved difficult. Eventually, when the Prince realised he was on the losing side, he more and more kept his own counsel, though Gladstone, out riding with him and Granville on 8 July 1864, recorded in his diary that the Prince 'showed a little Danism'.[21] When paying a visit to his in-laws in Copenhagen later that year, the Prince was compelled by his mother to visit Germany too, in an attempt to rebut claims of any hostility by him towards that country. However, the events put him on his guard for the rest of his life against Prussia and Prussianism; and, once his nephew William became Kaiser in 1888, he would not lack for evidence to justify his suspicions.

The simple fact was that Prussia turned from a medium-sized but powerful kingdom into the German Empire within a decade. English sensibilities were shocked by the progression, and slow to take on board its potential implications. A gap of culture was, though, the greatest problem. Not for nothing did Bismarck give Carlyle, the great British exponent of the might-is-right philosophy, the Prussian Ordre pour le Mérite: Carlyle understood what Germanism was about. His fellow countrymen, who were stopping reading him, did not.

His wife's family caused the Prince other new foreign exertions. His brother-in-law was elected King George I of Greece in 1863, and throughout a long and difficult reign (which ended, in 1913, in assassination) the Prince frequently importuned British governments to lend support and assistance to Greek policy and ambitions. Since the

Greeks routinely went about their national aspirations in an undiplo-
matic, not to say violent, way, this interest was not always welcomed by
the government. Indeed, Sir Sidney Lee writes that once the Balkan
crisis of the late 1870s was under way it 'revived in full intensity the
national aspirations of Greece, and the Prince's desire to help his
brother-in-law at times embarrassed his relations with Mr Disraeli's
government, whose policy scarcely favoured Greek aggrandisement'.[22]
King George tried to dissuade his subjects from invading parts of the
Ottoman Empire that they believed to be rightfully theirs, but to little
avail. The Prince invited King George and his Queen to stay at
Marlborough House in 1876, and in the course of the visit introduced
them to Disraeli. The following year, a return visit by the Princess to
her brother coincided with the threat of Greece joining Russia and
some of the Balkan states in an offensive against Turkey; and the
Prince was the official bearer of advice, via the telegraph, to his
brother-in-law from Beaconsfield (as Disraeli had become), warning of
the inadvisability of the Greeks becoming involved in a wider conflict.
It was advice the King heeded.

King George was not the only member of his wife's family to
exercise the Prince's diplomatic interests. His sister-in-law, Dagmar, in
1866 married the future Tsar Alexander III of Russia, and provided a
new emotional reason for the Prince to change one of his hitherto
firmly held views on foreign policy. Palmerston had brought him up to
believe that Russia, so recently the enemy in the Crimea, had
undesirable intentions towards India; but once he acquired the wife of
the Tsarevitch as a sister-in-law, and having heard many anti-Turkish
and pro-Russian protests from King George, the Prince began to
soften his views towards Russia. He was allowed to travel to Russia for
Dagmar's wedding in the autumn of 1866 only once he had given
assurances to his mother and to the Foreign Secretary, Lord Stanley,
that he would not voice his usual strong anti-Turkish sentiments and so
give the Tsar's court an entirely misleading picture of the British
government's policy. The Prince was determined to improve Anglo-
Russian relations, and even told Derby, the Prime Minister, in a letter
of 13 October 1866 that 'I should only be too happy to be the means in
any way of promoting the *entente cordiale* between Russia and our own
country'.[23] From such phrases it seems all too clear that the Prince, like
some royal personages after him, wanted to act like a roving
ambassador as a means of having a role, and to prove that his mother's

mistrust of him was undeserved. In an age when so much international diplomacy was most effectively conducted among royal families – because in the autocracies it was monarchs who, often, made the main political decisions – his willingness to be involved was far more understandable, and useful, than it might be today.

The Prince's deliberate cultivation of foreign ambassadors in London served a twofold purpose. It was a way of circumventing the deliberate exclusion from matters of state imposed upon him by his mother – these ambassadors often knew more of what was happening in British high politics than he did, never mind in matters of foreign policy. However, it also satisfied his rather childlike desire to collect significant people, a hobby that was the natural use of his rank, formidable charm and social talents. The result was that in his dealings with his extended family he was often peculiarly well briefed on the diplomatic and foreign policy issues concerning his country and theirs.

For all his ties of blood elsewhere, it was, paradoxically, with Bonapartist France that the Prince formed his closest affections. This sentiment was to have the most profound long-term implications. In June 1866, as Bismarck turned Prussia's attentions towards putting Austria in her place, the Prince told the French ambassador that the only way to keep Prussia in check was for the French and the British to forge an alliance. This view was to be sorely tested in 1870, when France declared war on Prussia following a disagreement about which of them should provide the candidate for the Spanish throne. The Prince felt that France had more right to be involved than Prussia in this matter, but was hampered publicly by Gladstone's declaration of neutrality, except in the matter of defending Belgium should either of the belligerents violate that country's neutrality. His sister, of course, was firmly identified with the Prussian side, and his mother's only regret, according to Lee, was that 'Prussians and Englishmen were not, as at Waterloo, resisting the French side by side'.[24] Bernstorff, the Prussian ambassador, almost immediately picked up word of the Prince's violent pro-French feelings on the society grapevine. Specifically, Bernstorff was informed that the Prince had told the French ambassador that he wished for Prussia's defeat, and had expressed similar views to Austria's representative too.

This rumour reached the ears of the Crown Princess, who speedily relayed it to her mother, Queen Victoria. True or not, the Prince wrote a letter of categorical denial to Gladstone on 21 July 1870, six days after the outbreak of war; and his mother ordered Granville, the Foreign Secretary and a long-standing friend of the Prince's, to send an unequivocal contradiction to Berlin. Granville, who as we shall learn had his doubts about the Prince's reliability, was not keen to lend his name to such an enterprise. He advised that the contradiction was best sent by the Prince himself to his sister. Gladstone, meanwhile, warned the Prince about 'the necessity of his keeping back at this juncture whatever private sentiments he may entertain on the subject of the disastrous war'.[25] Finally, Francis Knollys, who had just become the Prince's private secretary, called on Bernstorff and denied the truth of the story the ambassador had relayed back to Berlin.

Bernstorff was unconvinced. The whole episode simply showed the difficulties of two bodies, a future crowned head and a government, both trying to advance different foreign policies on behalf of the same state – for, however much the Prince spoke for himself, he could not but be seen to be speaking for his country. The Prince had great ambitions for himself, and a distinct evaluation of his own capabilities, that were so far unsupported by his attainments. On 21 August, as the French were taking a serious beating from the Prussians, he wrote to his mother begging her to allow him to act as a peacemaker between the French Emperor and the King of Prussia. The Queen dismissed the notion as impracticable: not surprisingly, given that the Prince's reputation for partisanship hardly qualified him as an honest broker. Ironically, when the following winter the Prince sent regards via a Foreign Office messenger to four of his German kinsmen stationed at Versailles, he was rounded upon by radical pro-French politicians, including his future friend Sir Charles Dilke, for apparently congratulating Prussia. He could do nothing right, which should have been a warning to him to act with more circumspection in forming his own private international alliances and giving vent to his ideas on foreign policy.

The Franco-Prussian War, despite having been started by the French, simply seemed to confirm the Prince's existing view that Germany, into which Prussia had now aggrandised itself, was a menace for the future and bent on continental domination. Relations were soon restored with his sister and her family, but the unease would never go away – an unease fostered among the paranoiac Prussians convinced that the Prince, with his well-known sympathy for the French, was determined to undermine them.

A LIFELONG FRIENDSHIP

The coming of a republic to France after the débâcle of the war with Prussia presented no great difficulties to the Prince. The Third Republic was recognised by the British government on 12 February 1871. The following year the Prince, at the urging of Granville, the Foreign Secretary, paid President Thiers a visit. The two men got on well, and the Prince followed up his visit by sitting in on the proceedings of the National Assembly. The Prince and the President met again informally later in the year when the Prince was cruising off the coast of France, and the frequency of their intercourse inevitably caused disquiet in Berlin. For all his cordiality to the Republic, the Prince still maintained good relations with the defeated Bonapartist royalty, as he did with members of France's older royal houses. Sometimes these relations, and those the Prince kept up with the old *noblesse*, were felt to be too good: in 1874, when the Prince planned an extended progress around the châteaux of the Loire, staying in the houses of the fervently royalist aristocracy, the Queen was sufficiently concerned to ask Disraeli, who had just become her Prime Minister, to talk the Prince out of it. Disraeli could not, but he sought to defuse the situation by asking the Prince to visit the new President, Marshal MacMahon, while in France. This the Prince did, but his visit still attracted fierce criticism.

He maintained good relations with the Republic's ambassadors to London too, helped by the fact that they were usually aristocrats whom he had encountered socially. When the last of these, the Marquis d'Harcourt, retired in 1879, the Prince tried to have his mother veto the appointment of his replacement, a reputed militant communist named Lacour. *Figaro*, which the Prince often read, had attacked Lacour; but Granville, at the Foreign Office again once the appointment came to be ratified, made his own enquiries and found that many of the allegations against Lacour were groundless. Ironically, he was put forward as envoy only because the first choice, the Marquis de Noailles, had been rejected by the Queen as morally unsound. In one of her sporadic fits of constitutionality she accepted Granville's advice and rejected her son's. As might have been expected, the Prince received Lacour with charm and courtesy once he had presented his credentials, despite having done so much to prevent him from taking up his post. His earlier hostility was the more remarkable because, from 1878, he had been on good terms with the main architect of the

Third Republic's success, Léon Gambetta. This relationship was forged out of the enduring understanding both men had about the dangers of Prussianism.

The Prince's early meetings with Gambetta during his May 1878 visit to Paris show him winning plaudits for his diplomacy, as Britain sought to allay French doubts over the recent Anglo-Turkish convention. Lord Lyons, the British ambassador in Paris, wrote to Lord Salisbury, the Foreign Secretary, that 'the Prince of Wales acquitted himself with great skill'.[26] Salisbury himself wrote to the Prince to thank him 'very earnestly' for what he had done with Gambetta, over whom the Prince's 'influence' had been exerted with 'skill', with a favourable result for French public opinion.[27] 'The crisis', Salisbury told him, 'has been one of no little delicacy: and if the leaders of French opinion had definitely turned against us, a disagreeable and even hazardous condition of estrangement between the two countries might have grown up, which would have been very much to be regretted.' The Prince, for so long patronised by his mother and her ministers, was genuinely thrilled to have helped, and was charmingly modest about what he had done. He replied to Salisbury that 'if I have in any way by the personal interview I had with M Gambetta tended to allay the irritation which was manifest in France by our taking Cyprus I am beyond measure pleased'.[28]

The Prince's anti-Prussian feelings were exhibited not just in the context of that state's activities against Denmark or France. His mother's cousin King George V of Hanover, ousted by Bismarck during the construction of the Second Reich, died in exile in Paris in June 1878. His funeral there was organised by the French government, and the King's remains were then taken to Windsor, at Queen Victoria's request, for interment. Given these close ties of kinship, it was hardly surprising that the Prince of Wales should have been at the funeral, where he was the most glittering of a long cast of European royalty, much of it dispossessed by Prussian expansionism. Berlin complained about the Prince's 'apparent leadership of an anti-Prussian demonstration in the French capital', but there was more to come.[29] The King's heir, the Duke of Cumberland, became engaged to be married to the Princess of Wales's youngest sister, Princess Thyra. The Prince took a close, almost paternal interest in his prospective brother-in-law's future, and it was with the Prince's encouragement that the Duke followed his father in denouncing the suppression of his hereditary throne and demanding the return of his family's confiscated fortune. Berlin, which was more interested in the Prince of Wales's activities than he, at first, realised, interpreted the friendship of the Prince for the Duke as a deliberate provocation to Germany, and the Prince, despite all the entreaties to him to be discreet in matters of international relations, did not hesitate to tell the Prussian royal family of what he felt about their state's treatment of Cumberland's family. However, so long as the Prince's brother-in-law, the Crown Prince, lived, successful efforts were made to bind the two royal families closer together. It was only when the Prince's headstrong nephew Willy came to the throne after his own father's tragically short reign in 1888 that the problem became endemic.

From the time of his father's death the Prince was keen to be included in the constitutional process by his mother, this being the only way in which he could have a proper insight into affairs of state. He wanted, above all, to be allowed to see some state papers. The Queen persistently refused to allow her son to see them as she felt he lacked the discretion needed to keep their contents secret. Over the years some ministers took pity on him, and let him see certain things, despite the Queen's furious opposition, and despite the Prince's occasional breaches of their trust. The Queen would, in time, choose items of a non-sensitive nature that she would allow her son to see, but only in the 1890s did she accede to ministerial advice and let him see whatever he wanted. He was then over fifty.

He had first felt the frustration of his exclusion in 1864, when Prussia and Austria invaded Denmark. Lord Russell, the Foreign Secretary, supported his request that the Prince should see the same official dispatches on the crisis as seen by the Queen and the Cabinet. The Queen refused, instead allowing her private secretary, General Charles Grey, to feed the Prince such titbits as she decided. She told Lord Russell that she would not allow the Prince to have a 'separate and independent communication with the Government'.[30] General Grey confided in Russell that the Queen's editing of the dispatches before the Prince saw them would allow her 'to exercise some control over what is communicated to Him – a control which is very necessary, as She must tell you confidentially, that His Royal Highness is not at all times as discreet as He should be'. The Prince protested, and was told by his mother that her decision was final. 'You could not well have a Government key,' she told him, referring to the dispatch boxes in which the details were sent, 'which only Ministers, and those immediately connected with them, or with me, have.' This forced the Prince to develop his contacts with ministers and diplomats, which, in the long run, were to provide far more scope for his involvement in politics. Gladstone, on taking office in 1868, was always available for private briefings, as was the Prince's friend Lord Granville, Foreign Secretary after 1870 and in Gladstone's second administration from 1880 to 1885. Later on, Sir Charles Dilke, whom the Prince befriended in the early 1880s, was to be a similar conduit of information.

Of these, Granville was the most cautious, because his fingers had been burned. When in 1872 the Prince was lobbying his mother's private secretary, Colonel Henry Ponsonby, about how much he wanted to see Foreign Office dispatches, Granville told Ponsonby this could happen only with the Queen's and the Cabinet's specific permission – a time delay that would make any news stale by the time the Prince was allowed to see it. Ponsonby told the Queen in July 1872: 'Lord Granville also whispered confidentially ... that he feared the Prince of Wales in his open and hearty manner had blurted out some information once which Lord Granville had communicated to him and this had always given him a mistrust of repeating private matters.'[31] This seems to refer to a note Granville had sent the Prince to keep him informed during the Franco-Prussian War. As the Foreign Secretary told Ponsonby, 'one evening I got four messages from different friends telling me to be careful. One of my first notes to him had been handed round a dinner party.'[32]

Continually excluded from the political process by his mother, the Prince persisted in trying to develop his own private involvement in politics. While the criticisms made of him by the Queen, and indeed by Gladstone – who felt he should be made to read more and to become more serious-minded – were largely justified, there was much within his bored and dilettante personality that thirsted for political life. However intellectually limited the Prince may have been, he knew that he had to be taken seriously, for his own sake and for the monarchy's, and some form of political gravitas was the obvious way for him to gain that credibility. For example, he wrote to his friend Lord Hartington, the Chief Secretary for Ireland, on 12 March 1873, curious for information about what the government would do now that it had been defeated on the Irish University Bill. 'Would you consider me very indiscreet if I asked you to let me know what steps the Govt are going to take since the meeting of the Cabinet. You can perfectly rely on my keeping secret any communication you may think right (with

Mr Gladstone's sanction) to make to me. Should you, however, think that my wish is an indiscreet one, please burn this and think no more about it.'[33]

AN UNEMPLOYED YOUTH

The senior politicians, such as Clarendon and Palmerston, who had befriended the Prince in his early adulthood saw the need for him to be found some gainful employment. The lesson of the youth and middle age of George IV was still potent, especially to Palmerston, who had seen some of it at first hand. It was assumed that the Queen would perhaps live another twenty or even thirty years after Albert Edward's coming-of-age (in fact, she survived for almost forty), and that it was not advisable or acceptable for the Prince to have nothing to do for such a length of time. However, his mother continued ruthlessly to exclude him from any possibilities of self-fulfilment. She made it clear to her ministers early on that the only functions the Prince could contemplate were purely ceremonial ones.

When Disraeli became Prime Minister in February 1868 he suggested to the Queen that the Prince, who was then twenty-six, should be sent to live in a congenial part of Ireland where there was plenty of hunting, giving him a base from which he could undertake public duties as the representative of his mother. The Queen, however, said the idea was 'not to be thought of', was 'quite out of the question' and could 'never be conceded'.[34] Her excuse was that, if Ireland had a resident Prince of Wales, all sorts of other dominions, not to mention Wales itself, would want one. Disraeli had self-preservation as a higher priority than philanthropy. He sensibly knew when to take no for an answer and, wanting always to remain on the right side of the Queen, did so in this case. It was to become the clearest example of why he prospered in his Sovereign's estimation and Gladstone did not.

In 1871 Gladstone, who was by now Prime Minister, came back with another suggestion for the occupation of the Prince. His motivation, as with much that he strove to do, was entirely altruistic. The plan was formulated for him by two of the Prince's closest friends, Lord Spencer and Lord Hartington – who just happened to hold the offices of Lord Lieutenant of Ireland and Chief Secretary for Ireland respectively.

Once more an Irish residence was suggested, with the Lord Lieuten-ancy being reformed into a non-political job and given to the Prince. The Prince would have a relationship with the Irish Secretary rather like the one the Sovereign had with her Prime Minister. Gladstone put the idea to the Queen in a long meeting with her on 25 June 1871. This time, encouraged by her incipient dislike of Gladstone, her opposition was put in even more colourful terms than she had used to Disraeli: that Ireland could not be treated like Scotland for the purposes of royal residences (though why not, since both were joined to England by Acts of Union, does not permit of a logical answer); that she 'doubted the Prince's fitness for high functions of state', though saw the benefits of having this apparently incorrigible wastrel out of London during the season; that her third son, Prince Arthur, would make a better viceroy; and, most bizarrely of all, that Lord Hamilton, a friend of the Prince's (and son and heir of the Marquess, later the Duke, of Abercorn, a pillar of Ulster society) was 'infecting him with Orangeism' – something for which there is no evidence at all, indeed quite the reverse, given the keenness with which the Prince had sought papal audiences and the enthusiasm with which he went among his mother's subjects in the predominantly Catholic south of Ireland.

Gladstone, whose relations with the Queen degenerated further because of his determination (as she saw it) to interfere in the arrangements for her eldest son, was motivated by his concern that the bored Prince had too much time on his hands in London to spend wisely, and that he was at best indiscreet, at worst liable to cause a scandal. Gladstone knew the potential, for he had been involved in extricating the Prince, during 1869–70, from the celebrated divorce case of Sir Charles and Lady Mordaunt, in which Lady Mordaunt (admittedly deranged) had claimed to be the Prince's mistress. The Prime Minister had also been told by Sir William Knollys that the Prince 'really desired some business' to do, so felt he was not, whatever the Queen might have thought, gratuitously interfering.[35] Gladstone had confided in Granville on 3 December 1870 that 'the Queen is invisible and the Prince of Wales is not respected'; and, being unable to do anything about the first problem, he nobly decided to see what difference he might make with the second. He gained the impression from the Queen at his meeting with her in June 1871 that she was open to persuasion. This was, unfortunately for him, manifestly not the case.[36]

When Gladstone's initial Irish plan failed, the Prince and his supporters had other suggestions. The Prince himself asked Ponsonby to suggest to the Queen that he might undergo a series of attachments to government departments, to see how they worked. The Queen, when Ponsonby put the matter to her on 7 March 1872, felt such an exercise would be pointless. Gladstone then suggested the Prince might join the Indian Council, which the Queen similarly thought was a waste of time. Despite renewed pleas from her eldest son, she refused to give him anything serious to do. He had been sworn of the Privy Council in the year of his marriage, 1863, but was seldom asked to attend Council meetings. Indeed it was not until 1898, in his fifty-seventh year, that the one occasion in his mother's reign arose when he was asked to deputise for her in the Council's chair – the Queen was abroad and the outbreak of hostilities between Spain and the United States necessitated a proclamation of neutrality to be issued urgently, in the Sovereign's name, by the Council.

In the winter of 1871–2, at around the time of the tenth anniversary of his father's death from the disease, the Prince almost died from typhoid. His recovery was taken as a signal by Gladstone to reopen the question of his proposed employment, despite the ferocity with which the Queen had treated his last attempt. The Cabinet discussed the issue during that winter.[37] Gladstone saw an opportunity not just to make something of the Prince of Wales, but also to capitalise on the new burst of loyalty towards the throne that had become apparent at the time of his deliverance from illness. The Prime Minister told the Cabinet on 9 March 1872 that they had a 'duty' to 'make a resolute endeavour at improving the relations between the Monarchy and the Nation by framing a worthy and manly mode of life, *quoad* public duties, for the Prince of Wales'.[38] Gladstone wanted the 'unanimous' support of his colleagues, and their approval for his then referring the matter again to the Queen.

In June 1872 he steeled himself to raise the question with the Queen again. He promised her he would not mention the matter to the Prince until she had let her Prime Minister know her views.[39] The Queen was appalled by Gladstone's impertinence, but Ponsonby tried to soothe her, saying the Prime Minister had only been trying to help. Ponsonby, in urging the Queen to let Gladstone tell her some concrete ideas for the Prince's future, made one great tactical error: he told the Queen that 'he believes that Mr Gladstone has ceased to entertain any ideas about Ireland – at any rate for the present'.[40] However, this was simply not the case. Despite Ponsonby's warning Gladstone not to raise the question, the Prime Minister did just that in a thirty-four-page letter to the Queen, in which he spoke of the 'admirable opportunity for giving the Prince the advantage of a political training' that the Irish plan constituted.[41] Ireland would occupy him for but a few months each year. For the rest of the time, he suggested that the Prince and Princess might live at Buckingham Palace, whence they might perform the 'social and visible functions of the Monarchy' that the Queen had chosen to forgo since her bereavement. She preferred exile from London at Osborne on the Isle of Wight, Windsor and Balmoral.

All this achieved was to upset the Queen still further. She told Ponsonby she had read Gladstone's submission 'with a good deal of irritation, because it is returning to the same subject on which she entirely disagreed with him last year'.[42] On the matter of her being represented socially by the Prince in London, she (invoking her late husband) expressed her disgust at the 'independent haughty faultfinding fashionable set' and thought it would not do 'the slightest good' for the Prince, as her official representative, to move among them socially. 'On the contrary, the Prince and Princess of Wales if they would but take the right course, which they very easily could, of excluding the doubtful characters from their house and society, could do the good which the Sovereign never for a moment could and it shows the extraordinary want of knowledge of the world of Mr Gladstone to enable him or make him even suggest such a thing [sic].' Gladstone's idea was, for good measure, 'absurd and quite wrong'.

Turning to the Irish matter, the Queen said that idea was 'quite useless': she had never taken the slightest interest in public affairs before her accession, yet, on becoming Queen, 'she bent her neck to the yoke and worked hard'. This ignored the point that this had happened to her at eighteen, whereas her son was already thirty and she had some years ahead of her yet. Her son, by 'necessity and responsibility', would be good when the time came. She complained that to take him away to Ireland for four or five months of the year would be 'very hard' on her, and there was no sense in sending him to the 'least loyal of the three Kingdoms'. However, her main gripe was that, as 'whoever knows the Prince of Wales's character well must know', the Prince 'will always lean to a party and in Ireland he would be unable to withstand this and would be beset with people who would force him into one extreme or the other'. As for everything else, she told Gladstone, in almost so many words, that it was none of his business, but would be sorted out within the family. However,

Gladstone would not take no for an answer, and sent back another long memorandum, seeking to answer all the criticisms the Queen had raised. This act of temerity only made the Queen hate Gladstone even more, and she buried the very idea by replying, after making him wait three weeks, that 'this plan may be considered as *definitely* abandoned'. It is not clear that she even bothered to read Gladstone's painfully composed missive, since Ponsonby sent her a short précis of it.[43]

In fact the Prince himself, for whom the idea of work was far more comforting than its immediate prospect, was not that keen on the Irish idea either. Not least, it would take him away from some of his regular amusements in the West End of London. He was determined not to be bounced into anything, and to have his cake and to eat it. He had Francis Knollys write to Ponsonby from Venice on 27 April 1872 to say it would be 'distasteful' to the Prince were a 'cut and dried' plan to be put to him.[44] The Prince would rather, Knollys said, have a chance to discuss any plan with Gladstone and Granville before it was settled. This, though, the Prince would not feel able to do until the middle of June, Knollys added, as he needed time to 'turn himself round'. He continued that the Prince's 'distaste' for the Irish plan 'is not so much Ireland itself ... as to the objection he would entertain of being either a nonentity, which would be the case were he to be sent merely to perform merely the social part of the duties of a Viceroy, or the humble servant of the Ministry of the day, which would ensue were any responsibility to be attached to his position'. Knollys himself, a man of caution, good judgment and 'sound' views who had quickly won the Prince's trust and respect in his role as private secretary, was against the plan too.[45] That was the dilemma that he presented: the Prince wanted a job, but it could not be a serious one, and if he could not have a serious job he did not want one at all. Ponsonby replied to Knollys that 'I entirely agree', and that he had mentioned the Prince's point of view to the Queen. This was no doubt why the Queen felt it safe to be especially horrible to Gladstone about it, not that she needed much encouragement.

The Prince saw his mother on her yacht off Cowes on 1 August 1872, and was told to forget Ireland. That was no problem for him, for he had told Ponsonby the previous day that he was delighted to hear his mother was so against it.[46] The Indian Council was mooted again by Ponsonby, but Gladstone now felt this 'hollow and insufficient' for the Prince.[47] He sent the Queen another lengthy memorandum at the end of August, trying to show how the Prince would not be a nonentity and how he would be prevented from becoming a partisan. Yet it was no use. The Queen had made it clear to the Lord Privy Seal, Lord Halifax, that she would not have any of Gladstone's suggestions for her son. Gladstone was initially defiant, telling Halifax he would not abandon his position on the question 'except in the last resort', and reminding him that 'what is wanted for the Prince of Wales is not a driblet of business coming up now & then but a plan of life'.[48] When the Queen still proved obstinate, Gladstone gave up. It was agreed that the Prince – not, it seems, with his mother's knowledge – would have a talk with Gladstone about how best to advance the matter; but it came to nothing. He and Gladstone failed, when Gladstone visited Sandringham in October 1872 ostensibly to discuss the question, to come up with any alternative. In the end, neither man wished to raise the subject. Gladstone accepted defeat at last on the Irish idea, reporting his failure to the Cabinet on 12 October.[49]

The spectacle of a Prince being supported by £100,000 a year of government funds while living a life of apparent luxury and indolence – the latter, though, not entirely of his own choosing – gave further stimulus to republican feeling, already fuelled by the extra-planetary behaviour of the Queen in her long and profound bereavement. The Prince was said to be heavily in debt already by the early 1870s, though this was denied by the Queen in 1874. It was also pointed out, in the Prince's defence, that he had to defray much of the cost of his foreign travel himself, and was performing many of the social duties that should rightly have been performed by his mother. But, in the general cause of fighting republicanism, the Prince did his bit, and more than earned his stipend from the government. He managed, at a dinner party given by Granville in 1872, to charm Frank Hill, the editor of the republican-leaning *Daily News*. In 1874 he took his wife to Birmingham, into the radical court of Joe Chamberlain, who (this was before Chamberlain's entry to the House of Commons) had recently been expressing veiled republican sympathies in some press articles. The visit was a great success and marked the end of Chamberlain's playing with the republican creed. In the toast he proposed to his royal guest as Mayor of Birmingham, 'Radical Joe' said that 'here in England the throne is recognised and respected as the symbol of all constituted authority and settled government'.[50]

Yet probably the greatest success for the Prince's policy of boldly confronting critics of monarchy was in the overtures made in 1880 to

Sir Charles Dilke, a prominent Liberal MP who for the preceding decade had been expressing almost incontinent republican opinions. Lord Fife, a friend of the Prince's, invited both men to his dinner-table, and Dilke fell immediately for the Prince's charm offensive. The two men became firm friends, with the Prince showing Dilke particular loyalty during his forthcoming, largely self-inflicted, troubles when involved in a particularly unsavoury divorce case that ended his ministerial, and almost his whole political, career. Dilke was useful to the Prince: when the Liberals came into office, he was able to keep him informed. Above all, the Prince enjoyed having among his circle of friends men his mother detested.

THE PRINCE AND THE CONJUROR

The Prince's relations with Benjamin Disraeli – a man ridiculed as a mountebank and an opportunist even by some of his own party, and branded (in a similar, if more extreme, anti-semitic spirit) a 'superlative Hebrew conjuror' by Carlyle – overcame the initial problem of the arch-sycophant's desire always to be associated with the views of the Monarch on any question on which she had a difference of opinion with her son. The Prince was easily seduced by Disraeli's immense charm and the act of mock-medieval courtliness that he put on, which revolted more sensitive observers. Also, the Prince had a soft spot for those, particularly Jews, who had made it to the heart of society in the face of prejudice and even legal disabilities. In some respects Disraeli was more royal than the Queen in the treatment of the Prince's political education. In 1876 the Queen agreed that her son could see certain selected Foreign Office dispatches, but Disraeli then contrived to have nothing sent to the Prince for three months, having told the Foreign Office that so indiscreet was the heir to the throne that nothing remotely important should be allowed near him. However, Disraeli was careful to ingratiate himself wherever possible with the Prince, which one so good-natured and as keen on making political contacts as the Prince found irresistible. Disraeli's love of power, and especially of the exercise of patronage, allowed him to tease the Prince and to deliver the occasional reminder of who, in a supposedly constitutional monarchy, was the boss.

In the winter of 1875–6 the Prince undertook a long and largely successful tour to India. Disraeli had played a substantial part in persuading the Queen that the Prince was fitted for this responsibility, and supporting her in her insistence that the Princess of Wales must stay behind, which put the Prince – whose leisure activities on the tour would not always be to his wife's taste – in his debt. This was acknowledged in a letter the Prince sent to the Prime Minister on 11 October 1875, just before his departure, thanking him for his advice, 'which I shall always be ready to accept at your hands'.[51] The Prince added that 'I am fully alive to the importance of my visit to India and hope that neither you nor anyone else in my land will have cause to regret that the honour of my country has been placed in my hands while in India.' By way of gratitude, the Prince had Francis Knollys send occasional letters describing the useful things the Prince had done on behalf of Queen and country in India – 'everybody I think, the Indian press included,' he wrote on 18 December 1875, 'agrees in saying that the visit has hitherto been a great success, unaccompanied by a single drawback, and that the feeling of gratification and pleasure which has filled the minds of the Native Princes who have been admitted into HRH's presence, far exceeds the anticipations that were formed on the subject.'[52]

The tour did go well – at least, the discretion of the Prince's suite and the diplomatic service ensured that some of the entertainments provided for the Prince were not revealed either to his mother or to his wife, which Disraeli had always understood would be a necessary aspect of the undertaking – and this emboldened the Prince to ask a favour of Disraeli towards the end of his trip. He wrote to him requesting substantial honours for some of those who had travelled as his official party and helped ensure that the trip went smoothly. Principally, he wanted a peerage or, failing that, a Grand Cross of the Order of the Bath for Sir Bartle Frere, a highly distinguished ex-Indian proconsul, who had led the Prince's party on the tour. Disraeli took weeks to tell the Prince what he had decided, specifically ignoring a request to settle the question before the party left India two months later. Disraeli refused to consider a peerage for Frere, who on his eventual return home was offered by the Prime Minister the choice of a baronetcy or the GCB.[53] Eventually the Prince's wishes prevailed to the extent that, after some more lobbying, Frere (having taken the GCB) got the baronetcy as well. On his way home, at Seville, the Prince received a cypher telegram from Disraeli, having one of his dear little jokes: 'Pray be careful Your Royal Highness is not taken prisoner like Coeur de Lion on your return home from your Crusade.'[54]

Three years later, when Frere had become high commissioner to South Africa and took the executive decision that led to Lord Chelmsford's troops being beaten by the Zulus at Isandhlwana, the Prince sprang loyally to his defence back in London. Sir Michael Hicks Beach, the Colonial Secretary, sent a dispatch to Frere rebuking him for having forced the issue by declaring war on the Zulus. He maintained 'almost daily communication' with Beaconsfield on the matter of the excellence of Sir Bartle, and wrote both to him and to Lady Frere urging him to tough it out and not to contemplate resigning. Whether the Prince, at several thousand miles' remove and with no experience whatever of the circumstances in which Sir Bartle was operating, would have been so extravagant in his support of anyone else to whom he had not felt personally indebted must remain a matter for conjecture. Certainly, the military force Frere had at his disposal was inadequate to take on the Zulus, and his push towards war was rash. But, as in many political matters, the Prince was happier to allow sentiment and admirable personal loyalty to overcome cool analysis. Only once Frere had made his stand and the damage to his reputation had been done did the Prince, eight months after the Zulu victory, suddenly realise the way the tide was flowing, and urge Frere to resign. Frere himself wanted to come home but, more at the Queen's insistence than anyone else's, he stayed at the Cape. The election of Gladstone's administration the following year brought an end to his service there.

In his tendencies the Prince was such a liberal that he showed, more than a century before its time, early signs of political correctness, though it was more a reflection of his extreme courtesy. Soon after reaching India in the autumn of 1875 he wrote to his mother that 'what struck me most forcibly was the rude and rough manner with which the English "political officers" (as they are called, who are in attendance upon the native chiefs) treat them. It is indeed much to be deplored, and the system is, I am sure, quite wrong. Natives of all classes in this country will, I am sure, be more attached to us if they are treated with kindness and with firmness at the same time, but not with brutality or contempt.'[55] A fortnight later he wrote to Granville on the same theme, advancing the distinctly radical ethos that 'because a man has a black face and a different religion from our own, there is no reason why he should be treated as a brute'; and he told Salisbury of 'the disgraceful habit of officers in the Queen's service speaking of the inhabitants in India, many of them sprung from great races, as "niggers"'.[56] Salisbury did indeed send out instructions to the government in India to display less arrogance towards the natives.

IMPERIAL ASPIRATIONS

Disraeli's childlike obsession with titles and honours, together with his gift for sycophancy, found their apotheosis in his decision to amend the royal titles and make Queen Victoria Empress of India. There had hitherto been a pleasing example of English understatement in the fact that, despite having much more of an empire, spread across five continents, than any of the European emperors, the Queen of England remained merely a Queen. Perhaps partly as a result of his not being English, this subtlety was lost on Disraeli. It was the Queen's idea to make the change – Prince Albert had suggested it to her as long ago as 1843, when India was still run by the East India Company. At home, the Prince's friends in the Liberal party fiercely opposed Disraeli's plans because of their unsavoury imperialist overtones, and images conjured up of Tsarist brutality and Prussian force; but far away in India, where he was on his long tour, the Prince heard nothing at all of the plan to change the title he would one day hold. As so often when something significant was happening, he learned of it from the newspapers.

He was angry with Disraeli, and wrote to Granville on 21 March 1876 about the pointlessness of the exercise and how he suspected it had been provoked by the Prime Minister's grandiosity. The following month he let Disraeli know directly how he felt. Writing from Seville on 22 April he told the Prime Minister that 'as the Queen's eldest son I think I have some right to feel annoyed that ... the announcement of the addition to the Queen's title should have been read by me in the newspapers instead of having received some intimation of the subject from the Prime Minister'.[57] Disraeli showed he had not got the point by replying to the Prince that he, too, could have a new title if it made him feel better – which the Prince took to be the offer of the title 'Imperial Highness'. This, understandably, further aggrieved the Prince, who replied that he would refuse any suggestion of a change in his style or title, and he trusted no such suggestion would be made. Knollys sealed the matter by writing to Disraeli, also on 22 April, that 'if it leaked out that such a suggestion had been made and refused by the Prince it would, though increasing his popularity, damage that of the Queen and her ministers'.

Disraeli at last got the message, and the Prince went out of his way to be friendly towards him on his return to London. There did appear to have been a breakdown in communications, for Sir William Knollys had corresponded with Salisbury as the Prince left England to ascertain that telegrams keeping him informed of developments about which he needed to know would be sent to him.[58] In the end, the Queen took the responsibility for not having told her son what was planned – an ignoring of his sensibilities in relation to high matters of state that was, after all, quite the usual practice. However, Sir Henry Ponsonby said it was an oversight – 'she blames herself for not having written to [the Prince] about the Titles Bill, adding, however, that she certainly thought she had done so.'[59] So converted was the Prince to the principle of the change, in fact, that when the Liberal Opposition attacked the Bill in the Commons the Prince told his mother that 'greater nonsense was, I think, never spoken in both Houses of Parliament'. The Prince was never an independent or an original intellect, though he was shrewd enough to know which side was likely to win any given battle.[60]

From then on, the relationship between the Prince and his mother's Prime Minister continued to grow closer, with frequent exchanges of hospitality that persisted until Disraeli's death in 1881, after he had left office. Disraeli, who on the Prince's return from India instituted a regular correspondence with him, would send the Prince titbits of political information, just to ensure that the heir to the throne maintained the correct level (in Disraeli's view) of respect towards the Prime Minister. The Queen was now listening more sympathetically to her eldest son, and Disraeli kept him increasingly (though unofficially) well informed until he lost office in 1880; occasionally, the Prince would call on the Prime Minister merely for a gossip, a habit Disraeli encouraged. By this unofficial means, the Prince was one of the first to know of the movement getting up among the powers for a congress to settle the Eastern Question (the problems caused by the weakness of the Ottoman Empire) about which Disraeli tipped him off in a letter of 29 May 1876.[61] The Prince was sure to write back at once, in his own hand, to say he was 'much obliged' for the information.[62] In July

Disraeli sounded the Prince out on the question of who might be an ideal Lord Lieutenant of Ireland, listing several possibilities. Disraeli's real intention was that the Prince might suggest to the Duke of Marlborough – whose son Lord Blandford's divorce case the Prince had been uncomfortably close to – that he might reconsider taking a post he had first declined two years earlier, to achieve 'the dignified withdrawal of the [Churchill] family from Metropolitan and English life'.[63] Disraeli justified his consulting the Prince by saying that 'Your Royal Highness encourages me to speak to Your Royal Highness frankly and confidentially on public affairs'. The Prince told him that he saw 'drawbacks in all those whose names you have mentioned', and instead advancing the name of Lord Hardwick. But Marlborough it was.[64]

In his private letters to third parties, Beaconsfield routinely referred to the Prince as 'Prince Hal': on one level just another expression of the Prime Minister's ludicrous campness, but also, it seems, meant as a sincere estimation of the popular King the young man would, he felt sure, one day become. As the two men came better to understand each other, so the Prince moved up a gear in his importuning of Beaconsfield for favours – though, in his princely way, not for himself but for others. One such example was an Arctic explorer, Captain Allen Young, for whom the Prince wanted a Knight Commandership of the Bath. 'Sir, and dear Prince,' the Prime Minister replied to him, on 7 November 1876, getting down to brass tacks, 'I have not a single KCB, or a single CB. I gave my last KCB to Your Royal Highness and my last CB except one.'[65] He did, though, promise not to forget the brave Captain – and nor did he, having him knighted two years later.

So good did relations become between the Prince and the Prime Minister that when Gladstone started his assault on Beaconsfield over the Bulgarian atrocities in 1876, the Prince – who was being carefully briefed by the Prime Minister in their correspondence – put aside his long-standing admiration for the Liberal leader to rebuke him for the intemperate way in which he attacked the Prime Minister for failing to come to the aid of Christians in Bulgaria who had been massacred by the Turks towards whom the government was now so well disposed.[66] However, the Prince had misread the Eastern Question: he confided in Sir Bartle Frere on 14 October 1876 his belief that, in the end, Britain would have to go to war with Russia for its perceived interference in Serbia which, the Prince felt, was destabilising the whole region; and there was the matter of Russia's designs on India to be settled too.[67]

The Prime Minister, though, was more than grateful for the Prince's support, and ensured he was kept up to date with the latest developments in the Near East as they happened, and also of important political matters at home. Indeed, so well informed was the Prince that he had real cause to regret it when Beaconsfield lost office, and was replaced by the more scrupulous Gladstone.

Beaconsfield did not allow himself to be too sidetracked by the Prince's sudden Russophobia, but he did tell Salisbury, in a letter of 10 November 1876, just how highly he rated the Prince's diplomatic abilities. At the imaginative suggestion of the Prince, Salisbury was being sent by the Prime Minister as a special envoy to the main European capitals, *en route* to a conference at Constantinople about the future of Turkey's rule in certain of its provinces, to gauge at first hand feelings among the leaders of the great powers about the development of the Eastern Question. The permanent under-secretary at the Foreign Office, Lord Tenterden, felt such a trip was so unprecedented – and would put so much out of the control of his department – that he protested it was unnecessary. The Prince urged Beaconsfield to take no notice of Tenterden, and Beaconsfield listened to him. He told Salisbury:

> I think on these matters HRH is a better counsellor than Lord Tenterden. The Prince of Wales is a thorough man of the world, and knows all these individuals personally. You must remember we suffer from a feeble and formal diplomacy and that there has been little real interchange of thought between the English government and foreign powers. I agree with the Prince and think it highly desirable that at this moment our communications with the powers should be lifted out of the slough of despond they have so long grovelled in.[68]

For all Beaconsfield's flattery of the Prince in these matters, he still ensured throughout the Eastern crisis that such information as the heir to the throne received was delivered, usually orally, by him. The bar on the Prince's seeing any remotely sensitive Foreign Office dispatches was still rigidly enforced; as snubs go, this was surpassed only by the fact that the Prince's youngest brother, Prince Leopold, who was just twenty-four, had been enlisted by his mother as a private secretary, and had therefore been given the key to the dispatch boxes the Prince of Wales so desperately coveted. Inevitably, the Prince complained, in the first instance to Sir Henry Ponsonby, his mother's private secretary, and to Lord Derby, the Foreign Secretary. 'The Queen says they should not be sent,' Ponsonby recorded and, knowing the Prince, added, 'I agree, of course, as regards the secret and confidential.' However, Ponsonby was more understanding than the Sovereign – 'I told her I thought they should send him what they could.'[69] Ponsonby knew that most Foreign Office dispatches 'might be read out by the clerks from the FO windows to the public without harm'.[70] The Queen emphasised to Beaconsfield, in a letter of 7 October 1876, that:

> it would be best *not* to *refuse* to send any despatches to the Prince of Wales but to send *such* as were *not* very confidential, making a selection and at the same time to let someone *report generally* at the end of a few days – the state of affairs quite *shortly* and never till after they are no longer required to be kept very secret. At the same time they should be marked 'Confidential and Secret' so as to impress upon the Prince of Wales the necessity of great prudence.[71]

THE EASTERN QUESTION

It was frequently useful for Beaconsfield to have the Prince as an ally. The Queen was unwilling to let her Prime Minister – then approaching the age of seventy-five – endure the strain of attending the Congress of Berlin, held between the great powers in the summer of 1878 to try to settle the Eastern Question. However, he enlisted the Prince to try to persuade his mother that he should attend, with Salisbury: and after some intense lobbying – 'now, do let me implore you to urge Lord B to go,' he wrote to her on 28 May 1878 – Beaconsfield was on his way to Germany. Earlier that year, on a visit to his sister in Berlin, the Prince had seen Bismarck – whom he had first met on a visit to Berlin in 1869, and with whom he had had cordial contacts over the years – and had a long political conversation with him.[72] Although reported by the Prince in a letter to Beaconsfield to have been genial in tone, the conversation was led by Bismarck to the subject of Germany's hostility to Russia, and the Iron Chancellor asked the Prince whether the Germans could depend on Britain's support should it come to a fight between them and the Russians. The Prince, certain of Beaconsfield's pro-Turkish sympathies and of his mother's belief in the importance of 'giving those detestable Russians a good beating', replied unequivocally that Germany could depend on Britain.[73]

In return for the Prince's support, Beaconsfield wrote him oleaginous letters from the conference table at Berlin describing how 'Turkey is in my pocket' and how Russia was 'now, more hopelessly than ever, excluded from the Mediterranean'.[74] Beaconsfield, with the hand of a master, exploited to the full all the additional opportunities the diplomatic activity in which he was engaged presented him for gross ingratiation. He wrote to the Prince on 6 July 1878 of how, in order to please the Princess of Wales by doing something for her brother, he had secured a minor extension of the Greek border. 'I did yesterday something for Greece. It was very difficult, but is by no means to be despised. It was all done for Her Royal Highness's sake. I thought of Marlborough House all the time....' One hopes, for his sake, that the Prince was not taken in by this.[75]

Throughout the time leading up to the Congress, Knollys had on the Prince's behalf taken every opportunity to complain that the Prince was not being kept properly informed; and indeed, the correspondence between him and the Prime Minister does, to judge from the Royal Archives, seem to dry up in the year or so before the Congress. In the spring of 1877, for example, the Prince had been ordered to return home from a cruise in the Mediterranean because of the international situation. Knollys wired back to Ponsonby:

> the Prince has no doubt that matters are 'critical', but he has no certain knowledge on the subject as the Government have not vouchsafed to send him one single word of information on the state of affairs since he left England, and had it not been for Prince Humbert [of Italy] who was good enough to place him a little *au courant* with what was going on, and for two letters which Borthwick of the Morning Post wrote to me, he would have been left still more in the dark than he even is at present.[76]

In the two years or so between the end of the Congress and Beaconsfield's fall the pitch of the correspondence stepped up, with the Prime Minister again occasionally sounding out the Prince on broad questions of policy. In January 1880 the Prince even invited himself to Hughenden, Beaconsfield's small but gracious country home, for a night; and, with the Queen usually out of London either at Osborne or Windsor, the Prince became an occasional conveyor of messages from the Sovereign to her Prime Minister.

CULTIVATING SALISBURY

For the best part of eighteen months Salisbury, who was at the time the Secretary of State for India, superintended the making of most of the arrangements for the Prince's Indian tour of 1875–6. The task had marked the beginnings of the professional relationship of the latest, and in many regards most distinguished, of a long line of Cecils to assist the Crown with the man he would one day serve as Prime Minister. Salisbury had the thankless job of acting as link man between the Queen, who was taking a close and not entirely helpful interest in the arrangements, and her son. He had the melancholy task of writing to the Prince on 5 June 1875 to report that 'at the Cabinet today, the Prime Minister read a letter from the Queen containing positive directions from Her Majesty that the detailed arrangements of the visit should be considered by the Government as an official question, and that recommendations in respect to them should be submitted to Her'.[77] There was no question of the Prince, now aged thirty-three, being let off the leash yet, even when thousands of miles from home. 'At the same time,' Salisbury continued, 'the Queen was pleased to lay especial stress upon the number and composition of Your Royal Highness's suite, as a matter of public importance, to which much attention would be inevitably directed, and on which therefore the consideration of the advisers of the Crown should be carefully bestowed.' In other words, there would be no question of the Prince packing his entourage simply with his friends, for the pursuit together of whatever passed in India for 'actresses'.

The Prince had cordial, but never close, relations with Salisbury from the time of the India visit until his death nearly thirty years later. He was quickly, though, on terms where he felt he could write to recommend honours: having read in the papers in July 1876 of the death of Sir John Kaye, the eminent military historian whose work on Indian regiments had led to his being invested with a Knight Commandership of the Order of the Star of India, the Prince noted that 'there is a vacant KCSI ... I trouble you with these lines to remind you of your promise to confer it if possible on the naval commander in chief of the East Indies (Rear Admiral Macdonald)'.[78] Nor was it just state honours for which he would ask Salisbury: he would write and ask for him to consider, in his role as Chancellor of Oxford University, the prospect of awarding honorary degrees to certain of his favoured friends.[79]

The Prince was painfully aware he still had no right to receive official information, and had Francis Knollys write to Salisbury on 13 October 1876 saying that 'The Prince hopes you will not think him indiscreet in asking whether you would have any objection to kindly let him know, privately, who the new Governor of Bombay is as soon as the appointment is settled.'[80] There are frequent letters of invitation in the Salisbury papers at this time for the Secretary of State for India to come to Marlborough House for an audience – the main purpose of which was for the Prince to extract what gossip he could. Salisbury humoured the Prince, but formed no high opinion of his capabilities in these meetings.

The Prince was always careful to thank Salisbury for services rendered, often writing to congratulate him for various diplomatic appointments he had made, and about which Salisbury had kept him informed. Salisbury let him see harmless but interesting foreign dispatches, sending him, for example, a cypher telegram of Lord Lyons's in May 1879. The Prince wrote to thank him, tipping him off in return that the Count and Countess of Flanders, brother and sister-in-law of the King of Belgium, 'have just arrived in London – and are staying at Claridge's Hotel'.[81] It was the best he could do, and a sad commentary on how little, relatively, a Prince starved of information *could* do.

That same month, the Prince sent further thanks for 'confidential papers' shown to him by Salisbury 'which cannot fail to be of the greatest interest to me', and reciprocating with a copy of a letter sent to him by his brother-in-law, the King of Greece, which he asked him to share with the Prime Minister.[82] It was but the latest of many such complaints from that quarter he had had to forward over the preceding months. George told the Prince that he had read political news the Prince had sent him with 'great attention and some astonishment.... I must confess I never expected to see such a change in the ideas of an English government with regard to Hellenic interests.' Yet he told the Prince, 'I was very glad to see in your letter that you wish me to accept the *territory which the Berlin Congress* recommended; Greece *never* asked for *more*, nor can she ask for a *smaller* territory, nor accept from Turkey anything less than that which was decided in congress.'[83] The King was aggrieved that Beaconsfield was merely going to 'press' the Sultan to abide by the frontier 'suggested' by the Congress, allowing him to keep a couple of frontier towns. The Prince simply passed the note on.

Although during the period of the Congress of Berlin the Prince had been sent the occasional document by Salisbury, who became Foreign Secretary in April 1878, he did not always have his information so directly. The Prince wrote to him on 4 February 1879: 'I read in the newspapers that Austria renounces Article 5 of the Treaty of Prague, and as it is a matter which concerns Denmark so closely – I write these lines to ask you if you have received any official conformation of this statement.'[84] For good measure, he added that were the news true it would be 'disgraceful' – 'and only shows how little faith we can place' in the whole process of treaty-making. He would also send Salisbury translations of German newspaper articles about Russia; he did this on 4 January 1879, and on the 14th sent him a separate account of a report made to him by a friend, the Marquis de Luce ('a legitimist and a thoroughly sensible man'), about the state of politics in France, 'for your perusal and for that of Lady Salisbury'.[85] The Prince, *comme toujours*, had an ulterior motive in writing, which he made plain. 'I shall be much interested in reading Lord Lyons' dispatches at the present time: but it is some months since his dispatches have been sent to me from the Foreign Office.'

DIPLOMATIC ACTIVITY

During the 1880s the progress of the Prince's desired Anglo-French entente was to be retarded by disagreements between the two countries over the control of Egypt. The purchase of Suez Canal shares, and the importance now of Egypt as a gateway to India, had led to British encroachment on what had traditionally been a French sphere of influence. A system of dual control between the two countries was implemented after 1879, and the Prince felt himself amply qualified to be the main Anglo-French go-between. He was assisted in this ambition by his growing friendship with Sir Charles Dilke, who in 1880 had become Under-Secretary at the Foreign Office in Gladstone's administration. Much of the Prince's diplomacy was conducted in the margins of dinner-parties, and it was at one such event, given by Lord Spencer in February 1881, that the Prince importuned Dilke on French matters. He offered to use a forthcoming visit he was making to Paris to meet Ferry, the French Prime Minister, and commend to him a new commercial pact the Gladstone administration was trying to conclude with the French, but which the French were resisting because of their policy of protectionism. Dilke accepted the offer, but the Prince's representations came to nothing: the technicalities of the matter meant he could, in effect, be of no help at all. At this time he was also (in order to promote the cause of entente) a partisan of the idea to build a tunnel under the English Channel to carry an underground railway, but Dilke talked him out of that, saying it would compromise national security.

Dilke was a friend of Gambetta's, and the Prince's connection with Dilke meant he met more often with the President of the French Chamber of Deputies. Gambetta could not understand why Britain should be worried by France's colonial ambitions, the first of which was the Protectorate established in Tunis in May 1881. Gambetta also surprised the Prince by revealing France's new warmth towards Russia, inevitable given their respective borders with the new Germany, but the Prince was a long way from grasping the need for better relations in that quarter.

Before his loss of office in early 1882 Gambetta had managed to secure the support of Gladstone and his administration for his promise to use whatever means necessary to protect the rule of the Khedive in Egypt. This was put to the test in June that year, when fifty Europeans were killed during an uprising in Alexandria by forces loyal to the nationalist dictatorship of Arabi Pasha. In London, neither Gladstone nor his senior colleagues displayed any wish to become involved, which the Prince thought regrettable. The issue found him torn between two friends, highlighting once more the sentimental nature of his approach to politics. Granville, the Foreign Secretary, wanted to keep Britain out of the quarrel; but another friend, Lord Charles Beresford, was commanding a British gunboat in a squadron off Alexandria, and wrote from there to the Prince stating that, unless resolute action were taken soon against Arabi Pasha, British rule in Egypt and the operation of the Suez Canal would be in jeopardy. At the behest of yet another friend, the Liberal Lord Dalhousie, the Prince sent Beresford's letter on to Granville, whereupon (as Sir Sidney Lee so delicately puts it) 'a commotion followed'.[86] Granville detected from the correspondence that Beresford had breached naval regulations, for in the letter he had admitted to the Prince that he had sent information direct to the Liberal-hating London newspaper the *Morning Post*, and promptly shared this intelligence with his colleagues. Not content with that, he asked the Prince, when replying to Beresford, to let him know that such behaviour incurred the royal disfavour.

The Prince did indeed advise Beresford to stop leaking to the *Morning Post*, but was far angrier at the breach of trust by Granville, for he feared it would rupture his friendship with Beresford. The Prince immediately wrote to Granville urging him to drop the matter, defending Beresford with, among other things, the phrase 'he is an Irishman, and in consequence hasty and impetuous'.[87] His plea was heeded, though this only encouraged Beresford to further indiscretions in the future. The outcome of the difficulties with Egypt had mixed results for the Prince. When it came to a fight Beresford so distinguished himself that he was promoted captain and became something of a national hero; but the French refused to have any part in the fighting and pulled out of Egypt, damaging Anglo-French relations into the bargain. The only European power which welcomed the British occupation of Egypt, completed in the late summer of 1882 under Sir Garnet Wolseley, was Germany, for Bismarck realised with glee the strain it would put on Anglo-French relations. France immediately started a process, which would drag on until after the Prince had become king, to ask Britain to set a date for leaving Egypt; and the Turks, who felt Egypt was naturally part of their empire, were aggrieved into the bargain, further destabilising the balance of affections within Europe. Still yearning for something to do, the Prince had offered to accompany the expedition to Egypt. The Queen had been 'disturbed' to hear of the idea – the Prince was not remotely qualified as a professional soldier – and saw that nothing came of the notion.[88]

From the time of the Congress of Berlin in 1878 until the death, after a tragically short reign, of his brother-in-law Kaiser Frederick III in 1888, the Prince had some reason to view Germany more favourably. Bismarck went out of his way, on several occasions, to be cordial and constructive in conversation with the Prince, which – given how susceptible the Prince was to personal charm – proved a good investment by the Iron Chancellor. The Egyptian adventures, plus a new upsurge of republicanism in France that led (after several attempts) to the expulsion from the country of various claimants to the French throne and their families, further alienated the Prince from France. However, a formal attempt to conclude an alliance between Britain and Germany, made in 1879, came to nothing, largely because of the Queen's wish not to alienate France.

Yet the Prince seems at that stage in his life to have been willing to grasp the challenge of improving relations between Germany and

Britain. He did not then see difficulties with the long-term problems of Germany's colonial pretensions, nor its desire, as a new country with a seaboard, to have a substantial navy. During the early 1880s one of his old friends, Lord Odo Russell (subsequently Lord Ampthill), was ambassador to Berlin, which helped improve the Prince's understanding of what was happening there. The Prince increased the frequency of his visits to his family in Berlin, and was made honorary colonel of a regiment of Pomeranian Hussars in 1883 – his first such distinction, coming almost a decade after his mother had refused to let him accept a similar colonelcy from the Tsar on the ground that it was unprecedented. On many of these trips Bismarck arranged to talk to him; once the Prince even went to witness the manoeuvres of the German army, which he diplomatically and probably accurately described as 'the finest in the world'.[89]

When Ampthill died in harness in 1884, the Prince took his by now customary leading role in seeking to influence the choice of a successor to one of the great embassies. He advanced the cause of Sir Robert Morier, an old German hand whom he had met on visits to his sister, Princess Alice, at Darmstadt. Another sister was most in favour of the appointment, and carried even more weight, since she was the Crown Princess of Germany. What made Morier especially sympathetic to the Prince was that, having spent much of his diplomatic career at such small courts as Darmstadt, he was no admirer of Bismarck's. The Prince told his mother on 28 August 1884 that Morier 'is the only one in our diplomacy fit for such an important post'; but Granville, precisely because of the strained relations between Bismarck and the potential ambassador, came down hard against the Prince's choice.[90] Thus thwarted, the Prince sought to rubbish the candidatures of several other prominent men – whether because, like Lord Dufferin, they were diplomats with no experience of Germany, or like George Goschen, an increasingly disaffected Liberal politician with whom Gladstone wished to do something, were not diplomats at all. In the end, the Prince had to put up with the appointment of Sir Edward Malet, the British minister at Brussels.

As if to prove a point, the Prince decided to pursue some other bauble for Morier. When the embassy at Constantinople became vacant, the Prince suggested Morier for it. When Granville pointed out that Morier had no experience of the East, the Prince said that to exclude him from a second embassy seemed to cast 'some slur' upon him. The Prince did not give up, and, given the obvious strength of his feelings about Morier's qualities, it is perhaps not surprising that the diplomat was appointed ambassador to St Petersburg in December 1884. The great significance of this somewhat accidental achievement was that Morier succeeded in making the Russians seem a more attractive prospect to the Prince than had hitherto been the case, and sowed in his mind the possibility of their use as a counterweight to the expansionist and aggressive Germans. One who realised this from the other end was the Prince's troublesome nephew Prince William of Prussia, now in his mid-twenties and being instructed by his mentor, Count von Waldersee, that the only way to secure Germany's future was first to attack and subdue England, and then to do the same to Russia. To this end, Prince William sought to prevent the possibility of Russia and England becoming too close: he wrote to the Tsar on 13 March 1885 that his uncle (and the Tsar's brother-in-law) had 'a false and intriguing nature' and would undoubtedly use a forthcoming visit to Berlin to plot against Russian interests.[91] Later that spring, he told the Tsar of his certainty that England and Russia would one day come to blows, but the Tsar does not seem to have been too affected by this counsel.

The Prince's attendance at Alexander II's funeral in 1881 had helped improve Anglo-Russian relations, which continued to ameliorate for all the attempts by Prince William to the contrary. The Prince of Wales, despite resistance from Granville, managed to persuade his mother to allow him to invest the new Tsar with the Garter while he was in St Petersburg, though this gesture paid no dividends for Britain. Russian manoeuvring on the fringes of Britain's Indian empire, and particularly in Afghanistan, was a constant source of tension throughout the new Tsar's relatively short reign. The defeat of an Afghan army by Russian troops at Penjdeh in March 1885 was especially explosive, breaching as it did undertakings given by Russia to Britain about its intentions in that region. The governments of both countries agreed to put the matter to arbitration by a neutral power, and the Prince urged the suitability of his father-in-law, the King of Denmark, for the job. In the event, no arbitrator was needed. However, the Prince was angry that the government had conceded to the Russians the right to remain in Penjdeh, and his growing warmth towards Russia subsided, temporarily, into froideur.

Throughout the last quarter of the nineteenth century the Prince was constantly importuning his mother's governments to do something to help the territorial claims against Turkey of his brother-in-law's government in Greece. King George was particularly upset about the redrawing of his country's borders with Turkey after the Congress of Berlin, and the Prince, lobbied by the King, did not hesitate to take the matter up with Beaconsfield; but he would not become involved, leaving it to Salisbury to pacify the Prince as best he could.[92] Salisbury even contravened the unwritten law by sending the Prince copies of Foreign Office dispatches on the question. The Gladstone administration was more helpful to him: the Prince and Granville engaged in diplomatic activity at the funeral in March 1881 of the assassinated Tsar Alexander II at St Petersburg, with the result that the new Tsar intervened to have Turkey cede Thessaly to Greece in July that year. King George felt this an inadequate gesture, though it at least had the effect of persuading the Prince that he had done more than enough in respect of these faraway countries.

Indeed, it would not be until 1897 that he would be disposed to seek to exert any influence in favour of that country. The people of Crete were again petitioning the Greek government to liberate them from the Turk. A small war broke out on the island on 15 February, the Greek navy having deposited a substantial number of troops there. All six great European powers – England, France, Germany, Italy, Austria and Russia – united in their condemnation of the aggression. The Greeks took no notice. Turkey was persuaded by the powers to agree to Cretan autonomy under Turkish suzerainty, and the powers told the Greeks to evacuate the island within six days. The Greeks refused this, and decided to declare war on mainland Turkey; but before they could the Turks, having had enough of this, declared war on the Greeks, with such ferocity that within thirty-four days the Greeks were suing for peace.

The Prince was a key player in persuading the powers to mediate between the Greeks and the Turks, and he was kept informed of how powerless his brother-in-law was to resist the swell of nationalist feeling in Greece. Once Greece was defeated, Salisbury, by then Prime Minister, was urged by the Prince to ensure that all the powers used their influence on Turkey to persuade the victor to behave leniently. The plan worked: Turkey took only small amounts of territory, and reparations of £4 million.

MAKING THE MONARCHY CONSTITUTIONAL

As heir to the throne, the Prince's main political interests were abroad: it would only be as king that he would be forced to concentrate more heavily on domestic matters. His principal activity in British politics before his accession was concerned not so much with policies as with personalities; and, notwithstanding the romance with Beaconsfield, most of his friends in politics throughout this period were prominent Liberals. His use of his position to seek preferment for those friends was perhaps his main preoccupation. He exercised it extensively for the first time when Beaconsfield's gamble in calling the election of April 1880 failed, and the Liberals were returned to office. Gladstone had stepped down as Liberal leader some years before, but had restored himself in the public estimation as *de facto* leader, and was the man to whom the party really owed its success. He had an unassailable claim on Downing Street as a result.

The Queen, adoring Beaconsfield and loathing Gladstone, was horrified by the result, and the prospect it brought. She told Ponsonby she would 'sooner *abdicate*' than have as her Prime Minister '*that half-mad firebrand* who would ruin everything and be a *Dictator*'.[93] Ever since Gladstone's attempts to find the Prince a job in the early 1870s the Queen had been affronted by him; and his histrionics in the Midlothian campaign before the election, particularly in his denunciations of her pet Beaconsfield, had ruled him out in her eyes. She had Ponsonby communicate these views unequivocally to the Prince in a letter, specifically not inviting his opinion: but he gave it to her anyway.

In a courageous, but apparently necessary, lesson in the art of sucking eggs, the Prince took it upon himself to remind his mother that, whatever her personal feelings, her constitutional obligations were paramount. The Queen wanted to persuade Lord Hartington, heir to the dukedom of Devonshire and one of the Prince's closest cronies, to form the Liberal government; and, in default of him, she wanted another of the Prince's friends, Granville, to lead the administration. The Prince, learning of his mother's intentions, talked to both men, and found them in agreement that the man responsible for the victory was Gladstone, and he would have to lead the ministry. As a second front, he wrote to Ponsonby, spelling out what a fine man Gladstone was – even though his recent anti-Turkish sentiment and pro-Russianism were utterly unsympathetic to the Prince. The Prince also identified his youngest brother, Prince Leopold, as the main poisoner of his mother's mind against Gladstone. Knollys wrote to Granville at this time that 'if the Queen would only look upon Mr Gladstone as a friend instead of as an enemy of Her Majesty and the Royal Family, which Prince Leopold deliberately delights in persuading her he is, she will find him all she could wish'.[94]

In the course of three long conversations at the Turf Club, Hartington made it clear to the Prince that Gladstone had to succeed, because of the massive public support he had registered at the election. Hartington also secured from Gladstone an assurance that he would not serve under any other Liberal prime minister, though he would loyally support the Liberal administration. The Prince told this to Ponsonby in a letter of 21 April 1880.[95] The Queen heard all the details from Hartington and Granville, jointly and separately; it was five days after Disraeli's resignation that she finally gave up and sent for Gladstone, who became both Prime Minister and Chancellor of the Exchequer. The Prince heard the news from Hartington, who wrote to him immediately upon his return from Windsor to London.

The Queen, who was not now in the best frame of mind, was outraged that her son should have played this part in the exercise of her most important prerogative. Just before her meeting with Hartington she had told Ponsonby, who had told his Queen of the correspondence with her heir, that 'the Prince of Wales may be told, but *very shortly* what the constitutional course is, which is *quite* clear. He has *no* right to meddle and *never* has done so *before*. Lord Hartington must be told, when he leaves, that the Queen cannot allow any private and intimate communications to go on between *them*, or all confidence will be *impossible*.'[96] Thus, in matters of state, was the Prince consigned to outer darkness yet again by his highly capricious mother. She would have been unamused to know that one of Gladstone's first visitors after he had accepted her commission to form a government was the Prince of Wales.[97]

Just as Gladstone's relations with the Sovereign were to deteriorate over the succeeding years, so his relations with the heir to the throne were to continue to improve, despite their policy differences. Unlike Beaconsfield, Gladstone did not go out of his way to solicit approval from the Prince for his political actions: that was simply not the way in which he operated. It meant that, although the two men enjoyed good personal relations, from which was stripped the unreal carapace of sycophancy that had encased the Prince's relations with the last Prime

Minister, the Prince's political influence over the ministry he had done so much to bring in was small. Where the Prince had friends in the ministry – notably Granville at the Foreign Office – he was able to exert a more direct pressure, and get the occasional result, but there was little he could prise out of Downing Street that Downing Street did not in any case wish to offer. His main activity with Gladstone, as usual, would be in seeking honours and jobs for friends. Yet even though Gladstone had long been well disposed to the Prince, his correctness and earnestness seem to have been a barrier to their having the sort of intimacy the Prince had enjoyed with Disraeli. Disraeli's vulgarity, showmanship and confidence-trickster air had put the Prince at his ease: he could never be so familiar with dear old Mr Gladstone.

The Prince's role for Gladstone, however, was to act as a public relations man on behalf of his appallingly rude mother (who crowned a career of casual, though at times meticulously calculated, offensiveness towards her greatest Prime Minister by failing even to thank him when, at the age of eighty-four, he finally resigned). By having the Gladstones to dine frequently at Marlborough House, by remembering the Grand Old Man's birthday and sending him Christmas greetings, the Prince at least ensured that he had some reason to feel benevolent to the royal house. The Prince carried his devotion to Gladstone literally to the Grand Old Man's grave, nobly acting as a pall-bearer at his state funeral, to the outrage of his mother.

His good relations with Gladstone also helped ensure that the Prime Minister did the Prince the occasional favour. His administration was additionally useful to the Prince in that he had several of his closest friends in high office: as well as Granville as Foreign Secretary, Spencer was Lord President, and Hartington Secretary of State for India. However, neither Carrington, who had nothing, nor Rosebery, who was merely given the under-secretaryship for Home Affairs more than a year into Gladstone's administration, had any immediate rewards. The Prince continued to badger Gladstone to promote Rosebery to the Cabinet – which, given he was only thirty-four at the start of the badgering, was even for those days pushing it a little – but it took until 1885 before Rosebery made it to the top table. Outside the aristocracy, two of the Prince's newer friends were given office – Dilke as Under-Secretary at the Foreign Office, and Chamberlain as President of the Board of Trade. In return for services rendered, the Prince made himself agreeable to Gladstone in the matter of some of his more contentious legislation. He told the Prime Minister in

September 1884, for example, that he very much hoped the government's Bill to extend the franchise would be passed.[98] It was only when Gladstone started propounding Home Rule for Ireland – a measure which, if implemented, might greatly have improved the history of the British Isles in the last hundred years – that the Prince would realise that there were limits to his espousal of radicalism.

THE PRINCE PLAYS POLITICS

For the duration of Gladstone's second administration, Dilke was the main conduit of information to the Prince. In return, the Prince chose not to mind Dilke's constant opposition to the support out of public funds of members of the royal family. When Gladstone's resignation as Chancellor in 1882 necessitated a reshuffle, the Prince sought to persuade him to promote Dilke to the Cabinet; but the Queen did not want Dilke as one of her senior ministers, because of his historic support for republicanism, and specifically vetoed his proposed replacement of John Bright as Chancellor of the Duchy of Lancaster. To try to concoct a plan that would meet with the Queen's approval – she had said that the Duchy was a 'personal' office that should be filled by a 'moderate' – the Prince asked both Dilke and Chamberlain to Sandringham in November 1882.[99]

Chamberlain, who himself was no slave to monarchy, threatened to resign unless Dilke were given office, a course the Prince implored him not to take. It was clear that Dilke would have to take an office in which, unlike the Chancellorship of the Duchy of Lancaster, he would not have to have dealings with the Queen; and the Prince tried, unsuccessfully, to persuade Chamberlain that he should take over the Duchy and let Dilke have his job at Trade. That notion having reached a dead end, the Prince suggested Dilke for the Admiralty, even though the current First Lord, Lord Northbrook, was perfectly happy in his work. The Prince, meddling far beyond his constitutional capabilities, thought Northbrook could take the India Office. Gladstone ignored this too. Knollys wrote to Gladstone on 17 December with another suggestion – Dilke for the presidency of the Local Government Board, a junior post in the Cabinet. Gladstone accepted this idea, which was something of a triumph for the Prince, though the whole procedure had displayed his limits in dealing not just with his mother, but also with Mr Gladstone.

In fact, Dilke was far from popular even within the government. On his appointment Horace Seymour, one of Gladstone's private secretaries, wrote to Ponsonby to tell him that 'I have no particular liking for Dilke, as I doubt his being very straight.'[100] The Queen was disgusted by Dilke's appointment, and made it a condition of his receiving office that 'he should say something to obliterate his "crude ideas"'.[101] Dilke made the promise, and the Queen waited impatiently for him to keep it. Nothwithstanding the Christmas holiday, she wrote to Gladstone on 28 December 1882, barely a week after Dilke's appointment, to ask him to 'pray remember that I accepted Sir Charles Dilke on condition that he took an early public opportunity of making a recantation or explanation of his former crude opinions'.[102] A speech was made, to the Queen's grudging satisfaction, within a few more days, but only after much more pestering.

The Prince's exact role in this affair, and his *modus operandi* in politics, was outlined by Dilke in a contemporaneous memorandum. 'During the whole of the month,' he recorded,

> while my position in the Cabinet was under hot discussion, I saw a great deal of the Prince of Wales, who wished to know from day to day how matters stood, and I was able to form a more accurate impression of himself.... The Prince is, of course, in fact a strong Conservative, and a still stronger Jingo, readily agreeing in the Queen's politics, and wanting to take everything everywhere in the world, and to keep everything if possible; but a good deal under the influence of the last person who talks to him, so that he would sometimes reflect the Queen and sometimes reflect me, or Chamberlain, or some other Liberal who had been shaking his head at him. He has more sense and more usage of the modern world than the Queen, but less real brain power. He is very sharp in a way – the Queen not sharp at all, but she carries heavier metal, for her obstinacy constitutes power of a kind.[103]

Dilke had made the correct assessment of the Prince of Wales's instinctive politics, for, ironically given how many close friends he had in the Liberal government, and how much he personally admired Gladstone, he was to find himself out of sympathy with much of Gladstone's domestic policy. When the Prime Minister's attempts in 1884 to extend the franchise were thrown out by the Lords, Gladstone's response was to announce that they would immediately be reintroduced in the Commons, and that the Lords would face drastic reform if it continued to impede the will of the Commons. This horrified the Prince, who for all the supposed Conservatism of his position had privately welcomed the Bill the Lords had just rejected, and had even asked Rosebery whether it would be constitutionally possible for him to vote for it in the Lords. This new threat to the Upper House changed everything, in his eyes. He believed the Lords was central to the constitution and, unlike some more contemporary politicians, saw an assault on the hereditary privileges of the aristocracy as an assault on those of the monarchy. He offered to act as an intermediary between Gladstone and Salisbury in order to help find a solution, which would have been a dangerously deep involvement for him in politics; luckily, both men were too mindful of the necessities to think of accepting the offer. The Prince was relieved when a compromise was reached in the autumn of 1884 that allowed Gladstone's measure into law, but his views on the Lords would not change, and would at the climax of his life and reign cause him much distress.

Granville used the Prince to try to obtain the Garter for Gladstone from an unwilling Queen. Little appreciating what fight the Grand Old Man had left in him, Granville and his colleagues thought that the success of the franchise legislation in 1884 would be his swansong, and that the Garter would be both an appropriate recognition of his services and a means of easing him into retirement. The Prince tried to choose his moment carefully to carry out this disagreeable task – he knew well what his mother thought of her Prime Minister – and was unsuccessful, not least because the Queen had, in a rare moment of compassion for Gladstone, offered him a peerage in 1883 during a period of illness, and he had turned it down. No Garter was forthcoming, but when Gladstone resigned office in 1885 after being defeated on the Budget the Queen (at the continued behest of the Prince of Wales) did offer him an earldom, which he again refused.

The events surrounding Gladstone's resignation in 1885 demonstrated that the Prince was starting to become, at last, a constitutional force. The Queen was at Balmoral, and had no intention of coming to London. Gladstone was in London, and had no intention of going to Balmoral. It was felt that the Queen should return to the seat of power, but no one was prepared to tell her this. No general election could be held, as a massive boundary change was under way following the Reform Act of the previous year. Either Gladstone had to soldier on despite this important defeat, or Salisbury had to form a government, albeit one not destined to survive for long. The Queen had to come to sort the mess out, but she was not minded to do so.

Gladstone's secretary, Eddie Hamilton, informed Knollys of the impasse on 9 June 1885. He dropped heavy hints that the Prince might like to join the chorus of opinion that believed the Queen should come south, and perhaps might even like to be the one to tell her. The Queen herself had started to see the other side of the argument, and wrote to Gladstone saying she would be on her way as soon as she could; but that was unlikely to be just yet. Her behaviour threatened to make a mockery of the normal constitutional procedures. The Queen told Ponsonby, who was in London, that she would not be hurried, and asked her private secretary to acquaint her son with the facts, in order to enlist the Prince's support.

The Prince, however, took a very high-minded and correct view of the whole matter. He immediately wired to the Queen that 'in present grave ministerial crisis your presence near London earnestly desired unless you do not accept Government's resignation. Fear your position as Sovereign might be weakened by your absence. Forgive my saying this but universal feeling is so strong I could not help telegraphing.'[104] The Queen was somewhat stunned, and sent further excuses: Gladstone was delighted the telegram had been sent, thinking it 'eminently judicious'.[105] It was another week before she appeared in the south, and as far as the political class was concerned the throne had been weakened by her attitude. It was just another act of constitutional neglect by his mother that diminished the respect in which influential people held the monarchy, and which, one day, the Prince himself would have to rectify.

OPEN GOVERNMENT

By 1882 the Prince was complaining to his mother that he was less trusted with official information than were the private secretaries of individual ministers, each of whom had a key to open his chief's dispatch box. So impressed was Gladstone by the Prince's conduct and statesmanlike behaviour on his visit to Ireland in 1885 (see p. 54) that he asked the Queen to reverse her decision and let the Prince, who was now after all nearly forty-four, see state papers. The Prince was a

willing conspirator in this plan. In May 1885 he had complained to
Eddie Hamilton that he was 'kept in the dark' too much and that 'he
would like important decisions of the Cabinet communicated to
him'.[106] Hamilton checked with Knollys, who told him quite truthfully
that the Prince had received all sorts of missives in Beaconsfield's day.
Knowing the late Prime Minister as they did, Hamilton and Gladstone
surmised that this flow of information had been without the knowledge
of the Queen; but, in fact, the Queen had advised Beaconsfield in
October 1876 that 'it would be best not to refuse to send any dispatches
to the Prince of Wales but only to send such as were not very
confidential'.[107]

Gladstone was quite happy for the Prince to see both Cabinet
memoranda and foreign dispatches, and was glad he had given him
the chance to raise the matter, for he was determined not to do it
behind the Queen's back. He had Ponsonby write to the Queen to
inform her that 'The Prince of Wales complains that the Government
tell him nothing. Mr Hamilton thinks Mr Gladstone would readily tell
His Royal Highness anything of importance that takes place in the
Cabinet – though he is not sure whether Lord Granville would concur.
But first he asks – would Your Majesty sanction this?'[108]

The Queen most certainly would not sanction it. The letter in which
it was suggested is marked in her handwriting 'not approved', with the
'not' underlined heavily, twice.[109] It may have interested her that
Granville, who knew her son better than most ministers, was uneasy on
the question, and she may have drawn the conclusion that he was
uneasy precisely because he knew her son so well. During his time as
Foreign Secretary Granville's correspondence with the Prince was
immaculately correct, usually merely acknowledging titbits the Prince
had supplied him with from his own conversations with diplomats or
members of other royal houses. There was no conspicuous traffic of
information in the other direction, as there had been in earlier days,
which says much about Granville's sense of propriety, or his
understanding of the Prince, or both. Indeed, at this time Granville
told Gladstone that 'the Prince of Wales is thoroughly though
unintentionally indiscreet – and he is especially abusive of our Foreign
Policy – and I doubt his being a little better informed would make
much difference – the Queen would I should think strongly object to
regular reports from the Cabinet'.[110] The Queen, also, had noted on
Ponsonby's letter to her that the Prince was 'not discreet'.[111]

Gladstone was not, though, one to give up, which was precisely why the Queen found him so tiresome. He had Ponsonby ask her whether the Prince could be allowed to see Cabinet reports. Writing to Ponsonby, the Prime Minister had said that 'I agree, respectfully and decidedly, in the opinion that communications to the Prince of Wales as to matters treated in the Cabinet should be by the immediate authority and under the immediate control of the Sovereign. On the other hand the admission of the Prince, at his time of life, to an interior knowledge of affairs, appears to me very judicious and desirable.'[112] Mindful of past objections, Gladstone added that 'I feel certain that HRH will receive the communications under a full sense of being bound, both towards the Queen, and towards the national interest, to the most careful secrecy.' The Queen, however, complained that her son could not be trusted with 'secrets', and said it would be 'quite irregular and improper' for the Prince to see documents that had hitherto been seen by herself alone.[113] If anybody was going to convey reports of what went on at Cabinet meetings to the Prince, it would be the Queen. It was still thirty years before the first Cabinet secretariat, and Gladstone in his own hand would write privately to the Queen after each meeting of the Cabinet informing her of what had passed.

Despite her objections, the Queen eventually agreed that her son could be informed of great decisions or changes of policy before they became widely known. The Prince, though, objected to the method of doing this – his mother making her own selections from what Gladstone told her and then having them passed on to him – because by the time he at last received the news, especially if his mother was at Balmoral, it was stale. Knollys and Hamilton made a joint approach to Ponsonby, to have him persuade her to be more flexible. They hoped that, in the first instance, the selection of news could be made by the Prime Minister, not by the Queen. The Queen objected, saying that under the constitution the Prime Minister 'can only report to the Sovereign, and it would not be desirable that W.G[ladstone] and HRH should have discussions which she knew nothing about. Whereas, on the other hand, it would be natural and constitutional that she should communicate with her son and take counsel with him on questions of public interest.'[114] She simply would not believe that her beloved Beaconsfield had regularly communicated with her son without her knowledge. 'Mr Gladstone must have been misinformed about Lord Beaconsfield sending regular reports to HRH as HM is convinced this was not done,' Ponsonby assured Hamilton on 28 May.[115] As the evidence of the October 1876 correspondence shows, the Queen's memory failed her. Hamilton replied that he and Gladstone were 'disappointed' by the Queen's attitude, 'and I am afraid the Prince of Wales will be similarly minded'.[116]

However, when the Prince's friend Rosebery became Foreign Secretary briefly in Gladstone's short-lived third administration of 1886, he routinely sent dispatches to him, without any authority from the Queen, 'in the red leather boxes which habitually circulated among ministers'.[117] Rosebery was quite nonchalant about it, as he was about so much else. 'It has occurred to me', he wrote to the Prince on 29 July 1886, 'that Your Royal Highness ought to have a cabinet key instead of your present one. If therefore it would be agreeable to Your Royal Highness to have one I will give orders that it shall be sent to you.'[118] Needless to say, the Prince did not have to be asked twice; however, as a bonus, the key he was actually sent was a special gold one made for his late father, and which had been retained at the Foreign Office since his death. This opened the most secret boxes, which Rosebery had sent to the Prince. The Cabinet key, which came too, opened boxes containing less sensitive material. Sadly for the Prince, Gladstone's third administration, and Rosebery's term at the Foreign Office, lasted but five months. The Queen, when (as was inevitable) she found out about this arrangement, protested at Rosebery's presumption, but the traffic of information to the Prince was not stopped. Salisbury, on becoming Prime Minister and Foreign Secretary again later in 1886, sent the Prince the second, less sensitive type of dispatch box only, though after three years he relented and allowed him, once more, to see all Foreign Office papers.

When Gladstone took office for the fourth and last time in 1892, he obtained the Queen's approval that his own private secretary, Sir Algernon West, should send the Prince copies of the reports of Cabinet meetings that Gladstone sent to the Queen. The Queen agreed on the understanding that the Prince would immediately send back the reports to Sir Algernon once he had read them. The Cabinet accepted this arrangement on 7 November 1892: from the 21st it was adopted, with 'Seen, A.E.' written in the margins of the reports before being returned.[119] There was a small hiccough before it happened: the Prince claimed that Salisbury, when he had been Prime Minister, had sent him Cabinet reports (something for which there is no documentary evidence, and which Salisbury had no permission to do), and Salisbury was consulted about what channels had been used – not by way of reproaching him, but simply to set out the least inconvenient arrangement for the future. On 14 November Salisbury told Ponsonby of his 'perplexity' at the Prince's claim – 'his statement refers to some incident that I have forgotten.... I cannot remember a single instance in which I sent him "the proceedings of the Cabinet".'[120]

There is no cause to doubt Salisbury's word. The Prince had often had quite substantial information from him other than purely on foreign affairs, but never regularly, even unofficially. What had happened was that Schomberg McDonnell, Salisbury's private secretary, had told Knollys – with whom he was on terms of close friendship – of any important developments, which had been passed on to the Prince. Now, at last, that veil had been lifted, though West, who would have the laborious task of copying out for the Prince the Cabinet proceedings, received one last warning from Ponsonby about how to present them to the Prince. 'I will be as discreet as possible,' West assured him, 'in a condition of things not altogether easy – I always mark my memos "secret".'[121]

The Prince made a visit to Ireland in April 1885 that was portrayed to the Queen and in parts of the British press as successful. The reality was a little different. As Fritz Ponsonby, son of Sir Henry and assistant private secretary to King Edward during his reign, put it, drawing on the folklore of the royal household: 'The Dublin City council flatly refused to take any official part in his reception, and his visit to the South was nothing more or less than a dismal failure.'[122] The Prince was, though, held to have behaved courageously and with great dignity in the face of provocations by militant nationalists. Gladstone had encouraged him to make the trip, hearing of the Prince's intention to do so with 'very lively satisfaction'.[123] When he returned, the Prime Minister congratulated him on the success of the visit 'cordially', which sounds more like a rare instance of the normally superhuman Gladstone feeling the need to save a little of his own face and the Prince's.[124]

There was a disturbance at Mallow and another at Cork, where the streets were draped in black and coffins were put out along the route. The Prince felt these incidents had been whipped up by local troublemakers. Expecting nationalist MPs to try to exploit them, he had Knollys fire a warning shot across the Irish Secretary, Henry Campbell-Bannerman, on 19 April. Knollys observed:

the Prince of Wales desires me to say that he feels very strongly that if any remarks of an offensive nature are made about him by the Irish members in the course of any questions that may be asked or of any motion that may be made in regard to the Mallow incident or the Cork visits, that reference should be made to the disgraceful allusions to HRH in the recent speeches of Messrs O'Brien, Deasy, O'Connor and Harrington. Nothing could have been more outrageous than the manner in which Mr O'Connor rounded on the mob on the quay at Cork.[125]

Whatever else, the Prince's mind was broadened. He told Gladstone, who debriefed him on his return, that 'I should not mind knowing Mr Parnell'.[126]

As, it seems, a consequence of the visit, the Irish plan, squashed so forcibly in 1871–2, arose again. It was hoped the Queen would have changed her mind. She had not. In May 1885 Spencer, in his second term as Viceroy of Ireland, had an audience of the Queen in which he argued the benefits of making the Prince a non-political viceroy, particularly in the light of the highly successful visit he had just paid there. The Queen listened sufficiently politely to make Spencer think he had won the argument, but within days he was informed that Her Majesty remained set against any such notions. Spencer despaired at the Queen's obstinacy. 'I feel inclined', he wrote to Ponsonby on 11 May, 'to throw up the sponge and retire to my plough in Northamptonshire.'[127] Despite Fenian agitation stirred up from America, the Prince nonetheless attained some considerable popularity in Ireland, renewing affections established on an earlier visit in 1868. Shortly after making that first visit he had discussed it with John Bright, the great Liberal statesman, telling him that the trip 'pleased him greatly'. In response to these complacencies, Bright had somewhat sternly told the Prince that 'there must be legislation as well as civilities', though he did concede the visit had been 'very wise'.[128]

What effect it might have had on Anglo-Irish relations had the Queen given way, and allowed the future King to identify himself explicitly with the Irish people, one can only speculate. There would always have been the danger of his being dragged to one side or other of the political argument, since political argument was much more to the fore in Ireland than in the rest of the United Kingdom. And, although the Prince was not a slave to 'Orangeism', he had (unsurprisingly) traditional views about the importance of the Union over which he hoped one day to rule. As his official biographer puts it:

'The Prince was convinced that the grant of Home Rule to Ireland was incompatible with the maintenance of the integrity of the Empire, and that coercion of the disaffected Irish was an essential safeguard of the Union.'[129] Although his old friend Mr Gladstone took the opposing view many of the Prince's other Liberal friends, led by Hartington, were very much of the same opinion as he was. They broke off and formed a Liberal Unionist party when their old party embraced Home Rule in 1886, and took Gladstone on – fatally, in that instance, since he subsequently lost office, for Gladstone.

SOLDIERS OF THE QUEEN

Of all the domestic policies Gladstone pursued during his second administration, reform of the army was perhaps the one that dragged the Prince most into political controversy. His mother's first cousin, the Duke of Cambridge, had been Commander-in-Chief since 1856. He believed in things in the army being done as they had always been done, with an obsessive concentration on drill and promotion according to seniority and not merit. Hugh Childers, Gladstone's Secretary of State for War from 1880 to 1882, was determined to liberalise and modernise the army, but first had to bring it under political control. The Duke would not hear of such impingement on his authority, and enlisted the Prince to help fight his corner. Ironically, the Queen gave way quite easily, not because she agreed with the planned reforms – she emphatically did not – but because even she was aware of the constitutional impropriety of ignoring the advice of her Prime Minister in this matter. The Prince, though, operated a policy of blind loyalty to 'Uncle George', at least to start with. He had always felt the close link that the royal house must have with the armed forces, all the more so since his mother had made him a field marshal in 1875.

One of Gladstone's early ploys was to have Sir Garnet Wolseley, a most popular soldier with the public, given a peerage – no less than his due, given his exemplary service record – so that he could give voice in Parliament to his own belief in reform. Cambridge said he would resign if Wolseley were thus honoured, a threat he delivered via the Prince. The Prince took Uncle George's side, and managed to persuade his mother not to elevate Wolseley – though it was a postponement of that honour, not its cancellation. Instead, Childers had Wolseley made Adjutant-General, which the Duke claimed undermined his authority. The Prince intervened again, suggesting to the Queen that Wolseley might be better employed as Governor-General of Canada. But on this Gladstone and Childers were not prepared to give way, not least because the heavy press were on their side, and the movement for reform was becoming unstoppable. The Prince, as on other occasions in his career of political interventionism, changed horses and persuaded Uncle George to accept the inevitable, which Uncle George did. One great factor in the Prince's switching sides was, as so often, the pressure of his friends. In 1882 Childers was succeeded at the War Office by Hartington, who was even more determined for reform than his predecessor had been. Not only did the Prince come to concur with him, but the act of conversion initiated an obsessive interest with modernising the army that was to make it one of the dominant themes of the Prince's reign.

The Duke survived in office until 1895, when he was seventy-six years old; it had long since been decided, and almost universally accepted, that when he gave up the commandership-in-chief the post would be abolished. However, on becoming Secretary of State for War a second time in 1892, Sir Henry Campbell-Bannerman decided to retain the office, but with greatly reduced powers. Although he had to tolerate various incursions into his authority, wholesale reform had to await the Duke's departure, and Campbell-Bannerman set about getting him out. The Duke made it clear he had no intention of going, and the Prince put his heart before his head again and, initially, backed him up. However, he soon realised the direction of the tide, and began a campaign to try to persuade Uncle George to go.

There was much plotting between the Prince and his mother about how best to go about this; the Prince tried on his uncle the line that if the Duke had to be forced out, the post of commander-in-chief, which both he and the Prince wanted to preserve, would be abolished too. This had no effect on the Duke. A plea to Rosebery, by then Prime Minister, to allow the Duke to serve a few months longer also failed. The Prince then tried more direct persuasion on his uncle, but his methods were not always the most diplomatic. Campbell-Bannerman told Rosebery how the Duke 'was very much hurt because the P of W on the way to the races told him in quite a casual picktooth sort of manner that the Q had come to the conclusion he ought to go'.[130] In the end, the Queen accepted her son's advice that she persuade the Duke to go in a private interview. Even this was not straightforward, since the Duke was not prepared to obey the injunction of his cousin and Sovereign. In the end, the Queen had to write to him after the interview to tell him to resign, which he at last did.

By the time his successor came to be appointed, Salisbury had replaced Rosebery as Prime Minister, and the Prince was determined to take an active role in the choice of the new Commander-in-Chief. One reason why the Prince had wanted the office retained was that he had hoped his brother, the Duke of Connaught, who commanded the garrison at Aldershot, might obtain it. However, various of the Prince's military friends persuaded him that the Duke was too young, and should gain more experience before acceding to this highest post in the service. It furthered the Prince's ambitions for his brother, therefore, that the government proposed to limit the commandership-in-chief to five years, without the prospect of reappointment. The Prince then adopted Sir Redvers Buller, the Adjutant-General, as his candidate, perhaps shrewdly because he was also favoured by Campbell-Bannerman. But there was then the change of ministry and Lord Lansdowne, Salisbury's War Secretary, wanted Lord Wolseley. Wolseley was promoted to the job, much to the dismay of the Prince and the Queen, who knew him as Uncle George's main adversary. Sensibly, as Wolseley set about some practical reforms – such as new uniform and equipment – he made sure to enlist the support of the Prince.

'KIND HEARTS ARE MORE THAN CORONETS'

The Prince's fascination with Beaconsfield had been not solely on account of the old mountebank's ingratiation towards him. The Prince, while correctly identified by his Liberal friends as a Tory, was on social matters very much of Beaconsfield's 'One Nation' school: in other words, hardly distinct from the social aspects of Liberalism, and embodying the hard-core traditions of *noblesse oblige*. The Prince let Prime Ministers from Beaconsfield onwards know that if they were considering inquiries or commissions to investigate possible means of social reform, he was only too glad to be asked to become involved with them. In this wish to do good works he may simply have been itching to satisfy his desire to have something serious to do, but he was also pursuing a path trodden by many of the aristocracy throughout the nineteenth century.

One motive for Conservatives to engage in this sort of politics – and it had started during the 1840s at the time of the Chartist agitation – was because of their fear of revolution. They had read their Carlyle too well, and lived in dread of the people of the slums, or the victims of an agricultural depression, turning on their employers or their feudal masters. More than a generation later, when a new industrial and agricultural slump was impending at the end of the 1870s, Beaconsfield engaged in a long correspondence with the Prince about the possibilities of establishing a committee to inquire into the reasons for the country's economic decline. The Prince was willing to sit on such a committee, provided it was non-partisan. However, the scheme came to nothing. The following year the Prince lobbied Beaconsfield to see to it that the country's water supplies were improved, and, although the Prime Minister showed no willingness to take up the matter himself, the government did introduce a Bill to establish a public water board in London instead of the various private companies there; but the Bill fell with the Conservative defeat in the 1880 election.

But perhaps the Prince's most direct involvement in politics was in May 1879, on the apparently minor matter of the Bill to allow a man to marry his deceased wife's sister. It was being introduced by an old friend of the Prince's, Lord Houghton: and when Houghton introduced the second reading of the Bill in the Lords, the Prince rose to present a petition signed by 3,258 farmers of Norfolk praying for the Bill to be passed into law. The Prince also made a short speech, saying he presented the petition because it was his 'firm conviction' that if passed the Bill 'would be of advantage to the community at large', and that Houghton had his 'hearty support'.[131] However, the motion was defeated by 101 to 81 votes, helped by the opposition of the established Church. It was reintroduced three years later, when the Prince again supported it, and it was again defeated. On a third occasion when the measure came to the House, in 1885, the Prince was again asked to present a petition, and did so: this time on behalf of the cab-drivers of London, appropriately so since he was one of their best customers. It was not, though, until 1896 that the Lords passed the measure, only to see it defeated in the Commons.

A far meatier subject was the condition of the housing of the working classes, and in 1884 the Prince accepted an invitation from Gladstone to sit on a Royal Commission on the subject, chaired by Dilke, after Dilke had sounded out Ponsonby about the suitability of the Prince's involvement. It had originally been hoped that the Prince would chair it himself, but he was too busy with other things.[132] For once, the Queen did not prevent her son from participating, Ponsonby telling Dilke the plan was 'excellent'.[133] The Prince urged the appointments of two others to the committee. One was George Goschen, the man whose qualifications for the Treasury Lord Randolph Churchill forgot when he thought he had snookered Salisbury by resigning in 1886. The other, in a display of his liberal credentials, was the philanthropist and reformer Octavia Hill.[134] Dilke too urged Miss Hill's appointment, but the Cabinet decided against it. It should be noted that, for all the Prince's enthusiasm to have women engaged on good works, he was fiercely opposed to their having the vote.

When the formal motion to establish the Commission came to the Lords on 22 February 1884, the Prince made his only full speech from the red benches. It was brief in the extreme – two or three minutes – and followed non-partisan assessments of the problem by Salisbury and Carrington. After a few platitudes, the Prince told the House that 'as your Lordships know, I take the keenest and liveliest interest in this question'.[135] With a charming modesty, he added, 'I confess I have not gone into the matter deeply enough for me to venture on giving an opinion,' but he was 'deeply flattered' to be asked to serve on the Commission. Citing his own credentials in this matter, he said that since acquiring the estate at Sandringham twenty-one years earlier, 'I have been much occupied in building fresh dwellings for the poor and the working classes.... I hope that now there is hardly one person on the estate who can complain of not being adequately housed.' He had, he added, been round 'two of the poorest courts and districts in St Pancras and in Holborn' a few days earlier, and had found conditions there 'perfectly disgraceful'. He trusted that the result of the Royal Commission would be 'to recommend to Parliament measures of a drastic and thorough character, which shall be the means not only of improving the dwellings of the poor, but of ameliorating their condition generally'.

The Royal Commission met thirty-eight times, and the Prince attended sixteen of its meetings. He took his fair share of questioning witnesses, one of whom, Mr Edmund Beck, was the agent from his own estate at Sandringham. Beck substantiated part of the Prince's speech to the Lords, telling the Commission of the 'sound cottages' that the Prince had built to replace the 'miserable hovels' on his own property.[136] Part of the duties of the commissioners was to tour slum housing: the Prince, owning much Duchy of Cornwall land in Kennington in south London, had some of his own, which he was seeking to improve; and his 1885 visit to Dublin was partly to obtain evidence of the problem from elsewhere in the Kingdom. The Prince signed the Commission's main report published in May 1885. However, he withheld his approval from an appendix that all but five of his colleagues had signed, for it argued for the furtherance of the rights of leaseholders at the expense of freeholders. He did sign a recommendation that landlords be compelled to keep their properties in an acceptably habitable state. Salisbury's administration enacted some of the proposals, though a first Act of 1886 proved to have so many loopholes that another was necessary in 1890.

The Queen had been concerned lest the Prince's participation in the Housing Royal Commission drag him into party politics; so when, in 1891, he seemed to be preparing to make another such excursion, she again voiced her anxiety. Salisbury set up a Royal Commission into industrial relations, to explore whether any legislation in this area was desirable. Hartington was the chairman, and the Prince volunteered to serve. On 21 March 1891 Knollys wrote to McDonnell: 'The Prince of Wales asks if it could be made known in any way that he wished to serve on the Labour Commission, but that it was not thought expedient that he should do so.'[137] He said that the Prince would 'quite understand' if Salisbury felt this was impossible. The Cabinet did indeed decline his offer, owing to the controversial nature of the subjects the Commission would discuss.

However, when Gladstone returned to power the following year, another less controversial opportunity presented itself. The new Prime Minister wanted to have an inquiry to decide what help the state should give to the poor who were too old to work; and, having been dropped a heavy hint by Knollys in a letter at the end of November 1892, asked the Prince to serve on it.[138] The membership of the Aged Poor Commission, as it became known, reflected the Prince's belief that the working classes themselves should be represented; and one such was the MP for the Prince's own estate at Sandringham, the radical Joseph Arch, who in 1872 had founded the National Agricultural Labourers' Union. Joe Chamberlain was the most prominent politician on the Commission, and the Prince, throwing himself into its deliberations, frequently invited his fellow commissioners to stay a weekend with him at Sandringham.

He attended thirty-five of the forty-eight sessions of the Commission over its two-year period of activity, and, as before, took an active part in the questioning. According to Sir Sidney Lee, the Prince's main concern was 'to ascertain the grounds of the strong prejudice harboured by the aged poor against entering the workhouses'.[139] Even a visit to the workhouse in Lambeth did not answer this question for him, for he later had to ask one of the witnesses before the Commission, George Lansbury, a future Labour leader, to explain why the inmates objected to workhouse dress and food. Many of his colleagues were urging the establishment of old age pensions, but the Prince called for this proposal to be properly costed. He put stress on the importance of thrift, and the operation of friendly societies, rather than create a bigger role for the state. When the Commission came to report in 1895 it was split, with a majority opposing state pensions. The Prince felt he could not support either side, but attached his own note:

> I have taken the deepest interest in the long and laborious inquiry of the R. Comm. on the Aged Poor, the meetings of which I have attended as frequently as possible. In not attaching my signature to the Report I do not mean to express disapproval of it. I feel however that as the subject has now to a considerable extent become one of party controversy, both inside and outside of Parliament, it has assumed a phase inconsistent with my position of political neutrality.

It would not be until 1908, under a Liberal government and in King Edward's reign, that the matter of old age pensions would finally be decided.

GLADSTONE AGAIN

Although the coming to power of Salisbury's administration in 1885 removed many of the Prince's cronies from office, it also put a new one in: Lord Randolph Churchill. As with his choice of Dilke as a friend, the Prince once more showed himself an uncertain judge of character. Churchill was broadly an unstable individual who had been a sworn enemy of the Prince until 1883, following a disagreement in the 1870s about the divorce of Lord Blandford, Churchill's elder brother, in which each man had, unwisely, all too publicly taken sides. The Prince became more and more to attracted to Churchill, who in the Commons was a formidable critic of Gladstone. By the time Dilke lost both office and his reputation after his own involvement in a divorce case, Churchill was on hand to fill the vacuum.

The Prime Minister remained, though, probably the member of the government best known to the Prince. Cashing in on his earlier professional relationship with Salisbury, the Prince was soon reporting to him his casual meetings with diplomats. With a nod towards what would soon be the burning political issue, the Prince also passed on a letter from an Ulster acquaintance, Lord Kilmorey, about the need to protect loyalists in Ireland. In another echo of their earlier intercourse, the Prince was soon recommending candidates for honours and jobs, including ecclesiastical appointments. As it turned out, the Salisbury ministry lasted only a few months, defeated by a combination of Gladstone's Liberals and Irish home rulers, to whom Gladstone was now prepared to offer concessions.

When the Queen had been through the distressing process of inviting Gladstone to form a government, he made it clear that one of this administration's intentions would be the achievement of Home Rule in Ireland. This split his own party, with the Prince's friend Hartington taking off his faction of Liberal Unionists. As a concession to her son, the Queen had Ponsonby keep him informed about the political situation as it had been relayed to her by Gladstone. The Cabinet-making that followed greatly excited the Prince, who foresaw massive difficulties for Gladstone if he persisted in his Home Rule plans. The Queen was also making her opinions known about who would or would not be acceptable in certain offices. She especially did not want Childers to return to the War Office, where he had pushed through reforms in the face of stern opposition from the Duke of Cambridge with the Queen's assent but not her approval. The Prince took advantage of his correspondence with Ponsonby to suggest that Sir Henry Campbell-Bannerman would be acceptable to the Duke for the post, and, indeed, Gladstone appointed him. Another success, though this was more pushing at an open door, was Rosebery's appointment as Foreign Secretary. The Prince also dissuaded the Queen from trying to make Gladstone appoint Lord Lorne, her son-in-law, as Under-Secretary for the Colonies. He wrote to Ponsonby, 'I hardly think that the Queen's son-in-law should form part of the Government, no matter what party is in power. And how could he form part of a "Home Rule" Government! I am very strong on this point.'[140]

Sitting in the Peers' Gallery in the Commons, the Prince watched the Liberal Unionists demolish Gladstone's attempt at radical legislation for Ireland. He became convinced it would not pass. He was right. Gladstone, on being defeated in the Commons on the Bill's second reading on 8 June 1886, went to the country, and lost heavily.

This defeat ushered in Salisbury for a second time, though now he would hold office for six years as Prime Minister and, within a year, as Foreign Secretary too. The Prince, perhaps more because of the second office Salisbury held than the first, immediately sought better relations with the new Prime Minister. The two men had little in common: Salisbury was a serious intellectual who could not understand the Prince's main role in life as the central figure of British, if not European, society. However, Sir Sidney Lee maintains that the Prince's extensive experience in foreign affairs, and his good contacts in the highest places around Europe, caused Salisbury to listen with respect to what he had to say on these matters. The Prince soon realised better than he had previously that Salisbury was a highly serious and strong-minded man who would not be pushed around: not that that would prevent him, on occasion, from trying. For his part, Salisbury authorised Iddesleigh, his Foreign Secretary, to let the Prince see some of the secret Foreign Office dispatches, a practice begun earlier in the year by Rosebery on his own responsibility.

The Prince had early successes with his now traditional recommendations about which of his friends – usually more distinguished as men of the turf or as socialites than as politicians – should join Salisbury's Cabinet. With Churchill immediately made Chancellor of the Exchequer and Leader of the Commons, there was no need for the Prince to expend energy on him. His attentions were turned to three others: Lord Cadogan, Lord Londonderry and, most controversially, Lord Charles Beresford. Cadogan became Lord Privy Seal, and was admitted to the Cabinet in April 1887, Salisbury having promised the Prince that something would be done for him; Londonderry became Viceroy of Ireland, the Prince having an opportunity to help after Salisbury had written to him on 27 July 1886 to say that he wished to make this appointment, though Londonderry was resisting: 'I venture to invoke Your Royal Highness' powerful assistance and advocacy to induce him to accept.'[141] The Prince got to work, and soon wrote back: 'I think he will accept your offer.'[142] Salisbury generously acknowledged his help.

Beresford, whose impulsive and not always subordinate behaviour

64

we have already noted, and who had returned from the sea to enjoy his second spell as a Conservative MP, was not regarded by Salisbury as such a catch. The Prince thought that he might, like Londonderry and as a fellow Irishman, find employment in Ireland. 'The Chief Secretary will be a very difficult post to fill,' he told Salisbury, dropping a heavy hint. However, he knew in his heart that Beresford was not suited to so delicate a post, so he asked: 'would you take his name into consideration as Head of the Irish Police Force? He is an admirable organizer and hard worker,' and the Prince felt it should 'carry considerable weight' that he was Irish.[143] Under some duress Salisbury made Lord Charles a junior Lord of the Admiralty, 'intermediately at all events', as he told the Prince, 'until some more agreeable offer becomes possible'.[144] On 30 July the Prince replied that 'it gives me greatest pleasure to hear that you intend offering C. Beresford a seat at the Board of Admiralty – I only wish his great capabilities of organization could have enabled him to be of some use in Ireland in opposing the Land League. Cadogan I know will be greatly gratified to receive a post in the Govt, as I know how anxious he is to be of use and have work' – a predicament the Prince knew all too well.[145]

Sadly, Beresford was almost at once engaged in violent disagreement with the First Lord, Lord George Hamilton, about the lack of speed with which Hamilton was engaging upon reform of the senior service. Having so recently been a serving senior officer, and one of some distinction, Beresford was hardly going to suffer fools gladly. Relations became so heated that the Prince, who realised he had rather misjudged this particular friend, was within two years writing to him to advise him to leave the Commons and apply for another command at sea; and was not best pleased when Beresford chose to ignore his advice, since his closeness to him caused the Prince to be embarrassed by his public criticisms of the government. Beresford was fanatical in his belief that the navy should be expanded, and used every means he could to propagate that message, including leaking to the press. He finally resigned in protest against the Treasury's refusal to contemplate higher expenditure on the service, but he stayed in the Commons a while longer to support and argue for the further strengthening of a Bill to expand the fleet.

The Prince became involved on the margins of Churchill's resignation as Chancellor in December 1886. Churchill had hoped his colleagues would agree to his plans to cut military and naval expenditure in order to fund some of the reforms of 'Tory democracy' for which he had long argued. They did not, and he fired off his resignation to Salisbury, expecting that he would not accept it. However, Salisbury did accept it, causing great shock to a number of people – Lady Randolph, who had known nothing, the Prince, and not least the Queen, since Churchill had dined and slept at Windsor and actually sent his letter of resignation on the Castle's writing paper. Churchill took the Prince into his confidence about the reasons why he had resigned, and, the better to defend his friend's actions, the Prince sent this letter on to the Queen. She was outraged by what she considered to be this breach of confidence between one of her former Cabinet ministers and her son, and ordered Ponsonby to tell the Prince to break off this 'most objectionable ... and even dangerous correspondence'.[146] The Prince, as was usual with those of his circle of whom his mother disapproved, did not drop Churchill: quite the reverse. This was to have an unfortunate diplomatic side-effect in 1887–8, when the Churchills visited St Petersburg and took Russian society by storm; the impression was created – and Churchill did nothing to dissipate it – that the Prince of Wales had authorised the trip, and that Churchill was acting as his representative in propounding the need for an Anglo-Russian entente. Again, the Queen urged her son to break off the correspondence, telling him: 'I cannot, I own, quite understand your high opinion of a man who is clever undoubtedly, but who is devoid of all principle, who holds the most insular and dangerous doctrines on foreign affairs, who is very impulsive and utterly unreliable.... Pray don't correspond with him, for he is really not to be trusted and is very indiscreet, and his power and talents are greatly overrated.'[147]

As the Prince's reputation grew with age, so too did the frequency with which his acquaintances – however distant – prevailed upon him for favours that required some element of political interference or manipulation. Modesty and discretion were seldom apparent in these requests, most of which were aimed at achieving another hoik up the social ladder for the supplicant, irrespective of merit. For example, Lord Kilmorey wrote to the Prince on 21 March 1888 from the Coburg Hotel in London: 'may I venture to ask Your Royal Highness to use your powerful influence ... in securing for me the vacancy in the Order of St Patrick.... I have consistently supported my party for 20 years in both Houses. I am the holder of an Irish title, dating from the time of Charles II – I am one of the largest landed (*resident*) proprietors in Ireland, and Your Royal Highness knows an active member of society on both sides of the channel. This is the only distinction I can aspire to.'[148] The Prince sent Kilmorey's letter on to the Prime Minister, saying that Kilmorey was 'an old Oxford friend of 28 years standing and I would be glad if you would take his name into consideration'. Kilmorey's importunate behaviour eventually paid off, and he received his Patrick.

Another typical example dates from 1891: a letter to the Prince from an acquaintance, William Francis Drummond Jervois, a former adviser to Palmerston and others on defence matters, who had noted that since his retirement from the colonial service two years earlier:

> I have received no recognition of the services which it has been my privilege to tender to her Majesty's Government during the last 50 years. I have continued to hope that some mark of Her Majesty's favour would be conferred upon me, but having been disappointed, I venture humbly to ask if it would be possible for Your Royal Highness to bring your great influence to bear on the Prime Minister, so that on the occasion of Her Majesty's birthday he may suggest my name to Her Majesty for some fitting honour.[149]

Lest one be too distressed by this hard-luck story, it should be observed that Jervois had been made a Commander of the Order of the Bath, a Knight Commander of the Order of St Michael and St George and a Grand Cross of the same Order, the last honour coming in 1878: his complaint was that he had nothing since then, 'although it is an acknowledged fact that the services I have rendered have been exceptionally great'. To spare any confusion, Sir Francis noted that, if a baronetcy were in the offing, he had the means to sustain such a dignity. Undeafened by the blowing of Sir Francis's own trumpet, the Prince nobly forwarded the letter to Salisbury.

If anything, the Prince's interest in honours increased as he became older, not least because of the expansion of his circle of friends and the range of personal and financial services he found himself occasionally being compelled to ask them to perform. After much lobbying, details of honours and appointments were sent to the Prince two days before publication from 1889 onwards: before then he had had to wait to see the lists on publication like the rest of the Queen's subjects. Sometimes he was disappointed. Knollys wrote from Sandringham to Schomberg McDonnell, Salisbury's private secretary, on 1 January 1890 that 'The Prince of Wales is very much pleased at seeing in the papers today that

Mr Mackenzie has been created a baronet, but he is greatly disappointed at finding no mention made of Sir Albert Sassoon and that his name is not included in the list of honours.'[150] Knollys said the Queen had told the Prince that Salisbury had agreed to the creation: he felt there must have been a mistake. There was: an immediate telegram assured the Prince that Sir Albert had been baroneted.

Sometimes, the possible recipients of patronage were close to home. In January 1892 the Prime Minister mooted to the Prince the possibility of the Duke of Clarence, the Prince's elder son, becoming Viceroy of Ireland. Clarence was, however, dead within days, from influenza. More usually, though, the intended recipients were members of the Marlborough House set. The Prince lobbied, for example, for a baronetcy for Christopher Sykes, giving as his justification Sykes's having spent £30,000 on elections, and having served twenty-seven years in the Commons.[151] He had also, incidentally, ruined himself financially by participating in the grotesque competitive hospitality in entertaining the Prince that was one of the less attractive aspects of the society of which he was the leader.

Later that year, the Prince told Salisbury he was 'desperately keen' on a peerage for Horace Farquhar, another crony whose business activities left something to be desired. At this, though, McDonnell warned Salisbury that 'it will be very ill-received by our people'. Nonetheless, in 1898 Farquhar had his peerage, though perhaps for reasons other than those of friendship with the Prince. He had for many years donated heavily to Unionist party funds, and was elevated after just three years on the backbenches of the House of Commons; he admitted to Eddie Hamilton, Gladstone's secretary, that the peerage was only his due for he had given more than 'the accepted tariff'.[152] So devoted was the Prince to him that, on his accession, he made Farquhar Master of the Household.

A CLASH OF PERSONALITIES

In March 1888 the old German Kaiser, William I, died in his ninetieth year. The Prince's brother-in-law Fritz became Kaiser Frederick III, and his sister Vicky the Empress. However, Fritz himself had cancer of the throat, and was too ill even to attend his father's funeral. He died in June after a reign of just 100 days. The Prince's nephew Willy, already regarded by his uncle as an arrogant, warmongering troublemaker, thus became Kaiser at the age of twenty-nine; and Sir Sidney Lee tells us that the Prince, on hearing of his brother-in-law's death, described it as 'a disaster, not only for his family and the country, but for the world'.[153] The Prince's role in making that disturbing prediction come horribly true would be one of the more disturbing themes of the next quarter-century.

When the Prince arrived at Fritz's funeral he found his sister under virtual house arrest, and the new Kaiser, Bismarck and Bismarck's son, Count Herbert, all united in apparent relief that this dangerous liberal had gone to an early grave. The Kaiser's dislike for his uncle as another such liberal was scarcely concealed; it had been practised since Willy had thought he was old enough to form such political opinions. It was to be one of the main diplomatic activities of the Prince for the rest of his life to keep his feelings about his nephew from causing great international breaches. By the time the Prince became king his concerns about his nephew's activities and intentions was to become a driving force of his approach to foreign policy. The hatred was largely prompted by personal considerations: the Prince was infuriated by the way the Kaiser treated his mother, the Prince's sister, and by his lack of respect towards him as an uncle and future sovereign. Sadly for British foreign policy, these considerations magnified an already delicate diplomatic problem between a power on the way up and another about to embark upon the way down. What must always be remembered about this relationship is that, although unfortunately it was competitive, the Kaiser was infantile in many of his attitudes to the point of mental imbalance, while the entirely sane Prince was all too often provoked beyond a point where none but a saint could be expected to turn the other cheek.

The first quarrel the two men had was the inevitable consequence of the collision between the Kaiser's touchiness and arrogance and the Prince's loose tongue. The Prince was visiting the Emperor Franz Josef in Vienna in September 1888, and learned that his nephew would be in Austria at about the same time. He wrote to Willy suggesting they meet. Willy did not reply, but a message was sent through diplomatic channels saying that the Kaiser expected no other royal guest at the Viennese court while he was there. It was a shocking insult to the Prince, who had to go to Rumania while his nephew was in Austria, and then return to Vienna to bid the Emperor farewell. The Queen, hearing of the slight, was angered, and told her son by telegraph that she was 'very anxious' that he should see Salisbury immediately on his return to England and tell him exactly what had happened.[154]

The British ambassador in Vienna, Sir Augustus Paget, investigated what had caused this diplomatic mess. On Salisbury's advice – having communicated the details to his master – Paget wrote to the Prince on 25 September 1888 to enlighten him. He spoke of:

> the *all importance* of Your Royal Highness being *more than guarded* in anything you say about the Emperor William. I am perfectly certain, from what has been told me, that all the present trouble comes from stories having been repeated to His Imperial Majesty of what Your Royal Highness has said. Some of these stories have been repeated to me. I need not say that I do not believe them, but it is necessary to avoid saying anything *whatsoever* which may be made use of as a foundation for the gossip of the malevolent or idle.[155]

As well as this, the Kaiser had, shortly after his father's death, been deeply irritated to hear that the Prince had demanded of Count Herbert Bismarck whether territory would be returned to Denmark and France won in the wars of 1864 and 1870–1, and whether the confiscated fortune of his cousin the Duke of Cumberland (who had backed the wrong side in the Austro-Prussian War of 1867) would be returned to him. Salisbury, no doubt reflecting on the wisdom of political matters being undertaken by professional politicians, informed the Prince of this at their interview on his return.

The Kaiser regarded this intervention in German politics as an impertinence by his uncle – which it was, despite the close family interest he had in two of the three matters – and was resolved not to let him forget it. Another of his complaints, relayed by Salisbury, was that the Prince treated the Kaiser 'as an uncle treats a nephew, instead of recognising that he was an Emperor'.[156] This last observation sent the Queen into orbit. She told Salisbury that this wish of the Kaiser's, 'to be treated in private as well as in public as "His Imperial Majesty"', was *'perfect madness'*.[157] His complaint, she went on, was *'vulgar'* and 'absurd'. 'If he has such notions, he had better not come here. The Queen will not swallow this affront,' she added. She hoped the relations between the two governments would not be affected 'by these miserable personal quarrels'. However, the atmosphere thus poisoned between the Kaiser and the next King of England would never, now, be cleaned up. That was to have serious implications for Anglo-German relations: and the rivalry between the two men encouraged the Kaiser to foul up his uncle's personal relationships with other European sovereigns whenever he could, which made a distinct contribution to international mistrust in the period leading up to 1914.

The Prince was not in a forgiving mood about the slight to him; and when, in 1889, Willy invited himself to Cowes, the Prince made it clear he could not take part in any official reception of him until he was given an apology. The Queen and Salisbury were worried about the political ramifications of this stand-off, and looked for a way to rectify it. It was settled that the Prince's brother-in-law, Prince Christian of Schleswig-Holstein, the uncle of the Kaiserin, would invite Willy to write a private letter of apology to the Prince. The Kaiser refused to do any such thing, claiming that the Viennese diplomatic channels that had communicated the message to the Prince the previous September had misrepresented his views and, indeed, that the incident had never happened. The Queen described this view as 'incredible'.[158] It would not be the last time the Kaiser resorted to the downright lie in his relations with his uncle. The Prince treated it with contempt; and Sir Augustus Paget was recalled to London to give the Queen a full account of what had happened at the time. The Prince made clear how unsatisfactory the Kaiser's reply to the Queen was in a letter he sent to Salisbury on 9 April 1889, in which he assumed that 'you will agree with me that the German Emperor's reply through Prince Christian ... is most unsatisfactory ... surely the Emperor might write me a few conciliatory lines which would end the matter. I have given him every chance.'[159] He added that 'the Emperor must have a very short memory' if he was denying that he had ever sought to have the Prince out of Vienna at the time of his visit. He wrote to Christian the following day, the letter being approved by the Queen, and sent a copy on 11 April to Salisbury – 'I hope that the young Emperor will accept the olive branch which I offer him ... I have no wish to ask for any more.'[160]

When this latest approach got nowhere, the Prince wrote to Salisbury that he would ask the Queen's permission to absent himself from any reception the Kaiser might be given on a future visit to England.[161] The Queen, having interviewed Paget, decided that Bismarck had been responsible, and that the Kaiser was trying to protect his Chancellor, but wrote a letter to her grandson advising him of the importance of treating Uncle Bertie with consideration. In reply to her attempts to extract a promise from the Kaiser that he would not repeat the offence, Willy wrote to his grandmother of his interpretation that 'you regard the Vienna affair as concluded, in which I heartily concur'.[162] In the interests of not aggravating Salisbury's attempts to have a decent understanding with Germany, the Prince reluctantly agreed to let the matter drop; but his and his nephew's enmity had been put on a new, more serious level from which it would never entirely recover. As the faultlessly loyal Knollys put it, his master had been 'sacrificed by Lord Salisbury to political expediency'.[163]

DOMESTIC DIFFICULTIES

As well as being adviser to the Sovereign on matters of state, Prime Ministers also find themselves involved in giving help and advice on what in most households would be purely family matters: inevitable, given the phenomenon (as identified by Bagehot) of a family on the throne, and the importance of maintaining that family intact. This has been more of a problem for modern Prime Ministers than it was for the late Victorians, but the Prince found himself having to entrust Salisbury with some of his family's more difficult secrets, because of the political significance of those in line to the throne. In an age before an intrusive press, the Prince's own philandering drew none of the attention it would merit or attract today. Salisbury found himself brought in on the margins of the celebrated Tranby Croft baccarat scandal of 1891, in which the Prince caused great shock to the religiously observant by admitting he played cards for money; and of at least one marital scandal, involving the Prince's friend, or former friend as this made him, Lord Charles Beresford. The details are beyond the scope of this book, but the affair caused to end up in Salisbury's papers a copy of the following difficult letter of 21 December 1891, from Beresford to the Prince:

> Sir, I cannot accept your Royal Highness's letter as in any way an answer to my demand. Your Royal Highness's behaviour to Lady Charles Beresford having been a matter of common talk in the two years that I have been away from England on duty. I am, Your Royal Highness's Obedient Servant, Charles Beresford.

No wonder Salisbury, not a man for society himself, had no great opinion of the Prince's moral character. Salisbury wanted to keep out of the Beresford business.[164] However, this was not perhaps the most embarrassing problem with which the Prince had to confront his mother's Prime Minister. His eldest son, Prince Albert Victor, Duke of Clarence, was a disaster. As well as being exceptionally stupid and so lacking in the normal powers of application that he was, by any normal measure, unemployable, the Duke had also been on the fringes of the notorious Cleveland Street homosexual scandal of 1890, and generally kept bad company, ran up debts and drank too much. All in all, it was a great patriotic service that the Duke – or Eddy as he was known to the family – performed in January 1892, when he died at the age of twenty-eight. The previous year, in order to get the next-but-one King under some sort of control, the Prince of Wales had decided to send him abroad. The Prince's idea was that Eddy should tour the colonies, particularly those famed for their complete lack of glamorous or sensuous diversions.

The Queen, however, felt it would prepare Eddy better for his future responsibilities if he were to make a grand tour of Europe. It would allow him to meet senior political figures and to renew acquaintances with much of his extended family, as well as to acquire some culture, thereby improving his mind. However, the Prince realised (drawing, without doubt, on his own experience) that the European capitals would be no better for Eddy than the West End of London. With the Queen seeking to have her way, the Prince, through Knollys, appealed to Salisbury for help. 'Unfortunately, her views on *certain social* subjects are so strong that the Prince of Wales does not like to tell her his real reason for sending Prince Eddy away, which is intended as a punishment and as a means of keeping him out of harm's way, and I am afraid neither of these objects will be attained by his simply travelling about Europe. She is therefore giving her advice in the dark.'[165] It must have been one of Salisbury's more thankless tasks.

RUSSIAN MOVES

Despite the greater closeness between the English and Russian royal families that had been forged by ties of blood, the Prince had still by middle age not shaken off the suspicion and hostility towards that country that had been bred in him by Palmerston and, later, Beaconsfield. Social as much as political forces moderated his view: M.

de Staal, the Russian ambassador from 1884 until 1902, was taken up by the Prince in a way none of his predecessors had been, on account of his popularity in society – a popularity which, ironically, could only blossom once the Prince favoured him. For the first time in his para-diplomatic career, the Prince had in his circle someone subtly and thoroughly advancing the Russian point of view on the main international questions, and this was matched by advice of a pro-Russian nature coming from his friend Sir Robert Morier, whom he had helped place in the embassy at St Petersburg. Morier, as a convinced opponent of Bismarck and his ways, had plenty of reason to see things from Russia's perspective, and to urge the Prince to work for a better understanding with that country.

In 1887 a family visit to Denmark put the Prince and Tsar Alexander III, the Princess of Wales's Romanov brother-in-law, together, and provided the Prince with the opportunity to dispel categorically all the mischievous stories Prince William of Prussia (as he still was) had been spreading to the Tsar about him. Thanks to his utterly defective understanding of human nature, the Kaiser had not realised that the Tsarina, being the Prince's sister-in-law, would inform the Prince of Wales in detail of the absurd allegations Willy was making against him. Willy was, though, so rattled to hear of the new Anglo-Russian friendship that, when the Tsar returned home via Germany, the Prussian Prince boarded the royal train at dawn to try to counter the English propaganda; but the Tsar refused, on the ground that he was still in bed, to see him.

In 1887 Lord Randolph Churchill took his wife on a prolonged holiday to Russia, and sent back enthusiastic word to the Prince that the international interests of Russia and Britain were now as one. Salisbury and his colleagues were horrifed by what Churchill was doing, since he risked helping to alienate many of Britain's friends who were hostile to Russia; and, as we have seen, the Queen was so incensed by Churchill's activities that she tried to persuade her son to stop corresponding with him. However, the Prince was coming more and more round to Churchill's view, even if he did not approve of his very public and loud means of expressing it. Over the next few years family ties with the Romanovs, via the Danish royal family, were to become closer, with more frequent family gatherings in Copenhagen than before; and by 1894 the Prince was urging on the Queen the 'excellent idea' of offering Tsar Alexander an honorary colonelcy in a

British regiment, though the Tsar died before anything could come of it.

His death, however, provided the excuse for a full-blown visit by the Prince and Princess of Wales to Russia, where the Prince stayed on for a month after the funeral to get to know the new Tsar, Nicholas II. He was seen constantly at Nicholas's side during the extensive funeral ceremonies, and had as the main item on his agenda the need for an Anglo-Russian rapprochement. As if to signify the inevitability of such a move, the Duke of York – now, since the death of his brother Eddy two years earlier, a prospective monarch, and a remarkable *Doppelgänger* for his cousin the Tsar – arrived in St Petersburg to join his parents. The presence of the Prince, the obvious trouble to which he was going and his obvious affection for the Russian royal family greatly improved Russian feelings towards the British. Ties were further strengthened by the marriage, a week after Alexander's funeral, of Nicholas to Princess Alix of Hesse, the Prince's niece; and there was, on the wedding day, an exchange of honorary colonelcies between the new Tsar and his uncle.

In political terms, what the Prince had done went down well. Rosebery wrote to him on his return to England 'to express my deep sense of the good and patriotic work that you have accomplished since you left England. Never has your Royal Highness stood so high in the national esteem as to-day, for never have you had such an opportunity. That at last has come and has enabled you to justify the highest anticipations, and to render a signal service to your country as well as to Russia and the peace of the world.'[166] Yet they were all being over-optimistic, not least the Prince, who could naturally foresee none of the terrible difficulties that lay ahead for the last of the Romanovs. Carried away a little by the success of his enterprise, he wrote during his Russian stay to an Austrian acquaintance that 'the character and personality of the new Tsar give assurance of the benefits which would come of an alliance between England and Russia'.[167] As with Germany at the time of the accession of his brother-in-law Fritz, the Prince hoped Russia would see political liberalisation of a peaceful nature under the new ruler, but he had not fathomed either the rigidity of Russia's politicians or the moral and intellectual weakness of his nephew. The main difficulty was the Russian Foreign Minister, Prince Lobanoff. So desperate was the Prince to advance Russian liberalism that he implored his mother to ask Salisbury whether he might suggest to the Tsar the appointment of de Staal as Foreign Minister when Lobanoff died prematurely in 1896. Salisbury, perhaps knowing the sort of reaction any interference by a foreign prince in the matter of who should be the British Foreign Secretary would provoke, responded that he had no intention of doing any such thing.

AN HONEST BROKER

When Gladstone became Prime Minister for the fourth and last time in 1892, the Prince's main concern was that Rosebery should be Foreign Secretary; and he was one of the leading friends of Rosebery who persuaded him to come out of the isolation he had imposed on himself after the death of his wife two years earlier. In approaching Rosebery, the Prince for a change had the goodwill of the Queen behind him, though was under orders not to mention her name. The Queen was acting on a request from Eddie Hamilton, who had asked Ponsonby whether the Queen could order Rosebery to serve. That was going too far even for the Queen, but, sensibly, she did suggest the use of her son's good offices. Rosebery, who had resisted all earlier pressure, and had gone to the lengths of setting off on a cruise when Gladstone won the election so as to be out of contact, was playing a game with Gladstone which involved frequent changes of mind and which drove the new Prime Minister to fury. In the end, on 14 August, by which time this saga had been dragging on for more than a month, the Prince wrote to his friend. 'Nobody', he said,

> dislikes more than I do to interfere in matters which not only do not concern me, but which might be looked upon as indiscreet; but we are such old friends and have so freely talked on so many subjects, especially regarding politics, you will, I am sure, forgive my writing to say with what deep concern I have learnt from public rumour that you are disinclined to accept office in Mr Gladstone's Government.[168]

The Prince said he understood how Rosebery disagreed with Gladstone's opinions on many subjects (Home Rule was the main problem), but that the country's good depended on Rosebery's becoming Foreign Secretary, and he added, despite his mother's orders to the contrary, that he knew how much the Queen wished Rosebery to agree to this. 'Let me therefore implore of you to accept office,' he exhorted his friend, concluding, somewhat histrionically, 'for the Queen's sake and for that of our great Empire!'

To an extent, Rosebery seemed persuaded by this intervention, although Gladstone (in direct contravention of the Queen's refusal to order Rosebery to serve) forced his hand by telling him his name would be submitted to the Queen 'today in conformity with her wish, and I trust you will allow the matter to terminate in this way for the advantage and happiness of all parties as well as for the public good'.[169] Meanwhile, Rosebery had told the Prince that 'the difficulty that I have found in going to the Foreign Office is not public but private: for I have the purest doubts as to whether my long loneliness and sleeplessness have not unfitted me for public life'.[170] The Prince of Wales's return on his investment was not what he might have hoped. In maintaining Salisbury's foreign policy of isolation, Rosebery was something of a disappointment to his royal patron.

Gladstone immediately set about a second Home Rule Bill, much to the Prince's dismay. Nonetheless, the Prince had Gladstone to dinner at Marlborough House shortly before the second reading of the Bill, and endured a long homily from the Prime Minister on the rightness of the measure. Again, the House of Lords came to the rescue, defeating the Bill by 378 votes. Within months Gladstone finally retired, exhausted, at the age of eighty-four, and the Prince was delighted to be asked by his mother to relay to Rosebery the message that she would like him as the replacement. However, the Rosebery premiership was to last just sixteen months and, beset as he was largely by internal problems of party discipline, the Prime Minister did not bring the Prince into his counsels. At the time, though, the Queen did come to rely more on her son. When Rosebery, faced with persistent sabotage of his measures by the Conservative-dominated Lords, warned the Queen that he might have to seek the Upper House's reform, she confided in her son that she was 'inclined to favour a dissolution sooner than consent to any step which implies tampering with the constitution, but I must first ascertain what the chances of the Unionists are, so don't mention this.'[171] She did ask the Prince to talk Rosebery out of it, but the Prince replied to her that there was nothing he could do or say that would improve the situation: Rosebery was far from being as extreme on this question as most of his colleagues. It was a problem that was to confront the Prince, as king, head-on fifteen years later.

ALL CHANGE

In 1895 the Prince marked Rosebery's loss of office, and Salisbury's return to Downing Street, with a banquet at Marlborough House for all the outgoing and incoming ministers, as a mark of his impartiality; but also as a mark of how, irrespective of who was in, he liked playing the game. He was helped in his equanimity in this respect by the number of his old Liberal friends who now, as Liberal Unionists, were welcomed into Salisbury's administration: Hartington, for example, who had now succeeded as Duke of Devonshire, and Joe Chamberlain. Salisbury maintained Gladstone's habit of keeping the Prince personally informed about events, or, if he could not spare the time, his secretary Schomberg McDonnell did so.

Hardly had Salisbury become Prime Minister – and Foreign Secretary – again than the nadir was reached in recent Anglo-German relations. The Kaiser would visit England almost annually during the first half of the 1890s, usually to race at Cowes, and each visit saw a progressive deterioration in his relationship with his uncle. In an act of impertinence incredible even by his standards, the Kaiser summoned his grandmother's Prime Minister to his yacht in August 1895 to receive an imperial onslaught of abuse for Salisbury's perceived failure to see Germany's point of view on international questions, notably the latest barbarities of the Turk. Through no fault of his own Salisbury was an hour late, which further annoyed his touchy host. The Prince, already branded 'an old peacock' by his nephew on this trip, was livid that Willy had sought to interfere with the British Prime Minister in this way. He was unimpressed, too, that the Kaiser had included two battleships in the flotilla he brought with him to Cowes and had harangued the sailors on them in floridly nationalistic style on the twenty-fifth anniversaries of two great naval victories over the French in 1870.[172] There seemed little hope of improvement for the future while the Kaiser insisted on behaving in so ill-mannered and provocative a fashion.

Once Salisbury had settled in again, the Prince quickly renewed his attempts to influence appointments and to secure honours, with a reasonable success rate. He began relatively modestly, lobbying in July 1895 for his friend Ferdinand Rothschild to become a trustee of the British Museum. He was also keen for a little something for the chairman of the Great Eastern Railway, who most helpfully and obligingly ran the line from Liverpool Street to Sandringham. The

Prince was especially generous in his recommendations for diplomats he met on his visits abroad, and who helped him in some way. His most notable achievement seems to have been in persuading the Prime Minister to stop the reappointment of the Italian ambassador to London for a second term. On 7 August 1898 Knollys wrote on the Prince's behalf to the Prime Minister:

> He directs me to let you know that he was anxious to see you for a few minutes respecting the proposed intention of the Italian Government to send Count Tornielli again as ambassador. HRH has received this information on what he considers is good authority, and he thinks you will agree with him that as a rule it does not answer for a man to return to the same post as Ambassador. He moreover thinks Count Tornielli is a great bore and very easily offended, and he has reason to believe he is not friendly toward England, especially as regards Egypt. Should you be of his opinion, he asks whether it is possible for you to prevent Count Tornielli from coming to London.[173]

Whether such views influenced Salisbury or not, Tornielli did not present his credentials in London a second time. Although Salisbury and the Prince were never intimate, the two men exchanged hospitality regularly during this last of Salisbury's premierships.

Before long, the Prince's views on honours were becoming quite far-reaching. On 26 October 1897 McDonnell told Salisbury that 'The P of Wales has asked me to mention to your Lordship that, when the present Garter King of Arms dies, it would, in HRH's opinion, be very desirable to institute one Chancery for all British Orders, as is done abroad, and so abolish the divided jurisdiction of the several existing officers. I said it would be an extremely difficult business but that I would speak to Y[our].L[ordship].'[174] When on 28 December that year the now traditional memorandum arrived for the Prince detailing the new year's honours, the Prince was gratified to see that there would be a knighthood for one of the 'new men' in his circle, the ever hospitable tea-merchant Thomas Lipton. Salisbury also explained in the memorandum why Lord Halsbury, the venerable Lord Chancellor, was being advanced to an earldom – he cited the precedents of previous occupants of the Woolsack who had received this accolade, and mentioned that Halsbury had served for longer than any of them.

When in 1898 there did not seem to be enough vacancies in the Order of the Bath to go round if some of the Prince's demands were to be met, he suggested an ingenious solution to McDonnell: the Queen would trade two of her household KCBs for two of Lord Salisbury's CBs, allowing him six instead of four knighthoods. Salisbury agreed. Such horse-trading was not always acceptable: earlier in the year, when the Prince had asked for Lord Sandwich to have a civil CB in recognition of his volunteer services as Colonel Commanding the South Midland Infantry Volunteer Brigade, Salisbury refused: 'This is scarcely possible: there are a certain number of military CBs and KCBs assigned by the War Office for this purpose.'[175] Tactfully, it was suggested that Lord Lansdowne, as War Secretary, be approached to recommend Sandwich instead.

THE JOYS OF EMPIRE

Much of Britain's foreign policy difficulties in the 1890s stemmed from colonial ambitions. The French were estranged over activities in North Africa, not least in the Sudan. Further south, the German settlers on the Cape and the fortunes of the Boers continued to excite German sympathy, with the Kaiser's open support of President Kruger being interpreted as the utmost hostility towards Britain. Throughout the late 1890s hostility from Germany never abated, as the Kaiser frequently let it be known that he regarded his uncle as the main anti-German conspirator. The Americans, with President Cleveland operating the Monroe doctrine (which proclaimed the USA as the dominant power in the Americas) threatened in 1895 to impose a solution on a border dispute Britain was having with Venezuela; tempers there were cooled partly by the Prince, who had retained an affection for America ever since his visit there of 1860 and who kept close contact with American ambassadors to London. As a stand-off developed between America and Britain, Joseph Pulitzer, the press proprietor, sent a telegram to the Prince and his son the Duke of York soliciting their views on the crisis. The Prince drafted a reply that said 'I earnestly trust and cannot but believe present crisis will be arranged in a manner satisfactory to both countries, and will be succeeded by same warm feeling of friendship which has existed between them for so many years.'[176] Salisbury, whom the Prince thought to consult before sending this message, was horrified. Nonetheless, the Prince sent the wire, which Pulitzer's paper, the *New York World*, duly published. As it turned out, the American public were more in favour of the

Prince's moderation than Cleveland's doctrinalism, and the temperature cooled.

THE BOER WAR

The Boer War was to be hard for the Prince in that, as his country's most prominent traveller abroad, he found that almost wherever he went during its two-and-three-quarter-year duration he was the target of protests. At the height of the conflict, in April 1900, he and the Princess were victims of an assassination attempt by a fifteen-year-old Belgian youth as their train passed through Brussels. The assailant fired at them four times. Twice his weapon refused to fire, and the two shots he did make good narrowly missed their targets, one of the bullets ending up lodged in the hair of Charlotte Knollys, the Princess's lady-in-waiting and sister of the Prince's private secretary. European views of the war were almost uniformly that Britain was acting as a colonial oppressor, and the Prince's would-be assassin said he regarded the Prince as 'an accomplice of Chamberlain [new Colonial Secretary] in killing the Boers'. The Prince, to his great credit, by all accounts kept his head during the incident, and behaved with great personal courage. However, he was rather bemused by the lack of reaction to the assassination attempt among the official classes back home. Salisbury soon learned from his secretary Sidney Greville – McDonnell, a territorial, had joined his regiment in South Africa – that 'the Prince had been a little surprised and hurt that no mention of congratulation on his escape at Brussels had been made in either House of Parliament'.[177] Salisbury noted that it had been discussed in Cabinet, and the precedents considered; the Lords had already adjourned for the day, and it was thought best not to draw extra attention to the difficulty by having a special sitting.

The Prince was also dissatisfied by the measures taken by the government to seek a speedy end to Boer misgovernment in the Transvaal Republic. In June 1899, four months before the outbreak of hostilities, he described the colonial policy of Chamberlain as 'somewhat ambiguous'.[178] When the war broke out the Prince was not slow to entertain Lansdowne, the Secretary of State for War, and other ministers with his views on the state of generalship and other strategic matters that had put British forces in South Africa on the defensive. He particularly urged the government to send out reinforcements after a spate of early defeats, though in this he only echoed the already hearty protestations of the Queen.

At least by the time the conflict came the precedents were established for the Prince to be kept fully informed of what was going on. Lansdowne and Chamberlain were in regular contact, and Wolseley, as Commander-in-Chief, reported to the Prince regularly. Nonetheless, the Prince still felt there were lacunae in his knowledge. Sidney Greville wrote to Salisbury on 9 September 1899 that 'I find the Prince of Wales much incensed with Mr Chamberlain for not having kept him informed of what was passing [in the Transvaal].' He urged that Chamberlain send the Prince a telegram 'from time to time'.[179] More irritatingly even than that, the Kaiser became a frequent correspondent of the Prince's and of the Queen's, wallowing in Schadenfreude as he wrote to commiserate in the latest British defeat, and to advise on military and political strategy. The Prince was given more active reasons to stir up enmity with Germany when he heard that the German Chancellor, Hohenlohe, had given a banquet on the Kaiser's birthday in January 1900 to which he had invited Dr Leyds, the Transvaal's Secretary of State, who happened to be in Berlin as part of a European tour to whip up sympathy for his people against Britain. Protocol demanded the presence of Sir Frank Lascelles, the British ambassador; and the Prince was outraged that Lascelles had been put in this position.

A memorandum from the Kaiser on the war had just been sent to the Prince, and in it the Kaiser had mused with barely concealed delight on the possibilities of a British defeat. He claimed it could be handled quite honourably, and could be of no more consequence than the defeat the previous summer of England by Australia in a test match: a choice of metaphor, coming from a German, of ultimate cruelty. The Prince replied to him on 8 February 1900, 'I am afraid I am unable to share your opinions expressed in the last paragraph of your Memo, in which you liken our conflict with the Boers to our Cricket Matches with the Australians, in which the latter were victorious and we accepted our defeat. The British Empire is now fighting for its very existence, as you know full well, and for our superiority in S. Africa.' And, in a suitably Germanic ending, the Prince closed: 'We must therefore use every effort in our power to prove victorious in the end!'[180] This forced a claim from the Kaiser that he had been misunderstood; and, as the British army went through

1900 reversing its previous humiliations, few were louder in their congratulations than Willy.

In fact, the Kaiser was throwing up one of his amateurish smokescreens, since he hoped at the time when the British were so heavily occupied thousands of miles from home to divide the Russians from them, and to improve his own relations with Nicholas II; if possible, he wished to make overtures to the French too. Largely because of jealousy towards British colonial expansion, the French press had been especially hostile over the Boer War, so much so that the Prince did not once visit his favourite holiday destination during 1900. It was unfortunate because Delcassé, the French Foreign Minister, had decided that an entente with Britain was essential, and the man most likely to be of assistance to him was not to be seen.

A KHAKI ELECTION

Salisbury called an election – the khaki election, as it was named – in October 1900, cashing in on the recent military successes; and, with the Liberals divided over the usefulness and morality of the conflict, the Prince was, according to Sir Sidney Lee, happy to see the unequivocal imperialist Salisbury returned to office with a majority of 134.[181] The best friends of the Prince in the government were Devonshire, the Lord President of the Council, Londonderry, who became Postmaster-General, and Cadogan, who remained Lord Lieutenant for Ireland. Although he did not socialise with him, he in many respects found Chamberlain the most interesting of the ministers, not least because he shared the Prince's views on imperialism and the importance of empire. Lansdowne, with whom the Prince had not always had a smooth relationship because he believed he imposed too much civil authority on military matters, became Foreign Secretary in succession to Salisbury, who at the age of seventy decided to be content just with the office of Prime Minister. The Commander-in-Chief, Wolseley, had, he felt, become 'virtually a cipher'; and he considered that the débâcles in the early months of the Boer War had demonstrated a lack of grip, and the urgent need for reform of procedures. Lansdowne was replaced at the War Office by one the Prince found, to begin with, quite congenial, St John Brodrick, heir to the viscounty of Midleton. Once Brodrick was properly installed, the Prince wrote to him and suggested a wholesale replacement of the senior officers in the army, as they seemed to be 'getting stale'. It was an argument he pressed also on Lord Roberts, the new Commander-in-Chief.[182]

He had done a useful service for Roberts, who in recognition of his achievements in South Africa had not merely been asked to succeed Wolseley as Commander-in-Chief, but had also been given an earldom. It was accompanied by the promise of a grant of £50,000 to maintain the dignity of the rank. On hearing of this, the Prince had Knollys write that it was not enough – £100,000 would be better. Salisbury noted that 'this question was much discussed – I doubt whether the Cabinet would reconsider its decision'.[183] The Prince also wrote to Brodrick in the same vein: '£100,000 seems to me the least he could receive. I feel sure the House of Commons will not grudge it him and will vote anything. I know the Queen feels as strongly as I do on the subject and has communicated her views to the Prime Minister.' Whether it was the Queen's or the Prince's doing one does not know, but Salisbury did persuade the Cabinet to change its mind, and Earl Roberts had his £100,000.

The Kaiser's antipathy to England having cooled with the run of British victories in 1900, and also because of his apparently genuine shock at the attack on his uncle in Brussels, some of Salisbury's ministers began to consider the prospect of a closer understanding with Germany. The great hostility to Britain during the Boer War by the other powers had worried some of those ministers – though not Salisbury himself – who had hitherto subscribed to the Prime Minister's policy of 'splendid isolation'. It was not a doctrine with which the Prince had ever agreed, and during a visit to Chatsworth in early January 1901 he learned from Devonshire, a member of Salisbury's Cabinet, that a thaw was beginning towards Germany. However, the Prince was not so willing to pursue a personal policy of friendship towards Willy that he was prepared to attend celebrations in Berlin in January 1901 to celebrate 200 years of the Prussian monarchy, for he regarded them as just another chapter in the Kaiser's campaign of self-advertisement; his brother Prince Arthur, the Duke of Connaught, went instead.

But the celebrations were interrupted by a telegram to the Kaiser on 18 January from his London embassy, informing him that the Queen's life was drawing to its close. He and his uncle Arthur rushed to England, to be met by the Prince in the full uniform of the Prussian Dragoon Guards at Victoria Station. On 20 January they all travelled to Osborne; at six-thirty on the evening of the 22nd the Queen died. In the third month of his sixtieth year, having undergone no formal training, and knowing only what he had acquired by osmosis from his mother and her ministers, the Prince who had for so long wanted to do something useful at last became the King.

INTERLUDE

There are those who will tell you that the role of the monarchy in the English constitution was definitively settled in the 1860s by Walter Bagehot. Do not believe them. The role of the monarch has never been settled: it has from the earliest times to the present day continuously evolved. It was, indeed, continuously evolving when in 1867 Bagehot wrote down his thoughts in *The English Constitution*. The institution has been shaped by the interaction of the monarch and his or her ministers and Parliament. Monarch and ministers have tested what the other will let them get away with: the result, at any one time, is the balance that exists between the powers of the Crown and the powers of elected politicians. Since the Civil War, the feelings of the electorate have influenced both parties to the deal. As the electorate has grown and the polity of Britain has become based more and more on the wishes of the people, so it has given an advantage to the elected politicians in their quest to take power from the Sovereign. This has not, however, happened as quickly as might be thought to be the case.

Britain has been a constitutional monarchy of sorts since the Restoration; but what George I and our present Queen would understand by their prerogatives in a constitutional monarchy would be likely to be very different. Edward VII showed in his short reign, and by his attitudes and attempts at political activity in his long apprenticeship for the throne, that he was rather more of the school of George I than of Elizabeth II. He was not an unconstitutional monarch, but, as we shall see, he was not a completely constitutional one either. He never passed the ultimate test of unconstitutionality, rejecting the advice of his Prime Minister on a vital issue – the last of his predecessors to do that was his great-uncle, William IV. However, he clearly reserved the right to do it and, had his death not intervened, may well even have done it in the Lords-versus-Commons crisis that accompanied the end of his reign. In some respects he certainly took Bagehot, if he had ever read him, with a pinch of salt. Nor was there any reason why King Edward should have treated the musings of this mid-Victorian journalist with any special reverence – despite the fact that one of the King's closest advisers would urge later in the reign that ministers should know their Bagehot, in order to treat the King with the respect he and his prerogatives deserved.

Had the King sat down in January 1901, on his accession, and read the two chapters of *The English Constitution* in which Bagehot sets out his opinions on what a monarch can or cannot do, he would have found much that was familiar. Equally, from his privileged view of how his mother had conducted the business of the Crown, he would have known that much of Bagehot's blueprint was an ideal and not a reality. Bagehot's genius lay in mapping out how, as the significance of Parliament in general and the elected House in particular increased with the widening franchise, the monarchy would become more constrained. By the time George V succeeded his father in 1910, a society existed in which, matched with an unassuming monarch reluctant to throw around his constitutional weight, Bagehot's vision could at last be achieved. King George had, indeed, studied Bagehot closely in a series of lessons he had had about constitutional matters in 1894, after becoming heir presumptive following the death of his elder brother. By the time he came to the throne Bagehot himself had been dead for over thirty years. However, his ideas were especially congenial to an elected political class that wanted more power at the expense of hereditary institutions, and that class would provide the main propagandists for those ideas long after the death of their originator. Like all good journalists, Bagehot was especially adept at spotting an opening, and providing the wherewithal to exploit it.

Edward VII came to the throne at a time when fewer than half his adult subjects had the vote, and when only the occasional eccentric thought there was anything wrong with the Prime Minister not being a member of the House of Commons. In such a climate it was more natural, and less controversial, for a King to exercise some latter-day form of divine right in active intervention in the political process: especially a king who had, during forty long years of adulthood, watched his mother behave in precisely that way. However, Edward VII's monarchy is special because it would come to represent a chapter of transition in Britain's constitutional history: it saw the last wholesale exercise of true political power in the Sovereign, through the King's initiative in international alliances and his *de facto* control over the reform of the army, and the first signs that elected government was determined to strengthen its mandate by completing the move to universal adult suffrage. George V's monarchy was to be far more on the lines that Bagehot had invented and suggested for those of his station; for with his accession the ruling politicians decided to test the relationship between Parliament and the King anew, and found little resistance to the movement of powers towards them and away from him.

LE MÉTIER D'UN ROI

By no means, however, did Bagehot's doctrine represent to Edward VII, in 1901, a set of rules by which he had to abide if he were to stay within the 'constitutional' limits. The King felt there were many areas in which he had a right to have his own way, and, by and large, he did, at least for most of his reign. The army was one, the navy scarcely less so. In foreign policy he got away with more than his ministers liked, and was a brooding presence on the issue in a way that no monarch since has been. As a result, he closely monitored and influenced appointments in the diplomatic corps. He had no such influence in domestic politics mainly because it bored him, and he chose not to have that influence: when, at the end of the reign, forced against his will and instincts to become involved in the utterly domestic matter of the People's Budget, he found it distasteful, but he proved largely intransigent. In other matters affecting the throne, such as honours, he took an especially close interest. All in all he was nothing like the monarch who, as Bagehot would have liked, sat meekly and waited to be 'advised' by his ministers, perhaps warning them if he felt they were going too far, but always in the end accepting that advice. That chapter in the history of the monarchy, which, according to taste, is either Bagehot's achievement or his curse, was to come later.

Some of Bagehot's main contentions about the monarchy were self-evidently wrong by the time of Edward's accession. In seeking to prove why 'the actions of a retired widow and an unemployed youth become of such importance', he claimed that monarchy – 'a family on the throne' – was an 'intelligible' form of government like no other.[1] The republican agitation at the time he was writing proved that another equally intelligible form of government had already been marked out by many as an alternative – indeed, many of the more extreme Chartists had marked it out more than twenty years earlier. By 1901 Britain's nearest neighbour, France, had lived successfully under a republic for thirty years. It was much admired by the new King of England, and its people were not visibly stricken by the 'unintelligibility' of their institutions. Bagehot had, though, warned that a monarchy was necessary in England because England had 'whole classes unable to comprehend the idea of a constitution', or, to put it another way, whose little minds could comprehend only a queen on the throne.[2] This is typical of his assumptions, and of the dangerous weight placed on assumption in the construction of his argument.

Bagehot never gave the English people credit for having higher reasons for preferring a monarchy to any other form of constitution. Even in the 1860s these were dangerous and foolish assumptions, as cheap newspapers, the creed of self-help and the organisation of the working classes spread across the country. Who is to say that the simple Tynesider to whom John Ruskin addressed his political thoughts – and who communicated his own back to Ruskin – in *Time and Tide*, in the very same year Bagehot was publishing *The English Constitution*, could not have grasped the alternative methods by which he might be ruled? Certainly no one who has read *Time and Tide*. Thirty-five years later, after Gladstone's Education Act of 1870 and the sequence of socially ameliorative legislation by Disraeli later in that decade, Bagehot's criticism was reactionary to the point of being meaningless. Edward VII knew that he ruled not by the complacent consent of the British people, but by the active interest of a large proportion of them now educated enough and involved enough in society, even if just through trades unions, who consciously supported what they regarded as a humane and sensible monarchy. Indeed, some of them may have been shrewd enough to conclude that one of the monarchy's main uses was to protect them from the sort of avaricious politician who read and enjoyed Bagehot. The inexorable ascent of such politicians in the twentieth century can in part be attributed to monarchs having read their Bagehot too literally, and being cautious to the point of inaction in tolerating behaviour from ministers that King Edward would have loudly condemned.

The King would not have taken it kindly to be told that the loyalty his people overwhelmingly felt for him on his accession was because they were too stupid to think or feel anything less conventional. Bagehot's patronising justification for his opinions – such as when he refers to the activities of the royal family as 'facts which speak to "men's bosoms" and employ their thoughts', and asserts that 'royalty is a government in which the attention of the nation is concentrated on one person doing interesting actions' – would have bemused a man engaged in the practical business of reigning, and, to an extent greater than his successors, ruling too.[3] Bagehot is on stronger ground when he speaks of the superior religious focus a royal family must have over a republic; but this is not, in the twentieth century, an issue greatly concerned with the mechanics of government. Nor is divine right of any significance, having taken a battering in 1688 and having, after the 1832 Reform Act initiated the spread of democracy in Britain, been replaced by the will of the people.

'The Queen', Bagehot wrote, 'is the head of our society.'[4] In 1867 that was, as he must have seen, true only *de jure* and not at all *de facto*. The 'retired widow', stricken still with grief and entombed at her own wish at Osborne, Windsor or Balmoral, played virtually no part in society at all. If the monarchy were to be rooted in the fact that she should, then it would be no monarchy at all. Nonetheless, Bagehot wrote that 'if she did not exist the Prime Minister would be the first person in the country. He and his wife would have to receive foreign ministers, and occasionally foreign princes, to give the first parties in the country; he and she would be at the head of the pageant of life; they would represent England in the eyes of foreign nations; they would represent the Government of England in the eyes of the English.' Well, the Queen for these purposes barely existed, and her place was taken mostly by her son, and partly by her First Minister. Bagehot himself admitted there had been a 'palpable' suspension of the court's activities since the death of the Prince Consort, but noted that things carried on largely as normal, even though the Queen was not visible. For Bagehot, her mystical presence in metaphor rather than in fact was enough.

It turned out, as King Edward would have reflected in 1901, to have made not much difference, and certainly not to have been the significant factor in the monarchy Bagehot had claimed it was.

Ironically, he claimed that society must remain under the leadership of the Queen and not of politicians because 'if the highest social rank was to be scrambled for in the House of Commons, the number of social adventurers there would be incalculably more numerous, and indefinitely more eager'.[5] He said, too, that 'in this present age and country it would be very dangerous to give the slightest addition to a force already perilously great'. However, this antique championship of the social status quo is a breathtaking pose; the limits Bagehot himself was to advertise for the monarchy could not but add more power, and therefore more social lustre, to the House of Commons he so affected to disdain.

What would most have amused King Edward was Bagehot's stricture that 'we have come to regard the Crown as the head of our morality'. What he meant – for he admitted the inadequacies of some of her more recent predecessors – was that the English had come to regard Queen Victoria as the head of that morality. It was very much a case of one swallow failing to make a summer. The new King was no moralist, never advertised himself as such, and in certain aspects of his sexual activity has given to history an unequivocal definition of Edwardian values. Lastly, Bagehot says that monarchy acts as a 'disguise', enabling 'our real rulers to change without heedless people knowing it'.[6] This, too, smacks of his underestimate of popular intelligence. 'The masses of Englishmen are not fit for elective government,' he continues. 'If they knew how near they were to it, they would be surprised, and almost tremble.' The 1867 Reform Act should have put paid to such widespread ignorance of current events; if it did not, the 1884 one certainly did. By King Edward's accession not only did the British people know who their real rulers were, but they knew when – and in most cases why and how – they came and went too.

So much for Bagehot's perception of the monarchy. When he moves on to detail Queen Victoria's functions he admits that 'there is no authentic blue book to say what she does'.[7] He does state, however, that the Sovereign is not an estate of the realm like the Lords and Commons. 'That authority could only be exercised by a monarch with a legislative veto ... but the Queen has no such veto.' In one of his most famous lines, he argues that 'she must sign her own death-warrant if the two Houses unanimously send it up to her'. In practice, of course, nothing from that region would ever be 'unanimous'; and in theory the right of veto existed for Edward VII, and exists now, and could be exercised if a monarch believed that in using the veto a majority in the House of Commons – and in Edward VII's day, before the 1911 Parliament Act, the House of Lords – would support him or her. In that respect the monarch's legislative power is not 'a fiction of the past'; it is, however abstract, part of the point of having a monarchy, and of it retaining reserve prerogative powers to protect the people, if necessary, against the caprice of an administration.

In talking of the prerogative and its mysteries, Bagehot said that 'some good lawyer ought to write a careful book to say which of these powers are really usable, and which are obsolete'.[8] Quite: for it is all about the balance between the Crown – which is an estate of the realm, every bit as much as the House of Lords remains one after the 1911 and 1949 Parliament Acts that so trammelled its powers – ministers and the two Houses of Parliament. That balance will change according to political circumstances, the personalities of the parties involved, the strength of mandates, and internal government discipline. Balfour in 1902 was far better able to get his way with the King than was Balfour in 1903, having been hamstrung by the crisis over free trade and the resignations from his Cabinet that this caused. The King in the early part of his reign, when relatively fit and active, was better able to exert his influence than towards the end, when frequently unwell, absent abroad, distracted and depressed. Despite trying to define the royal powers, even Bagehot admitted the danger in codifying them, of exposing exactly and to the letter what the Sovereign could or could not do. 'Above all, our royalty is to be reverenced, and if you begin to poke about it you cannot reverence it. When there is a select committee on the Queen, the charm of royalty will be gone. Its mystery is its life. We must not let daylight in upon magic.'[9]

Bagehot had had an important posthumous victory in 1880, when the Queen had been forced to send for Gladstone after accepting that neither Hartington nor Granville felt able to form the Liberal government the people had shown they wanted. In *The English Constitution* he had, in referring to the Queen's right to choose her First Minister, said that a monarch of 'singular discernment' could pick out the best leader of a governing party even when the party itself proved incapable, with the Sovereign acting as a 'thoroughly intelligent but perfectly disinterested spectator'.[10] However, Bagehot felt such people existed only 'in the works of certain moralists', and the Queen, three years after his death, proved she was certainly not one. She did, though, have her hand forced by the good sense of Hartington and

Granville in refusing to serve, both having recognised the obvious. Had either of them tried to govern, it would have been the Crown more than they that would have been damaged by any subsequent failure of the administration. That reality was as clear to the Prince of Wales as it was unclear to his mother, and he would not forget the lesson when he became king. Bagehot's assertion that the Sovereign 'certainly is not under the same motive to choose wisely' as a political party would be in choosing its leader is just not true. The Prince of Wales, when he warned his mother to accept Gladstone in 1880, knew that better than Bagehot.

In one particular respect King Edward's reign was especially unsuited to Bagehotian doctrine. Having just watched the methods of Palmerston's ministry after 1859, the Sage of Langport lauded a system in which moderate men of all parties joined together to support the ministry of the man who could best please all of them. When such a coalition was being put together, the aid that could be given by a monarch with 'a genius for discernment' would be 'great'.[11] This was not the sort of politics with which King Edward was to be confronted, and therefore his involvement was becoming far greater than Bagehot would have foretold. By the end of the reign a Liberal government wanted to emasculate the House of Lords while its Conservative opponents felt that the rights of the unelected landed interest should be left as they were. On such a matter – and it underpinned much that the government had tried to do since December 1905 – there was no room for compromise. Had the King not died, the proverbial coach and horses would have been driven through the Bagehot way. As it was, his successor had neither the temperament nor the motivation nor the knowledge to have the fight his father was pledged to have – though, as we shall see, he was denied one important piece of information that might have made the difference. In any case, by the time of King Edward's accession, the idea of party had become too firmly entrenched in British political life to admit of the Bagehot thesis.

THE 'THREE RIGHTS'

The main point of Bagehot's prescription concerns the conduct of a sovereign during the course of a ministry, not at its breaking up or formation. Here we have his most famous dictum: 'the Sovereign has, under a constitutional monarchy such as ours, three rights – the right to be consulted, the right to encourage, the right to warn. And a King of great sagacity would want no others.'[12] Queen Victoria had, additionally, the right to tell her ministers that she simply would not accept certain policies, or certain people, in certain circumstances – a breach of the Bagehot principles so wide-ranging as to make them specious. In her declining years the Queen became less insistent on certain things, and her son would try to wrest back his rights in some matters. Edward VII never tried to stop his government implementing a policy just because he disagreed with it, and there were some he disagreed with wholeheartedly. He did, though, feel he had the right to try to ameliorate them. He also felt he had the right to refuse to allow certain people to hold certain ministerial and other public appointments. He also felt he had the right to initiate certain foreign policies, which his ministers would then adopt as their own in order to maintain the fiction that they had advised him, and that he was acting on their advice. He lost some set piece battles, but he also won others, notably over reform of the army. By the end of the Balfour administration he had his Prime Minister willing to do exactly the King's bidding on questions affecting the military. He could, as on his trip to meet the Tsar at Reval in 1908, undertake political acts that had serious consequences for his ministers without bothering to consult them.

None of this is covered by Bagehot. The three rules certainly applied, and the King certainly insisted that they should apply – note his determination to be consulted throughout his reign – but sometimes his interpretation went beyond what Bagehot would have intended. It is unclear at what stage Bagehot saw the consultation of the Sovereign taking place. It was certainly interpreted by the ministers who came after him to mean that the King was told of things once the Cabinet had discussed them but before Parliament was told. The King received advice from his irregulars during the reign that he could insist on being consulted at the same time as the Cabinet was having its own discussion of policy questions, so that he could put in his own view, and in the hope the Cabinet would take that view into account. Bagehot's idea that a monarch could, when confronted with something he did not like, say that 'I do not oppose, it is my duty not to oppose; but observe that I warn', is simply fantasy. King Edward's treatment of the advice tendered to him in the admittedly minor matter of whether or not to make the Shah of Persia a Knight of the Garter is one example of this – though it was a minor matter that ended in a threat by a constitutionally provocative Prime Minister, Balfour, to tender the resignation of the government. The King's refusal to grant guarantees for the creation of peers at the end of the reign was another, more far-reaching instance. In the first case he gave way, and ministerial advice was acted upon. In the second he did not live to see the matter resolved, and his son took the Bagehot line. In both cases, though, Bagehot's end was not reached by Bagehot's means, for the King was not the supine individual this amateur constitutionalist designed him to be.

Neither, of course, was his mother. Bagehot based his rules on a memorandum Palmerston, as Foreign Secretary, had had from the Queen in 1850, complaining about the independence with which he was acting in foreign affairs. It was true that Palmerston, who had served the best part of sixteen years at the Foreign Office at that stage, often acted not just without consulting the Queen, but without consulting his ministerial colleagues either. The memorandum had been copied to Lord John Russell, the Prime Minister, and when Russell sacked Palmerston more than a year later, for the spurious reason that he had expressed sympathy with a *coup d'état* in France, he cited the memorandum as evidence of why he had to do so. In fact, Russell had been as keen as the Queen to have rid of Palmerston, and this provided him with an ideal excuse to do so – even though he, too, agreed with the view Palmerston had taken towards France. That the Queen had not been asked gave him the pretext he needed.

In something of a breach of etiquette, Russell had read the memorandum out to the Commons, by way of explaining why Palmerston had had to go. The Queen had wanted to know what exactly Palmerston had been proposing in matters of policy, so that she could know to what she was giving her sanction. That sanction given, the measure should not, she added, be altered 'arbitrarily'.[13] If it were so altered, this would mean the minister 'failing in sincerity towards the Crown, and justly to be visited by the exercise of her constitutional right to dismiss the minister'. This does not appear to be a constitutional right covered by the main three rights, but let that pass. The Queen had asked, as her son would ask his ministers fifty years later, to be kept informed of what passed between her Foreign Secretary and his opposite numbers abroad 'before important decisions are taken on that intercourse'. She wished, additionally, to receive Foreign Office dispatches in good time. The broadcasting of this memorandum was invaluable, as Bagehot said, for the way in which it revealed the unwritten rules of the monarch–minister relationship. However, it did not reveal all the rules; such rules as it did divulge concerned foreign affairs only, and the rules were open to all sorts of interpretations, especially in the hands of clever men like Bagehot. That he was able to win universal acceptance for his rules, in defiance of such matters, shows what a master of the moment he was. Also, this idea of the Queen's that she had a direct, almost executive role in foreign affairs – which Bagehot endorses – is hardly consistent with his other prescriptions for a constitutional monarchy.

Indeed, as Bagehot more or less admits, he would have been stuck for concrete evidence of the constitutional position had Russell not revealed the Queen's memorandum on Palmerston. It is another clue to how much elsewhere he relied on supposition, assumption and invention in propounding his thesis. The casual phrase 'a constitutional monarchy such as ours' is deeply misleading, for in 1867 there was no remotely comparable institution anywhere in the world. The three great European empires – Russia, Germany and Austria – were autocracies in some degree or other. Louis Napoleon's monarchy in France was unstable and unsupported by centuries of historical precedent in the way that the English throne was. Italy had only just become a nation. Neither Spain nor Portugal was politically, socially or economically comparable with Britain. Bagehot had no foreign examples upon which to rely: the case he outlined was one supported only by what little he could find out from within the 'magic', and by his own, admittedly intelligent, ideas.

In his approach to the advice tendered to him, and in his willingness to have policy (especially in regard to the army) initiated by him by certain backdoor means, King Edward was not remotely a king according to the letter of Bagehot. He would have been seen by Bagehot, had he survived to the Edwardian era, as the last unconstitutional King. Bagehot himself claimed that 'we shall find that it is only during the period of the present reign that in England the duties of a constitutional sovereign have been well performed', an admission that clearly gave King Edward less of a precedent to follow in being 'constitutional'. Indeed, as we now know – and Bagehot at the time did not – Queen Victoria might sometimes not be that 'constitutional' either. It is this false premise that would have made Bagehot so dangerous a guide for King Edward to follow.

Although he was no autocrat, he did not follow that guide. He took a high-profile role in active politics, mostly out of the public eye but occasionally, as in foreign affairs, in it, which none of his successors would have dreamed of taking. He proved Bagehot wrong in one respect in particular: he had written that if a prince came to the throne when middle-aged or old 'he is then unfit to work. He will then have spent the whole of youth and the first part of manhood in idleness, and it is unnatural to expect him to labour.' The King could hardly have been more active. The political class was not, however, passive in the face of this activity. The central theme of the nine and a quarter years of his reign was how a new breed of elected politicians, strengthened by the mandate from a widened franchise, sought to alter the balance of power against the unelected, hereditary forces of which the King was the ringleader. Bagehot had said that the 'divinity which doth hedge a king' still pertained, and gave a minister a disadvantage in argument with his Sovereign – 'now no man can *argue* on his knees'.[14] King Edward's reign, and the arrival in the highest reaches of government of such undeferential figures as Lloyd George, was to see the erosion of that safeguard. When the King died the battle for power was not yet won by either side: the victory would be Walter Bagehot's – even though it entailed the surrender of one of the few prerogatives Bagehot was prepared to name, that of creating peers – and it would not long be delayed.

KING

'BUT THE KING OF ENGLAND LIVES!'

The Queen's death was the first demise of the Crown in modern times that had not precipitated, within a statutory period of six months, a dissolution of Parliament and a general election. The 1867 Reform Act had put an end to that requirement, and so the accession of Edward VII was the first to take place in a climate of immediate political certainty. There did not, indeed, need to be an election until the summer of 1907. The King's first quasi-political act was to announce the name by which he would be known – Edward, like six of his predecessors, and using his second Christian name, rather than (as Queen Victoria would have wished) King Albert. Tactfully, the King explained that he felt his father should stand alone as history's leading Albert, so he had chosen another regnal name. It was a conscious repudiation of the cult of memory propagated by his mother, with all its connotations of ossification and sombreness. A new vigour marked the accession. When, in the royal yacht following the craft bearing his mother's coffin to the mainland from Osborne, he noticed the royal standard was at half-mast, he asked the captain why. 'The Queen is dead, Sir,' the officer answered. 'But the King of England lives!' retorted the new Sovereign, an assertion of the fact that the standard always flies at full mast, because there is always a monarch. Yet it was also an indication of the pent-up energy the new King, after almost a lifetime's wait, was now determined to release in his approach to statecraft.[1]

Paradoxically, throughout the reign to come, there was to be one constant truth concerning the rights and prerogatives of the Crown:

98

that the King liked things as they were – with certain limited exceptions – and saw no reason to change them. This was especially true in the matter of attempts by politicians to decrease the King's involvement in matters of state, either by seeking to erode his prerogatives or by neglecting their consultative obligations towards him. It did however ignore the fact that the late Queen had frozen the Crown's role in the constitution despite two major Reform Acts, both of which had progressed the democratisation of the national polity. This was an unreal situation, and could not last long.

Sir Francis Knollys, who had served the King as his private secretary since 1870 and whose father had served the Prince before him, was the King's principal adviser at court. Knollys was a careful man whose studiousness and dedication to his master over nearly forty years in the royal service had supplied him with a fund of experience and knowledge. He used these qualities to advise the King and to protect his position at all times. Though he had no great intellect, Knollys's innate discretion and acute powers of observation armed him to do his job well. Both he and his Sovereign came to their responsibilities at an advanced age – Knollys was in his sixty-fourth year at the time of the accession – and both had to learn fast. Thanks to his years at court, and the example and experience of his father passed on to him, Knollys learned faster than most. In his principal duty, of not exposing the King to any difficult or embarrassing constitutional situations, he was to complete the reign with his reputation largely intact. It was his responsibility to act as the King's mouthpiece, particularly with the Prime Minister and other senior officers of state. He was crucial because he had licence to interpret as he judged best the King's feelings and wishes for transmission onwards to those who had to act upon them. In so far as we judge the King's true political feelings, we most frequently judge them as expressed by Knollys.

The King's next most influential adviser, but who unlike Knollys had no official position, was Reginald Brett, the 2nd Viscount Esher. Possibly one of the most ghastly, yet most accomplished, men in public life in the twentieth century, Esher had been (like many of the King's most trusted inner circle) a Liberal MP. He had become, in 1895, Secretary to the Office of Works, thanks to a last act of Prime Ministerial patronage by his old friend Rosebery. Esher was to have a phenomenal career, more noted for the posts he turned down than for those he fulfilled – like the viceroyalty of India and the Secretaryship of State for War. He was by nature and inclination a toady and an addictive collector of the powerful. He was also a barely repressed homosexual, almost certainly (to judge from the tenor of their voluminous correspondence) in love with his younger son – though there is no evidence the King knew anything about that. The King had known Esher for some years, and been impressed by the roles he had played in the organisation both of the Queen's Diamond Jubilee in 1897 and of her funeral. Esher had first worked closely with the King directly after the accession, when he was put in charge of reorganising the royal palaces and had a hand in the arrangements for the Coronation.

The King found him highly congenial and quickly recognised his acute political intelligence and readiness to be totally loyal to him and to his wishes. Esher soon became a close adviser, sometimes writing to the King almost daily with information. Esher also gave regular advice to Knollys, who was likewise under the spell of this much cleverer and somewhat enigmatic man. This attitude of Knollys's made Esher, if anything, more influential at court than the King's private secretary himself. In 1903, to formalise the position at court of a man he now judged indispensable to him, the King made Esher Deputy Constable and Lieutenant-Governor of Windsor Castle. The most important aspect of this promotion was that it placed Esher in charge of putting the late Monarch's papers into some sense of order, as they had been left to deteriorate into a chaotic state during Queen Victoria's widowhood. Eventually, in 1912, the Royal Archives were established, and Esher became the first Keeper of them.

Esher's interest in the archives was highly active, and certainly not at all honorific. He became an expert on constitutional precedent, and after some time spent reading Queen Victoria's correspondence with her ministers sought to codify – from an empirical position far stronger than Bagehot ever held – the rights of a sovereign in superintending the executive. Since the King was jealous of his prerogatives, this further endeared Esher to him; and Esher was conscious of the power this gave him – 'The ignorance of historical precedent in men whose business it is to know is wonderful.'[2] Esher also acted as the King's informer-in-chief, faithfully reporting back to the King, via Knollys, any intelligence he picked up in private intercourse in society. While this made him many enemies – for his many influential contacts soon realised that anything told to Esher would end up quickly in the King's ear – it also secured his place of influence with the King. 'The King was more than kind,' Esher recorded of a meeting with him early in the reign; '[he] warned me that I must *never* leave his service.'[3]

DOWN TO BUSINESS

The King's first exchange with his Prime Minister, Salisbury, was to approve the message to both Houses of Parliament on the death of the Queen. Scarcely had the Queen died, however, than Salisbury had to press the King on more routine matters of state. In light of the royal family's bereavement, and his and his wife's own close relationship with their only surviving son, the King had said that a planned trip by the Duke of York to Australia, to open the first session of the new federal Parliament, would have to be postponed. Salisbury asked him on 24 January 1901, just two days after the Queen's demise, not to force a delay until the following year. Postponement would mean the Duke's being unable to discharge this unique and important duty, symbolising the imperial tie that remained with the new self-governing federation.[4]

The King was still not convinced, so the Prime Minister enlisted the help of his colleague and nephew, Arthur James Balfour, the Leader of the House of Commons. The King was to find that not the least of Balfour's distasteful attributes was that he was a supreme dialectician. After laying it on with a trowel in Disraelian fashion, Balfour advised his new Sovereign that there were:

> reasons to be urged which touch the deepest interests of the monarchy. The King is no longer merely King of Great Britain and Ireland.... he is now the great Constitutional bond uniting together in a single Empire communities of freemen separated by half the circumference of the Globe. All the patriotic sentiment which makes such an Empire possible centres in him, or centres chiefly in him: and everything which emphasises his personality to our kinsmen across the sea must be a gain both to the Monarchy and to the Empire.[5]

Balfour had, in fact, established some sort of new doctrine, one that would be completed during his own difficult term as Prime Minister: that the greater the expansion of British overseas power, the more symbolic and the less practical power the monarchy should have. In the light of such high-calibre insistence, the King gave way 'reluctantly'.[6]

Although no more a Bagehotian than his mother, the King made it plain that he would insist, as Queen Victoria had done, on the right to be consulted about what his government was doing. The idea was that the consultation took place after the Cabinet had reached a decision, though as we shall see the King would be advised by Esher that he could if necessary seek consultation before a decision was made. In the last decade of her life his mother had overcome her distaste for consulting her son herself, and she had especially sought his counsel on foreign affairs and the reform of the army. Naturally, the King expected no diminution in this involvement now he was on the throne, though in practice his more gregarious life in comparison with his mother's – a heavy social life at home and frequent long trips abroad – meant he simply did not have the time to scrutinise detail as she had done. Also, the weight of government business was steadily increasing in a more regulated society. Shrewd men like Balfour, seeing this, made sure not to give the King any details he did not expect to be given, thus diminishing his abilities to interfere with their political activities. In politics, especially, knowledge is power. Thus, by default over the nine years he reigned, went much of the interfering ability of the Monarch.

The King also told Salisbury that he was to be consulted on all Crown appointments: Salisbury's archive is full of correspondence between his office and the King about appointments to apparently minor deaneries as well as to grander posts. He expected full reports from his Prime Ministers of Cabinet meetings, in their own hands, and (when, under Balfour, he suspected the reports were becoming too brief) stipulated that they should run to four sides of quarto paper, as in his mother's day. However, whereas his mother had sent back to her Prime Minister 'voluminous criticism' on receipt of these reports, the King did not, preferring to raise any such matters in a personal interview.[7] The King's preference for conversation over written communication meant that the great correspondence Queen Victoria had had with her ministers was not repeated, presumably much to the relief of the ministers. Also, such written communication as did take place during the reign was mainly through Knollys – another boon to the recipients, as the King's handwriting was virtually illegible.

The King wanted, still, a report from the Commons at the close of each day's business, but allowed the Leader of the House, whose workload was heavy enough apart from this, to delegate the responsibility to the Home Secretary. It was the last reign in which such a procedure was important: King George V, who like his father received reports, found he could actually learn all he needed to know from the newspapers. Essentially, despite his long apprenticeship, and despite having been allowed to see state papers for most of the preceding decade, the new King was greatly inexperienced and, to an extent, at the mercy of his advisers. It was inevitable, therefore, that he should make one or two mistakes as he encountered the world of politics in his constitutional capacity for the first time; but, on the whole, and thanks to Knollys's assistance, he was remarkably sure-footed.

Until 1905 the position of prime minister was not formally entrenched in the constitution. Balfour had it formalised and his successor, Sir Henry Campbell-Bannerman, was the first Prime Minister to be formally accorded a place of precedence as such. The King was in the habit of talking directly to various ministers, who would in turn be sanctioned by his Prime Ministers to speak on behalf of the Cabinet to the Monarch. This changed somewhat once the Liberals came to power in 1905, partly because of the good relations the King had with Campbell-Bannerman, partly because he knew so few of his Liberal ministers socially, and could not stand the sight of one or two of them, notably Lloyd George. In communicating with his ministers, the King would usually append notes to their correspondence with him, and Knollys would then redraft this into a letter under his name, but embodying exactly the King's thoughts and wishes. Knollys would occasionally tone down particular notes of protest by the King and present his complaints in effective, though non-provocative language: it was ever the job of the Monarch's private secretary to have a clearer understanding of the constitutional niceties than the Monarch bothered to have. Knollys was fiercely loyal to the King and, egged on by Esher, he was rarely to be found advising the King to indulge in constitutional progress. He encouraged the King to take the greatest exception to any attempt by his ministers to use him as a rubber-stamp. If the monarchy of Edward VII became a time of transition, it was through no intention of Knollys's.

Since, unlike his mother, the King lived in London and was a social being, formal correspondence was much reduced compared with the previous reign, and the King was not averse to using the telephone. He would occasionally have audiences with the private secretaries of his

Conservative Prime Ministers – Schomberg McDonnell for Salisbury, J. S. Sandars for Balfour. Given the closeness of his contacts and the frequency of his intercourse with the political classes, the King had every right to be angry when important policy developments or appointments were made without his having been consulted. When one of his ministers, George Wyndham, the Secretary of State for Ireland, appointed a new under-secretary in October 1902, the King was angry not to have been told first. The minister replied that the oversight had been due to pressure of work, which the King magisterially crushed with the observation that 'the excuses of ministers are often as gauche as their omissions.'[8] The King would frequently sit up into the night reading the contents of his dispatch boxes, especially the foreign telegrams, which interested him immensely. It was because of his great interest in politics that he was as tough an adversary as he was to ministers determined to snatch some of his prerogatives for themselves.

Frederick 'Fritz' Ponsonby, his assistant private secretary, summed up the King's political interests thus: 'Foreign Affairs, the Army and the Navy interested him most, while internal politics and the Colonies bored him. He would rush through any question relating to the latter, but would read thoroughly through even insignificant letters relating to the former. He read through every dispatch from abroad, often when the subject was very dull.'[9] Like all generalisations this was only partly true: it understates the way in which circumstances forced the King to be interested in domestic politics in the latter part of his reign.

Much of his early intercourse with Salisbury was on the (for the King) endlessly fascinating subject of honours and appointments – arranging GCBs and other honours for foreign princes who would be attending the Queen's funeral, and dealing with some vacant bishoprics. For the first few years of his reign the King took a close interest in even the most minor of Crown appointments to ecclesiastical offices, and to other secular posts. However, the Boer War was the most immediate problem he had to face as king, and he warned Salisbury on 23 February 1901 that if he decided to raise the income tax from a shilling to one and twopence in the pound it would 'tend to make the war unpopular, but he presumes it cannot be helped'.[10] Compared with another suggestion made to his Prime Minister early on in the reign, this was quite conventional: in March 1901 the King, showing signs of his inexperience, told Salisbury – with, it seems, the intention of seeking the Prime Minister's approval – that he was thinking of sending for Rosebery and begging him to return to public life as Leader of the Opposition, for the good of the country. Salisbury, aghast both that he should be sounded out on such a thing and that the King was even thinking of it, managed to convince the Sovereign that he could not advise on such a matter. The same day the King heard of Salisbury's refusal to become involved, he saw Rosebery. If he tried to persuade him to become Leader of the Opposition, he failed.[11]

TELLING IT ABROAD

The Kaiser, who stayed in England for Queen Victoria's obsequies, engaged in several well-publicised protestations of friendship, which as usual cooled upon his return to Germany. The Tsar did not attend the Queen's funeral, but sent a message of hope that 'the new century bring England and Russia together for our mutual interests and for the general peace of the world'.[12] In keeping with court tradition, the King on his accession sent personal envoys to the other European powers. His friend Lord Carrington, who took his message to Paris, relayed back that the Republic's Foreign Minister, Delcassé, had urged him 'to assure the King that no effort would be spared on his part to foster and maintain happy relations between France and England'.[13] Furthermore the President, Loubet, told Carrington that 'I and my ministers would consider it a crime if any one, I care not who, were to make mischief between France and England.' Carrington relayed the messages, which were just the encouragement the King would need before embarking on his first great diplomatic project as Monarch.

The envoy the King chose to send to the heads of state in Greece, Turkey, Austria and the Balkans was Lord Wolseley, the distinguished soldier; and this indirectly led to an early ministerial rebuke. On 14 March the King complained to Salisbury about the 'acrimonious tone' of a speech in the Lords by Lord Lansdowne, the Foreign Secretary, in reply to a speech by Wolseley, because he felt Lansdowne risked discrediting his personal envoy by such treatment.[14] The King was especially angry because he had warned Salisbury in advance that Lansdowne should not attack the General, and Salisbury, having passed the warning on, told the King that 'Lord Lansdowne is especially cautious and pacific: and will doubtless not say anything of which Lord Wolseley will have a right to complain. The only difficulty will be if Lord Wolseley should make a vehement attack upon Lord Lansdowne – but Lord Salisbury hopes it will be possible to prevent any angry language passing.'[15]

The King and Lansdowne were destined not to get on, despite Lansdowne's being one of the grandest peers and richest landowners in the Kingdom. They had moved in much the same society, but never with any intimacy or friendship, for more than a quarter of a century. Lansdowne had some right to feel arrogant about his command of foreign affairs: in his late thirties he had been Governor-General of Canada, and followed that by being Viceroy of India. As Salisbury's War Secretary he was perceived to have made a botch of several important features of the Boer conflict, and when Salisbury had made him Foreign Secretary in 1900 the appointment had been accompanied by much adverse press comment. Certainly, the King seems to have harboured no illusions about Lansdowne's abilities and to have appreciated the point that Lansdowne's immense wealth and the position it and his experience gave him in the Conservative party were as much as anything the reason for his having attained one of the great offices of state. Balfour, under whom Lansdowne was to serve for more than three years as Foreign Secretary, regarded him as 'better than competent' but 'I shouldn't call him very clever'.[16] Balfour had been given an ideal vantage point from which to assess Lansdowne's capabilities, not just from alongside at the Cabinet table, but from having been his fag at Eton forty years earlier.

Lansdowne appears not to have rated the King's intellect and diplomatic abilities, and to have resented from the outset his single-minded determination to be, when it suited him, his own foreign secretary, reducing Lansdowne to the role of functionary. Fritz Ponsonby felt that 'possibly Lansdowne may have been jealous at the King being supposed to run the foreign policy of the country and felt he had been ignored, being only told when matters had so far advanced that it was difficult for him to do more than give his approval. I always had the impression that, if the King ever made a false move, Lansdowne, so far from defending him, would stand and look on.'[17] To be fair to Lansdowne, there is hardly anything in the copious correspondence between him and his Sovereign that suggests such Machiavellian intent. On the contrary, it shows great forbearance while being treated with impatience, disdain and occasionally anger by the King.

The King's interest in foreign affairs was inevitable: he was better travelled than almost any politician who served him, and spoke both French and German fluently. There were, as well, three powerful reasons for his involvement as a sort of chief executive in British foreign policy. The first was that, at the coal-face of foreign affairs, the activity was simply an extension of the social intercourse the King, as heir, had been having for years. By the time he came to the throne he not only had all the right contacts, but was well briefed about their backgrounds and about the domestic situations in, and international alliances of, the countries they represented. Second, and related to this, the King was a kinsman of the heads of state in most of the countries of Europe. Third, and related to that, Britain's main rival – Germany – had its foreign policy conducted principally by its autocratic head of state, as did Russia and Austria-Hungary. Although King Edward was not himself an autocrat, it would occasionally suit him and the foreign policy aims of his country for him to act as though he was. By no means could his ministers exert the pressure on, say, German foreign policy that he could himself, thanks to his relationship (however difficult) with the Kaiser. Making his ministers, especially Lansdowne, see the question from this point of view was, however, less straightforward.

NO POPERY

In another breach of his mother's traditions, the King opened Parliament himself on 14 February by reading the speech from the throne. It was, as Sir Sidney Lee puts it, an action that showed he was 'determined that the custom should now be resumed in the full panoply of state – a resolve that was evidence of his intention to renew all outward and visible signs of his central place in the Constitution'.[18] The Queen had not attended the ceremony since 1886, and had gone only six times in the twenty-five years before that. She had not read the speech since 1861, deputing that tiresome chore to the Lord Chancellor. The sudden aggrandisement of the occasion led to suggestions from Balfour, as Leader of the Commons, that the ceremony should take place in Westminster Hall, where there was more room for MPs who wished to witness it, as 'the House of Lords is totally inadequate'.[19] The King said he would perform the ceremony in the Lords, where it had always been performed. He would later make it clear, before opening Parliament in 1903, that he was deeply opposed to the Prime Minister's office briefing the press about the contents of the King's Speech in advance of its delivery, as to do so made the ceremony 'a perfect farce'. 'It is done in no country,' the King protested, 'not even in America.'[20] So keen was he to resume powers that his mother, through her disinclinations, had allowed to lapse that he refused in 1901 to nominate a member of his family to preside over a meeting of the Privy Council if one had to be called in his absence abroad: he said that, if such a necessity arose, he would come home to preside over it. By 1903 he was feeling less touchy, and made arrangements for the Prince of Wales, *in extremis*, to deputise for him.

He was not, though, always keen on doing things in the traditional way. Before reading the speech at his first appearance as monarch at a state opening, he was asked by Halsbury, the Lord Chancellor, in accordance with the 1689 Bill of Rights, to repudiate transubstantiation and to assert that 'the invocation or adoration of the Virgin Mary or any other saint and the sacrifice of the Mass as they are now used in the Church of Rome are superstitious and idolatrous'. These and further comments, to the effect that the Bishop of Rome had no jurisdiction in this realm of England, were regarded by the King as gratuitously offensive to his Catholic subjects. Salisbury, in a letter of 10 February 1901, alerted the King to the need to make this declaration, the matter having been drawn to his attention by the Lord Chancellor. 'Doubtless,' Salisbury observed, perhaps disingenuously and hoping to avoid any trouble, 'Your Majesty's attention has been called to this obligation.'[21] The King had no choice but to read out what he regarded as the offensive sentiments; but he determined, as a result, that none of his successors should be asked to 'make such a declaration in such crude language'.[22]

Immediately after the State Opening he wrote to Salisbury, asking for the abolition of the declaration against Roman Catholicism. It was, the King told his Prime Minister, 'not in accordance with public thinking at the present day'. Salisbury, never in favour of change for the sake of it, circulated the King's letter to the Cabinet, and managed to stall the King by pointing out that the Act of Parliament that forced him to make the declaration could be changed only by the passage of another Act.

It was not until June that a committee of nine peers, including

Salisbury and Halsbury, met to discuss a possible amendment to the declaration; and the amendment on which they decided retained much of the old 'no Popery' flavour. The Lord Chancellor had the report into the matter published, which further upset the King, who demanded to know why he had not been told the results of the study before everyone else. Halsbury apologised, to be told by the King that he was 'naturally much surprised that he had received no intimation, previous to having read it in the newspapers, of this Report, as it was an important matter concerning the Sovereign regarding which he ought to have been consulted'.[23] The King had a very clear idea of what a new declaration should say, for he had told Salisbury of it in a letter of 7 July 1901: 'it should be shorter and confined to his determination to uphold the Protestant faith, of which he is a member, and avoid those expressions which have caused such discontent, not only to his Roman Catholic subjects, but to many others besides.'[24] He accused Halsbury of 'bungling', urged Salisbury to get on with it, and warned that he expected to be fully consulted in future, before Balfour put the matter before the Commons.[25] He was also angry that among the committee that had considered the change there was not one bishop or archbishop. In his strictures he was coming dangerously close to party politics, making identical points to those made by Rosebery in a debate in the Lords on 8 July, points Salisbury had rejected.

Salisbury replied to the King on 8 July, saying he 'entirely' concurred with the desire for a shorter declaration, devoted to the upholding of Protestantism.[26] He stated that was exactly what the committee had sought to achieve. However, he warned the King that he had 'little doubt that both Houses of Parliament will insist on maintaining the Sovereign's declaration in such language as shall ensure the Protestant succession.... it was the object of the committee, having eliminated all insulting matter, to abstain from any further change'. Further pressure was put on the King to understand that the 'Protestant party' in the country would seethe if this Bill were sent back.[27] Eventually, Salisbury agreed that although he would make the findings of the original report the matter of a new Bill to be introduced in the Upper House, amendments could be made to it there if necessary.

This apparent concession – though in some respects a statement of the obvious, it did seem to show some private willingness on Salisbury's part to modernise the declaration – came as a result of direct pressure from the King. On 16 July 1901 McDonnell, Salisbury's private secretary, had been sent for by the King to be given the royal view on this apparently interminable irritation. The King told McDonnell of his concern about the draft Bill on the Declaration: 'though he was anxious that no handle should be given for a No Popery agitation, he was very desirous that the references to transubstantiation and the Virgin Mary should be omitted. The King then asked if the Bill could be altered accordingly.'[28] However, the King was told this was impossible; the Bill, McDonnell said, must embody the report of the Select Committee in which specific mention of these points was made. A change could now be made only by a measure going through both houses, which would draw unwanted attention to the matter. It could not really be whipped, and Salisbury himself could not be put in the politically impossible position of moving the amendments to a Bill he had introduced.

However, Salisbury promised the King, in advance of the second reading of the Bill on 23 July, that he would accept any amendments for which there was majority support. By the time the Bill went to the Commons the controversy surrounding it had become so strong that it was withdrawn. The King thought his government's performance on this issue lamentable, but in fact Salisbury had simply been observing the majority Protestant feeling in the country; subsequent attempts later in the parliament to introduce such a measure failed precisely because of the unwillingness of the Protestant constituency to brook this suggested dilution. It was not, in fact, to be until the summer of 1910, after the King's death, that an amendment was successfully passed. Sir Sidney Lee claimed that 'the episode illustrates an obvious weakness in the procedure of constitutional government,' which is manifest rubbish – at any rate, if one believes that constitutional government is about elected administrations taking more note of majority feeling in the country than of the views of one man, however important.[29]

While this controversy was building up, the Duke of Norfolk urged the King to receive a deputation of Catholics, that they might express their loyalty to him. Salisbury, once more betraying his Protestant fundamentalism, said they had no right to be received, but the King could grant them an audience, if he felt he had to. They referred to themselves as 'Catholics', but Salisbury warned the King that in his reply he was to refer to them as 'Roman Catholics'.[30]

MATTERS OF PREROGATIVE

The King was determined, as far as possible, to retain the royal prerogatives to himself. Sir Sidney Lee, going where Bagehot feared to tread, defines these as:

> the prerogative of mercy; the dissolution and convocation of parliament; the dismissal and selection of ministers (though this had been severely challenged in 1880 when Queen Victoria had to relinquish her choice of Lord Hartington as prime minister in favour of the more popular Mr Gladstone); the declaration of war and peace; the making of treaties; the cession of territory (though Queen Victoria was doubtful of the prudence of ceding Heligoland in 1890, and only consented 'that any of my possessions should thus be bartered away' on receiving from Lord Salisbury 'a positive assurance ... that the present arrangement constitutes no precedent'); the creation of peers; and the appointment of bishops, colonial governors, and judges.[31]

Sir Sidney also points out that the Sovereign had the right to veto any Bill brought for royal assent, but that this had not been done since 1707, despite much bluster on occasion by Queen Victoria.

The prerogative of mercy was of great interest to the King, even though it had long existed in name only. Unaware of the normal procedures, many seeking mercy petitioned the King direct, rather than going through the normal channel of the Home Office; and the King took a close interest in such petitions. An Act of Parliament in the first year of his mother's reign had removed from the Home Secretary the necessity of taking the Monarch's pleasure in matters of those condemned to death; and when the King's interest in these matters became a little too active, the Home Secretary, Aretas Akers-Douglas, wrote to him on 26 September 1903 to say that as the question of reprieves was often one of great public controversy, and as it was desirable to have the King's name kept out of such controversies, the matter had to rest with the Home Secretary. Nonetheless, the King continued to be informed of whether the Home Secretary had decided to commute a sentence, or to allow the law to take its course. He had long shown a liberal streak towards criminals. When, in 1882, a man named Bradshaw had written to him threatening his life unless he was paid £10, the would-be murderer was arrested and sentenced to ten years' imprisonment. Feeling sure the man was mad, and that ten years was somewhat extreme, the then Prince had written to Sir William

Harcourt, the Home Secretary, to ask him to have the sentence reduced. 'No doubt,' the Prince had written, 'in these days it is necessary to inflict punishment on those who write threatening letters, but at the same time I should be very glad if it were possible to lessen ... the sentence passed on Bradshaw.'[32] In that case, the Queen had intervened, telling Harcourt to do no such thing, and that was that.

One of the most celebrated cases during the reign was that of Arthur Lynch, an Irishman who had fought with the Boers, and who was sentenced to death for high treason in January 1903. Within five days this was commuted to a life sentence, and as the King prepared to visit Ireland later that year the Cabinet discussed whether an act of clemency was appropriate. The King was appealed to directly by his friend Sir Thomas Lipton, the tea magnate, to have Lynch released. The release took place, on licence, in January 1904. The King was indisposed to have the restrictions on Lynch lifted when further appeals were made to him by Lynch himself, but gave his assent when in March 1904 a conditional pardon was granted him; and Lynch wrote to the King to thank him. Two years later Lynch tried to have his remaining disabilities removed, but this time the King lost patience. He told his Home Secretary, Herbert Gladstone, that Lynch's original offences, not least ordering his men to fire upon English troops, were in 'the category of almost the worst of crimes'; and although he saw the importance of 'conciliating Ireland', it was 'contrary to the King's conscientious ideas of what is right and just' to allow any further concessions.[33] However, the King stated that if after a reasonable limit of time the case were referred to him again, he would give it new consideration; and a year later, in June 1907, he raised no objection to Lynch's having a free pardon.

The King was always prepared to cause trouble in these matters when he felt justice was not being done. In 1907 Horace Rayner was convicted of the murder of a W. Whiteley. Before his conviction and sentence he had attempted suicide, and there was a popular movement to have him reprieved on the ground of his insanity. Nine days after being condemned to death, Rayner had had his sentence commuted by Gladstone to life imprisonment. Gladstone sent the King a conditional pardon for his signature. On receiving it the King ordered an inquiry into the circumstances, and replied to the Home Secretary:

> the King has signed the Pardon which, as a Constitutional Sovereign,
> he is bound to do, but ... if Rayner was insane, the King cannot see

why the verdict of 'Temporary Insanity' which you think would have been brought in had Rayner committed suicide should not equally have resulted when he was alive and on his trial ... the murder of Mr Whiteley appeared to be a very cold-blooded one, incident on a failure to obtain blackmail, and this circumstance seems to have been lost sight of in the agitation which has taken place. The King is entirely averse to any form of punishment which errs on the side of severity, but he feels that as long as capital punishment is laid down as the penalty of murder, the commutation of that punishment should always be based on legal and moral grounds, and that the tendency nowadays to regard a criminal as martyr, and to raise an agitation on sentimental grounds in order to put pressure on the Home Secretary, is one which may eventually prove very inconvenient, if concessions are too readily made.[34]

Gladstone responded immediately, denying he had been motivated by anything other than cold reason, and certainly had not commuted Rayner's sentence for any of the reasons at which the King hinted. But Fritz Ponsonby, replying on behalf of the King, reflected the Monarch's lack of conviction on this point by saying that 'in this case His Majesty cannot help feeling that you have been actuated by sentiment.... His Majesty does not attach much importance to the letters and petitions in favour of the prisoner. They are usually the outcome of agitations organised by the halfpenny press, which invariably takes the part of the criminal. The point to be considered is the effect that such a reprieve will have generally, and this the King fears will not be for the best.'[35]

The King's attitude was one thing: the results he obtained another. He was powerless to prevent his Home Secretaries hanging or not hanging whomever they liked, once a murderer had been convicted. Throughout his reign his other prerogatives were often challenged, not least by Balfour, a Conservative, between 1902 and 1905: the Liberal party, which held sway for the rest of his reign, was docile by comparison, until the great confrontation in 1909–10 over the use of the prerogative of creating peers. Balfour made an unprecedented assault on the Monarch's role in dissolving Parliament. Although Queen Victoria had on occasion tried to prevent a dissolution, she had never refused one. Nor would her son; but, when there was the possibility of his dissolving Parliament in 1905 at Balfour's request, he was angered by Balfour's making a statement that the House of

Commons could insist upon a dissolution and that the Cabinet had ordered one. Balfour also argued that he could appoint or dismiss ministers without consulting the King, and he took the view that the cession of territory and the making of treaties were primarily the business of Parliament, though the main cession for which Balfour was responsible – of colonial territory to France after the *entente cordiale* of 1904 – was a result of the royal initiative that brought that treaty about.

Balfour also inaugurated an especially slippery slope in insisting that he could request the creation of peers: this was to have profound consequences in the crisis of 1909–10. The accretion of patronage to the Prime Minister was one of the great losses to the monarchy of King Edward's reign, and one feature that marks it out as a time of transition in constitutional history. Ironically, in his memorial address to the Commons as Leader of the House on the death of Queen Victoria in 1901, Balfour had said that 'in my judgement the importance of the Crown in our Constitution is not a diminishing, but an increasing factor'.[36] This was mainly, he argued, because the person of the monarch would bind together an empire whose future lay in the self-governing dominions, such as Canada and Australia. He cannot have meant he expected the sovereign to have more of a role in domestic politics, for as a senior politician he had no intention of allowing such a thing.

That said, the King early on overreached himself and attempted a trick that (had he been more experienced) he would have known belonged to earlier times. He tried to have a lord-in-waiting, Lord Laurence, removed, for no other reason than he had come across him socially and did not find him congenial. Laurence had been the Liberal Unionists' Whip in the Lords since the faction was formed in 1886, and had become a government Whip in 1895. The post of lord-in-waiting had long been a political one, but carried with it membership of the royal household, which was the King's excuse for seeking to intervene in this way. Salisbury could see no reason for sacking Laurence, since he performed his duties adequately. This gave McDonnell an awkward interview with the King, after which, having discussed the matter with Devonshire, Salisbury wrote to the King that he 'regrets very much that he finds himself unable to submit to HM that he should be authorised to acquaint Lord Laurence that his appointment as Lord-in-Waiting must come to an end.'[37] The Prime Minister wanted the King to know that he was 'anxious to serve' him in every way with respect to appointments, but that Laurence's dismissal would 'involve a novel procedure so much at variance with the constitutional principle on which these appointments were made', and Salisbury could not take it.

In his own hand on the draft of this memorandum to Knollys, Salisbury noted:

> for nearly a century it has been the habit to look upon the members of the Royal Household, having seats in parliament, as members of the administration of the day. They are appointed with the other members on the recommendation of the Prime Minister, and they resign when the Government is defeated. If at the instance of the Government any one of them is expelled from office, while the rest of the Government remains, it implies that the Government are satisfied that there is some grave reason why continuance in office is inexpedient.

That might have been the case with Lord Bagot, the only precedent Salisbury could find, because in that case there were personal scandals. 'But there is no fault to be found in the public or private conduct of Lord Laurence,' the Prime Minister observed. It would, he added, put an 'unjust' slur on Laurence's reputation for the King to insist on his removal, and there was no office of 'similar importance' available to which Laurence could be moved to take him out of the King's ambit. In the draft – the memorandum was not sent – McDonnell admitted the King could dismiss Laurence himself 'by causing the Lord Chamberlain to omit his name from the Gazette; but Lord Salisbury would earnestly deprecate so extreme a course'.

Despite the rumours that had swirled round late-Victorian London about the massive debts an extravagant Prince of Wales had run up while waiting to succeed his mother, he became king without owing a penny to anybody. Some financial prestidigitation by a few of his City friends, not least Ernest Cassel, had helped in this; but the King had no capital either. A generous settlement was made from the civil list by Parliament in 1901, which to everyone's satisfaction kept the King and his family in the style to which they ought to be accustomed. Parliament was satisfied the King was not engaging in any extravagances with the public's money. However, after six years of this arrangement working well, the Treasury started to have doubts about whether it should bear the cost of official visits to England by foreign crowned heads, most of whom were close relations of the King. The King saw this, quite rightly, as a dishonouring of the deal done in 1901:

these were not, whatever the appearance may have been, family entertainments, but often high diplomatic necessities. Knollys wrote immediately to the permanent secretary, Sir Edward Hamilton – the two men had known each other well for the best part of thirty years, since Hamilton had been Gladstone's private secretary – to tell him so. Having assured Hamilton that the original deal 'without doubt' covered this expenditure, Knollys warned him that 'the Treasury may, however, be assured that the King will not give in on this point, and if it is persisted in I hope His Majesty immediately on his return will send for the Prime Minister and tell him he will not stand such an attempted evasion by the Treasury of what was agreed upon in 1901'.[38]

That almost did the trick, though Hamilton asked that in future when the King considered a visit to be a state visit, of political importance, Knollys should write and tell the Chancellor so, who could then pass the matter on to the Foreign Secretary for adjudication. Knollys rightly saw this as an attempt to limit the King's influence, as 'His Majesty has ... his own views respecting the importance, from a political point of view, of visits of Foreign Sovereigns to this country, which might not coincide with those of the Secretary of State.... if the proposal in question were to be carried into effect, there might be constant conflicts between the King on one side and the Treasury and the Foreign Office on the other.'[39] That really did do the trick.

THE WAR CONTINUES

The Tsar wrote to his uncle, the King, at the end of May 1901 to warn him of the effect the Boer War was having on the reputation of Britain abroad. He said he had received many letters and other petitions begging him to 'interfere', and as a result he was asking the King to see what he could do to end the war promptly.[40] On 9 June 1901 Knollys sent the letter to Salisbury, asking him to circulate it to Lansdowne, Chamberlain (who as Colonial Secretary was directly involved) and Balfour. 'He thinks the letter is very kindly meant,' wrote Knollys, 'though he has probably been "put up" to it by his ministers.' The King wanted to know what to reply. He asked: '"How could we cease hostilities? Would the Russians have done so under similar circumstances? The answer is certainly in the negative".'[41] Nor did the King need to be made aware by anyone else of the unpopularity with which the war was regarded on the continent; in his travels abroad since it started he had not only been shot at in a protest about it, but had been subjected to the singing of the Boer national anthem wherever he went.

Salisbury himself drafted the memorandum of response, noting the Tsar's kindness, but observing that he clearly did not understand why the war had started, for it had been forced upon Britain.[42] On 19 June the King wrote back to the Tsar in those terms, outlining how the Boers in the Transvaal had for years been preparing for war, and how the British were used to fighting long-drawn-out colonial wars.[43] It was an example of how, in an age of autocrats, the government placed heavy reliance on the King to participate in the conduct of foreign affairs. At this stage in his reign, it was a responsibility he was glad to be given.

As a convinced imperialist and, therefore, a profound supporter of his government's policy in pursuing the war, the King was horrified when the leading Liberal 'pro-Boer', Sir Henry Campbell-Bannerman, made a speech in Edinburgh in May 1901 attacking the notion of unconditional surrender being forced on the Boers. Matters were further aggravated when, a fortnight later, he claimed that the war was being prosecuted by 'methods of barbarism': given that one of the methods Sir Henry was referring to was the internment of women and children in disease-ridden concentration camps, he was not entirely overstating his case. The King's first instinct was to send for Campbell-Bannerman and tell him to say nothing that might give encouragement to his country's enemies. Salisbury, however, talked him out of this prospective intervention in politics, not least because many of the Liberals themselves were unsettled by the attitude of Campbell-Bannerman and his faction. The Prime Minister argued that for the King to go on the attack against Campbell-Bannerman would be interpreted as an interference in the domestic strife of the Liberal party.

It was, though, only with the most severe reluctance that the King took Salisbury's advice. He continued to brood throughout the summer on what he considered to be Campbell-Bannerman's lack of patriotism, and sent for Rosebery on 8 July to discuss the matter with him. Rosebery recorded that 'he wished to consult me as to seeing C-B and impressing upon him the encouragement that his utterances about the war gave to the Boers and appealing to him as a patriot to desist. I urged him to do nothing of the kind, and he agreed to give up the idea.'[44]

In August 1901, being informed by St John Brodrick, the Secretary of State for War, that Lord Kitchener, chief of staff in the South Africa command, had great misgivings about whether he could bring the war to a successful conclusion if the government persisted in its plans for withdrawal of some of the troops in South Africa, the King urged that Brodrick see 'the extreme importance of being guided entirely by Lord Kitchener's advice in this matter'.[45] The following month the King was on the offensive again, this time against the Colonial Office, which he claimed had 'seriously hampered' Kitchener by not curtailing 'liberty of action in places where this freedom has been grossly abused'.[46] He claimed no action was being taken to restrict the flow of men, arms and ammunition to the Boers through ports in Cape Colony, and he told Brodrick that it was up to him to ensure that Chamberlain had the law enforced on the Cape. In reply, Brodrick assured him the situation would be tightened up.

However, the war dragged on, to the chagrin of the King, his government and his people. On 20 November 1901 he raised the issue in a memorandum to Salisbury:

> The King has read with great interest Lord Salisbury's account of the deliberations of his ministers at the Cabinet – and is very glad that they expressed such strong opinions on the inadequate information given by his officers in South Africa, which it is to be hoped may be remedied in future. The King shares with his Government concern at the continued prolongation of the war with apparently no hope for its coming to an end for a long time. The strain on the resources of the Country is becoming very great – additional taxation must ensue and the amount of troops now in South Africa is becoming most serious, should they at any emergency be required elsewhere.[47]

He took a close interest over the succeeding months in the question of the inadequate supply of horses to South Africa, and the incompetence with which the purchase of horses had been carried out – his patience finally snapping on 6 February 1902 with the remark 'no doubt someone will have to be hung for it'.[48]

Moving as he did in high social and diplomatic circles, the King occasionally thought he knew more about what was going on than he was being told by his ministers. On 6 November 1901 Knollys wrote to McDonnell: 'The King hears rumours that the Cabinet are very uneasy over the prospect of an insurrection in Cape Colony. Can you tell me for his information whether there is any foundation in these rumours?'[49] Salisbury replied to the King that there had indeed been rumours to that effect, but none so serious that the Cabinet was unduly concerned about them. It was further proof to him, though, that the King was determined to keep his ministers alert to their responsibilities towards him, and to exercise his right to know.

Kitchener was so fed up with the way politicians had conducted the war that he wanted to resign; and Lord Curzon, the Viceroy of India, convinced Brodrick that it would be a fine idea for the General to become, instead, Commander-in-Chief in India. Because of Kitchener's lack of experience of the sub-continent, and also his apparent physical exhaustion, the King described Curzon's idea as 'preposterous'. Yet the government persisted with it, and Brodrick tried to explain to the King that Curzon, who was turning out to be a first-rate viceroy, had had little previous experience of India either. The King, though, did not accept this. Writing to Brodrick on 2 February 1902, he said that 'I have still grave doubts about whether Kitchener is the right man for Commander-in-Chief in India, as he has absolutely no knowledge of the country and people.... the reason Curzon is making so good a Viceroy is that besides his great personal ability he has personal knowledge of the country!'[50] However, Kitchener stipulated that either he was given the India job or he would resign from the service. He was too valuable a soldier to lose, and so the appointment was made effective from November 1902. The King promised Brodrick that he would never refer to his doubts again, and no one foresaw that the relationship between Curzon and Kitchener would become so combustible and acrimonious that Curzon's viceroyalty would end as a result of it.

From his accession until the end of the Boer War, the close and detailed interest the King took in it was exemplified by the frequency with which he summoned Brodrick to audiences. To the Liberal Opposition it seemed unconstitutional: so much so that Campbell-Bannerman hinted to Balfour that the regular newspaper reports about the King's meetings with his War Secretary were so embarrassing to Parliament that he might feel compelled to ask a question in the Commons about them, and about their significance for the proper constitutional control of the army. It looked as though Brodrick was being made to take decisions not according to the Cabinet's collective responsibility, but according to the King's fiat. In fact, the King had no high opinion of Brodrick, whom he would later come to regard as having gravely mishandled the crisis that led to Curzon's resignation as viceroy in 1905. Even before that crisis came, so Curzon told his wife, the King regarded Brodrick as 'a most ridiculous personage' whom he could never consider 'without bursting out laughing'.[51] Fritz Ponsonby noted that 'the King never seemed to get on with Brodrick, although he always seemed anxious to please His Majesty. They had different types of mind.'[52] Throughout his reign, the King far preferred to talk informally with his ministers at social occasions than summon them for formal audiences. Indeed, Knollys observed in September 1905 that, with the exception of the Prime Minister, the Foreign Secretary and the War Secretary, the King had all but stopped giving formal audiences to ministers.[53] When, with the end of Balfour's regime that year, the office of prime minister became at last enshrined in the order of precedence, it effected the *de facto* establishment of the prime minister as the conduit through whom the monarch addressed his ministers. It increased the prime minister's power, at the expense of the king's.

The war ended in May 1902, with the Boers surrendering their right to govern the Orange Free State and the Transvaal independently, and with large resettlement grants offered by the British government. Given how critical the King had been about the conduct of certain aspects of the war, it might have been expected he would have welcomed the news, a month before the cessation of hostilities, that a Royal Commission of investigation was being set up into the war. In his Cabinet report to the King of 5 June 1902 Salisbury confirmed that the inquiry would take place. 'The feeling of the Cabinet, however, was that such an inquiry, though former pledges might make it necessary, ought to be restricted within the narrowest possible limits, and as far as possible held in secret.'[54] The King was not convinced. On 13 June 1902, having at an audience failed to persuade Salisbury of the wrongness of such a public washing of dirty linen, wrote formally to him to deprecate the inquiry. Showing a surprisingly naive grasp of political reality, the King argued that the government's large parliamentary majority meant that Salisbury had no need to go through this process. Salisbury replied the next day that promises had been made, and they had to be kept.

He proceeded to give his sovereign a sharp lesson in constitutional manners:

> YM speaks of your having urged Lord Salisbury 'not to consent to such an inquiry'. He has no power to interpose such a veto against the

decision of the Cabinet. His colleagues would have the right to refuse to be overruled by the Prime Minister, and in a matter which they regard as a question of honourable adherence to a pledge they would doubtless do so. If the Prime Minister were to decide rather to break up the Government than to consent to the inquiry, the public would inevitably conclude that so extreme a course had been taken for the purpose of concealing matters which would not bear disclosure.[55]

He continued, 'Your Majesty will doubtless remember' that in 1855 Ministers had tried to resist John Roebuck's Commons motion for an inquiry into the conduct of the Crimean War, 'which was held in spite of them'. However, Salisbury assured the King that 'every effort will be made to make the inquiry innocuous'. The King accepted the constitutionally inevitable, though furthered his own case by ensuring that Esher was a member of the inquiry. As usual, Esher acted as informant-in-chief, supplying the King with detailed information about the deliberations of the inquiry and the examination of witnesses every day that it met. His membership of this inquiry, and the slavish way in which he reported back to the King and seemed to be protecting the Sovereign's interests, was to have the effect of cementing his importance in the King's circle.

Long before the Commission reported in August 1903, however, one of the principal targets of the King's criticism of his part in the war chose to fight back. Brodrick, who throughout his time as Secretary of State for War had been on the receiving end of a robust correspondence from the King – usually for giving insufficient respect to the views of military personnel – wrote to him on 13 October 1902 to complain, in the usually respectful terms, that his difficult job was being made no easier by the King's interference. The letter followed an audience of the same day in which the minister had attempted to set out the same point. Brodrick had largely been handicapped by an army in need of reform, and which could hardly be reformed in the middle of a war over 5,000 miles away. The King appreciated the justice of Brodrick's protestations, and replied to him almost at once, in his own hand, promising full support in future, but he warned that his criticism would continue, in private, and that he was always available to Brodrick to discuss matters concerning the army – not least the reforms, the nature of which were part of the remit of the Royal Commission the King had been so set against.

MATTERS OF HONOUR

The King's almost childlike interest in the award of honours had never abated while he was Prince of Wales. Becoming King made him owner of the toyshop, though he had always to contend with the circumspection of the shop's manager, his Prime Minister. Salisbury, who had utter disdain for such things – easier to cultivate, perhaps, in a marquess with the Garter than in some of the King's other friends – was the perfect foil in this respect. His office was, almost from the moment of the accession, on the receiving end of a constant stream of suggestions and recommendations. Both the King and his Prime Minister claimed to share a view that appointments to orders of knighthood and to the peerage should maintain the quality of those institutions. The King, however, was more radical in his interpretation of this ethos than his Prime Minister; his definition of quality and his Prime Minister's did not always coincide, with the Prime Minister inevitably upholding the more staid view.

McDonnell wrote to Salisbury on 4 March 1901 that 'the King thinks Lord Haddington would be a good man for the Thistle. I represented to HM that Lord Haddington was fond of whisky and his *amours* were a local scandal.' The vacancy was instead filled by the far more respectable Duke of Sutherland. However, in the Coronation honours the following year, and after Salisbury had left office, Haddington had his Thistle.[56] On the same day, the King wrote asking Salisbury to procure the rank of an earl's daughter for Charlotte Knollys, sister of his private secretary, who had put in years of devoted service to Queen Alexandra. Salisbury, however, thought this would be difficult under the usually flexible peerage law. He counter-suggested that it would be easier to make her a baroness, not least because she was in her sixties and had no children to inherit the dignity. Unable to decide himself, he sent the matter on to Garter King of Arms, who was often kept busy by the King's exertions. Salisbury wrote to the King on 9 March submitting 'that the style and precedence of a Baron's daughter be conferred upon Miss Charlotte Knollys. He has ascertained from Garter King of Arms that precedents exist for this course.'[57]

The King was, sometimes, most conservative in his views about honours. Early in 1901 Knollys forwarded to Salisbury a recommendation sent to the King by a French friend of his, recommending Sir Edward Blount – a nonagenarian banker and promoter of French railways – for a baronetcy. The King's reservation was mainly, but not entirely, about the heir: 'young Mr Blount is a d—d bore and that he shewed the white feather at the fire at the Bazaar; also that Frenchmen have no business to recommend Englishmen for honours'. 'I respect-fully concur,' said Salisbury.[58] Later the same year, on 8 October 1901, Knollys wrote to McDonnell from Balmoral about the birthday honours the following month, saying that the King wanted a knighthood for his oculist, and a baronetcy for Sir George Lewis, who 'the King is aware has no public claims ... but he has done much work for HM and the Royal Family for a great number of years'.[59] Lewis was a prominent solicitor and one of those who attracted a certain amount of prejudice as one of the King's circle of Jewish friends: the baronetcy came in the following year's Coronation honours. On 20 October Knollys was writing again, the King having been importuned by Lord Hawkesbury, who asked to be created Earl of Liverpool. His grandfather had been the last holder of the title, and Hawkesbury had tried to become Baron Liverpool when his own peerage was created, but the city was too grand for a mere barony. He had asked the late Queen to consider his petition, and believed she was looking favourably upon it at the time of her death. The King thought 'the application might come under consideration' at the time of the Coronation, but Salisbury was advised by McDonnell that 'this is an extraordinary request: he is a Radical Home Ruler: and in the male line Sir George Jenkinson is the nearest descendant'.[60] In fact, Hawkesbury kept up his petitioning, and was rewarded with the earldom he wanted in 1905.

Yet all these matters were minor in comparison with the great honours drama of the early part of the reign: the selection of those to be included in the Coronation honours list. There was an additional distinction attached to inclusion on so rare a list, and it was supposed to be the moment to honour those who had rendered the most conspicuous public service. The King, though, had his own definition of what that service was, and, since he was the fountain of honour, any of his recommendations disapproved of by his Prime Minister might become the subject of a prolonged and difficult tussle. In fact, the provocative nature of the list – and he knew it was provocative by the lengths to which he went to explain away some of his choices – resulted in Salisbury in effect amending the prerogative as hitherto exercised by the monarch in respect of honours, by imposing his will much more forcibly than ever before. But then the old Queen had never had friends of the sort the King had, and nor had she been in the same sort of debt to them, both metaphorical and real, that the King often was.

The root of the problem was that the King wanted peerages for two of his wealthy friends who had performed him extensive, and generous, personal services in preceding years: Sir Ernest Cassel and Sir Thomas Lipton, for whom he had had a hand in securing a knighthood in the 1898 new year's honours and upon whom he had bestowed the KCVO in 1901. Cassel was regarded by the Conservative establishment as yet another member of the King's circle of Jewish friends, and in the prevailing mood of anti-semitism of the times in high Tory circles was not popular. Nor, at that stage, was it clear to anyone outside the King's circle what great public services Cassel had performed, other than massively enriching Cassel. This was unfair: Cassel had not only financed a number of imperial enterprises (for which he had been awarded the GCMG in 1899) but was also a great philanthropist, notably giving the then massive sum of £200,000 in 1902 to found a sanatorium in the King's name for tuberculosis sufferers. Lipton was a Glaswegian grocer turned tea-merchant who took the King yachting, and being a tradesman was regarded as quite the wrong sort of person for a House of Lords that was still almost exclusively made up of the landed interest, judges and distinguished servicemen. He, too, was a philanthropist, on a smaller scale than Cassel but nonetheless considerable, giving £25,000 to a charity of the Princess of Wales's for the feeding of the poor in 1897, and a few years later £100,000 for a pauper's restaurant. However, he was homosexual. The King, having correctly assessed the radical nature of what he was proposing, chose to explain the matter in detail to McDonnell, with whom he had by this time cultivated a confidential relationship.

McDonnell took up the story in a memorandum to Salisbury of 13 February 1902:

> The King sent for me yesterday and kept me 40 minutes. He began by saying that the conversation was to be considered absolutely confidential, that I was not to let a single word of it be known to anyone except Lord Salisbury, especially it was not to be known to anyone of his entourage – not even to Sir Francis Knollys. I promised to observe absolute secrecy. HM then said that he regarded his Coronation as a great national event: that he thought certain honours should be bestowed on that occasion: that they should be of a non-party character: and that the initiative in the matter should rest with himself

rather than with the Prime Minister! He would like to create two 'extra' Knights of the Garter, probably the Duke of Wellington, and the Duke of Marlborough: also two extra Knights of the Thistle, one of whom would be the Duke of Roxburghe: and two extra Knights of St Patrick, one of whom should be Lord Waterford. HM then went on to say that he should like Sir Francis Knollys made a Privy Councillor.

A pause followed, and I said that I would report his wishes to Lord Salisbury: HM's next remarks are best given in his own words.

'I now come to *Peerages*: and I wish Lord Salisbury to know that I have quite decided that two ought to be created personal to myself: one is a widower without a son: the other is a bachelor: neither are [sic] identified with any political party: both have rendered great services to myself and to the Queen: and both are most eminent in finance and in commerce. I refer to Sir Ernest Cassel and Sir Thomas Lipton! You may laugh if you like but no more suitable men could be found.'

McDonnell goes on to report:

I felt inclined to do anything but laugh: and my face must have shewn what I thought as HM at once proceeded to launch forth upon a valuable eulogy of both.

I will reserve some remarks upon this proposal until I see Your Lordship on Monday; if it should be carried out the scandal which would ensue would be positively dangerous.[61]

Salisbury, in a note back to his secretary, observed that while he did not think the alterations to the Orders were wise, no real notice would be taken of them. 'But the peerages! Neither would be a good nomination, but the second [Lipton's] is impossible. I would not accept the responsibility for either creation – the man has no services and his name and vocation are moreover ridiculous. I think we shall come to blows over that.'[62]

The Prime Minister made these views clear to the King. In the end, a compromise was reached, with Lipton receiving a baronetcy, and Cassel a Privy Councillorship. It was an honour Cassel kept only with difficulty and much expenditure of legal resources once the Great War broke out, as it was claimed that his being born outside the allegiance and without British parents – he was a German Jew – disqualified him from the appointment, which the King had had no right to make. In the end, in 1915, the courts found in his favour. That the King backed down, and that Salisbury held to the view he had outlined in the first instance to McDonnell, suggests that the popular myth that Salisbury left office in July 1902 as a result of a disagreement over the honours is precisely that. The King did not let up in his badgering of his Prime Minister, even when afflicted by the bout of appendicitis that caused the postponement of his Coronation from 26 June to 9 August: as soon as he could dictate, and just before Salisbury left office, he had Knollys soliciting honours again – a peerage for Sir Francis Grenfell, and knighthoods for Colonel Makins and for C. B. Maclaren MP.[63]

Sometimes the King could help Salisbury with honours. 'Lord Salisbury is very glad to see that HM is averse to Mrs Herbert's petition to be made Lady Hanover,' he wrote in March 1902. 'She has been bombarding him for years, but he always staved her off. Her pertinacity is phenomenal.'[64] The King was more generous when his Champion, Frank Seaman Dymoke, wrote to ask for a baronetcy to mark the Coronation. 'The King thinks a Knighthood would be sufficient,' McDonnell told Salisbury.[65] The King did, though, reconsider. 'HM does not hear a very good account of Dymoke and under these circumstances he sees no reason why he should obtain a knighthood.'[66] The Champion's function – discharged on a hereditary basis by the Dymokes since 1377 – was to issue a challenge to anyone who disputed the Sovereign's rights to succeed. The challenge was laid down at the Coronation banquet – but none had been held since George II's in 1728.

The details of the Coronation list kept Knollys busy for months, as a complex negotiation developed between the King and his Prime Minister. Knollys wrote to McDonnell to say that Sir Edward Lawson, a newspaper magnate, 'might wait for his peerage until 9 Nov, and that he will more appropriately come in then. He rather agrees that he is not an ideal Coronation peer.'[67] 'This is annoying,' McDonnell noted, 'but I suppose there is nothing to be done but to acquiesce.' Salisbury had his own suggestions for the list: a Privy Councillorship for Sir Alfred Lyall, an Indian civil servant of great distinction, and a baronetcy for Thomas Jackson, retiring head of the Hong Kong and Shanghai Bank. He also solicited a viscounty for Alfred Milner, High Commissioner of South Africa and one of the few concerned to emerge with distinction from the Boer War. There were also reports of personal difficulties arising from offers of honours: Salisbury reported that Sir Wilfred Laurier, the long-serving and distinguished Prime Minister of Canada, had turned a peerage down because it would eventually advertise the illegitimacy of his son.

Other matters concerning the Coronation list were more straightforward. The King had already, in his first birthday list the previous November, specified to Salisbury that he did not like the notion of party hacks receiving too many honours. His friend the Duke of Devonshire had, however, asked for a peerage in the Coronation honours for Michael Biddulph, a fellow Liberal Unionist who had sat in the Commons since 1865. On 18 May 1902 he had to let Devonshire know that he could not oblige because, as Knollys wrote, 'the list of proposed Coronation peerages is already sufficiently large, and.... Biddulph must wait, at all accounts until 9th November'. It was only a delay for Biddulph: the King kept his word and honoured him soon after the Coronation. Also, Knollys wrote, 'the King is not quite satisfied as to the advisability of making Sir Charles Tennant a peer, and would be glad if Lord Salisbury would "hold hard" in the matter, and kindly think of some other more eligible Liberal'. The King was keen to have all parties represented in the list, not just sympathisers of the Unionist government. One of the most prominent Liberals, Sir William Harcourt, was offered a viscounty, but turned it down on the grounds – which the King said he understood – of not wanting to leave the House of Commons.

Another prominent, though more discreet, Liberal received a peerage in the list: Knollys, who led the list of those honoured in the household. The King pressed his new Prime Minister to have the peerage fees, customarily paid for necessary heraldic services, remitted for Knollys, in recognition of his outstanding service to the Crown. Balfour agreed, with the caveat that 'such remission shall only be made in very special cases – but Sir F. Knollys' appears to be one of them'.[68] In fact, the King ensured the same favour was done to the soldier Sir Francis Grenfell, ennobled in the same list. As well as GCVOs being spread around some of his long-serving advisers, the King also asked for knighthoods for two senior officers of his household, Colonel A. G. Fife, the Standard Bearer, and Lieutenant-Colonel Reginald Rennell, the Lieutenant of the Yeoman of the Guard, citing the precedents of earlier coronations. The King's desire not to debase the currency by awarding too many honours was a vain hope. The total number of awards in all lists in 1902 was 1,540, compared with the 515 conferred in the year of the next Coronation, 1911.

A small part of the inflation was due to the creation, at the King's behest, of the Order of Merit. It was an idea he copied from Frederick the Great's Pour le Mérite, though stemming from a suggestion made by Esher nearly a year before the accession, as a means of creating a civilian equivalent of the DSO.[69] This was to be even more exclusive, however. It was to have a maximum of twenty-four members – so that, in Salisbury's words, it 'will keep its hold on public estimation' – and be in the gift of the Sovereign, not his Prime Minister.[70] Salisbury tried to suggest that military and naval men should not, as the King wished, have a special place reserved for them in this Order, as there were quite enough decorations available for them as it was. Acting at Brodrick's request, he wrote to the King on 17 April 1902 that the War Secretary, the First Lord of the Admiralty, Lord Selborne, and Lord Roberts, the Commander-in-Chief of the army, thought that extending such an honour to the military would be 'productive of confusion'.[71] His main concern was that soldiers might receive it for reasons not entirely connected with their military service.

However, the King had his own way, and the Order was established exactly as he decreed it. He wrote to Salisbury on 20 April 1902 that his letter had 'caused me some surprise' and that 'I fail to see any arguments brought forward by the Secretary of State for War and the First Lord of the Admiralty why the "Order for Merit" should not be conferred on officers of the Army and Navy who have greatly distinguished themselves on Active Service.'[72] The King stipulated that the only difference between the Order as conferred on military men and that conferred on civilians would be that the former would have two crossed swords on the badge. Salisbury informed Brodrick and Selborne, the First Lord of the Admiralty, of the King's view, and of an offer he had made that the War Secretary could have an audience of him to discuss it: but that, effectively, was that.[73]

The King did not, though, always get his way in matters like this. Salisbury thwarted a plan, put forward by the Royal Colonial Institute but approved of and referred to him by the King, that the Whit Monday bank holiday should be renamed Victoria Day, in honour of the late Queen. McDonnell replied to Knollys on 25 June 1901 that 'Lord Salisbury does not propose to suggest any further action at present: as yet it is not apparent whether there is a widespread desire for such a change.' The King fought back, with Knollys telling McDonnell the next day that 'the King thought it would be almost better to forestall public opinion by appointing the day'.[74] The groundswell of public opinion never, however, materialised, and the idea was dropped.

ON HIS TRIKE

For the most part, though, relations were constructive between the King and the Prime Minister. During early 1902 Salisbury kept the King closely briefed on one of his main legislative measures, the Education Bill – which, given how bored the King tended to become with matters of purely domestic interest, might just be evidence of the Prime Minister's sense of humour. The same day, having heard that Salisbury had taken up tricycling in London for his health, urged him to use the Buckingham Palace gardens for that recreation 'whenever and as much as you like'.[75] The King was always showing considera-tion to his aged Prime Minister; on inviting him to Sandringham the following November, and knowing he would be wearing his Privy Councillor's uniform, the King had Knollys pass on the message that he would expect Lord Salisbury to wear a greatcoat over his uniform as a precaution against the cold.[76]

Often, Salisbury was the conduit of the King's displeasure with the activities of certain ministers. On 7 January 1902 the King was upset that Lord Londonderry, one of the King's circle of friends and the Postmaster-General, should have written to *The Times* in reply to anonymous attacks on his department. The King thought that Londonderry's becoming involved in this way, in response to such low behaviour, was 'very objectionable' and wanted Salisbury to rebuke the minister.[77] Salisbury immediately concurred. 'He will speak to London-derry and to the Cabinet generally.'[78] At other times, the King was keen to press upon his Prime Minister ideas for legislative reform, albeit occasionally of a personally beneficial nature. On 27 February 1902 Knollys wrote on his behalf: 'The King thinks the proposed alteration in the law as regards quarantine for dogs is a most unnecessary one – it is admitted he believes that three months have answered the purpose; why then increase it to six? he confesses he should have liked a matter of this sort to be brought before him. Can anything be done in the matter?'[79] Nothing could be done, and the law pertains to this day.

The King had not been to Ireland since the 1880s, and was keen to visit the most troubled part of his realm as soon as possible. Much of the winter of 1901–2 was spent negotiating details – with, for example, the King insisting to Salisbury in January 1902 that he should go straight to Dublin on arrival in the country. Lord Cadogan, who had long wished to lay down his responsibilities as Lord Lieutenant, came to regard his part in the preparation of the visit as his swansong. The King, who as Prince of Wales had, of course, tiresome experience of attempts to design him a role in Ireland, now modified the old proposal in an interview with McDonnell. On 24 January 1902 McDonnell wrote to Knollys that 'the King spoke to me last Tuesday night about the Lord Lieutenancy of Ireland, and from what HM said I gathered that he had some idea that the Prince of Wales might undertake it when Lord Cadogan retires. Perhaps I was mistaken ... I mentioned this matter confidentially to Lord Salisbury and he was most agreeably surprised to hear that HM contemplated the possibility of HRH accepting the Lord Lieutenancy.'[80] Salisbury was, though, worried about the financial strains, as Cadogan was spending £15,000–20,000 a year above his official income doing the job. McDonnell's view was 'that HRH is a rich man however, and might afford this as he has no country place to maintain.'[81]

Salisbury, though, thought the financial strain on the Prince would be unreasonable; but later in the year, once Cadogan had retired, the question of a non-political lord lieutenancy was raised again in the Cabinet. Balfour, who by that stage had succeeded Salisbury, consulted William Lecky, the eminent Irish historian and Unionist politician, who strongly opposed the idea: he said Lords Lieutenant were invariably unpopular and the post was not able to be made commensurate with the dignity of royalty. So the idea was dropped. Cadogan proved difficult to replace; the King's chosen candidate, Lord Pembroke, declined the post 'on grounds of Lady Pembroke's health and his own financial position'.[82] Balfour fully consulted the King on alternatives before an appointment was made.

By this stage the King's visit to Ireland, which had been the subject of all that enthusiastic planning, had been postponed on the King's initiative because of reactions to a development in South Africa. When the news came to the Commons in March 1902 of Lord Methuen's defeat and capture at Tweebosch, the Irish Nationalist Members cheered it. The King was appalled. On 11 March 1902 he had Knollys write to the Prime Minister:

> I am desired by the King to inform you that after the manifestation of feeling expressed by the Nationalist members in the House of Commons yesterday on hearing of Lord Methuen's defeat and of his being wounded and taken prisoner, he thinks it would not be proper

that he should visit Ireland during the continuance of the war. His Majesty hopes that you, as well as the other members of the Cabinet, will agree with the view which he has taken on the subject.[83]

A statement – in which the King's initiative was concealed by the usual constitutional form – was put out on 12 March that 'the King, by the advice of His Majesty's ministers, has expressed his regret to the Lord Lieutenant that the visit of Their Majesties to Ireland cannot take place this year.'[84] It did happen in 1903: and the warmth of the welcome the King and Queen received raised vain hopes that the long feud between the two countries might be coming to an end. The King was so impressed by what he believed had been achieved that he went back, with the Queen and his daughter Princess Victoria, in 1904, and met with equal success. He was to remain popular in Ireland until his death, a rare symbol of English consideration for that unruly neighbour.

ADVISING THE ADVISERS

There were two main problems the King's ministers had in dealing with him in matters of foreign affairs. First, because of his ties of blood with many of the crowned heads of Europe, and because of the years he had spent cultivating diplomats, he was not so reliant on his ministers for information about what was happening in the world as they might have liked. Second, his long interest in foreign affairs had equipped him with his own opinions about what policies his government would be best advised to follow, and he was by no means always ready to accept those offered to him, on a constitutional basis, by his ministers. 'Not seldom,' says Sir Sidney Lee, 'he changed places with his constitutional advisers and offered advice instead of receiving it.'[85] And, although he could not make them take his advice, he was often in the position of having it offered back to him; and ministers could take the credit for policies that he, in his roving diplomatic role, had instigated, shaped and executed. Balfour, especially, was to remain touchy for the rest of his career about the suggestion, largely accurate, that without the King there would have been no *entente cordiale* with France.

The King paid special attention to the activities of, and the conduct of policy by, his Foreign and War Secretaries. He could be great in his praise and uncompromising in his criticism of failure. His principal impact on the foreign policy of his government was his success in causing the abandonment of the Salisburian ideal of 'splendid isolation', and its replacement by a system of alliances with foreign powers, notably the *entente cordiale* with France in 1904 and the conclusion of the triple entente between Britain, France and Russia in 1908. When the King came to the throne France and Russia were already allied, and Germany, Austria and Italy formed their own, separate grouping. King Edward's main political consequence was the role he played in inserting Britain in that structure of alliances, and the effect that had on Britain's place in the world at the beginning of August 1914.

Although the two sets of alliances in theory had antipathies that ought to have prevented them from coalescing – the historic enmity between France and Germany over Alsace-Lorraine, for example, and Russia's and Austria's conflicting ambitions in the Balkans – there was a residual fear that Britain, in 'splendid isolation', could act as the catalyst that united the alliances in hostility to it. Suddenly, the world's greatest power could find itself friendless or, worse, the object of organised multinational hostility. It was a far-fetched fear, but one affecting more and more politicians – notably, from inside Salisbury's own Cabinet, Chamberlain – in the early years of the century, not least because of the almost universal opprobrium Britain attracted on the continent over the Boer War. In so far as any encouragement was coming from the continent it was coming from Germany, which at times hoped to include Britain in a new quadruple alliance. For a while Britain entertained this prospect, thanks to a superficially more cordial relationship between the Kaiser and the King, but the tensions between the two men, almost all caused by the Kaiser's personality defects of vanity and inconsistency, overshadowed any such plan.

The King visited his sister the Empress Frederick, the Kaiser's mother, a month after his accession, and this seemed to set a tone of civility and constructiveness between the two nations. However, in April 1901 the King was furious that his nephew had described some British ministers as 'unmitigated noodles'. The Kaiser had used the phrase several times in a conversation with Britain's ambassador to Berlin, Sir Frank Lascelles, about Britain's refusal to co-operate with

Germany over German involvement in China. Lascelles, wanting to avoid trouble, had not mentioned this phrase in a dispatch, but the Kaiser had saved him the trouble by using it in a letter to his uncle anyway. The King sent for the secretary of the German embassy in London, Baron Eckardstein, to ask for an explanation. Eckardstein, who knew the King well and was on good terms with him, volunteered the view that 'wouldn't it be best if Your Majesty treated the whole thing as a joke?'[86] The King took the advice in good part, but told Eckardstein that he had already had quite enough of his nephew's jokes, and they were no longer that funny; and he wondered what the Kaiser would say if the King started making such remarks about German ministers.

Then, according to Eckardstein's report of the conversation, the King spoke of his frustration that his nephew was always causing such ill-feeling, because 'Great Britain and Germany are natural allies. Together they could police the world and secure a lasting peace.... there is room in the world for both Great Britain and Germany. Only we can't keep pace with these perpetual vagaries of the Kaiser.' He went on to say how he had been working on Salisbury to try to dissipate the distrust his Prime Minister felt for the Kaiser and Count von Bülow, his Chancellor, but this sort of behaviour by the Kaiser made such efforts pointless. 'Throughout the conversation,' Eckardstein reports, 'the King was more irritated than I had ever seen him before.'

As a naturally forgiving man, the King soon forgot the slight, and in June 1901 gave an audience to Count Hatzfeldt, since 1885 the German ambassador in London and a man trusted by the King, in which he urged him to co-operate with Lansdowne in securing a better relationship with the Germans. Hatzfeldt said he would work to that end with Lansdowne, but regretted that Salisbury was determined not to make matters easier between the two countries: an analysis with which the King agreed, but which he said was partly explained by Salisbury's age (he was eleven years older than the King). The audience further revealed the growing anxiety the King felt about his country's isolation. Some senior French officers had just been well received on a visit to Berlin, and Hatzfeldt detected concern that France and Germany might be about to combine to the exclusion of England.

Germany's neo-colonial excursion in China was to be the cause of further unrest. The Germans wanted to double customs dues in China to raise money, but the British – the longest-established European trading power in the region – refused to accept the proposal. The Kaiser's military commander in Peking, Count Waldersee, was already profoundly anti-British, and returned to Berlin to denounce Britain to the Kaiser. The Kaiser was only too willing to accept this view, and started to vilify the British government again. He began to make overtures to Russia, about becoming partners in a railway to Baghdad with Germany and France. Although Salisbury was prepared to countenance an alliance with Germany that did not formally wed Britain to any of Germany's allies, this was contrary to Germany's view, and it was finally agreed that the only hope of progress would be through what is now called a summit meeting, between the King and the Kaiser. This was arranged for August 1901. In fact, the two men had a meeting before the summit, occasioned by the death of the Empress Frederick from cancer of the spine on 5 August. It did not improve the King's view of his nephew when, at the funeral, he insisted that the 15,000 German troops lining the route should march past both sovereigns.

The official meeting took place on 23 August, after weeks of meticulous diplomatic preparations. Lansdowne had drawn up a detailed memorandum for the King on 10 August, briefing him on matters of German foreign policy. This memorandum, which outlined the stance Britain should take on German ambitions in China, Morocco, South Africa and Kuwait, formed the basis of a rare diplomatic *faux pas* by the King. Lansdowne had intended it for the King's eyes only, and it had been worded accordingly. But, to the Foreign Secretary's mortification, the King read it and handed it to the Kaiser, with whom he was staying at the time for the Empress Frederick's funeral. The Kaiser, understandably, circulated it to his ministers, and ordered the preparation of a counter-memorandum. He went to lengths to ensure that the British government did not hear of the contents of the counter-memorandum until it had been sent to the King. Two copies of it were dispatched to the German embassy in London, one for the embassy archives, the other to be sent to the Foreign Office after the King and the Kaiser had met. The King seemed willing to go along with this business of keeping the matter personal between himself and the Kaiser, without informing his ministers. As soon as he received the memorandum he sent it to

Lascelles, asking him to call to see him the following morning: 'and we can then discuss the advisability of it being sent to the Foreign Office'.[87] The memorandum itself looked a hopeful basis for negotiation, with Germany's intentions to go its own way on Morocco being the only obvious difficulty.

The Kaiser had a trump to play when the meeting took place on 23 August: he knew, as the King and Lascelles did not, that the Tsar was shortly going to visit France, to witness the manoeuvres of the French fleet, stopping *en route* at Danzig, where he would see the Kaiser. The Kaiser, in his report of the meeting, claims the King was agitated by this tripartite activity, and 'seemed seriously displeased' that the Tsar was doing this, and not visiting him in England, as his nearest relation.[88] The Kaiser further upset the King by saying all he knew of the Tsar's wishes was that he 'had expressed an urgent desire to see Count Bülow'. At this, the King supposedly said that the 'whole affair looked like a demonstration against England'. If the Kaiser's report is accurate – and he and the truth were not always the best of friends – the level of touchiness it reveals on the part of the King at this suspicion of Britain's deepening isolation is remarkable, and would explain much of what happened over the next few years.

The Kaiser then went on to accuse Britain of double-dealing with Japan, with which the British were negotiating an alliance to help protect British interests in China; and to accuse Salisbury of being of that old school of politician whose main foreign policy was to set foreign powers against each other. Using language that would resonate as much at the end of the twentieth century as at its opening, the Kaiser said that Britain would have to change. 'England', he said, 'cannot fail to observe that there is growing up on the continent a strong movement towards a continental economic union against those who are operating against the economic conditions of the continent. England will do well to take this into consideration'.[89] For good measure, the Kaiser also told the King that Russia and America 'are probably on more intimate terms than anyone in London can dream of'. It is not surprising, given that it appeared mainly to have been used as a means for the Kaiser to prey on the insecurities of his uncle, that the meeting achieved nothing for Britain. As if to mark this, the German press devoted itself for much of the autumn of 1901 to denouncing Britain for the way in which Kitchener was fighting the Boers. Tension was further heightened when Chamberlain responded by pointing out that no barbarity carried out in South Africa could match those of the Franco-Prussian War.

A tit-for-tat policy distinguished Anglo-German relations over the next few months, with the relationship between the two royal families at the heart of it. The King hoped to soothe matters by sending the Prince of Wales (as the Duke of York became on 9 November 1901, when his father reached sixty) to Berlin on the Kaiser's birthday in January 1902; the Kaiser concurred, though he told his uncle that he had had quite a job dampening down anti-British feeling in Germany since Chamberlain's speech. Indeed, he was not very successful, for as soon as the Reichstag reassembled after Christmas Bülow fiercely attacked Chamberlain and the British army in a speech, and Chamberlain rebutted this further a few days later, saying he intended to withdraw nothing. The King, also offended by the assault on Chamberlain, asked Lansdowne whether the Prince's visit should be curtailed, or indeed whether he should go at all.[90] Lascelles, ever keen to keep the peace with the Kaiser, wrote from Brunswick urging caution.[91] 'It is true', Lascelles wrote, 'that he [the Kaiser] has more than once expressed his disapproval of the actions of the Government, but he has never faltered in his expressions of friendship for the King and Royal Family.'

Nonetheless, and despite further urging from Lascelles that he could not believe the Kaiser would humiliate the Prince, the King wrote to his nephew on 15 January to say that 'it would be better for him not to go where he is liable to be insulted'; and so, given the strength of feeling in Germany whipped up by senior statesmen against Britain, it might be better if the visit were called off.[92] 'It is very painful for me to have to write this,' the King continued, 'but I feel I have no alternative.' Lascelles (who had also been rebuked by the King for not acting more swiftly to send him details of the Reichstag speech) was deeply depressed by the King's action, telegraphing to Knollys that it would be, 'to say the least, a great disappointment to the Emperor'.[93] He then wrote to Knollys saying that what would most upset the Kaiser was the King's allusion to the Prince being vulnerable to public insult. 'The police administration of Berlin', Lascelles noted, with admirable understatement, 'is such as to render such a thing almost impossible.'[94]

Lascelles – who also defended himself against charges of negligence in his handling of the affair, realising that without the King's confidence he might as well pack up and go – warned that while a 'rupture' might not take place because of the King's actions, 'I am afraid that we shall have to look forward to a period of strained relations which will not be of advantage to either country.' No word was received and the date of the visit came ever closer; but the King refused to budge until he had a reply to his letter, a delay which heightened the tension.[95] However, Lascelles met the Kaiser at a memorial service for Queen Victoria on 22 January, the first anniversary of her death, and the Kaiser claimed not to have received the letter – a claim which Lansdowne, on having it reported to him, described as 'extraordinary'.[96] Lascelles told the Kaiser what had been in the letter, and the Kaiser said that with all the preparations now so advanced such a cancellation 'would be a most serious matter'.[97] The Kaiser was instigating a search for the letter, and would reply to it. Lascelles makes no comment on whether the loss had been deliberate or accidental; back in London, he had come to his own conclusions, since he told the King he would 'not attempt to probe the mysteries of this occurrence'.[98] The King had made up his own mind: Knollys told Lansdowne that the King 'is bound to say that he does not believe one word of the story that his letter to the Emperor has been lost, and he looks upon it as an incredible one, especially as Lascelles in his telegram to me of the 17th instant, sent through the FO, says "immediately on arrival of messenger last night, I sent the King's letter to the Palace and obtained a receipt" '.[99] Knollys told Lansdowne that a telegram from the Kaiser, giving the assurances the King wanted about the good treatment of the Prince, would be enough to ensure the trip went ahead – and warned that 'of course the Emperor's letter must not be in any way aggressive or offensive in its tone'.

Meanwhile, Salisbury had sent the King a note on 22 January – before the missing-letter story had reached England – saying that a message from the Kaiser himself ought to be necessary if the visit were to proceed; if the Prince went without such a message being delivered, the Prime Minister continued, 'every newspaper in Germany will treat it as an act of English submission, and the English newspapers will reply in a similar tone'.[100] Salisbury also conceded that, if the Prince did not go, the press would represent it as a severe breach between the King and the Kaiser. Salisbury felt he had found a solution, in default of an 'overture' from the Kaiser. 'Lord Salisbury would submit', he continued, 'that it is better to avoid the issue if possible. He thinks it would be better – if the Emperor does not acknowledge Your Majesty's letters – to abstain from further correspondence: best to telegraph on Friday that HRH has a bad cold, and fears that he will be unable to accept the Emperor's hospitality on Tuesday. Your Majesty does not need to be told that this is an ordinary diplomatic device.' Salisbury did admit that this course was 'not wholly satisfactory', but was preferable to inflaming sensibilities. The King was concerned at the way in which some British newspapers stoked up anti-German sentiment – indeed, he would the following year make representations, unsuccessfully and through an intermediary, to the editor of *The Times* about it – but nonetheless he felt the overtures that had come were sufficient. With the end of the Boer War four months later – which prompted a congratulatory telegram from the Kaiser to the King – relations seemed to be less fraught, though there was still no prospect of a formal alliance.

Lascelles's informal interview with the Kaiser brought an immediate message via Count Metternich, who had just succeeded Hatzfeldt as German ambassador to London. Lascelles's pessimism about the Kaiser's reaction to his uncle's threat proved misplaced. Metternich had said that 'a letter is on its way from the German Emperor to the King written, he understands, in the most cordial terms', and that the Prince of Wales would be received by the Kaiser 'in a manner befitting a near relation of his'.[101] The King was appeased by this, and the visit went ahead. The Kaiser had little excuse for his displays of petulance. At the King's instigation, he was the first outsider to hear, at the end of January 1902, that a treaty had been concluded between Britain and Japan. The King, who knew his nephew would have no objection to the treaty, told Lansdowne that the Kaiser should be officially informed with 'no loss of time', and the Foreign Secretary took his Sovereign's advice.[102]

The next advance in the relationship that the King tried was to invite the Kaiser to stay with him at Sandringham in November 1902, for a shooting party around the time of the King's birthday. Every effort was made by the King to use the occasion as a time of healing political and personal fractures: one of the Kaiser's fellow guests was Chamberlain, with whom the Kaiser later admitted he had found it 'very difficult' to get on.[103] The British royal party felt the same about the Kaiser; when he left to continue on a progress to Scotland, all expressed voluble relief, from the King downwards.

THE UNDECIDED PRIME MINISTER

Salisbury was seventy-two by the time of the date set for the Coronation, and had decided to stand down as Prime Minister as soon as the South African war was ended. When it finished within a month of the Coronation, the Prime Minister chose to stay until the ceremony was over; but then it was postponed until 9 August, after the King was stricken with appendicitis. Salisbury therefore moved to resign without much further delay, and on 10 July 1902, as soon as the King was well enough to see him, he told him of his intentions. His sudden departure was a great shock to the public, and rumours abounded. One was that he had had a violent disagreement with the King over foreign policy, and on the question of the desirability of 'splendid isolation'; but, as we know, the Cabinet was already moving away from that policy. Then there was the rumour about the Coronation honours list, and about Salisbury's utter refusal to contemplate the Lipton and Cassel peerages; but that argument had been settled long before 10 July, and in Salisbury's favour.

Salisbury was succeeded by his nephew, Arthur James Balfour, a somewhat etiolated, languid, almost hermaphroditic Tory, who before commencing a long career on the Conservative front bench in the 1880s had been a philosopher. His most celebrated work, and one that set the tone for his premiership, was *In Defence of Philosophic Doubt*. A man of eclectic interests, he had in 1892 (when First Lord of the Treasury) accepted the presidency of the Society of Psychical Research. Lest he be thought a soft touch, his spell as Irish Secretary in his uncle's administration had earned him the nickname of 'Bloody Balfour'. He was not well known to the King – as one of the 'Souls', that collection of mainly Tory aesthetes and thinkers from the grandest families, Balfour moved in high intellectual circles a million miles from baccarat, racing and 'actresses' – and before long it was apparent that the two of them did not get on. As Sir Sidney Lee tactfully writes, 'The King had the typical English mind; Mr Balfour, a versatile Scotsman, had a very extraordinary mind, and while the extraordinary mind can often appraise the qualities of the ordinary mind, the converse does not follow.'[104] Balfour was bored by inferior intellects, which when married to what he considered preposterous flummeries and protocol – as in the case of royalty – closed down his interest completely. He had observed with an air of tedium to his confidante, Lady Elcho, at the time of the King's accession that 'the King will take up a good deal more of his ministers' time than did the Queen – and as the Prime Minister is always in the country this has meant, and may mean, that I shall have to go more to Marlborough House than heretofore'.[105] He was plainly not looking forward to it.

The two men had almost nothing in common, and Balfour's coming was a blow to a monarch used to laying down the law with his ministers. 'The King was privately conscious that Mr Balfour was easily his master in argument, and he avoided encounters in which he knew that he could not achieve victory,' explains Sir Sidney, unwittingly giving the reasons for much of the erosion of the prerogative that occurred under the new Prime Minister.[106] The root of the prerogatives was deference to the institution of monarchy. If Balfour chose to apply the logic of democratic practice to any of these, democratic practice would win: and he often did. The King, who must soon have realised he had cause to feel under threat, found Balfour condescending, and this made him feel uncomfortable and sensitive.[107] Not least will he soon have worked out that Balfour was one of those people, familiar at the top of any organisation, who in order to carry off one course of action successfully professes quite the opposite.

Balfour was fortunate, and the King unfortunate, that the Monarch was still convalescent at the time the new administration was formed. Balfour filled the vacancies caused by his uncle's departure, and by the retirement of three other ministers (including the King's friend Cadogan) without any help from the Sovereign, who merely agreed to the appointments. Balfour observed the traditional courtesies, writing to the King on 27 July that 'he fears that he cannot escape the painful task of explaining to some of [the government's] present members that the time has come when they ought to allow their duties to be carried on by others.'[108] He promised to communicate more details in a few days. However, the King had not the energy or the inclination to interfere when Balfour told him that the two 'new men' in the Cabinet would be George Wyndham, an immensely grand country gentleman (who later refused one of the better orders of chivalry because, it was said, he considered his social position already to be so elevated that nothing could possibly improve it), and Austen Chamberlain, son of Joe.[109] An important precedent had been set, and this accidental lack of interest in the appointments was an early sign of the transitional constitutional nature of the monarchy. Whenever Balfour was given an inch, he had the habit of taking the proverbial mile.

SHAH AND GARTER

The King was an assiduous reader of Foreign Office telegrams, and took the minutest interest in all areas of his country's external affairs. In 1902 his still-strong suspicion of Russia led him to send a warning to the Shah of Persia about what he believed were the designs the Russians had on that country. He was delighted when Lansdowne told him early in 1902 that there was to be an initiative to strengthen British ties with Persia, as he felt that the relationship had gone by default, and had allowed the Russians more influence than they should normally have had in the Middle East. The King was less pleased, though, when he learned that in a summer already crowded with events because of the Coronation, the Shah had chosen to explore the possibilities of a closer relationship with Britain – or, rather, to see what he could extract from it – by paying a visit to London beginning nine days after the postponed Coronation.

However, the whole relationship was almost torpedoed by a diplomatic crisis that looks farcical at this remove but which, at the time, threatened to bring down the British government. The British minister at Teheran, Sir Arthur Hardinge, had told the Shah that were he to visit England he would, like his father before him, undoubtedly be made a Knight of the Garter. This was innovative diplomacy: the King plainly should have been asked to approve the notion before the offer was made, for it was not within Hardinge's authority to make such an offer. This normally gifted diplomat, under pressure from an unscrupulous regime, had made a big mistake. The Prime Minister could recommend to the King that certain Garters be awarded, but the final decision was the Monarch's. Similarly, when the King wanted to take an initiative of awarding a Garter to an overseas sovereign, he would tell Salisbury purely as a matter of courtesy. On 20 March 1901, for example, Knollys wrote to McDonnell that he hoped Salisbury would approve of his desire to send the Duke of Connaught to Madrid to confer the Garter on the young King of Spain, thereby helping to cement relations between the two countries.

In the case of the Shah the King was to have an objection more fundamental even than the already profound one that he had not been asked. He felt the award should not be made to a non-Christian, since he believed the statutes of the Order made it explicitly a Christian one – though they were, in fact, vague on the question. The King ignored the fact that the late Queen had made three awards to Islamic potentates, twice to Sultans of Turkey and to the Shah's own father. Although technically (according to the weight of custom and practice in applying the statutes) he was right to deprecate the idea of an award to a non-Christian, it seems his main irritation was that he had not been consulted. As it fell to Lansdowne to sort the matter out, and as the King did not much like Lansdowne, the matter fast turned into one that (by the Prime Minister's own private admission) threatened the future of the administration. The Shah, having been made the offer, would not budge, and was not to be bought off by the lesser offer of the Order of the Bath; and the matter became urgent, as the date of the visit neared. Indeed, it seems that the only reason the Shah had agreed to come to England was in order to get his Garter. The King, though, was adamant: he could not have it, and that was that.

Lansdowne, desperate to try to find a solution without, if possible, acquainting the King with what exactly had happened between the Shah and Hardinge in Teheran, had on 18 June 1902 sent the King a long memorandum about the possible award of the Garter not just to the Shah, but to the Sultan of Turkey as well, and had warned that the Emperor of Japan might be asking for it soon too.[110] In it, he said he thought that maintaining the non-Christian rule would be 'almost impossible', given the precedents set by the late Queen, and added that an exception 'might be allowed in favour of Mahommedan Sovereigns of Imperial rank paying a personal visit to Your Majesty by Your invitation, and that such Sovereigns should be specially dispensed from the religious part of the investiture'. Lansdowne had doubts about these exceptions, not least since they would still rule out the Emperor of Japan, but suggested that a minor change to the statutes of the Order of the Garter might solve the problem. 'Should the change be carried out,' Lansdowne continued, 'Your Majesty might agree to confer the Garter on the Shah in connection with His Majesty's approaching visit.' The Sultan, he said, could wait, 'but he would have to get it sooner or later', and it would be 'an incentive to him to behave well towards this country'.

To his memorandum he attached letters from Hardinge and from Sir Nicholas O'Conor, the ambassador to Constantinople, about the expectations of the Sultan and the Shah. In his letter Hardinge made no mention of any promise having been made. All he did admit to, in an accompanying memorandum, was that 'the Grand Vizier stated to me at Teheran that "he presumed the Shah, on visiting the King, would receive the Garter as his father had done." I avoided giving a direct answer to this remark, but it is certain that His Majesty fully expects the honour, and that "getting his father's Garter" (as he puts it) has been one of his chief incentives in visiting England.'

Hardinge then referred to the rule made by Queen Victoria, on the recommendation of Rosebery, that no non-Christian could have the Garter: a disregard of her own practice, but a means of preventing her from having to give it to the Sultan. Hardinge dismissed this as 'a matter of policy and convenience rather than of a legal or binding obligation', and suggested that the start of a new reign was an ideal time to change the rules. He advanced arguments for why, in the Shah's case, this would be a good idea, not least the cosying-up to Persia being undertaken by the Russians. Hardinge warned that the award of the GCVO, as had just been made to the King of Siam, would be regarded as offensive and might not even be accepted, and would cause 'a feeling of dissatisfaction which may affect, to our detriment, the relations between the Palace at Tehran and His Majesty's Legation'. The Persians were, he warned, 'the vainest of Orientals', so the Garter would be a great help in appeasing them.

The King, irritated at being pressured like this when he had already made what he felt was a final decision in the matter, took further ministerial advice from Devonshire. His old friend told him he hesitated to disagree with Lansdowne, but that he did 'not think this an opportune moment' to alter the statutes of the Order.[111] The King's illness, and the postponed Coronation, interrupted the debate. It resumed late in July, as Lansdowne, by now greatly agitated and still, nobly, trying to protect the unfortunate Hardinge, communicated with Knollys about the Shah's now impending visit. The King had said the Shah could not have the Garter, and as far as he was concerned that was the end of the matter. But Lansdowne told Knollys on 22 July that 'as to the Garter, I shall of course not return to the question until I have the King's permission', and that he would buy time with the Persians by telling them that the King's illness made consideration of any 'controversial' decisions impossible.[112] However, he added that 'I still hope that particularly if the Shah behaves well to us in regard to various political questions ... he may be rewarded by the grant of the Garter one of these days.' The last paragraph of the letter is perhaps the most revealing: 'Hardinge is in the depths of despair and implores me not to send him back to Persia.'

Lansdowne was in scarcely less a state of despair, since he had still not worked out how he was going to explain to the Shah when he arrived the following month that the purpose of his visit would not be achieved. He wrote to Knollys on 25 July to say that if the King's wishes as he understood them – that the Shah should be told at once that he could not have the Garter, but could have the GCVO or the GCB instead – were implemented, 'the Shah would probably abandon his visit'.[113] Therefore, no such intimation was given, and the visit went ahead.

The crunch came at a luncheon on the royal yacht at Portsmouth on 20 August. This was the extent of the contact between the King and his visitor; the King was on his yacht convalescing after his appendectomy and the effort of the Coronation that had swiftly followed upon it, and was not in the best of spirits. Lansdowne had prepared a memorandum that informed the Persians that as the statutes of the Order might shortly be revised, no other order would be conferred on the Shah while he was in England, as His Imperial Majesty 'would naturally be one of the earliest recipients of the new order'.[114] He claimed he put the memorandum in front of the King in the Persians' presence, and that the King, his mind on other things, had nodded his assent. Lansdowne later said that he certainly was under the impression 'that Your Majesty had been pleased to approve it, and to authorise him to make known that it was Your Majesty's intention to revise the Statutes and to admit HIM to the Order of the Garter.'[115] This was news to the King, who had no recollection of approving the memorandum whatsoever. For Lansdowne, in his advanced distress, the wish appears to have been father to the thought.

When the King was told all this four days later he went into orbit. Not only had he made no such agreement to change the statutes; even if he had, there would be no reason why Lansdowne should assume the Shah to be a beneficiary. Matters had been made more incendiary when, in lieu of a decoration, the King offered to present the Shah with a beautiful miniature of himself that he would have specially painted. However, the Shah refused to accept the offer, despite the urgings of some in his suite, because his father had been given a picture of Queen Victoria only after she had awarded him the Garter. Hardinge suggested to Lansdowne that the Persians would be appeased if a public announcement could be made that the statutes were being revised to enable the Shah to receive 'a de-Christianized Garter'; many of the Shah's entourage were disconsolate that they had been unable to accept British honours because their ruler had been given none, and were making life hot for Hardinge.

Lansdowne admitted, without apportioning blame, that 'the situation was one which lent itself to misunderstandings and misrepresentations and both have been prevalent'. More to the point, he said that political considerations must now come first. At the best, though, Lansdowne was guilty of a misunderstanding in the matter of the King having assented to the memorandum: the King was scrupulous in reading Foreign Office material, and would never have agreed to anything unless he had had a chance to read it thoroughly first, a chance he certainly did not have over a tense and protocol-laden lunch table. The Shah, now back in London, was giving Lansdowne a hard time; the Foreign Secretary had reported on 23 August, 'Shah still very unhappy about Garter and his dull mind cannot understand why, if his father was eligible, he is not'.[116]

Determined in his desperation not to take no for an answer, Lansdowne then went so far as to have the Lord Chamberlain draw up a design – the crude draft of which is in the Royal Archives – of a non-Christian Garter insignia. He even told the King that Garrard, the Crown jeweller, could make up such an insignia within three days of receiving the order.[117] It was when the King received this material on 24 August that his wrath ignited: 'there was an explosion', Fritz Ponsonby recalled, having the misfortune to be present to witness it. 'He was so angry that he flung the design across his cabin and it went through the porthole.'[118] Luckily, it landed on another craft whence it was retrieved by a stoker. A letter containing 'some very violent remarks' was then dictated to Ponsonby. The assistant private secretary, who had learned from experience the wisdom of toning down the King's invective in letters that a member of the secretariat, rather than the King himself, would sign, then sent Lansdowne 'a bowdlerised version'.[119] 'The King hoped ... the subject of the Shah receiving the Garter was at an end ... when Lord Lansdowne drew up the hasty memorandum at Portsmouth during the Shah's visit last week, the King assented to give it his fullest consideration but nothing more, and after giving the matter his fullest consideration, he is loath to make any change,' he said. 'It is an unheard-of proceeding,' he said, 'one Sovereign being dictated to by another as to what Order he should confer on him.'[120] He added that 'the Shah forced himself upon the King when he knew his visit this year was most inconvenient on account of the Coronation and since by the King's serious illness. If the Shah leaves this country in the sulks like a spoilt child because he cannot get what he wants, it cannot be helped.'

The King was determined not to give in to pressure from the Shah, fearing particularly that it might lead to his having to give the Garter to the Sultan of Turkey, who had just conferred a high honour on the King.[121] Rather menacingly, he had also told Lansdowne, 'I cannot have my hand forced.' Lansdowne should have known better. One of the first letters he had sent to the King after the accession had been to advise against the award of the Garter to the Sultan, as it was 'laid down by Her late Majesty that the Garter could not be worn except by Rulers of the Christian faith'.[122] The King had by this stage had enough of Hardinge, as he made clear in his 24 August letter to Lansdowne: 'We should not have lost the hold which Russia now possesses if the Government of the day had kept their eyes open and had had more competent representatives at Teheran to maintain its interests and those of our country.' Lansdowne was also being criticised by none less than his own permanent secretary, Sir Francis Bertie, who wrote to Knollys on 24 August of how pleased he was the King had not given the Shah the Garter, as 'its bestowal should not be in consequence of promises from the would-be recipient, but for something tangible'.[123]

Lansdowne then compounded his offence. He wrote to ask the King to permit a statement to be made to the newspapers about the Shah's having been given no honours because of the revision of the Garter statutes, in order to prevent 'mischief' being made.[124] He also wrote a hurried defence to Balfour against the King's attack on him, which he described as 'a singular production'. He added: 'He is wrong.'[125] He claimed the memorandum he had written for the King on his yacht was for immediate use 'and for the purpose of smoothing the ruffled temper of the Shah. This the King quite understood at the time.' The King, as we have seen, understood nothing of the sort. Lansdowne also accused the Monarch of 'not quite understanding the immense importance which Easterns attach to such matters'. At this point the King opened a new front on Lansdowne, having Ponsonby write to him on 26 August to say he was 'much vexed at the proposal to alter the statutes of the Garter having been communicated to the Shah.... the King promised to consider the matter but it never occurred to His Majesty that you seriously contemplated making such an important change in the oldest order in the world simply that it might be conferred on the Shah before he left. The King hopes you will understand how distasteful it is for him to be dictated to by the

Shah.'[126] The instruction at the end of the letter was to 'allow the matter to drop'.

Lansdowne was too far gone to do anything of the sort. He still protested his innocence, replying to Ponsonby (in what the King's assistant private secretary termed a 'stuffy' letter)[127] that he was 'absolutely convinced' the King had authorised him to act upon the memorandum.[128] 'My whole object in going to the King was that I might be able to do something to put the Persians into better humour.' If the memorandum was not to be acted upon immediately, Lansdowne asked, 'what on earth was the object of my writing it in such a hurry, and obtaining the King's approval in the midst of the Shah's reception?' He said it had never been his intention to have the statutes amended so quickly that the Shah could have the honour before going home, but 'when you tell an Eastern that you will do something for him one of these days, he thinks you are putting him off with a civil refusal'. Having said all this, Lansdowne at last agreed that it might be best, for the moment, to 'let the matter drop'. Again, this was not to happen.

The Foreign Secretary now had to draw Balfour into the argument. By now on holiday at his Irish estate at Deneen in County Kerry, Lansdowne wrote to the Prime Minister on 28 August that the King's order to close the matter 'is to say the least of it awkward and places me in a very difficult position which I shall bye and bye have to ask you to consider.... If the King remains obdurate there is so far as I can see only one way out for me, and that will be "out" in the most literal sense of the word.'[129] The next day he wrote to the King of 'the deep concern which it gives him to find that his action has incurred your displeasure'.[130] Chancing his arm rather, he added that 'he feels sure however that Your Majesty will accept his statement that, at the conclusion of his second interview with Your Majesty on board the Royal Yacht, he remained under the impression that he had been authorised to communicate the substance of the memorandum which Your Majesty had permitted him to draft'. Lansdowne also said that when the Grand Vizier, attendant on the Shah, had asked him 'whether the Shah was likely to receive the Garter soon, he replied that he could name no date as the matter must depend solely upon the King's pleasure'. Knowing this would still not be enough, he wrote again to Balfour and told him, 'I am afraid it will not only be desirable, but indispensable, that you should intervene sooner or later.'[131]

Writing yet again on 4 September – poor old Lansdowne was not having much of a holiday – and enclosing further background information from Hardinge, the Foreign Secretary said that the minister 'dreads showing his face in Teheran after what has happened'.[132] The King wrote to Lansdowne, for once in a kinder tone, and said it was only the thought that Lansdowne had promised the Shah the Garter that had 'put him out'.[133] Nonetheless, for all this show of forgiveness, the King's mind was not about to change. Balfour discussed the matter with Knollys, though not with the King, when he visited Balmoral in mid-September. He reported back to Lansdowne that the King was still intransigent, regarded the matter as political rather than personal, and 'he does not admit, apparently, that he gave any assent to the Memorandum which you showed him, and thinks he has been "rushed"'.[134]

For a while, the matter indeed dropped; but Lansdowne stuck to his point that, unless the Shah got the Garter, he would have to resign. Balfour could not contemplate such an embarrassment, and realised he would have to force the issue. After a short interval he therefore reopened the matter, writing apologetically to Knollys on 20 October for having to come back 'to the wretched question of the Shah and the Garter'.[135] 'Of course,' the Prime Minister continued, 'if it were a mere question of misunderstanding on Lord Lansdowne's part of what the King had directed, or on His Majesty's part of what Lord Lansdowne had suggested, I should not re-open a subject which everyone would gladly see dropped. Unfortunately, this is not the case.' It was, of course, but this letter is a masterpiece of Balfour's fundamentally dishonest rewriting of history as a means of conducting policy. He went on: 'Lord Lansdowne, acting on what he believed to be His Majesty's commands, gave a distinct and explicit pledge to the Shah that though he could not receive the Garter until such additions to the constitution of the Order had been made as would admit non-Christian Sovereigns, such additions were about to be effected, and that, when effected, he should receive the Order, as his father had done before him.' Balfour said he was not concerned with whether or not this was good for British policy in the region: 'the difficulty lies in the fact that the Minister for Foreign Affairs has, on behalf of the Crown, made a definite promise to a Foreign Sovereign, and that it seems almost impossible to evade it without laying this country open to the charge of a breach of faith.'

The guilty emissary, Sir Arthur Hardinge, was about to return to Teheran, and Balfour – rather typically putting the onus for the mistakes of others on the King – told Knollys it would be as well, before he reached his post, that Sir Arthur was informed 'what language he is to use in explanation of a *volte face* which the Persians will find it impossible to understand and which, until it be explained, they will, I fear, regard as a deliberate affront'. Lansdowne was willing to come up with the form of words, but felt he could do so only on the King's authority – 'and he tells me that His Majesty has virtually forbidden him to mention the subject again'. So the problem was put back on the shoulders of Knollys, who will have been unaffected by the Prime Minister's peroration – 'the position is one, as you will see, of great difficulty, and is causing me much anxiety'.

Knollys replied testily the following day, saying that the King 'could only repeat what he wrote to Lord Lansdowne'.[136] The King had said that he 'distinctly refused' to give the Garter to the Shah 'for reasons which are well known' to Lansdowne and Hardinge. He also resented the fact that Lansdowne had tried to 'force his hand' when the two men had met at Portsmouth in August. Moreover, the King was convinced he had never given Lansdowne any reason to suspect that he was in favour of the statutes of the Order being changed – 'HM only told him that he would consider the matter, as it was obviously a question which could not be settled in two minutes.' There was worse to come. 'The King', Knollys continued, 'thinks therefore that he has not been fairly treated by Lord Lansdowne, and that he has grounds for complaint against him in this respect. He does not either consider that Sir A Hardinge has behaved well to him in the matter' – though, when the King had seen Hardinge two days earlier, neither man had mentioned the matter, an admirable act of self-restraint on the part of the Monarch, perhaps because as yet he had no proof to support his suspicions of Hardinge's deviousness.

'To give way now,' Knollys continued, 'would, the King thinks, show great weakness on his part, and in doing so he would moreover be acting dramatically contrary to his convictions, and he believes that the Shah would not alter his attitude towards this country and would only "laugh in his sleeve".' The King had taken it as an affront that the miniature and the other decorations he had offered to the Shah and his suite had been refused, and asked Knollys to say that 'HM desires me to put it to you whether a Sovereign of any country has ever before been treated in such an insulting way, notwithstanding which he is ready to have his portrait painted for the Shah, or to give him anything short of the Garter – as regards the Garter he must stand firm.'

After this blast – and given Knollys's legendary tact, one can only imagine how the King had actually expressed himself – Balfour might have been expected to retire hurt. His first instinct was to send the correspondence to Devonshire – who, although the King had sounded him out on the question earlier, like all rest of the Cabinet had no idea the drama was still going on – to ask for his opinion. He warned Devonshire to maintain utmost secrecy, and said that Lansdowne had not seen Knollys's letter. 'I feel convinced that if you *down* it,' Balfour wrote, 'he will resign at once.'[137] Devonshire spoke to Lansdowne about it, and told Balfour that if the King stayed intransigent 'I do not see how Lansdowne can possibly remain, and I think this is his own view, although he does not want to do anything precipitate.'[138] He added, shrewdly from his long and close observation of the King, that 'the King is evidently irritated, and I daresay would part with Lansdowne without much regret, but can we sacrifice him? My own impression is that if we stand by him the King will give in.'

Balfour took Devonshire's advice, being careful to keep the matter as secret as possible in the interests of the King's having as little face as possible to lose by giving in. He opened his next assault on the King on the matter on 3 November. With his famed ability to see no problems where many arose, Balfour suggested there was 'no case of conflict between the views of the Sovereign and the views of his ministers': a philosophical trick of the sort that was to lead to his administration ending in chaos and disaster three years later, after Balfour had used his agile mind to decide that there was no real difference between free traders and protectionists.[139] He said that Lansdowne's promise of the Garter to the Shah was not the root of the problem. Blithely, he added that 'still less are we concerned with the question whether Lord Lansdowne had or had not Your Majesty's authority to make the promise to the Shah which in fact he did make': a question with which the King was very much concerned. 'No one of course doubts', the Prime Minister continued, 'that Lord Lansdowne acted in perfect good faith': something the King, according to Knollys's recent letter, very much appeared to doubt.

Yet there was no end to Balfour's sophistry. He said, not for the first time, that he would not have dreamed of raising the subject again if it been a straightforward question of Lansdowne's misunderstanding the King's wishes (which the King, remember, thought was the best possible interpretation that could be put on his Foreign Secretary's actions). No: Balfour was raising the matter again 'because Mr Balfour is convinced that Your Majesty is solely concerned with the not unfamiliar problem of having to deal with a public servant who by mistake has exceeded his instruction. The question in such cases inevitably arises: is he to be "thrown over" or is he not?' Never mind, Balfour went on, that Lansdowne had made this explicit promise in the King's name: what would be his position if he now had to go back on his word? 'Could his promises carry with them any weight in the future?' asked Balfour, now attaining a high level of moral blackmail. 'Could he usefully endeavour to carry on the work of a difficult department? And if he resigned' – at last Balfour reached his point – 'could the matter stop there, in these days of Governmental solidarity?'

Thus Balfour delivered his ridiculous threat that the whole government might fall on Lansdowne's and Hardinge's bungling over this very minor matter. With painfully obvious subtlety, however, he hurriedly dismissed the point that Lansdowne's, or his colleagues', fate was the matter at issue (which, of course, it was). 'There is the question of Your Majesty, and there are the interests of the country.' Lansdowne's sacking would not alter the fact that a promise had been made in the King's name: 'the disavowal of the agent can hardly get rid of the obligation into which the agent has entered'. Then there would be the offence to the Shah and the dwindling of British influence in Persia – 'we have a very difficult game to play there. Russia has most of the cards, yet it may be disaster for us to lose the rubber,' he said, using a metaphor he trusted the King would understand.

Balfour concluded, unsurprisingly, that Lansdowne should be supported, that to do so set no precedent, and that the award could be 'the last of its kind': it just required the King to do 'what all governors of men are obliged by circumstance to do, when a situation is unintentionally created for them by their subordinates, which in the public interest and their own, as well as out of the generous regard for those who rank under them, they cannot otherwise than accept'. Brilliantly and utterly dishonestly, Balfour had thrown the whole responsibility upon the King, and in doing so proved that the use of such casuistry in public life, much deprecated and reviled in the 1990s, is nothing new. Resistance to this sort of blackmail was pointless, since Balfour seemed to hint that if the King were to stick to his guns (as he had every right to do) he would not shrink from provoking a full-scale constitutional crisis.

In reply to Balfour's exercise the next day, Knollys grimly wrote: 'My dear Balfour, you may like to know that the King will I think give way, but he is much depressed about it all.'[140] The King did give way, making it clear that he did so 'from patriotic motives and a high sense of duty, though with the greatest reluctance'.[141] He also stressed that his government should never again ask him to bestow the Garter on a non-Christian, and that he would not stand for Sir Arthur Hardinge performing the investiture in Teheran – 'he is much displeased with Sir Arthur for the way in which he has acted in this affair'. Instead, Sir Arthur was explicitly snubbed by the act of the Garter's being conferred on the Shah by a special mission to Teheran, when such investitures were a normal ambassadorial function; Sir Arthur no doubt got the message. On other of his stipulations, the King's memory was shorter: three years later he happily assented to the Garter for the Emperor of Japan.

This was not the only time Balfour threatened to leave the King without a government over a single issue. Also that autumn the King urged leniency in the case of a court-martial of an officer who, during the Boer War, had mistakenly surrendered, and who was being cashiered for cowardice. The King felt the officer's action to have been just an error of judgment, and that the man should be allowed to resign. However Brodrick, the Secretary of State responsible, refused the overturn the verdict, as it had been reached on the advice of the Commander-in-Chief, Lord Roberts. He would not budge even when Roberts told him he did not mind. Brodrick informed the King that, if the Monarch insisted on reversing the decision, he would have to resign. For a moment, the King was content that he should resign; but Balfour used exactly the same line of argument he had with Lansdowne, saying that if Brodrick went, they all went. Admittedly, by present standards, Balfour was more justified in issuing this threat in this case than he had been in the case of Lansdowne, who had been incompetent. The King said he would, of course, put the matter entirely in the hands of his advisers. As Fritz Ponsonby put it, the officer concerned 'was cashiered and disgraced, and the British Constitution saved at his expense'.[142] Both incidents, however, gave Balfour ideal opportunities in the early days of his premiership to display to the King the realities of constitutional monarchy, and to gain a psychological advantage over him in the wielding of true political power: that the King could have his way on matters of no significance, but his advisers had to prevail on anything else. What the Garter issue showed – though the King had not given up yet – was that his sway over foreign affairs, which he had thought was considerable, was in his Prime Minister's view merely supervisory, as it was in everything else.

The main beneficiary of the King's climbdown about the Shah's Garter, apart from the newly Gartered despot himself, was Lansdowne; so no wonder he should write to the King on 6 November 1902, 'Lord Lansdowne cannot thank Your Majesty sufficiently for the decision at which you have arrived. It is one which relieves him from a most embarrassing position which he felt acutely: he will never cease regretting that in dealing with this question he should have failed to apprehend Your Majesty's wishes, and occasioned you so much trouble and anxiety.'[143] Hardinge, keen too to try to salvage things, wrote to the King from Teheran to say that the honour 'has produced a most excellent political effect here'.[144] It did nothing to alter the King's view of the whole episode, which was that 'no Sovereign had ever before been so treated or so insulted'.[145]

MINDING HIS BUSINESS

However much Balfour might be his better in dialectic, the King was no more reluctant to acquaint him with his views on foreign affairs than he had been with his predecessor. When, for example, Balfour let him know that the Cabinet favoured a conciliatory approach to Russia over Tibet, the King was adamant that this would be a mistake. 'The question of Thibet is no doubt a very difficult one,' he wrote on 20 February 1903, 'and the King fears that Russia cannot be trusted, as she has but one desire, and that is to increase her power and territories in Asia.'[146] In the same letter he rebuked the Cabinet for its 'grievous mistake' in not finding further employment, preferably as Quartermaster-General, for Sir William Butler, a hero of the Zulu wars and the Sudan and, more recently, a Boer War general. The King regarded him as 'an officer of such undoubted military capacity, of which we possess so few alas!' He had read the correspondence between Butler and the War Office about the General's future, circulated by Brodrick, which had served only to convince the King that Butler 'had the best of the arguments'.[147]

As in many matters, the intriguing of Esher, who had been lobbying Brodrick about Butler, played an important part in the King's judgment.[148] He reported to the King on 12 February that the

Secretary of State for War had invited him for a chat that evening, which turned out to be on the matter of Butler. Brodrick had assured Esher that he had no personal prejudice against the officer, but that the Cabinet simply felt he was not appropriate for the post of Quartermaster-General. Esher had replied with a ringing defence of Butler, with a view to Brodrick trying again. He ended his letter to the King: 'Lord Esher ventures humbly to ask Your Majesty not to mention to Mr Brodrick that he has spoken of this interview; but Lord Esher, as Your Majesty is aware, conceals nothing from his Sovereign': which just about summed it up.[149] Butler did not get the post.

The King did not stint in his determination to know what was going on in non-martial matters either. Nominations for deaneries and candidates for bishoprics flowed across his desk, which he would take up with the Prime Minister; and when more serious matters were not drawn to his attention, he was swift to complain. Selborne, the first Lord of the Admiralty, had forgotten in March 1903 to tell him about the building of a naval base on the Firth of Forth, for which the King rebuked Jack Sandars, Balfour's secretary. Balfour immediately wrote to atone for this 'unfortunate mistake' and 'on his own initiative, ventures to anticipate the more detailed apologies which Your Majesty will receive from the responsible minister'.[150] This did the trick, though Knollys reminded Balfour that 'the King takes such a deep interest in the welfare of his Country, especially in all matters connected with defence, that he was naturally much surprised, and he might even say pained, to have received no information on the subject previous to Mr Balfour's important statement in the House of Commons'.[151]

Nor had Lansdowne exhausted the King's interest. When the Austrians let some Russian ships through the Dardanelles, the King wanted his Foreign Secretary to engage in some bellicose rhetoric, and was disappointed that he did not. In a letter to him of 28 December 1902 the Sovereign explained that 'The King's object in urging stronger language to be used in Lord Lansdowne's despatch of 23rd instant ... was merely with the object of impressing upon the Austrian govt how much we deplored the passage of Russian men of war through the Dardanelles, and how strongly we felt that treaty rights had been discarded, in which Italy concurred. ... the King cannot help feeling that Austria is afraid of Russia, and will therefore not protest.'[152] It often seemed as though the King was more alert to the nuances of foreign relationships than his ministers whose job it was to conduct them.

ENTENTE CORDIALE

Once it was apparent that an Anglo-German alliance was an impossibility, an alliance with France came back on the agenda, and in the climate of the times, with senior politicians becoming increasingly paranoid about Britain's having no firm friends on the continent, the prospect became even more attractive. Delcassé was determined to bind England to France; and had a useful agent in Paul Cambon, from 1898 the French ambassador to London. Cambon took it upon himself to try to convince leading British politicians of the value of an alliance: failing with Salisbury, succeeding with Chamberlain. He also worked on Lansdowne, who had discussions with the King, who in turn took the trouble to communicate to Cambon his enthusiasm for an entente. On a visit to Paris at the end of October 1902 the King gathered from various luminaries with whom he spoke that 'there exists a much greater wish to come to an understanding with England'.[153] In this letter to King George of Greece, written from Vienna on 2 November 1902, the King revealed that 'Monsieur Loubet [the President], especially, spoke most warmly and in the highest terms about England, and how sincerely he wished that people in France might understand clearly that it would only be in the interest of France to be on the most intimate footing with England.'

Conflict over colonial ambitions, notably in Morocco and Egypt, had been a great cause of estrangement between the two countries. France envied British influence in Egypt; Britain resented French interference in Morocco, with which country the British had much commercial traffic. In March 1903 it was reported that Cambon had asked Lansdowne to act as arbitrator in arranging the partition of Morocco between France and Spain, a report that caused some embarrassment to the government. Lansdowne had discussed the matter with Cambon, who, he reported to the King on 7 March, 'at once admitted that there was nothing to justify the imputation of such designs to Your Majesty's Government'.[154]

At the same time, the King was planning his own itinerary for a European tour, without any reference to his ministers, and on his own initiative. It was to begin in Lisbon, at the urging of perhaps the King's closest friend, the Portuguese Marquis de Soveral, the first person the King had consulted about his journey. The royal yacht would then go on to Italy, and from there he would travel by train to Paris. There was nothing apparently unusual in that: the King had been in the habit of visiting Paris. When the King eventually told his ministers that the French had asked him to make his visit official rather than private they were unimpressed, Lansdowne warning him of the risk of a hostile reception. The Foreign Secretary had spoken to Cambon earlier and the two men had agreed the visit would best be informal, but the President would entertain the King to dinner nonetheless. However, the King was already upping the level of formality: when his ambassador to Paris, Sir Edmund Monson, acting on an enquiry from Delcassé, asked the King how he would like to be received in Paris, the King replied: 'As officially as possible, and that the more honours that were paid to him, the better it would be.'[155]

Lansdowne was put out not just to be one of the last people to be consulted about the journey, but to be told that the King would break with precedent and travel without his Foreign Secretary. On the trip, therefore, the King would routinely meet and discuss matters with other heads of state without having any of his own ministers present. There could be no better demonstration of the King's determination to be, if necessary, his own foreign secretary, nor of his view of Lansdowne. To make matters worse for the Foreign Secretary, he had been on the receiving end for some time of letters from a somewhat wounded Monson. The ambassador, too, was offended at being kept in the dark, having picked up through various channels in Paris rumours of what the King was planning. Still smarting from the Shah and Garter incident, Lansdowne was in no mood to take the King on again; however, he made his displeasure plain as best he could. The King, who manifestly did not want Lansdowne's society for the best part of a month, 'insisted and refused to yield'. Eventually, Lansdowne gave way, formally protecting the constitutional niceties by 'advising' the King to proceed as the King had planned all along. The long-term consequence of Lansdowne's omission, however, was that for the rest of the reign the King was perceived abroad as holding the reins of foreign policy, a not always helpful perception, but a confusion easily made in an age of autocrats about a monarch who now and again chose to behave like one.

Having taken no minister with him, he entrusted much of the detail in planning and executing the trip to a diplomat with whom he was well acquainted and whose presence he had requested as his sole foreign affairs counsellor. Charles Hardinge was a cousin of the unfortunate Sir Arthur, and at the remarkably early age of forty-four one of the four under-secretaries at the Foreign Office. Hardinge, in an earlier posting at St Petersburg, had closely monitored Franco-Russian relations, and fully understood the importance of Britain's friendship with its neighbour.[156] The King had noted Hardinge's career for some time, and had pressed Lansdowne to have him brought back from Russia to serve at the Foreign Office in 1902.[157] Jealous colleagues – of whom there were a few – also had it that Hardinge had been favoured because his wife was one of the Queen's ladies-in-waiting. However, the evidence of his subsequent career (which included the headship of the Foreign Office and the viceroyalty of India) seems to suggest that the King was justified in preferring him. By his own admission, Hardinge was a success in the diplomatic service because, in those leisurely days when senior Foreign Office men were rarely at their desks before eleven o'clock, he worked much harder than his peers.[158] It should be noted, though, that not least among Hardinge's qualities was a gift for discreet self-promotion, accomplished largely on the evidence of his achievements (which were not hidden under the proverbial bushel) but also partly through suave ingratiation, and on occasion through managing to take credit for the achievements of others.

At the King's command he was accorded the temporary rank of minister plenipotentiary. Lansdowne was aggrieved by this too, as Hardinge was the most junior of the four under-secretaries. The Foreign Secretary appears to have had fears, which were partly justified, that he was being supplanted, and told Hardinge of his special mission 'very unwillingly'.[159] Hardinge recognised that the Foreign Office, which had referred less and less detail to the old Queen in her declining years, was now aggrieved by the new King demanding to have what he considered to be his constitutional rights restored to him: a wish for which the obliging and ambitious Hardinge had every sympathy. The unconventional nature of the suite did cause a little difficulty for the government, and after a decent interval – at the end of July – a statement about Hardinge's role was made to the House of Commons to the effect that 'no ministerial responsibilities devolved either on the King or on him during the foreign tours, and that the foreign policy of the country was unaffected by the royal progresses'. That statement reflected the touchiness of the government more than the curiosity of its opponents, and was, as we shall see, true only up to a point.[160]

Arriving in Portugal on 2 April 1903, the King's main achievement there was to end fears that Britain would interfere with Portuguese

colonial ambitions. While at Lisbon, he started to plan the arrangements for Paris, leaving the detail to Hardinge. Paris was in a state of
great excitement at the prospect of seeing 'The Prince of Wales' again,
and President Loubet cut short a trip to Algiers to be back in Paris in
time. The King enjoyed himself in Lisbon but, according to Fritz
Ponsonby, who was travelling with him, 'has not been much struck
with the Portuguese nobility. He thinks they look like waiters at second
rate restaurants.'[161] From Lisbon the King sailed to Gibraltar, his first
overseas possession visited since his accession. After five days there he
headed for Malta, though not before sending the four battleships that
had joined his escort over to Algiers to salute the arriving Loubet – a
brilliant gesture of friendship to warm him up before the King and he
met in Paris. From Malta he sailed to Naples, whence he took a train
to Rome. There he met the King of Italy and, after a great diplomatic
performance, the Pope too.

It had been the King's original intention that he should see the
Pope, Leo XIII; but the Cabinet, as usual convinced of impending 'no
Popery' agitation at home, had argued against such a meeting when, at
the King's request, Balfour had sounded them out on the question. On
17 March the Prime Minister had reported back that his colleagues
were 'greatly disquieted at the suggestion'.[162] He continued: 'They were
unanimous in thinking the "Protestant feeling" (so called) which such a
visit would arouse, most irrational; but they were agreed as to its
probable strength, as to the vehemence of the professions it might
arouse, and as to the undesirability of making any action of Your
Majesty the theme of attack on the part of some of Your Majesty's
most loyal subjects.' Balfour also agreed it would be difficult for the
King to go to Rome without visiting the Pope; and so they hoped that,
if the King had to go to Italy at all, he would stop off somewhere else in
that country, helpfully suggesting Naples. As a trump card, Balfour also
revealed that he had discussed the matter with Salisbury in confidence,
and that his eminent uncle had concurred with him. However, the
Prime Minister, showing his weakness of leadership, told the King that
he did not press these views, merely laid them before him. The King,
urged strongly by Knollys, decided not to see the Pope, which
produced another letter of marvellous ambiguity from Balfour. 'I am
glad of the King's decision,' he wrote to Knollys on 4 March. 'Much as
I detest the excessive bigotry of a certain class of opinion in this
country, I should be sorry if HM should unnecessarily offend it.'[163]

However, once the King was on his travels, he became convinced of the discourtesy of his going to Rome without calling on the Pope. He sent a cypher telegram to Balfour saying that as Prince of Wales he had met the Pope and saw no reason why he should not do so as king. Minds were being changed at home too, following representations from Hardinge. Sir Eric Barrington, Lansdowne's private secretary, sent Hardinge a 'very confidential' message on 8 April to say that 'the King will receive telegram from Prime Minister about Pope – my conviction is that it is intended as a loophole in case King thinks informal visit desirable.'[164] Balfour was prompted to reopen the subject after being rattled by the tone of an interview with two of the grandest Roman Catholics in England, the Duke of Norfolk and Lord Edmund Talbot. They had spoken to the Prime Minister about the prospect of a royal visit to the Pope, and had urged that it should happen. Balfour had, as usual, radiated confusion on the subject – and, as Ponsonby put it, 'the FO do not want to be responsible for advising the King to see the Pope'.[165] Balfour, in his telegram to the King of which Barrington had warned, spoke of the 'deep emotion' with which the Duke and Lord Edmund had spoken to him of their belief that the King should meet the Pope, and that not to do so would be a 'deliberate slight put on an old and venerable man'.[166] However, Balfour stuck to his guns, reminding the King of the 'great danger of inciting Protestant sentiment'; but quite clearly, and unconstitutionally, threw the whole onus for making the final decision on to the King. 'Mr Balfour had at one time hoped that by visiting Naples instead of Rome the difficulty might have been avoided,' he wrote. 'This however is now clearly impossible and though he does not see his way out of the dilemma, Mr Balfour thinks it necessary to inform Your Majesty how matters stand.' This was indeed, as Barrington had correctly surmised, a 'loophole', and Hardinge presented it to the King as such.

Meanwhile, back at home, Knollys had had a letter from Sir Francis Bertie, newly installed ambassador to Rome, in which he warned of the effects on 'The King's Catholic subjects' of his possibly going to Rome to see the King of Italy but not seeing the Pope. Hardinge advised the King that the various new communications from Balfour showed that, while the Cabinet would not change its advice, it would 'not mind so much' if the King saw the Pope. Barrington wrote to Hardinge on 10 April to say that he hoped the visit would take place, and Lansdowne 'certainly does' hope it would because 'it is impossible to find a decent argument to support a refusal'.[167] Barrington explained that 'the Cabinet dare not recommend the King to go, but evidently AJB

[Balfour] wished the King in such a matter to "*passer outre*" of his advisers'. The King sent a wire back to Balfour saying that he 'entirely shares' Norfolk's and Talbot's arguments, adding: 'The King deeply regrets to be in divergence with you and the Members of the Cabinet but would like to hear from you again on the subject.'[168] In other words, he wanted Balfour to pull himself together and give him the go-ahead to see the Pope. Backing up this message, Hardinge wrote to Lansdowne on 12 April to say that 'from the manner in which the King would carry out his visit it would be impossible that it should be regarded even by the most bigoted Protestant otherwise than as an act of civility'.[169] Since Hardinge was well aware by this point that Lansdowne needed no persuasion, the purpose of this letter can only have been to give the Foreign Secretary more ammunition to use against Balfour. It would not, however, be needed.

Hardinge had added that 'the King feels very strongly on the subject', underlining the word 'very' twice. That same day, Easter Sunday, Ponsonby wrote to Knollys, who was still set against the visit, to warn him that 'the King is now very violently in favour of visiting the Pope'.[170] Balfour was seeking to protect the constitutional niceties, but also (and probably more importantly) his and his colleagues' faces. The King felt this 'unfair', and, as Hardinge continued, 'quite made up his mind that he would get a distinct assent from Mr Balfour for an informal visit to the Pope before taking any further action'. Luckily, also on 12 April, Balfour obliged with a suitable telegram. It was a masterpiece of Balfourian reasoning: 'He thinks it would be altogether outside his duty', the Prime Minister wrote in the third person, 'to offer any advice to Your Majesty as to what private and unofficial visits it might be Your Majesty's wish to pay and if proposed visit could really be made private and unofficial Mr Balfour would think it an impertinence to offer any observation on it.'[171] Balfour revealed one of the real causes of his worry: that the visit might be interpreted at home as 'part of a settled plan to buy off Roman Catholic opposition and secure passage of Irish Land Bill and success of Your Majesty's visit to Ireland [scheduled for later that spring]'. If that aside was meant to provoke the King into thinking again, it did not. He will instead have taken at face value Balfour's assurance that he 'will do his best to get matter properly presented to public here'.

So it was that the visit could go ahead. As a precaution, Hardinge told Knollys about Balfour's telegram, just in case the Cabinet protested when the change of course became apparent. Knollys was still upset. 'I shall be very sorry if it takes place,' he wrote to Hardinge on 23 April.[172] Even at that late stage the visit had not been confirmed, because of an insistence by all on the King's side that, to protect the proprieties, the initiative for this 'private' visit had to come from the Pope: and the ninety-three-year-old Pontiff was being slow in issuing the invitation, despite furious diplomatic activity between Hardinge, Bertie and the Vatican. Knollys rubbished the King's idea that, since he had seen the Pope as Prince of Wales, he could see him as king – 'an heir apparent can do many things which it is not advisable a Sovereign should'. Knollys did not blame the Monarch for the problem, but rather Balfour, for writing to him after the meeting with Norfolk and Talbot in a tone of such 'vacillation' that it opened the way for the King to change his mind. The 'vacillation' was, added Knollys, 'the more surprising as no-one in the Cabinet was, I believe, so strongly opposed to the visit as he, except Chamberlain'. However, Knollys was coming to understand the Prime Minister.

The incident also provided an example of how the King's closest advisers worked to moderate his wrath, usually with his *post facto* approval. The crucial message from the King to Balfour asking him to give new advice was originally dictated to Ponsonby. It was such an unpleasant tirade about the need for Balfour to stop vacillating and make up his mind that Ponsonby realised the Prime Minister might feel he ought to resign in the wake of so violent a rebuke. So Ponsonby, much to the uninitiated Hardinge's shock, toned it down to the point where it was merely a request for the King to act on his own responsibility in visiting the Pope: it elicited the happy, almost relieved note of compliance from Balfour.[173] Displaying the acumen and technique that won him a peerage and no fewer than six separate orders of knighthood, Hardinge, who had strongly objected to Ponsonby's intervention, in his memoirs makes no mention of the assistant private secretary's crucial role in the affair, but takes all the credit to himself.

When the Pope and the King met, the Pope thanked his visitor for his consideration towards Catholics and for the toleration that pertained throughout the British Empire. As Britain failed to be swept by 'no Popery' riots, Balfour sent his congratulations to the King on a successful visit, making, naturally, no mention of his recent warnings against it. On 1 May he wrote that 'no irritation of a serious kind has been produced by Your Majesty's private visit to the Pope.... the better opinion among all classes of Your Majesty's subjects seems content'.[174]

Appeasing the various denominations within his realm was not, though, the purpose of the King's trip. The Germans knew what it was, and their ambassador in Paris, Count von Radolin, wrote salivatingly to Bülow on 20 April about how the French press, still hostile to Britain after the Boer War, were opposing an Anglo-French alliance.[175] The Germans would have been elated at the muted reception the King received when he reached Paris on 1 May ('sullenly respectful' is how Sir Sidney Lee describes it), but the King was unperturbed. When Ponsonby noted, in response to some boos, that 'the French don't like us', he replied 'Why should they?'[176]

In a speech later that day to the British Chamber of Commerce in Paris, the King expressed the hope that 'the days of conflict between the countries are, I trust, happily over.... I trust that the friendship and admiration which we all feel for the French nation and their glorious traditions may in the near future develop into a sentiment of the warmest affection and attachment between the peoples of the two countries.'[177] The King continued his charm offensive that evening, attending the theatre with Loubet and his wife, and mingling among an unenthusiastic crowd and winning them over. At every public and private opportunity he praised Paris and the Parisians, France and the French. At a banquet on his second evening he said, in reply to a speech by Loubet, that 'our great desire is that we may march together in the path of civilisation and peace'.[178] By the time he left for home two days later the crowds were cheering where they had earlier been booing. The Kaiser and his ministers preferred to ignore this, and wallowed in the conviction that the Anglo-Russian antagonism would prevent a formal alliance between England and Russia's great friend, France. However, the Kaiser – who following the success of his uncle's trip to the Vatican was about to go there in great state himself – asked Lascelles to find out whether the King would be coming to see his nephew that year and, if so, when.

For the moment, though, international intercourse with the French was the first priority. Loubet and Delcassé came to England in July 1903 for a four-day visit. It was a great success, and after they left the King telegraphed to Loubet that 'it is my most ardent wish that the rapprochement between the two countries may be lasting'.[179] More crucially, in the margins of the visit Delcassé and Lansdowne had started to sketch an outline of a possible treaty, and Lansdowne had more detailed discussions in August with Cambon. Although in the last months of Salisbury's administration some of his ministers had been softening towards such an initiative, they did not take it. The King took it; he instigated the policy and gave it its spur and motive; his ministers, who were either enthusiastic or who could see no harm in it, simply filled in the details. Hardinge – a diplomat and not a politician – noted that the entente was down 'entirely to the initiative and political flair of King Edward who, had he listened to the objections of his Cabinet, would never have gone to Paris'.[180] Ponsonby observed that 'it was all very well for Lord Lansdowne to claim afterwards the credit for the Entente Cordiale, but neither he nor the Government could ever have got the French people round from hostility to enthusiastic friendship in the way King Edward did'.[181] Ponsonby quoted the observation of Cambon that 'any clerk at the Foreign Office could draw up a treaty, but there was no-one else who could have succeeded in producing the right atmosphere for a *rapprochement* with France!'

Needless to say, public recognition of such a fact was unpleasant to the ministers' *amour propre* – and not just temporarily. Long after the King's death, on 11 January 1915 as the war raged in Flanders, Balfour, who had lost none of his shiftiness with advancing years, wrote to Lansdowne asking him to confirm that the King had not originated the *entente cordiale*, and that 'during the years which you and I were his Ministers, he never made an important suggestion of any sort on large questions of policy'.[182] Sir Philip Magnus, the King's second official biographer, notes that 'that was true'; but to believe that depends on an interesting and novel definition of the adjectives 'important' and 'large'. The activities surrounding the inception of the entente suggest that Balfour was rewriting history, and the King's pre-emptive involvement in certain other matters, such as army reform, also gives the lie to the statement. The fact was that, until Grey became Foreign Secretary at the end of 1905, the King could legitimately detect a vacuum in his country's pursuit of foreign policy at a crucial time in world history, and proceeded to fill it.

The trip greatly strained relations between the King and Balfour, a point perhaps not adequately appreciated hitherto. On 2 May 1903 Knollys wrote to the Prime Minister to hint at a means of improving relations. 'I hope you will forgive me', he said, 'for venturing to make the suggestion that you should meet the King on his arrival in London on Tuesday – I am sure that your doing so would please him and would mitigate any little feeling of soreness he may have owing to the causes which I mentioned to you last night' – which were presumably more than just the contretemps over the visit to the Pope, and may have touched on a lack of appreciation on the part of his ministers for what the King had actually achieved in Paris.[183] It was a wound that even time and the King's own passing seemed destined not to be able to heal.

CLINCHING THE DEAL

Many of the details to be resolved before the entente could be concluded concerned potential or actual conflicts of interest arising out of the colonial ambitions of the two powers, from Canada to the Far East via Africa. However, Lansdowne's negotiations with Cambon went sufficiently smoothly for him to draw up a minute for the Cabinet in September dealing with the possibilities of concluding a treaty with the French. The main concession was that Britain should recognise France's influence in Morocco, while France gave way to Britain in Egypt. Lansdowne's minute was circulated to the King, who approved its thrust but made two main corrections. The first was the striking out by the King of an observation by Lansdowne that his government had no intention of annexing Egypt;[184] the King saw no need to be so specific, but Lansdowne in his final draft still included the phrase 'His Majesty's Government have no desire to alter the political status in Egypt.'[185] The other correction concerned Lansdowne's observation that the commercial liberty of that country's open ports should be 'absolutely respected'. The King wanted to go further, saying that the liberty was 'absolutely indispensable', and Lansdowne agreed.

Further negotiations then ensued through the winter of 1903–4, with most arguments rapidly solved. Balfour wrote to the King on 26 February 1904 to say that all could be settled if England gave up Ile de Los, an island off Konakry, the capital of French Guinea. Balfour was nervous of this because the Cabinet did not want to give up the island, but the King squashed all objections. 'I am delighted that we intend giving up Ile de Los to France. It is in the first place right that we should do so, and secondly, *more than ever now* we must leave no bone of contention between ourselves and France.'[186] After a few more squabbles about fishing rights off Newfoundland, Lansdowne was able to tell the King on 7 April 1904 that the Treaty would be concluded the following day. The two Foreign Ministers signed it on time, and its terms, with the King's express approval, were immediately made public, even though Lansdowne had counselled waiting until Parliament returned from its Easter recess.[187] The King was overjoyed, writing to Lansdowne that 'I sincerely congratulate you on having brought these difficult negotiations to a successful termination.'[188]

There was an after-effect that touched on the King's prerogatives. When Parliament met the following week to discuss the Treaty, Balfour told the Commons that a Bill formalising the arrangements and cessions of territory would be submitted to Parliament. He then found *The Times* rebuking him for constitutional malpractice, drawing attention to his part in the decision to cede Heligoland in 1890. That had been done with the permission of Queen Victoria and without reference to Parliament. Knollys, having read this article, telegraphed the King in Denmark and warned him what was afoot, observing that what Balfour was up to was 'constitutionally not so' and that 'it appears to be a mistake that the Crown should surrender this power'.[189] The King agreed with his private secretary, and said he felt Balfour had treated him with 'scant courtesy'.[190] In a telling insight into the relationship between King and Minister, the King added that Balfour 'is always so vague that probably he is wrong, but I must insist, if he is, and as a matter of principle, that he admits it'.[191]

He told Knollys to see Balfour immediately, and then in a cypher to the Prime Minister from Copenhagen on 16 April 1904 objected vehemently to what Balfour had done: 'I have not yet seen the newspapers, but you stated in the House of Commons that the consent of parliament was necessary in connection with the Anglo-French agreement. Constitutionally, power to cede territory rests with the Crown independently of Parliament. I should gladly hear from you why this statement was made as I feel sure you would be careful to safeguard my rights.'[192] Balfour wired back that he had spoken only after consulting law officers and the Foreign Office, but would 'have the whole subject further examined.... Mr Balfour need not say that it is his earnest desire to preserve prerogative intact.'[193] He claimed he had no wish, either, to spend legislative time unnecessarily. However, after taking further advice, he stuck to his position; and an important part of the royal prerogative was eroded.

Knollys told the King that while the government (with Queen Victoria's approval) had set a 'dangerous precedent' in 1890 by seeking the assent of Parliament, there was no need for it to happen in this case.[194] Balfour's involvement then, Knollys mused, was typical, and matters had only worsened in the intervening fourteen years. 'Mr Balfour was even then a regular "House of Commons Man",' he told the King, 'and he is now more than ever pronounced in the idea that very little signifies outside the House of Commons and that every possible question should be brought before and decided by that body – this is a dangerous doctrine and one which tends to diminish the proper influence and authority of the Throne and to decrease the responsibility of ministers.' Knollys also felt the King should rebuke Balfour for not having discussed this with him earlier. The King was determined to be more vigilant in Anglo-French matters in future, as if taking it upon himself personally to protect the entente. To this end in July 1904 he let it be known that he wished Sir Francis Bertie, the ambassador to Rome and a long-time trusty of his, to succeed Monson at the Paris embassy. Bertie was deeply grateful to be yet another beneficiary of the King's determination to have his own men in such senior diplomatic posts.[195]

When the Bill establishing the treaty went through both Houses it was almost unanimously applauded, the one dissenting voice, iron-ically, being one of the King's oldest friends in Parliament, Lord Rosebery. Virtually alone in seeing King Edward's profoundest political consequences, he said that sooner or later the formal alliance would lead to war. For the alliance was King Edward's responsibility. Though Delcassé had made the overture, and he and Lansdowne had settled the details, without the King's enthusiasm and diplomatic activity it is unlikely that the climate would have been created in which the entente was possible – either in terms of public opinion in both countries, which the King greatly helped to soften, or in terms of His Majesty's ministers realising that such a thing was possible. The King had made it his project, and his ministers had acted following his impetus. When assessing the results of the alliance, it is not merely the politicians who must take the praise, or blame. For their part, the Germans professed, at the time, to be unworried; but the Kaiser was later to class what had happened as the 'beginning of the English encircling policy against Germany'.[196]

CONFRONTING THE TURK

The next great issue in European affairs to arise after the exchange of Anglo-French pleasantries in 1903 was caused by Turkish attacks on Macedonia. These attacks – of a blatantly religious, Moslem-on-Christian nature – caused the King some concern. He urged on 27 September 1903 that the British military attaché in Constantinople join the Turkish forces in Macedonia to supervise their behaviour. The King, justifiably, adhered to the provisions of the Treaty of Berlin of 1878, which called upon the main signatories to guarantee the freedoms of Macedonia, and to take on Turkey if necessary. Liberal opinion in Britain was calling for something to be done to protect the Macedonian Christians, and the King, not for the first time, felt the government and particularly the Foreign Office were acting pusillanimously towards the Ottoman government. On 30 September he asked Lansdowne to have British ships sent to the Dardanelles, a step which he felt would 'have a very wholesome effect on the Porte, and prove to her that we insist on her carrying out her promised reforms. It would have the best possible effect in England.'[197]

Lansdowne, however, baulked at this attempted coercion, and told the King so, arguing that he would 'deprecate isolated action on the part of this country of the kind contemplated by Your Majesty', and hinting that the King did not quite understand what was going on.[198] This prompted the King to thunder in reply:

> he never wished to propose that British Ships of War should be sent into Turkish Waters in order to coerce the Porte, but he still thinks that some Naval demonstration might be made which, without attempting to 'coerce' the Sultan, might have the appearance at home that we were doing something actively (not merely in words) to show that we might eventually be obliged to take stronger measures than to put pressure on the two Powers which, even if any good results from it, must necessarily take some time to effect any benefit.[199]

He warned Lansdowne that public opinion at home would become stronger on the matter, and possibly even get 'out of hand'; and after some vivid newspaper reports over the next two days about the 'cruelties' in Macedonia, he telegraphed Lansdowne again to warn him that if this 'drift' by Britain continued 'the growing feeling of indignation in England will make it very serious for our Government.'[200] Not for the first time, though, the King was overestimating the interest of the British public in faraway countries of which they knew little.

The Foreign Secretary replied that the government did have an attitude of its own, and had demanded definite improvements from the Porte. What Lansdowne did not tell the King was that the government was reluctant to interfere with the plan being designed by the Emperor of Austria and the Tsar of Russia, whose countries were two other signatories of the Treaty of Berlin, to reform the Macedonian government.[201] The Porte accepted the plan in principle that autumn, but by February 1904 the King was still dissatisfied by the rate of progress in the Balkans, where he felt the situation could 'hardly be worse'.[202] He told Lansdowne on 23 February that 'diplomatic action up till now had proved fruitless'. He felt that conferring with other powers about what to do would be 'a waste of precious time'. The Foreign Secretary, who (however much he had asked for it) must by now have become somewhat tired of being kicked around by the King, reported back to him that such a conference of the signatory powers 'may become inevitable notwithstanding His Majesty's objection to this mode of putting pressure upon Turkey'.[203] One could understand the King at such times, though, envying the autocratic powers of his nephews in Russia and Germany.

The situation still did not improve; and while taking his now regular annual cure at the Bohemian spa of Marienbad that August the King consulted on the matter with some high-powered visitors, notably Emperor Franz Josef and Prince Ferdinand of Bulgaria. As a result of his discussion with the Emperor, the King telegraphed Lansdowne on 21 August 1904 to ask for more British officers to be sent to what would now be called the Macedonian 'peace-keeping' force – 'it would not be advisable that Austrian and Russian officers should predominate'.[204] By November, however, the King had abandoned all hope of Britain exerting any influence for the good in the Balkans. He wrote to Lansdowne on 23 November that 'reforms in Macedonia will never be carried out in the way wished or hoped for'.[205]

Prince Ferdinand provides another, microcosmic example of the King using his ties of blood and his pan-European social leadership to improve British relations with another country. The King had long loathed 'Foxy' Ferdinand, whose father was a first cousin to both Queen Victoria and the Prince Consort, because of his double-dealing, gossip and snide tongue. He had complained about his precedence when attending the Queen's Jubilee in 1897 (he was placed as a minor Saxe-Coburg royal, not as a reigning prince), and when he could not have the question settled for the Queen's funeral he refused to attend it, ostentatiously entertaining the Russian minister to Sofia to a gala luncheon on that day instead.

Although the removal of Bulgaria from Russia's sphere of influence was important to Britain, the King could not overcome his personal detestation of the Prince in order to do what was necessary. George Buchanan, his minister in Sofia, had however worked out the Prince's susceptibility to ingratiation, with the result that the Marienbad meeting of August 1904 was engineered and was a great success. An invitation to Ferdinand to come to England ensued, and the visit took place in March 1905. The Turks were most discomfited by this, but the King made a point of seeing his cousin again at Marienbad in August 1906.

Earlier on, in the autumn of 1904, Ferdinand had been distinctly less popular with the King. His crime had been to invite the new King of Serbia, Peter, to visit him in Sofia. Peter, a Serb prince, had been in exile at the time the previous year of the assassination of King Alexander and Queen Draga of Serbia by army officers in league with the radicals; so hated had the former King been that it was not difficult to raise so unlikely a coalition against him. King Edward had laid down to the Foreign Office that there was to be no support for what had happened; and even when Austria and Russia recognised the new King, King Edward pointed out that they, unlike Britain, had special interests in the area. There was no need, he said on 13 June, 'for England to recognise a Government consisting of assassins'.[206] The murders had been particularly horrible: Bonham, the British minister at Belgrade, reported in his dispatch to Lansdowne that 'the King had twenty-eight wounds. The Queen was ripped open by a bayonet and had seventeen other wounds.'[207] There had also been 'the extraordinary brutality of throwing the bodies from the windows', to satisfy the soldiery massing outside that the mission had been successfully accomplished. A fortnight later, the new King had telegraphed to King Edward informing him 'que le peuple Serbe par la voix unanime de ses représentants Legaux' had elected him; and he invited the King's recognition. The King, after consulting Lansdowne, sent back his wishes for 'peace and prosperity', but added that 'I hope your Majesty will succeed in restoring the good repute of your country upon which recent events have left so regrettable a stain.'[208] The King had discussed with Lansdowne whether Bonham should be recalled, but it was decided to leave him there – partly for the protection of British subjects, partly to monitor the situation.

The King's view was that no normal relations would be possible with Belgrade so long as the senior military officers who had killed the last King – however atrocious he might have been – were still in their posts. But Peter would not be rid of them and only moved them on the following year by promoting them. During the spring of 1904, the Foreign Office started to press the King to change his mind, as they wanted a British minister back in Belgrade. In April he told Lansdowne that Britain should be 'in no hurry' to restore relations; unable to take the hint, when urged to reconsider the following month he declared: 'Till they know how to behave themselves no British Minister should be sent to Serbia.'[209] He forbade any British representation at Peter's Coronation, which took place that September: most other European countries were represented. When, the next month, Peter met Ferdinand, Sir George Buchanan, as minister resident, boycotted his reception and the banquet given for him. The King had wanted Buchanan to go further, and leave Sofia for the duration, a course with which Lansdowne had initially agreed.[210]

Although King Peter professed public indifference to Britain's attitude, his anxiety that relations with London should be restored was severe. The Serbs had kept a minister in London, but there was little he could do. Eventually, the Italian and Russian ambassadors came to his aid: the Italian because Peter's sister-in-law happened to be Queen Helena of Italy, the Russian because the Tsar had befriended Peter long since. Once it was made clear to these agents that the King was the main obstacle to a resumption of relations, they requested a joint audience with him to discuss the matter, which took place at Windsor in the summer of 1905. However, the King told the ambassadors that he could not change his mind; not least because he felt that Kings should stick together, and he could not treat lightly the assassination of a member of the same club. Nothing changed until July 1906 when the regicide officers were placed on the retired list, and Britain resumed relations within days. The King had had his way.

THE RUSSIAN FRONT

The King spent much of the early part of his reign watching with some concern the activities of the Russians. He saw them as a permanent threat to British power in India, but also to the stability of Britain's vital trading relations with China. When Count Benckendorff took up his post as ambassador to the Court of St James's after the Coronation, the King expressed the hope to Lansdowne that the new man would bring with him promises of no further Russian activity in Afghanistan – the main area of provocation hitherto – without prior British consent. When, the following year, the King embarked on his project with France, he and his advisers all realised the importance of a thaw in Anglo-Russian relations to the success of the entente, given France's understanding with Russia. The King played his part, notably in seeking to propitiate Benckendorff, but other difficulties were in the way. The greatest of these was that England and Japan had recently forged their alliance, which was anathema to the Russians, who would have their own disastrous war with Japan in 1904–5.

The King had been alarmed to hear, in a Cabinet report from Balfour of 27 November 1903, that the Russians were about to buy two battleships, belonging to the Chilean government and lying on the Tyne. An international arbitration between Chile and Argentina had compelled the sale of the ships. Selborne, the First Lord of the Admiralty, had asked the Japanese to buy them, and they had tried to raise the money to do so, but before they could the Russians had stepped in with ready cash, and offered £200,000 more. Balfour was distressed at how this would change the balance of naval power, and asked the King whether, even though the ships were not really suitable for the Royal Navy, Britain should buy them. There was, though, the problem of money too: taxes were already set to rise, and such an outlay would put them up to unacceptable levels.[211] The King, however, had a ready answer. 'We must have these ships at any cost if Japan will not buy,' he said in an immediate cypher from Sandringham. 'I strongly advise asking Sir E. Cassel to lend the money. Feel sure he will do so if you mention my name. We must show Russia a firm hand as there is no doubt they mean mischief by trying to outbid the Japanese.'[212] He urged Balfour to put his suggestion before the Cabinet at once, which Balfour did, and the Cabinet did not rule out buying the ships. However, it emerged that the Japanese believed the Russian offer 'is not *bona fide*' but a 'contrivance by the Chilians to raise price of ships'.[213]

On 30 November an offer was made to the Chileans of £1,650,000 – £100,000 more than Japan was bidding, as it was established the Russians had made an offer. On 2 December Selborne sent a cypher to the King saying that he 'has the honour to report to Your Majesty that the two Chilian Battleships have been secured for Your Majesty's Fleet', to which the reply was sent: 'The King is very much relieved.'[214]

The Russo-Japanese War, which began a matter of weeks later, was mainly over Russia's ambitions in Manchuria and refusal to recognise Chinese independence. When it started, with the torpedoing of two Russian ships by the Japanese at Port Arthur in February 1904, the suspicion was that Britain had egged Japan on. The King, on Lansdowne's advice, sent for Benckendorff and told him to take a personal message to the Tsar repudiating any such notion: 'a few words from Your Majesty repeated to HIM the Emperor of Russia may have an excellent effect. It is hard to convince the Russian Government that Your Majesty's Government has not mitigated that of Japan or even given it indirect assistance.'[215] However, the King also told Balfour that Japan, as an ally, should be afforded any diplomatic assistance Britain could provide.

The Anglo-Japanese alliance inevitably strained British relations with Russia, despite the King's categorical denial of more martial involvement. However, the King's now traditional spring visit to his wife's family in Copenhagen in April 1904 allowed for some of the damage to be repaired. The Tsar, who was normally at this gathering, was absent due to the war. However his minister there, Isvolsky, was present and met the King for the first time. It was during this visit that the King heard that the entente had been concluded. He and Isvolsky, in the course of a forty-five-minute talk after lunch on 16 April, hit it off well. The King told Isvolsky that the entente should be good not just for Britain, but for international relations generally. He mused that it would help for Britain and Russia to conclude a similar understanding, something that was, he claimed, 'l'objet de mes plus sincères désirs'.[216] He added that his new ambassador to St Petersburg, Sir Charles Hardinge – whom the King was propelling up the promotional ladder, and on whose appointment he had insisted – was charged with the express task of improving Anglo-Russian relations, a most necessary part of the King's international project following the successful conclusion of the *entente cordiale*. The King urged Isvolsky to try to find a way of ending the war with Japan, as a first step to the restoration of international harmony; and when he reported this latest diplomatic initiative to Lansdowne, his Foreign Secretary assured him that 'Your Majesty's language to M. Isvolsky seems to Lord Lansdowne, if he may venture to say so, to have been most opportune and judicious.'[217]

Remarkably, Isvolsky let the King see the draft of his dispatch to St

Petersburg in which he described the conversation with the King, and the King approved it without question. He sent it on to Lansdowne, who was somewhat taken aback to realise the extent and scope of his Sovereign's intercourse with the Russians, and immediately consulted Balfour about it. What especially shocked Lansdowne was Isvolsky's report that the King had told him that the British government had tried to stop Japan going to war with Russia; and that the alliance Britain had concluded with Japan had had as one of its main objects the application of some restraint to Japan in that country's international conduct. 'In both cases,' Lansdowne tactfully told the King on 18 April 1904, 'M. Isvolsky has probably imputed to Your Majesty statements in excess of Your Majesty's actual observations; for, as Your Majesty will remember, your Government was careful to avoid, while the Russo-Japanese negotiations which preceded the war were in progress, putting pressure of any kind, moral or material, upon the Japanese Government for the purpose of inducing them to moderate their demands.'[218] On the contrary, Lansdowne said, the government had considered the Japanese demands reasonable, and aimed at safeguarding Japan's security as a nation – something the government had not wanted Britain to be blamed for preventing. In order to keep on the right side of the King, however, Lansdowne concluded by reminding him how Balfour, 'like Lord Lansdowne, feels how much Your Majesty has done to promote peace and goodwill amongst nations'.

Lest the King should think of trying to mediate in the Russo-Japanese War, however, the Tsar (who had, it will be recalled, been full of advice during the conflict with the Boers) wrote to him strongly. 'There is not a man in the whole of Russia who would tolerate another country mixing in this affair of ours and Japan's. This seems to be quite just, my dear Uncle Bertie. No-one hindered England at the conclusion of her South African War. I hope you won't mind my telling you this so frankly, but I prefer you should hear it privately from me than in any other way.'[219] The King was somewhat startled, since he did not see that the terms of any peace were exclusively a Russo-Japanese question, given Britain's extensive Asian and oriental interests. He pointed this out to Lansdowne on 29 April 1904, asking for his advice, and arguing that, because no other country had a sphere of influence in South Africa, the analogy with the Boer War was meaningless. 'Could we,' asked the King, 'without loss of prestige, allow Russia to make terms with Japan as she considers right without any other country interfering?'[220] Lansdowne and he crafted a response, sent on 12 May, in which the King said he understood his nephew's feelings, and was sure that all the powers would view it the same way – 'none of them would desire to interfere unasked *unless their existing rights were menaced* by the *proposed terms of peace,* an eventuality which I am sure neither they nor you see any reason to regard as probable'.[221]

The King had two new avenues through which to pursue his desire for better Anglo-Russian relations. One was via his new French allies; the other was via the trusty Hardinge. Hardinge himself reported that his new appointment at St Petersburg was regarded by the Tsar's court as having been made on the King's intitiative – which it was – and therefore a great and helpful compliment to Russia. The Kaiser, ever on the outlook for new trouble that he could cause, wrote to the Tsar to disabuse him of any such notion: Hardinge had been sent, he warned his cousin, to pave the way for British mediation in the war with Japan.

As it happened, the King and the Kaiser were to meet at Kiel at the end of June, on board the German royal yacht, and the occasion was an excuse for superficial displays of familial friendship. The Kaiser in his memoirs says that the King stated on this occasion that an alliance between Britain and Germany was unnecessary: 'This refusal to make an alliance was a plain indication of the English policy of encirclement.'[222] Chancellor von Bülow, who had a long talk with the King, saw things differently: the King had said that conflicts such as had been resolved by the Anglo-French Treaty did not exist between Britain and Germany, he quite openly admitted that he would like a similar deal with Russia, and he stressed the policy was not aimed at isolating Germany.

During the summer of 1904 there were incidents of Russian ships arresting British and German vessels carrying ammunition, even though many were headed for neutral ports and not for the Japanese. The King wanted joint Anglo-German action against Russian ships, but was warned off this by ministers who felt that German feelings in the matter were different from British ones. The Cabinet discussed the question and Balfour kept the King, who was off to Marienbad, informed. The King wrote to Balfour from his spa on 17 August, saying that while approving of the messages of warning Lansdowne had sent to Count Lamsdorff, the Tsar's Foreign Minister, 'the moment has no doubt come when England must put her foot down and give Russia clearly to understand that we cannot tolerate her high handed conduct at sea regarding our ships, or else our trade will greatly suffer'.[223] The King did, though, strike a conciliatory note towards his Russian family, saying that 'I feel sure that neither the Emperor nor Lamsdorff approve [sic] of what has lately taken place, but I fear the former has most injudicious advisers who are blinded by that disease (so prevalent in Russia) called Anglophobia. I rejoice to see that my Government is acting so strongly.' The King also told Balfour he had just proposed himself as godfather to the Tsar's new son, an offer that was accepted, and so there was hope that relations would improve.

However, then came the North Sea incident. The Russian Baltic Fleet, sailing off the Dogger Bank on a long haul to Japan following the destruction of much of the Tsar's Pacific fleet, managed to mistake some British trawlers for Japanese ships, and opened fire on them. One was sunk with the loss of two lives, including the captain's, while others sustained damage and injury to the crews. The Tsar quickly telegraphed to the King expressing his regrets, but saying that his navy had been warned of 'Japanese ... hiring fishing smacks and other vessels for purpose of destroying our squadron on its way out'.[224] The King, despite these apologies, was furious that the Russians had made no attempt to stop to pick up the survivors, 'as searchlights must have revealed to your Admiral that the ships were British fishing vessels'.[225] He showed this missive to Lansdowne, who endorsed it as 'most appropriate'.[226] The Foreign Secretary contacted the King the next day with a further explanation from Benckendorff, relayed via Hardinge in St Petersburg, where Hardinge found Benckendorff 'evidently much distressed'.[227] This the King dismissed as 'too flippant', adding that 'the Russian Government does not treat the matter with that gravity of importance which it invites'.[228] He told Lansdowne that apologies were not enough; those responsible had to be punished. The Foreign Secretary, with the King's approval, duly sent Benckendorff packing with a demand for an apology, a disclaimer, an inquiry and full reparations.

However, remembering that he wanted good relations with Russia, the King soon backtracked on the demand for punishment of the Admiral, Rozhdestvensky, saying that 'Russia could not accept such a humiliation'; he was also bemused by the Admiral's claim that the Japanese had pursued him in the North Sea with a motor torpedo boat, and the King asked Lansdowne to discover from the Japanese whether they had such a craft in the North Sea.[229] He felt a genuine mistake had been made, though this did not explain the failure to pick up survivors. Russia quickly accepted its responsibility in the matter, and paid £65,000 compensation, so it was as well that the King suppressed his initial bellicosity. It also meant that, once the details had been cleared up, Hardinge could continue on his course of steering his country and Russia towards the King's desired entente. However, once Russia's Baltic Fleet too was smashed by the Japanese in 1905, bringing the war to an end, it could not immediately afford an alliance with anyone that would alienate any of its continental neighbours – as one with Britain would have done.

The revolutionary movement in Russia, whose sudden growth was a direct consequence of the beating the country was taking in the Japanese war, also hindered progress. Hardinge, acting very much as the King's personal envoy as well as his government's, did all he could to find opportunities to further relations. On 21 October 1905 Hardinge telegraphed the King to say that the Tsar had summoned him for a rare audience, and the King wired back:

> When you are received by the Emperor pray express to him my earnest desire that the best and most durable relations should be established between the two countries, and that all important points should be discussed in the most amicable spirit and arranged as soon as possible. I need not assure the Emperor what my personal feelings are towards him as they are already well known to him. You can at the same time convey to him my hope that he may find himself able to grant a more liberal form of Government to his Country.[230]

Within two months, however, Hardinge's mission came to an end, and he returned with another impressive promotion to become permanent under-secretary at the Foreign Office. The King had wished for the move, as it led to his having his own man at the head of the permanent establishment in the Foreign Office, and it meant, among other things, that Hardinge could continue to pursue closer Anglo-Russian ties, but from Whitehall. The King had complete trust in Hardinge, who during his time at the Foreign Office supplied him with regular briefings about the state of Britain's relations with the world. Sir Edward Grey, Lansdowne's Liberal successor, had Hardinge to thank for the King's giving him a far easier ride in the job than he had given Lansdowne. Neither Grey (to start with) nor Campbell-Bannerman, in contrast to the attitude of the previous administration, made any objection to Hardinge's accompanying the King on his foreign trips. The King justified it because Hardinge was an ex-ambassador and a Privy Councillor; but Hardinge was sensitive to the criticism of his role in relation to the constitutional niceties 'since, although I fully represented the Foreign Office, I had not the responsibility of a Member of the Cabinet'.[231] However, so long as the King's ministers approved the arrangement, and he technically acted on their advice in having Hardinge in the position of minister plenipotentiary, there could be nothing 'unconstitutional' about it.

GERMAN TENSIONS

As was probably inevitable, the King's relations with the Kaiser deteriorated after the *entente cordiale,* however much the visit to Kiel had been intended to prove that in forging this alliance Britain had no hostile intent towards Germany. This tension was clear even after the North Sea incident, which did not ostensibly involve Germany at all. On 5 November 1904, after the incident, Metternich wrote to Knollys:

> if it were not so serious a matter to observe how systematically public opinion is poisoned in this country against Germany it would have been amusing to see that within days of the North Sea incident the papers, headed by *The Times*, hinted more or less openly that Germany was morally responsible for the outrage because she had given timely warnings to the Russian Government and the Russian admiral as to plots against the Baltic Fleet. Hence their nervousness and the firing on English fishermen. The warnings of course given with the sinister intention to embroil England and Russia.[232]

This conspiracy theorising aside, Germany's attempts to interfere in Morocco and to set itself up as the guarantor of Moroccan independence, in a land which Britain recognised as a French sphere of influence, were also regarded by the King as highly provocative. This German interference would lead to the constructive dismissal of Delcassé in the summer of 1905, which was seen as a great moral victory for the Kaiser. Therefore, when the King took his annual cure at Marienbad that August he made no effort to see the Kaiser, who was staying only a few miles away. This action was perceived as a snubbing of his nephew by the King and occasioned much mischievous comment in the press. Lascelles, still Britain's man in Berlin, had urged the King to meet his nephew in the interests of lessening tension between the two countries, but the King had told him in reply that such a thing was 'difficult to carry out at present'.[233] Lascelles reluctantly concurred, which prompted the King to write back to him from Marienbad, 'I am very glad that you agree that the moment has not yet arrived for me to meet the German Emperor.'[234] Lascelles was coming under pressure from Count von Seckendorff, one of the Kaiser's ministers, to organise a meeting, and had even suggested to Lascelles three days in September 1905 when the King and the Kaiser might meet at Homburg on the King's way back to England. This suggestion the King regarded as 'a great piece of impertinence', and he sent word to Knollys to have him write to Seckendorff at once to tell them there could be no such meeting.

Knollys's masterful tact was demonstrated once more. He wrote to the minister that the King 'has no quarrel whatever with the German Emperor of any sort'.[235] There was then the distinctly double-edged comment that 'The King is on the same terms with him now as he has always been since his accession.' Knollys did, though, make it clear that no direct contact could be resumed until Germany improved its relations with France; and even his diplomatic skill was stretched with his peroration: 'His Majesty in conclusion directs me to tell you that he does not know whether the Emperor retains any affection for him, but from one or two things which he has heard recently, he should *say not*, so that it would do no good if he were to pay him a dozen visits in the year.'[236] This letter, justly motivated though it was, initiated a spell of tit-for-tat insults, the cancellation of invitations by both families to junior members of the other, with the unfortunate Lascelles used as punchbag in the middle. After falling victim to a severe flow of invective from the Kaiser, the ambassador passed on the details to the King, who had Knollys send back to Lascelles word that there could be no change in the attitude of the court in London to the court in Berlin. The King was right to mistrust his nephew: some of the Kaiser's advisers were urging on him the idea that with Russia defeated and in turmoil, and with upheaval in France following Delcassé's removal, this was the ideal time for the Second Reich to take on France and Britain in war; and the Kaiser was writing to the Tsar at this time referring to their distinguished British relation as 'the arch mischief-maker of Europe'.[237]

TRADING DIFFICULTIES

The first great domestic political controversy in which the King became involved was when the Conservative party, in 1903, risked splitting over free trade. Chamberlain had just defied his party's policy on the question by arguing for tariffs that favoured trade with the colonies. He had not resigned, and other senior Unionists had expressed their sympathies for him, which created a severe disciplinary problem for the leadership. Balfour, in a demonstration of the weakness of purpose that was to be his downfall, tried to unite the Cabinet by adopting a confusing policy of ambiguity. The King, who was by inclination a free trader, feared a collapse of a government that still had four years of its mandate to run, and had a strong majority; all his instincts were against such instability, not least given the mess he all too vividly remembered the last Liberal government, under Rosebery, making of running the country. Esher (acting, *comme toujours*, with massive impropriety) was also letting his friends in the higher reaches of the government know that the King had told Charles Ritchie, the Chancellor of the Exchequer, that he would never agree to any taxes on food.[238]

Holidaying in Marienbad, the King wrote to Balfour on 18 August 1903 that he 'much regrets' the dissension in the government over tariff reform, and, apparently having the measure of his Prime Minister, suggested to him that the whole question might be referred to a Royal Commission, to spare the Cabinet having to decide.[239] Quite rightly, Balfour refused: it was not so much that such a procedure might lead to a decision being imposed on him that would split his party, as that it would be a complete abdication of the political leadership a Prime Minister was supposed to exert. Nonetheless, although the King let the matter drop for the time being, he raised it again the following March, only for Balfour to retail the same objections to him.[240] He wrote to the King on 15 September of 'the very complicated position' in which the government found itself.[241] In fact, Balfour largely agreed with Chamberlain, but he pointed out to the King that Britain's terms of trade with many other nations were governed by treaties. In September, as he should have done much earlier, Chamberlain resigned, the better to take his case to the country. The King was so concerned when he heard that Chamberlain was going that he asked Balfour to consult him about the Cabinet changes 'without delay' – trying to ensure that his former habit of being involved in Cabinet appointments could be resumed after the lapse caused by his illness in July 1902.[242] He wrote to Chamberlain of the sincere reluctance with which he accepted his resignation, but he had no choice, both constitutionally and politically. Initially, Balfour was determined to act without having to have the King hold his hand, but soon his position was to become too weak to allow such an attitude.

Worse came imminently. Balfour's mishandling of the situation meant that the most avid free traders in the Cabinet – Ritchie, Lord George Hamilton, the India Secretary, and two others – thought Chamberlain (of whose resignation they did not know) was about to prevail, and they resigned. They had come to this view because Balfour had talked to them of fiscal changes he was planning to make, and which they had told him they could not accept.[243] Balfour told the King that to propitiate the Chancellor and others would lead to even more resignations – not just Chamberlain, but his son, Austen (whom Joe had persuaded to stay on), the Lord Chancellor and several others. Devonshire submitted his resignation too, but the King enforced the Old Pals Act and talked him out of it – temporarily, as it turned out, since he went for good three weeks later after being shamed and goaded by several old Liberal friends for whom free trade was the ark of the covenant. Balfour had told the King of his optimism that Devonshire would stay in the Cabinet, which did not, when Devonshire left, improve the King's respect for his First Minister.'[244]

When the initial clutch of resignations had taken place Balfour had asked for permission from the King to reveal news of the resignations to the press, as he was being further debilitated by rumours. He expected it to be granted, but the King telegraphed back at once: 'I cannot approve of resignations being announced until I have thoroughly discussed the matter with you on Saturday, and also the question of the filling-up of the places. This great haste is to be deprecated and appears to be unnecessary…. it would not look well in the eyes of the public that a matter of such importance should be settled without my having seen the Prime Minister.'[245] To the King's 'regret', this message did not reach Balfour in time to prevent the Prime Minister from announcing the resignations – or so it was claimed. The tussle for political mastery between Sovereign and Prime Minister was on again.

Having lost so many of the Cabinet, Balfour was highly vulnerable, and those ministers who remained were compromised by their being associated explicitly with the vague and indefinite position from which

Balfour was trying to hold the party together.[246] Whereas in private the King would have had every excuse to give Balfour a rocket for his incompetence, he instead acted entirely constitutionally by giving his Prime Minister complete support. However, it seems that both he and his Prime Minister saw that the crisis presented an opportunity for each of them to try to claim the strategic upper hand: the King taking advantage of Balfour's vulnerability to assert himself and his prerogatives after a fashion that had gone by default in the Queen's declining years, Balfour seeking to handle the crisis in his own way and at his own pace without taking direction from the King.

It has to be said that, in this context, the King had the better of a draw. Balfour wrote to him at Balmoral with some initial suggestions for replacements for the ex-ministers. The King asserted his authority, and without commenting on them wrote back to Balfour that the appointments 'naturally will not be offered until after full consultation with me'.[247] Thus alerted, the Prime Minister wrote to ask the King 'if there be no objection to be allowed to approach Lord Milner for the Colonial Office'. However, the King would not let Balfour approach Milner for the moment, on the ground already expressed that he wished to discuss the whole question with him first.[248] It was a good move by the King: Balfour, as the King had been told by Knollys and Esher, simply did not have the political strength to refuse his Sovereign's wishes.

MANNER MAKYTH MAN

The one aspect of the big reshuffle Balfour had to undertake with which the King could not bring himself to agree was the proposed replacement for Brodrick, whom Balfour wanted to leave the War Office to become India Secretary. The King, for all his earlier differences with Brodrick, at least believed he had the weight and the experience to see through the badly needed reforms of the army. He had hoped that Aretas Akers-Douglas, the Home Secretary and one of whom the King had a high opinion, would inherit the post; but Akers-Douglas asked to stay where he was, and Balfour did not have the luxury of being able to give him an ultimatum. Then both the King and Balfour tried to persuade Esher (who had once sat as a Liberal in the Commons) to take the post, but Esher, who preferred his career as an intriguer and who was being heavily bankrolled – £5,000 a year plus various commissions – by Sir Ernest Cassel, refused in a way that he admitted was 'purely selfish'.[249] 'It is not in my line to go back into politics and become identified with party strife,' he told his son on 21 September 1903, hours after the King – not, note, Balfour – had asked him to become one of his ministers.[250]

When finally refusing the post, in a letter of 25 September, the throne-struck Esher came dangerously close to revealing his true motivations. 'We are too intimate', he told the Prime Minister, whom he had known for years, 'for us to depart one iota from perfect frankness, and I know that as Sec of State I should fail in the double capacity as a servant of the King and as your colleague.'[251] As Esher saw it there were two governments in the country, one operating from Whitehall and Westminster and the other from the court. Sometimes – most of the time – they were on the same side. At others, they were in conflict. In that conflict, Esher knew which side he wanted to be on. It was the side on which the favour and patronage of one man – one easily influenced, at least by Esher – counted for everything, and not the side where the will of an electorate, and time and chance, dictated the terms. This was the basis of all the advice that he gave the King, and upon which the King was so abnormally reliant.

So the post went instead to the Secretary of the Admiralty, Hugh Arnold-Forster. The King instinctively felt that this was an over-promotion – he told Balfour he would accept the minister as Under-Secretary – and he had personal, or rather social, objections to Arnold-Forster too. Austen Chamberlain, who was a friend and admirer of Arnold-Forster's, noted that 'his great failing was his inability ever to see another man's case or to get into another man's mind. He was so full of his own ideas that he scarcely listened to what others had to say or, if he listened, failed to understand it.'[252] This self-absorption was to turn out to be a substantial problem, given how many ideas of his own the King had about the army. However, Balfour went strongly in to bat for his nominee: 'Mr Balfour does not underestimate the force of the criticism urged by Your Majesty; it is undoubtedly true that Mr Forster's manner is not his strong point. But though he wants manner he does not want tact; as is proved by the regard in which he is held in the House of Commons.'[253] The King claimed he had repeatedly told Balfour of his objections to Arnold-Forster, and that Balfour had concurred with them: 'the King therefore sees no reason why he should change his mind now'.[254]

Sir Luke Fildes' portrait of King Edward VII in his Coronation robes

Lord Esher in characteristic pose

Lord Knollys: his master's voice

Sir Charles (later Lord) Hardinge: when the King was not
his own Foreign Secretary, Hardinge usually was.

The King was not convinced that Arnold-Forster was a reformed character, and, prompted as usual by Esher, asked Balfour to consider Lord Selborne instead. However, when Selborne then threw his weight behind Arnold-Forster, the King had no choice but to back down – not least after a pained reply from Balfour about his 'plain duty to Your Majesty to give the best advice he [Balfour] can under circumstances of considerable difficulty', and expressing his 'dismay' at the King's views on Arnold-Forster.[255] The King sent back a sharp note, effectively asking Balfour what right he had to be dismayed, when the King thought he had agreed with him all along about the proposed minister.[256] The King had also observed, with apparent amusement, how the press had, for some reason, started to canvass Arnold-Forster's name as War Secretary, adding to the pressure to appoint him: he appears to have suspected Balfour of leaking.[257] When the King gave up the fight, the Prime Minister wrote to him promising that although 'manner may be a real and serious obstacle to success', he was sure Arnold-Forster would succeed.[258] As an insurance policy, Balfour wrote to Knollys to implore him to 'do everything you can to make Arnold-Forster's difficult job easy. He suffers from serious faults of manner, but *really* has in him the making of a first-rate public servant.'[259] This last claim was, though the King would scarcely recognise it, completely true.

The King probably did not know that Esher, with typical arrogance, had advised Brodrick to leave the War Office earlier in the year, since he would not win the argument Esher was hoping to arrange for the King to have with him about the abolition of the post of Commander-in-Chief – of the efficacy of which Esher had by then persuaded both the King and Balfour.[260] Esher had lobbied the King in memoranda and in conversation for some months about this aspect of army reform. In presenting his own minority report at the conclusion of the deliberations of the Committee into the Boer War, he had argued that the commandership-in-chief embodied such inflexibilities that it had been one of the causes of British military unfitness for that war. However, as the King had privately been urging Esher on throughout the year, advising him of the importance of building a climate of radical intentions for when army reform came to be broached, he was hardly likely to dissent from any move that might have taken an important obstacle or two out of the way. The following year, as a sweetener, the King was glad to assent to the offer of the GCB for Brodrick.[261] Brodrick refused, but hinted in refusing that he would be glad if his family's peerage, the viscounty of Midleton, were raised to an earldom.[262] It was: in 1920, thirteen years after Brodrick had succeeded to it.

Milner refused the post of Colonial Secretary, which prompted the King to tell Balfour that he was 'extremely sorry', and to express the view that he 'does not think he ought to have done so'.[263] Later on, the King expanded on his reasoning, and the doctrine was clear: 'when a public servant of the Crown is asked by the Prime Minister to undertake a duty which the latter considers him well qualified to fit, it is in the King's opinion decidedly wrong of him to decline it, especially at a moment when it is so very difficult to fill adequately the different offices vacated by four Cabinet ministers – the King will not forget it now, nor in the future.'[264] Balfour's suggested replacement was Alfred Lyttelton, a gifted Liberal Unionist (and even more celebrated amateur batsman) who had won praise for his ability while sitting on an important commission into South African affairs. However the King urged, instead, the appointment of Lord Onslow, a former deputy of Chamberlain's. Of Lyttelton, he asked Balfour: 'what real experience has he? and will he give strength to the Government? At the same time the King will not object if Mr Balfour has quite made up his mind on the subject.'[265] Balfour had.

Although he had lost the Arnold-Forster battle, the King was to have some opportunities, arising out of Balfour's weakness, to assert some serious influence. He and Esher had been closeted together for several days at Balmoral in late September, discussing army reform but also devising ideas of ministerial movements for the King to suggest to his Prime Minister. When, on 3 October, just as he thought he had stopped the rot in his party, Balfour then lost Devonshire too, he was told straight by the King that 'this will greatly weaken the Government'.[266] The King told Balfour too that he would be wise to make Londonderry Lord President in the Duke's place, and that Sir William Anson, the Parliamentary Secretary to the Board of Education, should replace Londonderry. Balfour agreed to Londonderry's promotion after the King had rejected the appointment of Lord Salisbury, who had just succeeded his father as 4th Marquess, and was Balfour's cousin. Balfour did not want to move Londonderry from Education, but he concurred in the King's view that to appoint Salisbury, irrespective of his merits, would once more raise charges of the 'Hotel Cecil' – the abusive nickname given to Salisbury's 1886 administration, on account of the number of relations he included in it – at a time when the government had enough problems as it was.[267] It was hard on Salisbury, who in a thin year was an outstanding candidate; and Balfour hoped, later on, that the King would agree to his being appointed to a Cabinet post. For the moment, he had to be content with being Lord Privy Seal outside the Cabinet, though the King thought this a little provocative too, and was surprised when Balfour presented him with 'un fait accompli'.[268] So Londonderry it was. One interesting by-product of Londonderry's appointment was that the King, on 19 October 1903, held a meeting of the Privy Council at his house, Wynyard, late in the evening, at which his host's appointment was declared. It was the first time a Council had been held in a country house belonging to a subject since 1625, when Charles I had held one at Wilton.

In an attempt to try to heal the breach in his party, Balfour suggested to the King in November 1903 that Chamberlain, whose initiative had caused it, would be an ideal candidate for the vacant lord wardenship of the Cinque Ports. Knollys wrote back that while the King 'has a great regard for Mr Chamberlain, and ... a high admiration for many points in his character' he was unable to support the suggestion.[269] Given the recent strife, it was not, the King felt, a 'judicious moment' to appoint Chamberlain to such a post. 'He is conducting', the Monarch felt, 'a heated political campaign in furtherance of a policy which has excited great animosity among a large portion of the community.' Instead, at the King's personal initiative, the post went to Curzon, who was just returning home on a two-month leave of absence from India, where he had agreed to extend his five-year term as Viceroy by another two years.

SOLDIERS OF THE KING

When at last a committee came to be established on army reform in the autumn of 1903, the King was fully consulted on its composition and kept informed of its progress. He had urged Balfour on to the extent of telling him, on his return from Marienbad that autumn, that it would be impossible for him to meet Parliament again without having a scheme for reform.[270] Balfour, quite weakened enough as it was and wishing to have no further fronts on which to have to fight, took no chances. Two of his friends, Esher and Admiral Sir 'Jackie'

Fisher, were appointed to the three-man committee, Esher (at his own suggestion to Balfour) as chairman: the committee had been his suggestion too, springing not least from the great public interest in the inquiry into the South African war, on which he had also sat. He saw it as one of the great bonuses of his not having accepted the offer of the War Office – he told his younger son on his appointment that 'now I think I shall be able to carry through my scheme, whereas as Sec of State I doubt if I should have done so. It is the old story – Power and Place are not often synonymous.'[271] Esher had sent the King an extensive memorandum the previous March on what should be done.[272] The King had agreed: Esher's task was now to ensure that the committee did too, and was made easier by the small size of it.

The King's main concern about the army at this time was that, while men were being trained properly, the officers to run them were not. There were also reservations about the role and function of the War Office. Ironically, Arnold-Forster, the King's *bête noire*, was as keen on reform as his Sovereign was. The King was insistent that the committee should answer to the Prime Minister, not to the Secretary for War, who had a vested interest, since part of the deliberations would be concerned with the interplay of civil and military authority. Similarly, the King requested that Arnold-Forster be not a member of the committee, but have a right to attend its deliberations whenever he wanted. As constituted, the committee was thus more powerful than the government, and more powerful largely as a result of the King's determination to dictate its terms.

The appointment to it of a representative from the army proved troublesome, as all suitable men were engaged in important commands; and on 23 October 1903 Balfour had to write to the King, who was impatient for the committee to get under way, to apologise for the 'hitches' that had held its progress up because of the difficulty of finding a senior soldier who was not 'strongly identified with any particular military clique, nor with the existing War Office administration'.[273] He asked the King to approve, however, the appointment of Lord Grenfell, who had one such important command, as otherwise the committee would founder. However, Grenfell said he could not accept the post, as he would have difficulties as a soldier on full pay serving under officers whose posts he would have a hand in abolishing. The King, who had secured a peerage for Grenfell in the Coronation honours just a year earlier, was livid, and retailed his public service doctrine again: 'when the Prime Minister desires a senior Officer of the

Army to assist the Government, the request should be complied with.'[274] However, once Grenfell had an audience of the King and explained his difficulties the King understood, and did not press the point further. Lord Roberts was suggested but 'the King would not hear' of him, according to Knollys, because he felt Roberts would not be objective about the abolition of the commandership-in-chief.[275] The result was that Colonel Sir George Sydenham Clarke, the Governor of Victoria, was brought all the way home from Australia to become the third man.

The committee's composition and remit were publicly announced on 7 November 1903. As its deliberations proceeded, and the Prime Minister realised the radical nature of its likely recommendations, he sent a memorandum to the King on 28 January 1904 suggesting that the name of the War Office should be changed to reflect the fresh start that would occur in British military arrangements after the Esher committee had reported. The King would not hear of it, ordering the retention of the name that had pertained since the mid-nineteenth century, since the country was used to the term and knew what it meant.[276] The same day he received a full account from Balfour of the changes proposed by the committee, and the next day sent the Prime Minister a detailed reply.[277]

The speed of his response was attributable to the fact that the King already knew well what was planned before his Prime Minister told him formally. He had been in receipt throughout the process of backdoor briefings from Esher either directly – the flow of informative and devotional letters remained regular – or via Knollys. Esher also kept the King informed about Cabinet reaction to such proposals as had been confided to them. It was no surprise, therefore, that the King approved the radical changes – the establishment of a Cabinet defence committee and of an Army Council modelled on the Board of Admiralty, and the abolition of the post of Commander-in-Chief, with appropriate decentralisation. The Army Council would answer to Parliament, removing the previous conflict and struggle for supremacy between the Secretary for War and the Commander-in-Chief. The King, welcoming the report when it was presented at the end of February 1904, urged the government to approve it before Parliament met to discuss it – which it did.[278]

Many in the military were horrified by the suggestions, not least Kitchener; but the brio and speed with which Esher was able to force the changes through demonstrated the terrible weakness of the government in general and Balfour in particular, a weakness upon which the King had been allowed to capitalise. The King was so pleased with the committee's work that he urged Balfour to agree to honours for the three men concerned. Balfour refused, saying that the work had been accomplished in far less time than that taken by the average Royal Commission, whose members were not normally so rewarded – which rather ignored the fact that Esher had spent months before the formal constitution of the committee planning the new shape of the army, and consulting with the King about it. To give these men an honour would, Balfour said, set an 'extremely embarrassing' precedent.[279] He clinched the matter by telling the King he was sure that Esher (who habitually turned almost everything down, so Balfour was on safe ground) would agree. One might also note that by not honouring the committee the government was not drawing additional attention to a long-overdue job that its ministers had been incapable of doing themselves.

The wider implementation of the reforms, especially those concerning decentralisation, helped renew the conflict between the King and Arnold-Forster. There had been hopes, earnestly shared on both sides, that the two men would, after all, get on. On 24 January 1904, a few months after Arnold-Forster's appointment, Knollys had written to Balfour that 'the King said to me this evening that he found he had made a mistake about Mr Arnold Forster and that the more he saw him the better he liked him. Could not Mr A Forster have a hint given him that he had made a favourable impression, as he is I believe a sensitive man.'[280] The King had come to this new estimate of his minister after 'two long talks'; it seems to have been a rushed judgment. Some remarks Arnold-Forster made about Esher's report when it was published, to the effect that it was a censure on some parts of the civil service, gravely annoyed Esher. He proceeded to make his displeasure known to Balfour, and to the King by sending him a copy of his complaint to the Prime Minister.[281] It was downhill for Arnold-Forster from then on.

As the implementation of the reforms went through the King felt he was not being consulted about the detail. He had Knollys write to the Secretary for War on 22 October 1904 to ask, in the first instance, that minutes of Army Council meetings should be sent to him routinely, as was done with the minutes of the Cabinet's defence committee. Knollys added that the King:

is a little sorry to find that he has not been in any way consulted on the questions of the best mode of promulgating decentralisation and of the General Staff Scheme, both of which he believes are now practically settled.... during the late Queen's reign not a step was taken at the WO in connection with the Army of the slightest importance without her being informed of what was going on, and the King hopes the same course will be pursued with him.[282]

Arnold-Forster tried to defend himself, saying he had gone to lengths to keep the King informed, and would 'consider it a privilege to be permitted at any time to give him further detailed information on any point...': no failure of 'manner' there.[283] When the Army Order was finally submitted to the Head of the Army – the King – the King suspected that the Order was more or less in its final form, and he wanted to know why he had not seen it earlier. Once he had read it, a huge traffic ensued between the King and Arnold-Forster, who felt obliged to answer each of the King's points thoroughly, and to turn down (to the King's chagrin) some of his suggestions. One such was the King's hope that, in order to encourage the recruitment of more young officers, the minimum entry age to the Guards should be set at eighteen. Arnold-Forster was loath to drop it below nineteen, for the very good reason that even a reduction to eighteen and a half would 'practically preclude the entry of any candidates for the Guards through Sandhurst'. The King took this in bad grace: Knollys wrote a one-sentence letter of reply to Arnold-Forster in which he said that 'the King desires me to say that he will give way on the age question, but that he does so reluctantly'.[284]

Simultaneously, another matter was starting to come between the King and his minister, though it was one that seems to exemplify how Arnold-Forster was used as a lightning conductor by Knollys. Knollys wrote to Balfour on 21 October 1904 to say that 'a little cloud is gradually arising between the King and Mr Arnold Forster'.[285] It was because the War Secretary, and Brodrick, wished to recall a senior soldier, Sir Ian Hamilton, from Japan (where he was monitoring the Russo-Japanese War) to take up the command of Southern District at Salisbury. The King wanted Hamilton kept where he was and wanted a friend of his, General Kelly-Kenny, given the post instead. Kelly-Kenny, as Knollys agreed, was unpopular in the army – there was 'dislike and distrust of him in certain quarters' – but that was not the whole point. Arnold-Forster had told the King that there were other officers who could perfectly well do Hamilton's job in Japan, and Brodrick had already telegraphed to him telling him to come home. 'This I have not repeated to the King,' Knollys revealed, 'as it wd set him against Brodrick.' Arnold-Forster could do that job for both of them. 'The King is beginning to feel very sore on the subject,' he continued, imploring the Prime Minister: 'Can you privately intervene?' The argument dragged on for months, with the King losing. The following April, just as Hamilton was due to embark, the war between Russia and Japan entered its decisive phase, and Knollys asked Balfour to reconsider the logic of the posting 'when a fresh campaign is commencing'.[286] Still Balfour was not moved. Normally the King took the loss of a battle manfully. Any battle lost to Arnold-Forster was a notable exception.

Knollys continued to receive pacific sentiments from Balfour about Arnold-Forster. He had, however, come to share his master's opinion of the man. He wrote to Sandars on 9 November to say that 'A Forster will assure you, as he invariably does me, that his only object in life is to meet the King's wishes, and he will not admit that he has not done so on any occasion.'[287] When, that month, another memorandum on decentralisation was sent by the War Secretary to the King, the King sent it back with criticisms in almost every particular, saying that the plans served neither to implement the Esher proposals nor to maintain a 'striking force' and making the general observation that he 'regrets' not having seen it earlier.[288] Reasoning that these serial acts of provocation were getting nowhere, Arnold-Forster did his best to tolerate the King's truculence, which was now bordering upon caricature and was less than ever rooted in intellectual considerations. A new memorandum was sent, which Knollys applauded with the observation: 'AF's tone is good and he has appeared anxious to meet the King's wishes as much as possible.'[289]

As always, Esher was on hand to give an already turbulent mixture an unhealthy stir. He was especially quick to point out to Knollys when anything of remote significance had been done in the army without being brought to the King's attention. To justify this, he sent a memorandum to the King on 16 November 1904 that began: 'It was the universal practice of Ministers from 1837 to the end of the Queen's life to lay before the Sovereign all proposals for important administrative changes; and suggested nominations for important posts, before formal submission.'[290] More to the point, Esher said there were 'volumes' of letters to the Queen on these subjects simply canvassing her opinion, long before matters reached the stage of formal submission. This consultation was useful, because 'over and over again the Minister gave way to the arguments used by The Queen.' The message to the King was clear: he had a perfect constitutional right not just to superintend the smallest details of what Arnold-Forster was doing, but to have him do it according to the King's wishes.

The next bout of hostilities between King and minister came when Arnold-Forster tried to respond to the call from the Treasury for economies, at the same time as addressing the problem that the system of enlistment was virtually breaking down, with an especial shortage of young officers. By suggesting two different sorts of service – a general service army where men enlisted for nine years followed by three on the reserve, and a home army of six years' service and two years' reserve – he hoped to solve the problems of enlistment and of the decline of the militia. The King, however, was not satisfied. On the one hand, he wanted a period in the army 'free from disturbance and constant change'. On the other he would have liked more radical measures, after a consultation 'with the most eminent soldiers here and in India'.[291] He viewed 'with regret' the present 'half-measures', and could not see the need for them. Conscious of the constitutional proprieties, he said that 'the King cannot withhold his consent from the proposals which he is advised by the Cabinet to approve, but he cannot conceal his strong misgiving as to the effect which the announcement will have upon the Army'.[292] Balfour, however, reported to the King on 12 November 1904 that 'recruiting appears to be extraordinarily brisk and, at present, there is no difficulty in securing men for nine years' service'.[293]

On 30 December 1904 the King wrote to Balfour from Sandringham conceding that 'to make the Army really efficient and at the same time to keep the estimates down appears to be a task which it is almost impossible for any Government to carry out. Unfortunately, Mr A Forster's Army scheme, at which he had been working for a year, has been abandoned owing to his military advisers having proved to him that it was not practicable owing to its great expense – which this Cabinet agreed. What is to be put in its place? What will satisfy the country when the matter is discussed in Parliament?'[294] Meanwhile, the King was enlisting Esher more and more in his tussles with his elected minister, and Esher seemed to sense that this was not wholly proper constitutionally. Discussing with Knollys an army order with which the King was not happy, Esher noted that 'I gave A.F. a chance of speaking to me about this Army Order, of which he did not avail himself. I could not betray the King's confidence by assuming knowledge of the documents.'[295] The War Secretary would have had every right to be irritated by Esher's interference, and plainly was: Esher complains to Knollys that 'as the Prime Minister admitted to you, A.F. takes every criticism to be either opposition or personal affront'. During the Ian Hamilton affair, Knollys had observed to Esher that 'what makes it difficult to give even a hint to A-Forster is that he always takes up the "hurt line"'.[296]

Writing to the King on 2 February 1905, when Parliament was still in recess, Balfour had to admit that 'he is not at all satisfied with the present position of Mr A-Forster's army scheme.'[297] He had decided to take the drastic action of appointing a sub-committee of the defence committee to investigate what could be done, on which he himself, and Lord Roberts, would serve. Esher was also investigating the matter; the sub-committee had, as usual, been his idea, suggested to the King at Christmas 1904.[298] The King had been 'all in favour' of it.[299] As soon as he knew of the Sovereign's interest, Esher promptly set out the proposed details to Sandars, for Balfour's attention, in a letter of 6 January. It will not have surprised anyone concerned that Esher's own name was on the suggested list of members.[300] Balfour, although initially objecting strongly, had no choice but to agree. Predictably, given the embarrassment Balfour was in, the Prime Minister added a footnote to his memorandum to the King in which he said: 'Mr Balfour has respectfully to add that he is very anxious, at least at present, that the existence of this informal committee should be kept very secret.' The King replied that he 'highly approves' of the plan, 'and though he is glad that Mr Forster gives his full consent, he is much surprised that the latter does so, as it is virtually putting his important office "into commission"'.[301] In other words, the King might have thought he had picked up the scent of Arnold-Forster's being forced to resign because of the snub dealt to him. The committee sat more or less continuously for several weeks, Esher once more supplying the King with lavish accounts of its deliberations.

There were various other matters that strained the relationship between the King and Arnold-Forster, not least his suggestion that there should be an army journal in which officers could raise their own plans for reform. The King, who strongly believed in the traditions of the silent service, was appalled, and gratified when the publication folded after a little more than a year. However, in 1905 two more serious issues almost ended the King's patience with the man whose appointment he had never wanted. The first was a new set of army pay scales, sent to the King in July 1905 without any warning, which represented worse terms and conditions of service for some officers than they had had before. The King wanted an assurance that no officer would be worse off, and when he received what he regarded as an ambiguous reply, he had Sir Arthur Davidson, his assistant private secretary, send a note of supreme stiffness: 'Put into plain English, the matter stands thus: The King will not sign the new Royal Warrant for Pay and Promotion, etc, until he knows whether it reduces the pay and allowances of those who serve under its provisions.'[302] The minister had not clarified to the King's satisfaction whether new entrants to the army would be worse off than they would have been under the old ordinances. Still no clear information was forthcoming, so still the King would not sign. This provoked a complaint from Arnold-Forster that the King by his delay was causing severe difficulties for the War Office; but the delay went on for a few more weeks still, until the assurances the King wanted were received, which meant the Treasury backing down, and a fundamental reversal of policy against the 'advice' to the King of his ministers.

The second, simultaneous affront to the King was caused by Arnold-Forster's sending another warrant for signing to him, this time affecting General Officers Commanding Districts and Accountants, through his civil service private secretary. It was accompanied by a request to sign it urgently, which the King did; but he had Knollys write at once to Balfour, claiming that the King 'thinks that he had a right to receive an explanation written by the Secretary of State for War himself' since the matter of principle had been considered by the Esher committee and was vital to decentralisation. The King said that this was 'not the form which communications between the King and his ministers should take'.[303] The incident provided a further opportunity for Esher to cause trouble. Shown the documents by Knollys, he reported back that Sandars, on Balfour's behalf, had been 'shocked' by the approach made by the private secretary, 'a person of whom His Majesty has no cognisance whatever'.[304] Esher pronounced semi-regally that 'such a proceeding is derogatory to the Sovereign, and a distinct lack of duty on the part of the Minister'.

Esher said that, of course, the King would have wanted to talk to Balfour about this, and Knollys duly took his cue. He claimed, in a letter to Balfour, that the King would have wanted to consult both

Balfour and the Chancellor about the warrant, but had been left with no time to do so. 'The King hopes', he continued, 'that you will kindly make such arrangements with Mr Arnold-Forster as will in future prevent these informal communications on most important subjects being laid before him without the constitutional advice on which the King has a right to rely, and without time being afforded him for conversation with his Prime Minister.'

Arnold-Forster apologised prostrately, saying that his being detained in the Commons had led to the matter being delegated. It was not a masterpiece of tact, and the King would probably have upbraided any minister who had treated him so casually; but in the case of Arnold-Forster he was by this stage apparently searching for faults, and rebuking them with especial sternness. Balfour was sufficiently embarrassed to tell the King that, if Esher would replace Arnold-Forster, he would sack his War Secretary. Esher, breaking the habit of half a lifetime, had been dropping hints that he was, after all, prepared to serve in this capacity. He had told his son in July 1905 that there was about to be a 'War Office crisis' that would spell the end of Arnold-Forster. 'Then,' Esher had added, 'the question will arise whether I shall take his place or not. I am rather inclined to do so.'[305] The King, who also picked up these vibrations, was delighted. 'I am glad', he wrote to Knollys on 18 August 1905, 'that A. Balfour at last sees the necessity of getting rid of A-F, and that Esher is willing (at last) to succeed him.'[306] However, it turned out that Esher was not willing: not the least of his many female characteristics was the prerogative of changing his mind, and he did. He told Knollys on 6 September that he did not believe Balfour would sack Arnold-Forster, because of the embarrassments this would cause at a difficult time for the government. Nor, he felt, would the minister resign, for that would mean 'an end to his political career: and he is eaten up with ambition'.[307] The old bitch, not for the first time, underestimated Arnold-Forster's over-developed sense of public duty (to which his career pays ample testimony), confusing it, perhaps, with some of his own motives. In any case, the government was doomed. The King would have to tolerate Arnold-Forster for a few more weeks only.

The apparent entertainment the King derived from his regular exchanges with Balfour about the honours system seems almost to have been necessary light relief from the grimmer matters of high policy with which that administration became nearly exclusively concerned. When in July 1904 he suggested baronetcies for the Lord Mayors of Liverpool and Birmingham, Balfour delivered a philosophical exegesis on the problems of bestowing hereditary honours, 'which always present difficulties when perhaps little is known of those in succession to the title'.[308] Balfour said that to make these awards would risk lowering the value of hereditary honours, and that the award of such honours, already fraught with difficulties, would become yet more complicated 'if the mayors of certain great cities were to expect such marks of distinction'. It was yet another sign of the Prime Minister being far grander by inclination than the King, whose willingness to kick aside class barriers in these matters had already been amply demonstrated at the time of his Coronation. The Lord Mayor of London by custom had a baronetcy, but was always drawn from that class of wealthy financier who could, in the Prime Minister's view, naturally support such a distinction. Balfour feared that if these two Lord Mayors received such an accolade, the Lord Mayors of the five other cities entitled to appoint one would also expect it. Balfour said, as he often did, that he would abide by the King's wishes in the matter. However, having read the arguments, the King scribbled 'I agree' on the top of the letter, and the two Lord Mayors had to be content with knighthoods.

Sandars wrote to Knollys on 18 March 1905 to ask him to confirm that the King was against special remainders – the means by which others than heirs male of a peer, such as his daughter or his brother, could succeed to the title – except in the case of certain military peerages and other cases of exceptional national service. 'I have mentioned', Sandars wrote, 'that such is the case in the course of a conversation I have had with a supplicant; but it will strengthen my hand if I have your authority.'[309] Knollys obliged the next day, writing that 'on no account could he [the King] agree to such a remainder except in the case of a very distinguished soldier or sailor, or of a civilian who has performed eminent services to his country. HM has a strong dislike to these remainders which he thinks have been too lavishly given of late years.'[310] Nor was this the only peerage question in which the King was determined to display his ultra-conservatism. Balfour wrote to him on 1 December 1905 arguing for the creation of life peerages for civil servants, a group first honoured by Gladstone. He cited the precedent of Law Lords, the only group for which there were such creations.[311] The King, ever conscious of his own dependence upon the hereditary principle, turned the idea down.[312]

CONSERVATIVE DECLINE

In the two years between the ructions over tariff reform and the final collapse of the Balfour administration, the King progressively lost patience with his government. In December 1904, when Balfour asked for a postponement of the new year's honours until the following June, the King commented: 'Will the present government then be in office?'[313] It was, but only just. It lost a vote in the Commons on the working of the Irish Land Purchase Act, after which Balfour refused either to resign or to ask for a dissolution. The King, after summoning Balfour for a discussion, supported him in this. He had been told by Esher, now established as the ultimate authority on these matters, that Balfour had done nothing unconstitutional, citing a precedent of Gladstone's staying in office after two defeats in the same week in 1872; but Balfour was vehemently attacked in the Commons by the Liberals and the Irish Nationalists for unconstitutional behaviour.[314] No further vote was taken on the issue, but the variance between the Prime Minister's actions and the letter of the constitution became a matter of acute concern to the King, despite Esher's assurances.

Up until the prorogation of Parliament on 11 August 1905, for a recess scheduled to last until the following February, the Opposition continued to maintain that the government had lost the confidence of the country, and that Balfour should ask the King for a dissolution. Balfour said one defeat was not conclusive, and that so long as the government maintained the confidence of the House of Commons, it could stay in office. This doctrine, commonplace within thirty years, caused further anxiety to the King, for it seemed that Balfour was challenging his prerogative of dissolution, and instead placing it with the majority in the House of Commons. Not only was the King distressed to be told he counted for nothing in this hitherto important respect, he was annoyed that Balfour had expressed this belief in the very public forum of the House of Commons. In a reply of 2 September to a letter in which the King raised these points, Balfour was not to be swayed.

The King had been upset by a report in 'an intelligently conducted paper like the *Spectator*' that Balfour had 'laid down an entirely novel view of the Constitution'.[315] Sandars, his secretary, writing to Knollys on 2 September, repudiated the construction the *Spectator* had put on Balfour's words, and added that in not resigning after a single defeat he was merely following precedents set by various nineteenth-century

Prime Ministers from Pitt to Palmerston. It was not, he argued, remotely 'novel' to act as Balfour had: 'it is the House of Commons deciding the initial step whether the Government is to continue or whether the Prime Minister must repair to the King, and either ask to be relieved of his office or propose to His Majesty the dissolution of Parliament'.[316] Sandars blamed John St Loe Strachey, the editor and proprietor of the *Spectator*, 'whose personal abuse of Mr Balfour is notorious'.

The abused Balfour had little further to go, however. The Conservative party conference in November 1905 ignored an appeal by him for unity. Soon afterwards the Prime Minister told the King that he wished to resign. The King wanted him to meet Parliament – not least in light of the doctrine Balfour himself had recently outlined. Chamberlain then joined the attack on Balfour, censuring him for his indecision and evasiveness, which brought the press down hard on Balfour too. As usual, Balfour was unsure what to do, and unsure even after a meeting of the Cabinet to discuss the possibilities, for the Cabinet was divided, and Balfour was not prepared to break the habit of a lifetime and overcome his sense of doubt. On 16 November, the day before Balfour had an audience of the King to review the situation, he had a long discussion with Sandars about it. Since by a happy chance he was visiting Sandars at the time, Esher was present. The three men tried to clarify the options; the question was not whether there would be a resignation of the government, but when.

'There were two courses,' Esher recorded in his journal; '(a) To resign in the middle of December. (b) To call Parliament early together, i.e., Jan '06, and resign after the first bad division.'[317] Esher favoured the first course, 'as it forces the Opposition to show their hand'. However Balfour was unconvinced, and was uncommunicative to the King, who told Esher on 20 November that in his audiences with Balfour 'he could get nothing from him'.[318] Hearing this, Esher immediately saw Balfour, and persuaded him to talk the matter through with the King. This, though, still resolved nothing. Balfour wrote to the King on 24 November to reflect on the possibility of meeting Parliament as opposed to immediate resignation. 'He now inclines to take the resignation alternative,' Balfour wrote.[319] He explained that this would give the party that won the election an uninterrupted session. However, he was still waiting to judge whether the 'vigour and unity' of his own party, which he had sought to bolster in a big speech to activists, was equal to carrying through further legislation. 'A final judgment on this point cannot yet be arrived at; and Mr Balfour is carefully watching the trend of public opinion, and endeavouring to estimate the degree of success his appeal for unity at Newcastle is likely to meet with among his supporters. At present the success seems but moderate!' The letter ended with a familiarly ambiguous note: referring to the comparable strength of conflicting views, he said 'he may bring up the question again: or he may decide it on his own responsibility. No immediate steps need in either case to be taken.'

The King replied that 'as a Constitutional Sovereign it is naturally not for the King to give advice to his Prime Minister.... but he cannot help regretting that Mr Balfour should not have abandoned his idea of resignation and of his decision to meet Parliament'.[320] He said that with the press calling for Balfour's resignation, if he did resign the newspapers would take the credit for it; and nor did the King understand why a single speech by Chamberlain, whose following in the country was substantial, should change anything. He reiterated his view that Balfour should meet Parliament, and did not see any need to consider the convenience of the Opposition. At a Cabinet on 2 December, the government formally endorsed the decision to resign, though Balfour had told Esher on 28 November that, despite division in the Cabinet, that would be the course.[321] Balfour had also told Esher that the King did not want him to resign, so Esher had Knollys come to Downing Street – incognito, entering through the back door – to be persuaded. He was, and therefore so too was the King. It just remained for the King to approve Balfour's resignation honours.

The King had been concerned – a concern prevalent at the time, but harder to understand today – that the Liberal party would refuse to accept power, but would demand a dissolution and an election. He also wished Balfour to be spared any further embarrassment. The King saw no point in having an election two years before one was strictly necessary: if the Liberals could win a vote of confidence in the Commons, they could, in the prevailing constitutional view, continue to govern without an immediate appeal to the electorate. When the choice came down – and it was Balfour's choice – between requesting a dissolution immediately, at the end of November, or waiting until January, even that matter could not be decided unanimously by the Cabinet. The whole thing was becoming a farce, with many nominal Conservative MPs no longer supporting the party, but at last Balfour performed an act of leadership, and handed the reins over to Campbell-Bannerman, pending an election.

THE CURZON PROBLEM

The King had corresponded frequently with Lord Curzon, the Viceroy of India, ever since his accession, and had formed the highest opinion of Curzon's qualities in his post. However, after Curzon returned to India from his leave of absence early in 1904, he progressively fell out with the Balfour administration over the conduct of foreign policy affecting India. The flashpoint, though, was to be a power struggle between Curzon and Kitchener, the man whose appointment he had urged as Commander-in-Chief, over dual control of the army shared between Kitchener and the Viceroy. In May 1905 Brodrick, the Indian Secretary, briefed the King fully about the growing problem between the two men. He also informed the King that a committee of senior military men would be established to consider possible reforms, and they concluded that the Commander-in-Chief should have exclusive control of certain military sections of the administration. The King approved the changes; Curzon did not.

The Viceroy wrote to the King and to Knollys in June 1905 complaining about the changes, and offered to resign; the Cabinet refused to accept his resignation. Curzon continued to complain to Brodrick, and to make semi-public his views in India. His letters to Brodrick became militant, and the King expressed regret at Curzon's tone. On 25 July Brodrick told the King that the differences between the two men were irreconcilable, and on 13 August the King received Curzon's resignation. The Viceroy could not be dissuaded, and the decision was made public on 21 August. The King, in Marienbad, sent an immediate message to Curzon recognising his services, and although the King had not involved himself in the fight between his government and his Viceroy, he now decided that Curzon deserved proper recognition for his work.

On 1 September 1905, still in Marienbad, he had Ponsonby send a cypher telegram to Balfour: 'The King desires me to inform you he thinks the Viceroy of India should be offered an earldom and at once. He hopes, considering the Viceroy's character, such an offer made immediately might soothe his feelings.'[322] Balfour replied immediately:

I quite sympathise with the King's wish that as little soreness as possible should result as a consequence of recent events, but there are manifest difficulties in the course proposed – GC has resigned because he differed with the policy of the Government. Under the most favourable construction he cannot be said to have behaved well. To reward him now would be equivalent to a public intimation that the sure road to honours was disobedience to instructions.[323]

He said he was conscious of Curzon's immense services, but that 'he is young and may well wait until the time comes when an honour can be given him without implying approval of his proceedings during the last eight months. The sooner this time comes the better I shall be pleased.'

On 6 September Balfour wrote at greater length that the point that had to be determined was not whether 'some mark of His Majesty's favour' should be given to Curzon, but whether it should be given immediately.[324] Curzon's eligibility was, he wrote, 'unquestionable'. He repudiated the popular interpretation of the reasons why Curzon was going: he had been engaged for months in trying to implement a policy with which he did not agree, 'but which he declared himself ready to accept'. He argued that to give an honour immediately would suggest that Curzon had been right and Kitchener and Brodrick wrong. Balfour's opinion was, though, that 'Lord Curzon will be lauded by the impartial historian as among the greatest of the British Rulers of India.' It would be wise, he said, to have a postponement, 'but only so long as is absolutely necessary to obviate any understanding as to its significance'.

Knollys wrote to Sandars disagreeing, saying that opinion in India would be upset if Curzon were not honoured. Sandars challenged that; and Knollys, in his next letter on 9 September, conceded that there was 'something to be said on the other side'.[325] However, he pointed out that Curzon had resigned, not been recalled, that his 'brilliant services' deserved some reward, and that he should not be 'completely ignored'. Curzon had turned down the Grand Cross of the Order of the Bath in 1903, but Knollys said that he did not think that 'has anything to do with the question of an honour on his retirement in 1905'. He claimed he did not know what line the King would take, but added that 'if I were in his place I should fight the question stoutly'. In fact, Knollys and the King were both being egged on by Esher to get Curzon his earldom.[326]

When Sandars discussed the matter with the King the following week he found him keen to have Curzon honoured in the forthcoming birthday list, but said he noted the points made in Balfour's explanatory letter to Knollys. The King also warned Sandars about 'poor Curzon, with all his faults a great man – a popular man – but more – very likely a dangerous man if he is allowed to come home with no laurels on his brow'.[327] He was also apprehensive lest Curzon come home 'to seek election in some constituency with a view to laying his grievances before Parliament' – the peerage he had taken in 1898 before leaving for India had, at his insistence, been an Irish one, which did not debar him from the Commons.[328] The King summoned Brodrick and told him sternly that he expected right to be done by Curzon, and that he simply did not believe the propaganda that the India Secretary poured out against a man the King considered, with some justification, to have been a great Viceroy and public servant. At the King's request, Balfour continued to consider the matter, but he would not budge. Nor, for a time, would his successor, Campbell-Bannerman: it was 1911 before Curzon received the earldom the King wished for him, after the King was dead, and in the Coronation honours list of his son.

Balfour's line, in a letter to Knollys of 7 October 1905, was that 'George on his return home may think it right, in his own or in the public interest, to continue the late unhappy controversy in the press or on the platform. He may cross swords with Kitchener or denounce Brodrick and the Government.'[329] This was all straightforward: but Balfour, being Balfour, had to complicate matters with deep philosophical considerations too, arising as usual out of the perceived sensitivity of his own position. 'A further embarrassment arises', he continued, 'out of the fact that I cannot explain to George himself how matters stand. To do so would lay me open to the interpretation that I sought to close his mouth by the offer of a Peerage, and conceived him to be the kind of man to whom such a transaction would not be offensive.' For Balfour, the fundamental consideration was that, until he was sure the ex-Viceroy would not attack him, he could do nothing.

Knollys replied to this letter on 10 October saying that the King understood Balfour's problem, and that the King had himself written to Curzon three weeks earlier urging him not to wash any dirty linen in public, but had as yet had no reply. 'Though I deeply regret that you are unable to be in accord with the views expressed by my Government at home,' the King had told him, 'I cannot but hope that on your return you may consider it advisable in the interests of the

British Empire at large, and especially as regards India, not to enter into any further controversy regarding the different issues with my Government which compelled you to resign, as the effect would be very serious.'[330]

'George' in fact behaved like what the Edwardians used to call a white man, but the change of government in December 1905 complicated the matter further. By the time his good behaviour was manifest, it was no longer up to Balfour to rectify matters in accordance with the King's wishes. However, he told Knollys on 24 February 1906, from the safety of the wilderness as he had lost not just the premiership, but his seat, in the landslide defeat for his party the previous month, that 'bygones may be regarded as bygones, and certainly if this be the case, and I were in office, I should respectfully recommend George Curzon for an honour'.[331] Knollys had confidentially asked the Liberal statesman John Morley, both as a friend of the King's and as the new India Secretary, for his views on the subject. Morley replied on 16 February 1906 that he had discussed it with Campbell-Bannerman, who wished for 'a little time to consider his part in the matter'.[332] Morley did, though, make it clear to Knollys that 'it would be rather odd for a minister to recommend a rival for an honour, of which his own party and the authors of his Viceregal being, did not think him worthy'.

At the same time Esher (who had had a crush on Curzon when the ex-Viceroy had been in the sixth form at Eton) was sounding out Campbell-Bannerman, on the King's behalf, about the question, and Morley's information had given the right clue. The new Prime Minister would not reverse the decision taken by his opponent and predecessor. Esher urged him to explain this to Knollys, which he did in a letter of 1 March.[333] Knollys, though, had been forewarned of Sir Henry's view in a letter of 27 February from Morley.[334] Now, the Prime Minister wrote that Curzon's being 'an active political opponent' was only a small part of the problem. 'Lord Curzon resigned while his friends were in power, and resigned without receiving any sign of favour or approbation, which was frankly – I was about to say ostentatiously – withheld.... How could I explain my action if, many weeks afterwards, I advised the King to take a view of his career which Lord Curzon's friends had refused to take?'[335] Also, he noted that 'my political friends have not always viewed with sympathy the methods and actions of Lord Curzon'. Knollys sent back an acknowledgment of the problem, and registered the King's regret. But for now the matter was closed.[336] Knollys was furious, and complained privately to Esher: 'It is all very well Balfour saying he was quite willing to recommend Curzon for a peerage, but when; and why did he not take advantage of his last chance to do so when he left office?'[337] The King had found as early as his Coronation honours list that, for all his supposed status as the fountain of honour, if his ministers did not wish him to confer a peerage on someone, he could not confer it. Thus what had been true for Tommy Lipton and Ernest Cassel was to be true of the blue-blooded ex-Viceroy.

Curzon, meanwhile, was livid with Balfour for his vacillations, and confronted him with a copy of Campbell-Bannerman's letter explaining that as Balfour had not wished to act, he could not oblige either. Found out in his web of sophistry, Balfour at once had a fit of the vapours, writing to Knollys that Campbell-Bannerman 'has unintentionally quite misrepresented my attitude'.[338] However, it was not so simple as that: with Balfour, it never was. Nor was this to be the last or worst disservice he would do his friend George. In 1923, when Curzon and many in his party felt he must become Prime Minister in succession to the dying Bonar Law, it was Balfour who impressed upon King George the importance of keeping the job in the Commons, and giving it instead to the nonentity Stanley Baldwin.

ENTER THE LIBERALS

After Balfour's resignation in December 1905 the King had a vital constitutional duty to perform: resolving the question of for whom to send to try to form his government. Balfour had not asked for a dissolution – he had simply decided he could no longer command a majority in the Commons, and that the King's government would better be carried on by someone who perhaps could. His ulterior motive was to expose the divisions which existed in the Liberal party over Irish Home Rule, and which had caused Rosebery (despite the private and somewhat unconstitutional exhortations of the King) to refuse to come back to serve, thus handicapping the Liberals. The tactic did not work, as his party was shortly to be on the receiving end of a landslide approached in this century only by that of 1997. Sir Henry Campbell-Bannerman, who had served Gladstone and Rosebery as Irish Secretary and Secretary of State for War, had been acknowledged as Liberal leader in the Commons since 1899. After promising Asquith during 1905 that he would not introduce a Home Rule Bill if he became Prime Minister, he had looked able to unite the party.

When Balfour resigned the King had Esher brief him on the procedure followed by Queen Victoria in such circumstances, and the King followed it to the letter.[339] He appears, though, to have ignored some of the encouragement Esher gave him in the memorandum, such as 'the Queen frequently exercised a Veto upon the appointment of the Minister'. Esher had, as a sort of last vain hope, been to see Rosebery on 28 November at his country house, where he found the faded statesman 'in a state of great mental dejection' since he felt that Grey and Asquith were now acting independently of him – hardly surprising, Esher noted, since he had resolutely refused to enter into cabals with them.[340] Esher told the King that the support Rosebery's former friends now had for Campbell-Bannerman constituted 'an understanding which cannot fail to have much influence on the formation of Your Majesty's next Government'.

Therefore, Knollys wrote to Campbell-Bannerman on the afternoon of 4 December inviting him to come to see the King the next morning.[341] Campbell-Bannerman duly came to the Palace and kissed hands as Prime Minister – under an arrangement made during Balfour's term of office at the suggestion of the then Prime Minister, the new First Lord of the Treasury was the first to be accorded formal precedence as Prime Minister, ending an ancient anomaly. In fact, 'kissed hands' was purely a metaphorical statement, because in the course of an involved and friendly discussion the new Prime Minister had no chance to perform that ceremony. Knollys, ever practical, assured him it did not matter, and that it would be recorded in the Court Circular that he had.

The King was quite happy at the change of government, and not just because he had had enough of the squabbling and incompetent Conservatives. Early in 1905, Carrington, long a friend of the King's, had written to Campbell-Bannerman to tell him that 'the King looks on a Liberal Govt. with serenity'.[342] In June that year Carrington had given a dinner-party at which the King met the Leader of the Opposition; the King had never quite forgotten the 'methods of barbarism' attack during the Boer War, but found Campbell-Bannerman deeply agreeable, the conversation continuing until one in the morning. Carrington impressed on the King that 'if we come in Sir

Henry will make your Majesty a first-rate prime minister'.[343] At Marienbad that summer the King at times monopolised Campbell-Bannerman, dining with him more or less daily for a fortnight, telling him that he 'must soon be in office and very high office'.[344] He said nothing of the government, except that he was 'free in denouncing much that they do'.

The only difficulty about Campbell-Bannerman's appointment was that three of his most senior and gifted colleagues – the former Home Secretary H. H. Asquith, Sir Edward Grey and R. B. Haldane – were keen for him to go to the Lords, leaving Asquith to lead in the Commons. Campbell-Bannerman's doctor joined the lobby, telling his patient that his health would not stand being both Leader of the Commons and Prime Minister. (The doctor was right: Campbell-Bannerman was dead a little over two years later.) The new Prime Minister was, however, resolute, even when the King, on appointing him, made polite enquiries about Sir Henry's own views on the matter. He mentioned that neither he nor his Prime Minister (who was five years older than the King) was a young man any more. The King was wise in the ways of ministerial life and its pressures. He once told one of his ministers 'that what broke men down was not the work of their offices, but big dinners, late hours, and casual speechifying after the office work of the day was over'.[345]

The triumvirate of Sir Henry's colleagues had hatched their plot at Relugas in Scotland the previous summer, where Grey had been on holiday fishing. It fell to Haldane, who was on good terms with the King, to tell him of their deliberations, and of the stipulation in the 'Relugas Compact' that if Sir Henry did not listen to them they would not serve under him. Haldane's work for London University and the Imperial Institute had been noticed by the then Prince of Wales in the late 1890s. He had been taken up by the Prince from then on. He was a brilliant polymath, a Germanophile and a fine conversationalist, all of which made him good company in the King's estimation. He broke the news to the King via Knollys, his fellow Liberal, to whom he had written on 12 September 1905, and with whom he had had a preliminary discussion of the problem the previous July: it never seems to have occurred to him that such an act was not just improper, but absurd. He did have some finer feeling about it. He notes in his *Autobiography* that 'the only thing that made us pause over our decision was whether it could in any way embarrass the King' – though Haldane, having given the matter some thought, decided it could not.[346] Also, in writing to Knollys now, Haldane took as his cue a remark Knollys had made to him when they had last spoken, asking him 'to let you know if any new development took place in the situation of the Opposition'.[347] This gave him his excuse.

Haldane's letter outlined the plans the senior Liberals had made for themselves – 'what we would try to bring about is that, if the situation arises and Sir H.C.B. is sent for, he should propose to the King the leadership of the House of Commons with the Exchequer for Asquith, either the Foreign or Colonial Office for Grey, and the Woolsack for myself.' Lest that last remark look too appalling, Haldane added that 'I am merely recording for you the wish of others.' What will have attracted Knollys, and the King, to the idea was Haldane's claim that 'one longs for Rosebery', and that the idea was that, without this spiritual leader, the three men of Relugas should rebuild and reform the Liberal party as Rosebery and his admirers would have liked.

Knollys therefore realised the importance of not telling this importuning trio to get lost. Keen to stop the incoming government being too provocatively radical – which it would be if such men as Asquith, Grey and Haldane were not part of it – he wrote to Haldane on 16 September:

> if you and your friends refused to join the Government, HM would be placed in an awkward position. A Cabinet of which Sir H C-B was the head, without the moderates, would, it appears to me, be disastrous both for the Country and the Party.... of course what the King would desire would be the presence of a restraining influence in the Cabinet, being aware that many members of it would be men holding extreme views, and this could only be effected by the presence in it of men like yourself, Asquith and Sir E. Grey.[348]

Knollys told Haldane he was sure the King would urge Sir Henry, without any help from them, to go to the Lords and conduct his ministry from there, or would extract from him a pledge to go there once the foundations of his administration had been properly laid. Knollys urged the men to think of the good of the country and not to carry out their threat in the event of Campbell-Bannerman staying put. He reassured Haldane with the notion that 'the King might well ask him [Campbell-Bannerman] to give a pledge that he would go into the House of Lords within a certain time, say a year for instance'. Although this was a clever letter, effectively morally blackmailing the three men to stay inside the Cabinet should it be formed, Knollys was for once presuming a little more than he should: he seems not to have been aware of the conversations the King and the Leader of the Opposition had had in Marienbad, where no mention had been made of Sir Henry's going to the Lords once he obtained the highest office. Haldane was well pleased with what Knollys told him, replying that 'your most friendly letter ... is a source of very real satisfaction'.[349] Haldane was sure that 'you hold so clearly the broad view that is strongly ours' about the 'redemption of the Liberal Party from its present condition'.

Perhaps unwisely, and certainly outside the letter of the constitution, the King summoned Haldane to Balmoral to talk the matter over with him, at dinner on 5 October. He told Haldane that he had read his correspondence with Knollys 'with much interest', and revealed that, having talked much with Campbell-Bannerman that summer in Marienbad, he had found him 'in his talk far better than in his speeches'.[350] Haldane stayed for three days – he and the King were, after all, old pals by now – and at the end of his stay the King summoned him into his private room. 'He wholly approved of our ideas, and was favourable to what we suggested,' Haldane recalled.[351] This visit to Balmoral was important for another reason. During it Haldane made the acquaintance of Esher, who decided – luckily for Haldane – that he liked him. How far he reached this decision thanks to knowing that the King already favoured Haldane we cannot know. Esher certainly saw in Haldane a man committed to further reform of the army, and, although brilliant in his own right, willing – too willing – to defer to the wishes of others. This made him an ideal man to act as a cypher for Esher in his continuing programme of ensuring that the King got what he wanted in military matters. It was partly at Esher's urging to both the King and another new friend, Campbell-Bannerman, that Haldane would become Secretary of State for War when the Liberals gained power.

Haldane reported back to Asquith that 'the plan is thoroughly approved in all its details.... I think that the K will ask CB to Sandringham in Nov and say that he doubts, from recent observation, whether any one but a young man can be both PM and Leader in his H of C'. Haldane said that the King would then 'suggest a peerage'. He advised Asquith to try to discuss the matter in vague terms with Sir Henry 'but not to go so far as to let him surmise any connection between your conversation and what may be done here. They are fully alive to the importance of secrecy and reticence.' One can only believe what Haldane says, in which case the King and Knollys were most unwisely getting up to their necks in the internal affairs of a political party that was not in government. 'I think', Haldane told Asquith, somewhat smugly, 'that we have secured very cordial and powerful assistance.'[352] The King also sounded out Haldane on possible future ministers: Haldane was careful, respecting the King's prejudices, to note that it would not be difficult to find a War Minister or First Lord of the Admiralty from the Commons, and that 'the name of Sir Charles Dilke naturally occurs in this connection as that of a man of ability and position'.[353] In fact, when the King was later to mention Dilke, now aged sixty-two and still on the Liberal backbenches, to Campbell-Bannerman, Sir Henry said his inclusion in his ministry was out of the question. The matter dropped.

When the time for Sir Henry's high office came, the King remained relatively aloof from the question of ministerial appointments, confining himself to an enquiry about the new Foreign Secretary. He was delighted to hear that the post was to be offered to Lord Cromer, formerly Sir Evelyn Baring, and one known to and, although not particularly liked, admired by the King. However, Cromer rejected the offer on grounds of health. Instead Grey, son of a former courtier and godson to the King, was appointed. He would hold the office for the best part of ten years. In fact, the King had unwittingly made it harder – much to the chagrin of Knollys, who knew how difficult some of his new Liberal ministers might turn out to be – to influence the process of forming the government. Going to Sandringham for the weekend immediately after Campbell-Bannerman's appointment, he had offered to cut his trip short if that would be of assistance to his new Prime Minister. Sir Henry had, though, 'pressed' him to 'remain away until Monday'.[354] Knollys told the King that, had he stayed in London, 'Your Majesty would, I am sure, have had more direct control over the negotiations, and Sir H could then, without any difficulty, have referred to you from time to time the proposals which were made for the filling up of the various offices.' The King had missed some drama – 'yesterday Sir E Grey positively refused to join, this morning he gave way, persuaded it is said by Mr Haldane'.

When the final list of Cabinet members was drawn up it appeared in *The Times* before the King had given his formal approval, which was not the best start to the new ministry's relations with him; but Campbell-Bannerman told a colleague that the King had been 'first rate' about the mistake and there had been 'no difficulty' in that quarter.[355] The new Prime Minister was, though, 'horrified' by this unfortunate beginning to his relations with the King. 'I cannot explain it,' he told Knollys on 9 December, 'nor can I, after efforts, trace its source.'[356] He asked Knollys to convey to the King his 'extreme regret that so great an impropriety has been somehow committed'. Two of the King's friends received office: Carrington as President of the Board of Agriculture, and Althorp, son of Earl Spencer, as Lord Chamberlain. The King had orginally sought this post for Carrington, whom he had described to the Prime Minister as being 'as a brother', and who had been Lord Chamberlain before. However, Carrington, when Campbell-Bannerman tried to go along with the King's wishes, refused on what appeared to be diplomatic 'medical grounds', supported by a doctor's letter that was forwarded to Knollys.[357] The King was disappointed, but happy with Althorp; interestingly, Carrington was well enough a day or so later to enter the Cabinet as Minister of Agriculture. The King was particularly pleased that Haldane had become War Secretary, writing to the Prince of Wales that 'Mr Haldane with sound common-sense and great powers of organising ought to make an excellent War Minister, which is much needed as his predecessor was hopeless.'[358]

For all the King's confidence in Haldane, he nonetheless had cause to pull him up quite early in his tenure of office. It was the usual gripe – the King felt he was not seeing War Office papers that should have been put before him. In a mood of conciliation (Haldane was not, after all, Arnold-Forster) Davidson wrote to Haldane on 15 September 1906 to say that this was no doubt the fault of Haldane's staff:

> During the last half of Queen Victoria's reign, the Military authorities were unwilling to trouble Her Majesty with too much detail, and as The Queen had perfect confidence in the Duke of Cambridge's ability to guard her interests and privileges, occasionally there were omissions to obtain The Sovereign's sanction for alterations &c, and the King feels sure you will agree with him that these lapses should not be regarded as constituting precedents.[359]

In forming the government, Campbell-Bannerman further appeased the King by leaving the choice of lords-in-waiting – Whips in the House of Lords who, by tradition, were attached to the royal household and had certain ceremonial duties to discharge – in the hands of Carrington, who knew the King's likes and dislikes. On 22 December 1905 Knollys sent the names of four peers to the Prime Minister, tactfully asking whether they would be suitable – Lords Kenmare, Lock, Suffolk and Russell. 'Any of these would be agreeable to him,' Knollys said with reference to the King, 'but he is not sure about their politics. The fathers of all of them were however Liberals.'[360] The King's main fear concerning the new administration was that few of them, especially at junior level, had ever held office, and might not therefore conduct his government with the discretion required. The change of government brought the King into contact with a group within the party that he might have regarded as foaming radicals – such as John Burns, tactfully described by Sir Sidney Lee as 'an extreme radical, if not definitely a socialist', and one with whom the King was soon on good terms ('me and 'im get on first-rate together' was how Burns described the relationship).[361] Burns was the first working man ever to hold Cabinet rank. Sir John Simon, one of the law officers and a future Lord Chancellor, remembered him attending a court function for the first time in his full Privy Councillor's uniform of cocked hat and braided coat, and telling the King that 'it is not the first time, Sir, that I have worn Your Majesty's uniform'. Asked by the King whether he had served in the army, Burns replied, 'No, Sir, I was in prison.'[362]

The King was not for the moment to find his position or dignity placed in any peril by the new men. The Liberal ministry was well disposed towards the King personally and had, in Knollys, a prominent political partisan next to the throne. Lee comments that 'the Government of the last four-and-a-half years of King Edward's reign, however radical and democratic, in no way diminished the legitimate influence of the monarch in affairs of state'. That, though, is a highly debatable point, not least because that same government was ready to move soon after the King's death to limit, by subtle means, the influence of his successor. Yet at the outset King Edward found his new ministers readier than their predecessors to consult his wishes in ceremonial and other matters that touched his *amour propre*.[363] Lee goes on to note that with many of his Liberal ministers, notably Campbell-Bannerman and John Morley, 'the King encouraged relations of familiarity which exceeded in warmth and frankness anything that had been experienced in the earlier days of his rule while the Conservatives held sway'.

In certain important regards, the way things had been done under the Conservatives continued. Campbell-Bannerman had no qualms about Esher's somewhat ill-defined and unusual role, taking the trouble to see Esher to discuss various matters of mutual interest soon after taking office.[364] 'I explained my relation to the King,' Esher noted in his journal, 'and the confidence in which I was honoured. CB said he welcomed all the help I could give him; that he had no sort of objection to the confidence with which the King chose to honour me.'[365] Esher was to enjoy a brief honeymoon with the new government; even his old and close friendship with Balfour had not stopped him being uncordially detested by most members of the previous administration by the time it expired. For example Salisbury, the Lord Privy Seal, had written to Balfour in April 1905 after spending some time as Minister-in-Attendance to the King to say that 'I think Esher's relations with the King are in the highest degree unsatisfactory. He ought either to be a responsible minister and defend his views in Parliament or (at the very most) he should confine himself to intensely confidential communications with yourself.'[366] It would not be long before the Liberals took the same view.

Esher turned down a GCB offered him by Balfour, reasoning that if he was to work well with the new regime he did not wish to appear in an entirely partisan resignation honours list, looking like 'a spy left behind by Arthur'.[367] One of his strengths was that he had sufficient self-knowledge and *savoir faire* to see how he was regarded by others, and he tailored his judgment accordingly. He was quick to cultivate the new ministers, soon acquiring John Morley – with whom he had been on good terms since the 1880s – as his principal informer in the Cabinet. As a result, Morley, after only Haldane, became the King's favourite minister, regarded by him as 'wonderfully agreeable and sensible'.[368] During his tenure of the India Office, Morley became one of the King's most assiduous ministerial correspondents, thereby fulfilling his Sovereign's ideal of how a loyal minister should conduct himself – by keeping the King informed. Esher was voluble in his praise of Morley to the King, which helped. 'Although a confirmed Home Ruler,' he told the King at the end of 1906, when Morley was threatening to resign because of differences he had with Campbell-Bannerman, 'Mr Morley, upon Imperial questions, and especially upon the Indian question, is so sound and broad minded, that he would be a great loss to Your Majesty.'[369]

A LEAP IN THE DARK

Colonial policy provoked the first disagreement between the King and the new ministry. Showing impeccable liberal credentials, the new Prime Minister, within a fortnight of taking up his office, announced that the government would immediately stop the importation of Chinese coolies to act as indentured labour in South Africa. The King was upset for two reasons: first, he thought the indentured labour was on economic grounds a good idea, and second, he regretted that Lord Selborne, the High Commissioner and *de facto* Governor-General, had not been consulted. When Lord Elgin, the new Colonial Secretary, sent details of the policy change in a dispatch to Selborne he neglected to tell the King, which prompted a strong rebuke from Knollys when the details appeared in the King's morning newspaper. 'His Majesty directs me to point out to you that it is his constitutional right to have all dispatches of any importance, especially those initiating or relating to a change of policy, laid before him prior to it being finally decided upon. This "right" was always observed during Queen Victoria's reign, and likewise by the late government since the King succeeded to the Throne.'[370] For good measure, Knollys added that the King objected to the policy anyway as 'a leap in the dark'. In fact, no disastrous consequences came of the policy reversal despite the King's fears, the last coolies being repatriated to China in 1910.

The King's interest in South Africa brought him into professional contact with the new Under-Secretary for Colonial Affairs, Winston Churchill, son of his late friend Lord Randolph. The two men had known each other since Churchill's childhood, and had corresponded sporadically over the years: in the late 1890s, when Churchill was bored out of his wits playing polo at an Indian hill-station, the then Prince of Wales had recommended to him that a career in Parliament and in literary life would suit his temperament far better.[371] Since entering the Commons, Churchill had been a guest at Balmoral. Now, in the summer of 1906, in the course of a new correspondence about the Transvaal Constitution with the thirty-one-year-old MP, who had gravely offended many Tories by crossing the floor to join the Liberals over free trade in 1903, the King offered him some fatherly advice: 'His Majesty is glad to see that you are becoming a *reliable* minister and above all a serious politician, *which can only be attained by putting country before party*.'[372]

The previous year the King had been dismayed when Churchill, entering his brief and (in the context of his later life) uncharacteristic anti-military-expenditure phase, had made a speech in the House about 'those gorgeous and gilded functionaries with brass hats and ornamental duties who multiply so luxuriously on the plains of Aldershot and Salisbury': remarks the King had dismissed as 'what good words for a recent subaltern of the Hussars!'[373] Since then, in March 1906, the Under-Secretary had offended the King, and many others besides, with some injudicious remarks about Lord Milner's record in South Africa in a debate on a motion seeking to have Milner censured over civil unrest on the Cape arising out of problems with Chinese labour. The King wrote at the time to Lord Crewe, the Leader of the Lords and an old friend, that 'it is a pity that Lord Elgin does not seem to be able to control the violent and objectionable language of his Parliamentary Under-Secretary. It has made a painful impression on most people.'[374]

One assistance to the relationship between the King and the Prime Minister was that Sir Henry, like the King, took the cure in Marienbad every August. In Marienbad society, indeed, the King was a Johnny-come-lately; his first visit had been in 1899, whereas the Campbell-Bannermans had had an August fixture there since 1870. The King and his Prime Minister never talked much politics there: a sketch was published of them during one of the visits showing the Prime Minister listening intently while the King punched his fist into the palm of his other hand. The portentous caption was 'Is it peace or war?' Campbell-Bannerman revealed that, in fact, the incident depicted had been during a discussion he and his Sovereign were having about whether halibut was better baked or boiled.[375]

Lee explains the good relations with the Liberals generally as being partly due to the King's innate ability easily to adapt to circumstances, but partly because the Liberals were more willing to enter into the spirit of constitutional monarchy than the Conservatives had been. Such a theory would, though, be tested by events at the end of the reign. From the start, too, the King was concerned about the brevity of the communications between his Prime Minister and himself. Esher had already warned him in the autumn of 1905 that Balfour was falling short in this regard; and, with his omniscient grasp of how Queen Victoria had been treated, had advised the King to demand better of his Prime Minister. Esher had warned the King not to allow this tradition to go by default when a new government, unused to these constitutional practices, came in, and the King was especially keen to find out about the matters relating to Cabinet decisions before those decisions were taken. The previous year Esher and Knollys had agreed that the main fault of members of Balfour's administration had been that 'mainly through defective training and carelessness, [they] do not adhere, as part of their duty and not the least important part, to the old practice of writing fully to the Sovereign upon important questions, before Cabinet decisions are fully taken'.[376] Knowledge was power, in this case the King's power. Esher and Knollys were holding the line against erosion of that power, but the forces of history and human nature were against them.

In the matter of getting reports of meetings of the Cabinet, the King insisted on his rights, and Esher put down the deficiencies in Campbell-Bannerman's manner to his innate laziness – though to be fair the new Prime Minister was seventy, with a terminally ill wife and in failing health himself. The Cabinet reports, which had run to four quarto pages under Balfour, were often just one page – albeit of smaller, neater handwriting – under Campbell-Bannerman. But after three months of this concision the King scribbled testily on one such report: 'the information as usual is meagre'.[377] A month later, in April 1906, a one-paragraph report on a meeting about 'two difficulties of detail' – unelaborated upon – in the Education Bill is endorsed with the sarcastic note: 'what valuable information'.[378] When, the following year, Campbell-Bannerman became exceptionally ill, the Cabinet reports became even more skeletal. Knollys, always careful of his master's rights, wrote to Esher on 29 November 1907 to say that the reports were 'really making an absolute fool of the King; but whether he ought, constitutionally, to know *everything* that passes in the Cabinet, I cannot say. There is no use in Ministers *liking* the King if he is to be treated as an absolute puppet.'[379] Knollys felt that 'of course the King *himself*, not me, ought to have it out with him. I shall try to induce him to do so, but I don't know whether I shall succeed.'

Esher was fixated by the relationship Queen Victoria had had with Peel and Aberdeen, never worrying that that was two Reform Acts ago. He seems to have failed to appreciate that the reform measures had not simply widened the franchise: they had also shifted the balance of power from the centre towards the periphery. Once a government was seen to be accountable to the people, it was they and not the monarch who needed to be the prime point of consultation. Esher maintained that the King, like his mother, had a right to be consulted on Cabinet decisions while they were in the process of being taken, not merely afterwards. He contended that 'in the interests of tradition and the Monarchy ... the practice which prevailed under the Queen should be adhered to, because the position of the Sovereign should be altogether independent of the personality of the Monarch, if the Monarchy is to stand. The King's personality is the great factor nowadays, and this is a stumbling block in the way of his successors.'[380] Better to prove his difficult point about Queen Victoria's relationship with her ministers, he persuaded the King to allow him to prepare for publication an edition of the late Queen's letters, not least as a means of shaming Peel's and Aberdeen's successors for their want of care and duty. Meanwhile, Esher became a one-man intelligence network on behalf of the King, insinuating himself into the confidence of Cabinet ministers and then reporting to his master what they had to say. It was not a formal consultation as Peel and Aberdeen had done it, but it at least armed the King in advance of anything controversial arising.

Esher impressed upon Knollys not just the breach of precedent involved in failing to consult the King at the start of a decision-making process, but also ministers' 'carelessness (almost amounting to making it a dead letter) about the sanctity of the Privy Counsellor's oath'.[381] He even started quoting Bagehot at him, an interpretation of whom by Esher would have had to be pretty unique if he and Bagehot were to end up agreeing.[382] What interested Esher was the right to be consulted; but Bagehot never intended this to be a right of veto, if the King did not like the decision towards which the Cabinet was moving. That was why, as we have seen, Queen Victoria was not a Bagehotian, and Esher, had he but known it, would not have had his master be one either.

While by nature and politics a Liberal, Knollys's first loyalty was to the King and to the upholding of his position. Armed with these arguments from Esher, he further entrenched the King's position in relation to his ministers, but by 1907 it was too late. The only force that could alter established custom and practice was a newly established custom and practice. One point neither Knollys nor Esher took into account was the enormous weight of government business, and the sheer growth in the size of the state, in Edwardian England compared with the 1840s and 1850s. The King was not always by-passed because of rudeness on the part of his ministers, or because of their determination to seize what were rightly and by law his prerogatives: he was by-passed because, had he been presented with even a portion of the new mass of detail, he and his staff would simply have been overwhelmed.

After Knollys's letter to Esher about the King's ministers making a fool of him, Esher replied expressing sentiments that show him at his most typical. 'No-one can make a silk purse out of a sow's ear – and C-B is incurable,' he said, just days after the Prime Minister had had a serious heart attack.[383] 'The indolence of senility is upon him. I don't for a moment believe that he wishes to keep the King in the dark, but he cannot bring himself to write. His ignorance of precedent, the fact that he has had no real training in Government, and the fact that the King never writes to him direct, all tend to make him perfunctory. The result is deplorable, both in the interests of the Country and of the Monarchy.'

THAT MAN, AGAIN

Esher's role in the household had, as we have seen, long since been an irritation to ministers, who were powerless to do anything about it. One of the King's closest friends, Carrington, noted of Esher in 1905 that 'he certainly is an extraordinary man, and has a wonderful footing in Buckingham Palace. He seems to be able to run about as he likes and must be a considerable nuisance to the Household. He is a clever, unscrupulous man, who might be dangerous; and he is not trusted by the general public, who look on him as an intriguer.'[384] Given that Knollys, too, seems to have been in thrall to him – Esher was the answer to the question 'who advises the advisers?' – it is hardly too much to say that, into the bargain, it was Esher who almost single-handedly prevented the transition of Britain to a fully constitutional monarchy being completed during the reign of Edward VII. Indeed, the very fact that Esher had his place at court, and was charged by the King to undertake the missions he did, can be seen to be utterly inconsistent with what we now understand by a constitutional monarchy. Esher's retention by the King and that concept were simply not compatible. Brodrick, in his memoirs, noted that 'by the time any decision had come to the point when the Cabinet could lay it before the Sovereign, the issue had been largely pre-judged on the incomplete premises of an observer who had no official status. In other words, Esher, whether intentionally or not, had constituted himself the unofficial adviser of the Crown, and ... it would be tedious to record the endless contretemps to which this usurpation of power by an outsider gave rise.'[385] While allowing for the politician's knack of insulting another for no reason other than that that person disagrees with him and holds him to account, ministers still had some cause for complaint.

What mattered – in fact, all that mattered – was that by this stage the King had reached a point where he would scarcely contemplate a bowel movement without seeking Esher's counsel on the matter. Esher's judgment had, in the King's eyes, virtually never been found wanting; and, like many unclever men, the King's main talent lay in his being clever enough to see the importance of enlisting his intellectual superiors to help make his life easier and his position more secure. Above all, Esher treated him like a king. In 1906 he wrote to his son that 'in parting the King said to me, "Although you are not exactly a public servant, yet I always think you are the most valuable public servant I have," and then I kissed his hand, as I sometimes do'.[386] As Lord Esher's finest biographer, James Lees-Milne, has pointed out, kissing the Sovereign's hand was not commonplace even in 1906, but it is not entirely fair to use this passage as an illustration of Esher's appalling toadyism, and of the King's possible moral defectiveness in being the willing recipient of it. Esher continued the letter to his unhealthily beloved son (though this line, understandably, is suppressed from the published *Letters and Journals*): 'But in doing it I only thought how little all this meant including the kiss, compared with a kiss upon another hand, and a few words of affection or appreciation from other lips.'[387]

In March 1907 the *Standard* published a long attack on Esher in relation to his work with the army, saying he was 'neither a permanent official accountable to the Secretary of State, nor liable to the criticism of Parliament.... "Lord Esher", writes one of our correspondents, "has considerable influence, and even, to some extent, an executive power without any sort of responsibility." '[388] Although Esher deserves credit for having helped significantly with the modernisation of the army, he knew too well that his position was, to say the least, controversial. He had had an assault of this sort coming for some time, and wrote to Knollys to tell him authoritatively (though without a scrap of evidence being supplied) that it was the work of Arnold-Forster.[389] Despite the lack of proof, the King was told this information, and pronounced himself 'shocked that an ex-Cabinet Minister should have lent himself to this underhand form of attack'.[390] Knollys consoled Esher with the news that the King was 'very indignant' about the affront to his trusty.[391]

The Liberal government, and the civil service establishment, came to see Esher as the archetypal over-mighty subject. He was regarded as a high-class sneak who, even worse, was quite shameless and unrepentant in his sneaking because he subjugated everything to his ultimate master, the King. Whatever these higher loyalties, he excited the mistrust of ministers and officials who felt they had to guard their tongues in front of him, and who were convinced – usually rightly – that he was intriguing behind their backs. Esher even divided the King's own private political court. Charles Hardinge, who benefited directly from the King's patronage possibly even more than Esher, did all he could as permanent under-secretary at the Foreign Office to keep Esher's nose out of his department's affairs. In June 1906, for example, Esher sent a telegram to Hardinge requesting 'for the King's information' a 'short statement' about the Baghdad railway.[392] Hardinge replied magisterially to Esher that, having consulted Grey, he could not comply with Esher's request. Rubbing it in, he added that 'any information which the King may desire on foreign politics will always, as heretofore, be gladly supplied if HM will make known his commands through one of his Private Secretaries.'[393] For good measure, Hardinge told Knollys how 'astonished' he had been by Esher's request which, if complied with, 'might cause a very inconvenient precedent'.[394] He added that 'Sir E. Grey feels very strongly that Esher is not the proper channel between him and the King. I feel certain that you will agree.' Esher certainly did represent a by-passing of the normal constitutional functions, but rebukes such as this seem to have done nothing to deter him from those activities.

THE NEW ORDER

Some of the democratising, radical policies that the Liberals intended to pursue in office were sure to offend one of the King's natural conservatism, but he was willing to support his government in its intentions, provided Ministers sought to execute them in a way that persuaded rather than alienated the people. Campbell-Bannerman

realised in a more profound way than many of his colleagues the great
benefit of having the sympathy of the King in this way. It was one of
his less experienced colleagues, John Burns, who provided the King
with his first bout of apoplexy under the new government. With the
administration settled, Campbell-Bannerman called an election for
January 1906. The new President of the Local Government Board
included in his election address his opinion that the House of Lords
would be better off abolished, though had helpfully clarified this on the
hustings by saying that he was quite happy with the retention of the
monarchy. This prompted the King to write to Campbell-Bannerman
from Chatsworth on 7 January 1906 that as the Prime Minister 'has so
recently recommended several prominent members of the House of
Commons to be peers, the King is somewhat surprised that a member
of the Cabinet should have made this declaration'.[395] The Prime
Minister hastened to smooth things down. 'That is the worst', he
replied, 'of the abrupt appointment of men to the Cabinet without
serving an apprenticeship in subordinate office. I have had two or three
cases of want of discretion already from the *novi homines*, including the
Secretary of State for War.'[396]

The King was determined to make sure that Burns, the novice in
these gentlemanly arts, knew he had done wrong. He took up the
matter with Lord Tweedmouth, the First Lord of the Admiralty, who
asked Campbell-Bannerman to have Burns make a personal apology,
in addition to the one made by the Prime Minister on his behalf.[397]
Burns, an unassuming man who must have been deeply intimidated by
the whole performance, wrote at once, on 10 January 1906, to confirm
'my intention to adhere to my oath as one of His Majesty's Privy
Councillors'.[398] Even this act of prostration was insufficient for the
hidebound Knollys, who as one peer to another told Tweedmouth that
the apology was 'not I think very satisfactory – I really do not quite see
what more I could say'.[399] This, somewhat absurdly given everything
else he had to do in fighting the election, brought Campbell-
Bannerman into the fray again. He wrote to the King on 11 January to
say that he had directed Burns's attention to the matter (as if that was
necessary) and told him that 'it is incumbent on a Cabinet Minister to
refrain from the expression of extreme views unless with the consent
and leave of the Head of Your Majesty's Government'.[400] We do not
know whether the King noted how Sir Henry reserved the right to
sanction the expression of extreme views. As the Prime Minister had

already told the King, the episode was 'due solely to the inexperience in official responsibility of the Minister concerned'. In time, Burns's indiscretion would come to appear ridiculously minor, compared with what else would be said.

One prominent 'want of discretion' manifested itself in David Lloyd George, the President of the Board of Trade, long regarded by aficionados as the man most likely to cause trouble to the established order. The King had met the uncompromising Welshman socially at a dinner given by Tweedmouth two years earlier, an event much commented upon at the time as marking Lloyd George's apparent passage to social respectability. Such ideas were premature. The minister said something in the proceedings of the Education Bill in the Commons in July 1906 that led the King to suppose that the government was about to appoint a 'Minister for Wales'. This was the first the King had heard of it, and the next day he wrote to Campbell-Bannerman that he was 'much astonished' to read a report of this in his newspaper.[401] 'I have heard nothing on the subject', the King continued, 'from the Prime Minister. This proceeding is most unconstitutional and I cannot pass it over in silence.' Lloyd George protested to his chief that he had been misunderstood – he had meant only to signify that a minister would have independent charge of Welsh education – an excuse the King dismissed as 'a very meagre one'. Having obtained assurances that there would be no special Welsh or Scottish ministers, the King lamented that 'it seems inconceivable that the PM has so little control over the members of his cabinet'.[402] Sir Henry admitted that when Lloyd George made the remark 'I should have been on the spot, aware of what was going on, and ready to correct misapprehensions'.[403] It was especially noble of the Prime Minister to take the blame, since his absence from the front line was caused by his being with his dying wife. Acquainted with this news, the King had Knollys tell Sir Henry that his absences from the Commons were 'very natural' and that 'he entirely absolves you from all blame in the matter'.[404]

For all his goodwill towards Campbell-Bannerman, the King did not take long to start to feel uncomfortable with some of the activities his new government was carrying out. In reply to a letter from Esher in April 1906 – in which, usefully, Esher had briefed the King confidentially about the precarious state of the Prime Minister's health – the King let rip about what he called, without being specific, 'the ill-timed measures they [the government] are bringing forward'.[405] He added that it was 'simply deplorable' that 'young and inexperienced ministers' were allowed so much leeway because of the rather casual attitude Sir Henry adopted to the business of governing. For the moment, though, the old order would hold fast and protect the King's sensibilities from the excesses of radicalism; the great affront would not come until Sir Henry was gone.

MEETING THE ARREARS

One thing did not change with the colour of the administration: the King maintained his flow of advice to his Prime Minister. Hearing there would be a Trades Disputes Bill, he wrote to Sir Henry on 13 February 1906 to say that he presumed it was to alter the law as laid down in the Taff Vale case, in which a railway company had in 1902 won substantial damages against a trade union for having damaged its business by industrial action – 'but he trusts sincerely it will not include a clause allowing what he thinks is rather absurdly described "peaceful picketing", as if it could possibly be ensured that any form of picketing could be free from occasional acts of violence and at any rate of constant intimidation'.[406] Sir Henry replied that 'the details of it are not yet drafted' but added: 'I hope that the consequence you indicate will be guarded against.'[407]

The King and the Prime Minister soon had a difference of opinion over honours. With the Liberals painfully weak in the Lords – it is estimated that in 1905 there were 462 Conservative peers to 77 Liberals, the Liberal benches having been seriously depleted after the breakaway of the Liberal Unionists twenty years earlier – Campbell-Bannerman asked for ten peerages to be created, including a necessary one for Sir Robert Reid, the new Lord Chancellor.[408] Then, within six months, he asked for another clutch to coincide with the King's official birthday at the end of June, because, his party having been out of office for so long, 'there are naturally arrears to be met'.[409] Of seven peerages suggested the King objected to only one, for W. J. Pirrie, a Belfast shipowner, as the King 'does not consider [he] is altogether the stamp of a man who should be created a peer, and as far as HM knows, he has done nothing special to merit the honour. The King does not moreover think he behaved very well or patriotically when an English fleet of steamers, of which he was the part proprietor, was sold to an American company a few years ago.'[410] Knollys explained all this in a letter to Campbell-Bannerman on 17 June. Furthermore, he said the King felt that seventeen peerages in six months was 'excessive', and asked for four of the next seven to be created in June and three on his actual birthday in November; 'but he would be glad if some other name could be substituted for that of Mr Pirrie'.[411] No reason was given for the King's dislike of Pirrie, which without one seems rooted in pure snobbery. In any case Campbell-Bannerman did not give way, either on the timing of the creations or on the people being elevated. He was similarly robust with two objections the King made later in the year about prospective birthday honours: one radical MP was thought to be 'a rather violent and mischievous man', another to have a disreputable heir.[412] The King did, though, wrest from his Prime Minister an assurance that there would be no more political peerages that year.

For all the new mores of a supposedly radical era, the King was determined to do what he could to uphold what he regarded as the traditional basis of the peerage. His vain attempts to prevent the elevation of Pirrie, 'not quite a gentleman', were the first evidence of this. Then in October 1907, when the Prime Minister solicited a peerage for Sir Henry Fowler, the seventy-seven-year old Chancellor of the Duchy of Lancaster and one who had given a lifetime of service to the Liberal party, the King raised a different objection. 'He will, of course,' Knollys wrote to the Prime Minister, 'approve of the proposed Peerage if you have satisfied yourself that Sir Henry Fowler's eldest son is reputable. When it was proposed to confer a Coronation Peerage on Sir Henry in 1902, the idea had to be abandoned on account of the son's character, and HM imagines that this objection must still hold good.'[413] Campbell-Bannerman wrote back in defence of the son, but Knollys replied on 6 November that the King 'cannot, he is afraid, consider the account of young Fowler ['young Fowler' was, in fact, thirty-seven] very satisfactory, and he is glad therefore that the question of conferring a peerage on Sir Henry Fowler is postponed for the present'. In fact, Asquith ensured that Sir Henry became Viscount Wolverhampton at the change of premiership the following April; his son succeeded him in 1911, having married the previous year, and lived the rest of an undistinguished life in the wilds of Norfolk. It is not clear at this remove what exactly was held against him. The only obvious item on the charge-sheet is that he was an Old Carthusian.

The new Liberal government inherited a difficult economic situation from Balfour. A programme of spending cuts was immediately implemented, including the cancellation of one of four Dreadnoughts – the new heavily armed, turbine-driven, oil-fired battleships – being built for the navy, as well as three destroyers and four submarines. In July that year Campbell-Bannerman told the King that Asquith, the Chancellor, was saying that even the three Dreadnoughts were unnecessary, and that even if both France and England combined against Germany the existing resources of the navy would be enough to beat them. The King commented that 'evidently the cheese-paring policy of the Government is also to be extended to the navy'.[414] One of the King's closest service friends, Admiral 'Jackie' Fisher, the First Sea Lord, was deeply concerned at the expansion of the German navy, and he urged the King that the navy's Atlantic and Channel fleets should be combined into a single North Sea Fleet. The King was sympathetic, though the Prince of Wales, as a naval man, could not see the point. At the King's behest Fisher wrote to tell him, presciently, that the change was necessary because 'our only probable enemy is Germany'.[415] Fisher fully accepted the need for economy, and argued that much money was being used to subsidise inefficiency; but, when his suggestions for the redeployment of ships were resisted in Whitehall, he immediately sought to enlist the King on his side of the argument. The King found himself in a difficult position because another one of his trusties, Charles Hardinge, now head of the Foreign Office, profoundly disagreed with Fisher. Privately, though, the King supported Fisher, and was relieved when in January 1907 the Cabinet endorsed his proposals too: a victory Fisher acknowledged could not have been won without the support of his Monarch. In a series of tussles the flamboyant Fisher was to have with the government until his retirement in 1910, the fact that he was the King's man seriously handicapped the resistance politicians could mount against him.

The King was rarely willing to allow his own good opinion of someone to be obstructed by practicalities. It was true with Fisher: true, too, with Sir Charles Hardinge. On 20 November 1906 he wrote in his own hand to Campbell-Bannerman recommending Hardinge for the vacant Washington embassy, and for a peerage – 'the only good choice that could be made'.[416] Sir Henry agreed to consult with Grey on the matter, adding that 'the only doubt will perhaps be whether Sir C Hardinge does not better serve Your Majesty in the very important position which he was so recently appointed to fill'.[417] The Foreign Secretary did not agree with the King. He told the Prime Minister that he found the suggestion 'the very best arrangement – for Washington. But what we should gain there we should lose here.'[418] Grey added that Hardinge's current elevated appointment in charge of the Foreign Office was 'such a success that I now consider him invaluable where he is, and he really cannot be spared'. More to the point, it was Hardinge's 'own strong wish to stay at the Foreign Office'.

Unperturbed by all this, the King then petitioned Campbell-Bannerman again, on 23 November. He pressed his reasons more cogently: 'German influence, and indeed successful intrigue, has been so paramount at Washington, that it wants the ability and Diplomatic tact and knowledge possessed by Sir Charles to counteract the first, which is *so* important for the maintenance of our good relations with the United States and the peace of the world.'[419] Nonetheless, thanks largely to Hardinge's own resistance, the King did not have his way, and accepted the Prime Minister's own suggestion, James Bryce, the Irish Secretary and one of the most intellectually distinguished men of his day, with some magnanimity – 'under the circumstances, no better choice could have been made'.[420] Hardinge was relieved, writing to Knollys on 24 November to thank him for helping talk the King out of the notion.[421]

The King soon realised how fortunate he was to have someone so loyal as Hardinge acting as his eyes and ears within the Foreign Office. Understandably, Grey seems to have come to feel some discomfort at the closeness of the relations between his permanent secretary and his Sovereign. He eventually started to object to Hardinge being sent with the King wherever the King went abroad, a matter Hardinge dealt with by briefing Knollys to see that, effectively, Grey was given a command to let him. Cleverly, when the command duly arrived – Hardinge having stressed to Knollys that 'I send you very privately these suggestions which I trust you will keep suitably to yourself as having come from me' – Grey naturally discussed it with Hardinge, who talked him round until Grey believed it had largely been his own idea.[422] Hardinge would occasionally have audiences of the King without Grey's knowledge, and which, with Knollys's complicity, failed to be reported in the Court Circular.[423] By early 1907 Hardinge and the King were corresponding far more frequently than the King and Grey ever did, with the King insisting on being given the details of all intended diplomatic appointments and vacancies, and Hardinge being in no position – nor, apparently, having the inclination – to refuse him. Ever the master of tact, Hardinge sought to protect his chief's *amour propre* by hinting to Knollys that it would be good for the King to receive Grey regularly, notably after the King's occasional absences from London. 'Grey likes being received by the King,' he told Knollys on 6 May 1907, as the King returned from Biarritz.[424] 'It also helps make things go well.' It also helped remind the King that he should go through the motions of hearing what his Foreign Secretary had to say, even if he had already been told it all by Hardinge.

The King was glad to hear that Bryce would be replaced by Augustine Birrell, whose 'conciliatory manners and disposition, with his tact, will have an excellent effect on the Irish'.[425] The King was not an impeccable judge of character, and was too often swayed in those judgments by social considerations: Birrell's tenure of the Irish secretaryship was to end in ignominy, through some fault of his own, after the Easter Rising of April 1916. The King had had cause to criticise the former President of the Board of Education only a few weeks before his promotion, in November 1906, for his having expressed his distaste at schoolboys learning rifle shooting. 'Nearly everyone who has given any thought to the subject of national defence will take the same view as he does in the matter,' Knollys wrote of the King to the Prime Minister.[426]

> The idea that teaching boys how to shoot encourages militarism is absurd. His Majesty is afraid that the radicals in the House of Commons are opposed to the teaching of military exercises of every description, extending their dislike even to Rifle Shooting, because it is called 'military', which he regards as curious considering that in Switzerland (a Republic) Rifle practice among the youth is universal, as was also the case under the Boer *Republic*, which we discovered to our cost during the late war.

It is interesting that Knollys, or the King, or both should have been undergoing a period of persecution mania that caused them to think that the assault on military training by the radical fringe of the government was coupled with a hidden agenda to remove the trappings of monarchism, and that militarism was perceived as one of those trappings.

HEREDITARY RIGHTS

It was, as we have seen, a conviction of the King's that any assault on the hereditary privileges of the House of Lords was an assault on the hereditary privileges of the monarchy. Although subsequent governments, in their attempts to reform the Upper House, have routinely denied the truth of this assertion, the fact that both these parts of the constitution self-evidently exist and function according to hereditary right seems to suggest that the King had a point. He believed that, like the Crown, the Lords should be above party attacks; but this was entirely unrealistic, given that the Lords, unlike the Crown, engaged in party politics. From quite early on, long before the People's Budget controversy, it was clear that Lloyd George was to be a serial offender in this respect. He attacked the constitutional status quo ante in a speech at Llanelli on 29 September 1906, saying that in opposing the government's Education Bill the Lords were taking on the British people; and Lloyd George made it clear that he was prepared to fight back on behalf of those people. The King complained immediately, and on 16 October the Prime Minister wrote to Knollys that 'I have passed on to him [Lloyd George] the objection taken and admonished him to avoid such a tone in future.... he has not yet learned that once he gets inside an office his sword and spear should only be used on extreme occasions, and with the consent of his colleagues.'[427] He added that he thought what Lloyd George was doing was 'wretchedly bad tactics'.

However, an assurance from Campbell-Bannerman that the offence would not be repeated proved optimistic. Lloyd George made what was in the King's view 'another indecent attack on the House of Lords' during November, which prompted Knollys to issue the following threat: 'Mr Lloyd George is very anxious that the King and Queen should go to Cardiff next summer to open some new docks there, and they have given a half consent that they would do so, but the King says that nothing will induce him to visit Cardiff unless Mr Lloyd George learns how to behave with propriety as a Cabinet Minister holding an important office.'[428] This made no difference. In Oxford on 1 December Lloyd George raised the threat of dissolution and an election to settle whether or not the Lords had the support of the people in blocking the Education Bill. 'Whether dissolution comes sooner or later, it will be a much larger issue than the Education Bill. It will come upon this issue: whether the country is to be governed by the

King and his Peers or by the King and his people.'[429] The King was outraged at having his name dragged into the debate; and, one has every cause to believe, at the debate itself being conducted by one of his most senior ministers. He protested at once to Campbell-Bannerman, saying that 'the King sees it is useless to attempt to prevent Mr Lloyd George from committing breaches of good taste and propriety by abstaining from attacking, as a cabinet minister, that branch of the legislature.... it is difficult for the King to understand why he has paid no attention either to the wish of his Sovereign or to the warning addressed to him by the Head of the Government.'[430] The King insisted that 'Mr Lloyd George shall not introduce the Sovereign's name into these violent tirades of his, and he asks you, as Prime Minister, to be so good as to take the necessary steps to prevent a repetition of this violation of constitutional practice and good taste'.

However, the Prime Minister defended Lloyd George for expressing the popular frustration at the way in which the Lords had chosen to overturn the will of the people. He said Lloyd George had said 'nothing disrespectful' to the King, and that he felt 'profound regret' that his words had caused offence.[431] In what the Palace must have regarded as an especially provocative use of an adjective, the Prime Minister also claimed that, in his speech, Lloyd George had striven to be 'moderate' in the 'exasperated circumstances' of the Education Bill.[432] Knollys replied to this defence, on behalf of the King, by saying that Lloyd George, as one of his ministers, 'cannot with propriety indulge in that freedom of speech which if he were a private member he would be at liberty to gratify'.[433] The King also suspected that the President of the Board of Trade was trying to provoke the Lords deliberately, and gave his quite weighty evidence for this supposition: 'Some of his speeches were delivered even before the Bill was introduced into that House, others while it was being discussed, and ... the speech at Oxford was made previous to the third reading, when it is possible, though the King is afraid not probable, some of the amendments may be modified or withdrawn by the Opposition.'[434] Knollys said the King would have no objection to ministers criticising the Lords once they had done their worst; but for Lloyd George to take the line he was suggested an implicit desire on his part to have them abolished, and such constitutional dynamiting, without a mandate, by a minister of the Crown was simply unacceptable. This fusillade did for the moment restrain Lloyd George, but only for the moment.

The King himself had not been happy with the Education Bill, whose main aim was to remove all religious tests for teachers and to put local education authorities in charge of religious instruction, redressing the complaints of a main Liberal constituency, the nonconformists. In April 1906 he had written to Esher that 'this new Education Bill is deplorable, and has driven the Church of England and R. Catholics to despair. What can the Govt be thinking of – in excluding teaching Religion in our schools? Do they wish to copy the French! I look with considerable alarm to the way the Prime Minister is going on, and needless to say, he never brings anything before me – never consults me in *any* way.'[435] The Archbishop of Canterbury was especially offended by its provisions, since what he had been told would be included in the Bill was radically different from what actually was in it, and he wrote to Knollys on 13 April 1906 to protest. As he was clearly expected to do, Knollys drew the letter to the attention of the King, who was on a Mediterranean cruise. The King agreed the Archbishop 'has not been well treated by this Government', but then asked, 'who has by this Bill?'[436] He termed the measure 'unfair and dangerous' and forecast it would 'produce violent dissensions between the Church of England and Roman Catholics on one side and the Nonconformists on the other'.

Already aggrieved at not having been consulted properly on the detail of the Bill, the King was even more annoyed to learn from other than his Prime Minister that the measure threatened to provoke the thing the King dreaded most: conflict between the two Houses of Parliament. In November 1906, shortly before the extent of the problem became apparent, the King had had Sir Henry down to Windsor, where apparently no mention was made of the gathering storm. Knollys wrote to the Prime Minister on 23 November to say that he thought the King should have been made aware of the difficulty – 'His Majesty can however hardly suppose, after what you told him at Windsor, that no discussion took place [in Cabinet] on the probability of an important and serious conflict.'[437] Knollys laid down a marker for the future, warning Sir Henry that 'this is a matter which must closely concern the Sovereign, and the King directs me to let you know that he is naturally anxious to be informed if any discussion occurred which would enable you to ascertain the views of your colleagues on the subject in question'.

When that month the House of Lords amended the Bill out of all recognition, Campbell-Bannerman told the King that the Commons simply would not accept the changes. The King advised his Prime

Minister to swot up on the tussle over the Irish Church Bill of 1869, in which Queen Victoria had intervened. Sir Henry replied that he would, and spoke of his 'earnest desire to avoid unnecessary friction and conflict, and to spare Your Majesty trouble and anxiety'.[438] The King, who regarded this as a 'prompt and satisfactory reply', now suggested that the Archbishop of Canterbury might mediate between the Lords and the government – although his qualifications for mediation, since he was a fierce opponent of what the government was proposing, are not immediately clear.[439] This, however, was another one of Esher's schemes, born of his love of precedent, because Queen Victoria had done something similar over the impasse with Gladstone's Irish Church Bill in 1869.[440] At the King's request, the Archbishop went to meetings of the Cabinet sub-committee considering the Bill.

The King urged Campbell-Bannerman to try to find a compromise over the Lords' amendments, and hoped he might work this out with the Archbishop; the 'threatened collision between the two houses' was, he warned, 'deplorable from a constitutional as well as from every point of view'.[441] Sir Henry replied that he would certainly try to come to an arrangement with the Archbishop; he also promised the King, in response to the rebuke about lack of information, that 'I have every desire that he should at once be made aware of every decision of importance.'[442] However, the Conservative peers in the Lords, led by Lansdowne, would not be appeased. They amended the Bill in committee, and gave it a third reading in its new form by 105 votes to 28 on 6 December 1906. Campbell-Bannerman now warned the King of the wholesale redrawing of the Bill that would be necessary in the Commons, in rejecting the Lords' amendments. The hope of compromise was still being held out, though the King observed that he doubted whether 'so drastic and novel a measure as the rejection *en bloc* of the whole of the amendments of the House of Lords' could be regarded as a conciliatory step.[443] The King was worried that the government was not talking to Lansdowne and Balfour about the problem, but the Prime Minister assured him that such talks were taking place – fruitlessly. The Commons rejected the amendments *en bloc*, in return for which the Lords passed a motion insisting on their amendments. In response, Campbell-Bannerman had no alternative but to kill the Bill. The King's attempts at avoiding a deadlock had failed, and the failure depressed and demoralised him, for it provided him with evidence of an impotence whose existence he had determinedly not hitherto recognised. He also realised, as did the rest of the political establishment, that this would not by any means be the last outing for this particular argument.

LOOKING FOR A SOLUTION

In the next speech from the throne, opening the new session of Parliament on 12 February 1907, the King announced that his ministers were looking at ways to avoid a repetition of the constitutional problems of the previous session. The King himself, in the interests of the smooth running of the constitution and the government, was keener than ever to avoid confrontation between the two Houses. For this reason he himself took a more democratic view, and wished the Conservative majority in the Lords would be a little more open-minded towards the wishes of the elected chamber. Campbell-Bannerman, more realistically, saw that no such gentlemen's agreement was likely to work. He instead wished to legislate to limit the Lords' veto. He established a Cabinet committee to consider this question. It was one, inevitably, in which the King took a strong personal interest, so he was doubly irritated when Campbell-Bannerman starved him of information about it. He picked up what he could from Esher, whose networks of informants gave him a relatively clear picture of what was happening. Esher had told the King on 18 March 1907 that the committee 'has put aside – in deference to your Majesty's known wishes – all idea of making proposals which involve touching the hereditary principle upon which the House rests, and have limited their enquiry as to the method by which a serious deadlock between the two Houses is in future to be avoided'.[444] Sensibly, Esher warned the King that the 'more extreme' members of the government would find this inadequate – in a letter to Knollys, being more candid, he said the moderation was 'much to the disgust of Lloyd George'.[445]

Nonetheless, the King would have liked to hear all this through the appropriate channels. Knollys told Esher that 'between ourselves, I don't think that the King will ever like CB politically. I do not believe the latter understands him any more than Mr G[ladstone] understood the Queen.'[446] Knollys added that 'I have just heard from the King who says: "I hope the Prime Minister will not abolish the House before I return. I think the least he could have done would have been that I should have been consulted on this question instead of which I have heard nothing." ' Knollys wrote to the Prime Minister on 23 March 1907 to express his 'regret that no information should have been given him [the King] respecting the proceedings of the Committee on the House of Lords. He says that the question is one of a grave constitutional character and that he should therefore be kept *au courant* with what goes on at the Committee, and further that he should be consulted before any recommendations are approved of by the Cabinet.'[447] Campbell-Bannerman was scrupulous in future to keep the King informed; as Knollys also told Esher: 'I think the Cabinet would make a great mistake if they made an enemy of him [the King] as their difficulties are increasing all round.'[448]

The first fruit of this deliberation was a resolution on 26 June 1907 in the Commons, to precede a Bill, declaring that the power of the Lords to alter or reject Bills passed by the Commons 'must be so restricted by law as to secure that within the limits of a single Parliament the final decision of the Commons should prevail'. This wording was a toned-down version of the original suggestion, which the King had questioned. Knollys had written to the Prime Minister on 16 June to say that 'the King desires me to say he thinks the expression "to give effect to the will of the people" savours more of a Republican than a Monarchical form of Government, but no doubt you had to consider the feelings of the left wing of your party.'[449] The revised resolution was carried by 432 votes to 147, but no Bill followed. The committee investigating what might be done had made some radical suggestions, such as establishing a number of 'delegate peers' who would have voting rights in proportion to the Commons majority.[450] The Lords showed what they thought of such moves by so amending the Small Landholders (Scotland) Bill that it had to be abandoned. The Prime Minister included a paragraph in the King's Speech at the prorogation of Parliament expressing regret that this measure had failed to come into law, but the King objected to having to express such regret, and the paragraph was dropped.

Two prospective measures that arose in 1907 excited the King's conservative prejudices. The first was a private Bill to promote a Channel Tunnel scheme, which the King, heavily lobbied by naval and military friends, strongly opposed. It was another issue on which Campbell-Bannerman starved the King of information, to the extent that the King began to make sarcastic remarks to Knollys about the pointlessness of Sir Henry's sending him Cabinet reports if they were going to be so uninformative. In a letter of 15 January 1907 the King had Knollys write to his Prime Minister, just to be on the safe side, to say that 'he directs me to express the hope that you are not now in favour of the Channel Tunnel scheme – he is greatly opposed to it himself, seeing but little advantage in such an undertaking, and from a national point of view very much disadvantage'.[451] The King thought a better ferry service would suffice. Knollys, showing an insight that later developers of the fixed link would have done well to note, expressed disbelief that the money would ever be raised for the project, or that it would prove financially viable.

The second incident that aggrieved the King, while he was making one of his early spring visits to Biarritz in March 1907, was to read an article by his Prime Minister in the new radical weekly the *Nation*, in which Sir Henry appeared to be supporting a reduction in armaments – and this coming hard on rumours, horrific to the King, that the Prime Minister was also in favour of votes for women. The King proclaimed himself 'disgusted' by the article, and said the women's franchise business was, like defence reductions, 'unnecessary and the matter very undigested'.[452] He complained vituperatively to Hardinge: 'I wonder if the Prime Minister realises how he has angered the French and German Press by his most injudicious article in *The Nation*. Ministers nowadays seem to forget the responsibilities of their office and ventilate their opinions as if they were private individuals.'[453] In fact, Hardinge had been aware of the article before it appeared, since the Foreign Office (of which he was permanent head) had approved it.

At the end of that month, however, the royal temper was improved by word that his government would, after all, oppose the Channel Tunnel. The King wrote to Sir Henry that 'I rejoice to see that you "put your foot down" regarding the Channel Tunnel.... I only wish you could have done the same regarding Female Suffrage. The conduct of the so-called "Suffragettes" has really been so outrageous and does their cause (for which I have no sympathy) much harm.'[454] Writing to the Prince of Wales on the matter, the King was characteristically blunt: 'thank heaven those dreadful women have not yet been enfranchised'.[455] The King's antipathy to this cause was intense. When the Home Secretary, Herbert Gladstone, wanted to release from prison women on hunger strike, the King wanted to know why they could not be force-fed rather than have their sentences cut. Writing from Marienbad in August 1909, Fritz Ponsonby told Gladstone: 'His Majesty is inclined to think that this short term of Martyrdom is more likely to attract women than deter them from joining the ranks of the militant suffragettes.'[456] The following month the King was 'glad to hear that strong measures were going to be taken' against these women.[457]

The King's relations with Lord Minto, who early in 1906 succeeded Curzon as Viceroy of India, were correct and civil, but less warm than those with Curzon had been. There was a problem of growing sedition in India, about which Minto kept the King informed. In these matters, the King was an arch-conservative. When Campbell-Bannerman told him in August 1907 that the Commander-in-Chief wanted curbs on the press in India to help restrict the stirring up of unrest, the King was annoyed to hear that Morley, the Indian Secretary, and the Cabinet were against such censorship. He had Ponsonby, accompanying him in Marienbad, write to the Prime Minister on 19 August to say that 'the King hopes that the Cabinet realise the grave responsibility they have assumed in refusing to accede to a request put forward not only by the Commander-in-Chief in India, but also by the Viceroy and his council'.[458] He understood the inflammatory nature of such a law, but expressed the hope that:

> the Cabinet will carefully consider the question whether some stringent laws should not be passed with regard to the press generally. The freedom of the press, although an undoubted boon to a free people under self-government, is apt to be abused by a people under the autocratic government of another race. There is no doubt the disloyal press is mainly responsible for the trouble we have had in India, and the King would, therefore, impress on you the importance of discussing this question with as little delay as possible.

The King eventually had his way, for it was not until a new Prime Minister, Asquith, was in office, that the Cabinet discussed the matter, and brought the new Press Act in.

However, the King did not always prevail in Indian matters. On the fiftieth anniversary of the Mutiny in 1907 he suggested, somewhat tactlessly, that there might be a distribution of honours to some of the surviving officers; but the India Office, fearing the effect such triumphalism might have on the native population, refused. The following year he had a difference of opinion with the government over the programme of reforms drawn up between Morley and Minto, which would allow the Indians themselves a larger share in the government. The King's objection was to the prospect of Indians being admitted to the Viceroy's council, an objection he had in common with many members of the House of Lords. The objection was made not on racial grounds – as we have seen, the King was unusual in his time in being unencumbered by such prejudices – but because he feared the reform would cause offence to native princes, on whose goodwill the Raj greatly relied. Nothing happened, though, until 1909, when Satyendra Prasanno Sinha, a prominent Hindu lawyer, was nominated. The King protested, and begged Morley to reconsider; and with two former viceroys, Lansdowne and Curzon, on the King's side, Morley was forced for a time to have second thoughts.

Knollys wrote to the King, who was at Biarritz, on 6 March 1909, to say that Morley had told Esher he was thinking again, and Esher thought Morley would back down if he could; but the effect of such a disappointment on native opinion in India would have been grave. On 10 March, Morley put Sinha's nomination to the Cabinet, which approved it unanimously, and Morley explained to the King that not to have done so would have endangered the support for the reforms that had been growing up in India. He implored the King, whose favour he was desperate to keep, to support what he had done, defending this 'act of high policy' as best he could.[459] 'Nothing but a strong conviction of its expediency – almost amounting to necessity – for the contentment and stability of Your Majesty's Indian Dominions, would have induced Lord Morley so earnestly to ask for an assent which Your Majesty, on grounds most easily understood by him, may hesitate to give.'

The King, to begin with, said he could not change his views. He thought the step 'fraught with the greatest danger to the maintenance of the Indian Empire under British rule'.[460] He accepted that he had 'no alternative' but to accept the unanimous decision of the Cabinet, but 'wishes it clearly to be understood that he protests most strongly at this new departure'. He also conveyed his dislike of the step to Minto, admitting that he may well have 'very strong and possibly old-fashioned views on the subject'.[461] He told Minto that at a time of unrest there were all sorts of dangers in including a 'native' on the Viceroy's council; and he also wondered why, if a Hindu were to be included, a Moslem were not to be included too. He closed his letter to Minto with the rather minatory exhortation 'that you never repent the important step now made is the ardent wish of yours very sincerely, Edward R&I'.[462] For a moment, the business strained the King's relations with Morley, who had written in abasement and gratitude when the King had given his reluctant assent. Morley, thinking of assurances given by the late Queen of greater involvement in Indian affairs by Indians, defined this act as a 'marked fulfilment of Queen Victoria's historic promise' which 'will win for Your Majesty an exalted and enduring place in the deepest affections of the Indian subjects of the British Crown'.[463] The King, ensconced appropriately at the Hôtel du Palais in Biarritz with his *maîtresse en titre*, Mrs George Keppel, was nonplussed: 'why he should bring in the name of Queen Victoria I cannot see – or how it bears on the question. I myself do not think she would have approved of the new departure. I have had to sign the objectionable paper.'[464]

HOUSEHOLD CONCERNS

Although the King had accused his Prime Minister of a promiscuous approach to the award of honours, he maintained the heavy traffic of recommendations of his own. In March 1907 he had a disagreement with Campbell-Bannerman over the post of Lord Steward, made vacant by the death of the Earl of Liverpool. It was a political post, but the King wanted it filled with someone congenial to him – his friend Lord Farquhar, a Liberal Unionist and acting Steward during Liverpool's final illness.[465] Sir Henry, who had earlier readily agreed to the acting appointment as 'most desirable', however wanted a fully paid-up supporter of his party, Lord Chesterfield. Finding this uncongenial, the King tried to compromise by suggesting that Farquhar remain acting Steward, unsalaried.[466] But Campbell-Bannerman continued his habit of putting his foot down, and had Lord Beauchamp appointed instead, to which the King assented.[467] He managed to secure a Privy Councillorship for Farquhar as a consolation. Normally, in matters concerning the household, the King exercised more tact than in seeking to influence appointments that did not so directly concern him. Knollys, for example, in a letter to the Prime Minister of 16 February 1907, wrote that 'the King has of course no idea whom you propose to recommend to him for the appointment of Vice-Chamberlain, but he desires me to mention to you, please understand as a suggestion only, the name of Dalmeny, but HM has no wish whatever to press him in any way upon you'.[468]

The end of Arnold-Forster's reign at the War Office was for the King one of the happiest by-products of the change of ministry in December 1905. He quickly warmed to his successor, Haldane, whom he perceived as having none of the faults of 'manner' that had so coloured his view of his predecessor. Haldane was keen to establish a strong territorial army, and instituted a committee – sensibly, given his desire for the King's support, under Esher – to consider how best this might be done. The old defence sub-committee established under Balfour continued, with Esher still a member and still reporting its every activity loyally to the King. Since Haldane also listened to Esher with great respect, and acted on much of his advice, the King was soon happy that he had the army under control again after the Arnold-Forster nightmare, when a minister had dared show independence of thought and regard for his party's democratic mandate. Haldane could not have been more compliant, effectively handing over the entire manufacture of policy to Esher, whom he told on 10 December 1905 'he is "willing to be nobbled" by our Committee'.[469] Two days later, at luncheon with the King, Esher reported not just his 'very satisfactory talk' with Haldane, but that Haldane – for which read Esher and the King – had been promised 'a free hand' by Campbell-Bannerman.[470]

Haldane consulted the King regularly throughout 1906 about the nature of the reserve he was planning, and in January 1907 showed him the draft Territorial and Reserve Forces Bill. Ironically, the King was far keener on this than were Haldane's own colleagues, some of whom harboured distinctly pacific tendencies and did not like the idea of hitherto harmless civilians playing soldiers. Haldane found himself enlisting the King to persuade Campbell-Bannerman of the rightness of the proposals. This the King did, to good effect, reversing once more the supposed constitutional procedure of the King acting only on the advice of his Prime Minister. When the Bill establishing the Territorial Army was enacted later in the year, he summoned all the Lords Lieutenant of Great Britain to a meeting in London at which he impressed upon them the importance of their helping to launch the County Associations of the Territorial Army. To press home his point further, the King announced on 18 November 1907 his command that no one should become a deputy lieutenant of a county unless he had served ten years in the forces, or in connection with a County Territorial Army Association.

Haldane obeyed the King's injunction to keep him informed in detail about all that went on in the army; and in the spring of 1907 the

King's attention was seized by a report Haldane sent him of the proceedings of a court of inquiry into the activities of a Lieutenant F. C. H. Tryon of the Dorsetshire Regiment 'who absented himself from his duty and enlisted as a private in the Seaforth Highlanders at Edinburgh under an assumed name'.[471] Tryon was in charge of his company's funds and had dipped into them, the deficit becoming obvious because he had kept the accounts honestly. Stricken, too, with influenza, he had an attack of panic and ran off, but, so as not to desert (he thought) joined another regiment. A young officer going missing – his effects were found at the Metropole Hotel, London – was quite a story, and a resemblance was noted by some of his brother soldiers between the photograph of Tryon in the newspapers and one Private John Fraser of the Seaforth Highlanders. Confronted with the accusation, Fraser denied he was Tryon, but had to admit it when Tryon's father and uncle turned up to identify him. Tryon's father repaid the missing sum of £26 13s 9d. Medical evidence from an army doctor said that while Tryon was sane, 'his nervous system had been affected by an attack of influenza, and he was not entirely responsible for his actions'.[472] The Court took pity on him, not least because the money had been repaid, and invited him to resign rather than be court-martialled. Haldane urged the King to endorse this 'merciful' course.

The King, normally the most liberal of men, would do nothing of the sort. Ponsonby wrote to Haldane:

> His Majesty ... cannot see any grounds for the very lenient course you propose to adopt. This case has excited so much interest that the King fears that it might have a very bad effect on the rank and file were Lieut. Tryon to receive exceptional treatment simply because he was an Officer. If a non-commissioned Officer was to be tried for desertion, fraudulent enlistment and for having a deficit of £26 in the money entrusted to him, the plea of influenza would hardly hold good. The fact that Lieut. Tryon's father made good the money can hardly be taken in extenuation of the offence. And his having enlisted as a private soldier makes it all the more necessary that he should be tried by Court Martial.[473]

The bond with Haldane became closer the more radical some other elements in the Liberal administration grew. Haldane took great trouble to write lengthy but entertaining memoranda to the King, not just about domestic departmental matters but also about his overseas trips – notably to Germany, where he would watch the manoeuvres of the Kaiser's army – which satisfied the main demand the King had of any of his ministers, that they keep him fully informed. Unlike Arnold-Forster, Haldane also knew when best to back off: such as when early in 1906 the King had made it clear that while he might consent to the reduction in size of certain colonial garrisons, in the interests of economy, he would never consent to reductions in the size of those garrisons in South Africa. The Foreign Office had long been telling the King that, in the event of an Anglo-German conflict, troops in German South-West Africa were poised to invade the British colonies, with assistance from still-disgruntled Boers.[474] Also, as the King told Esher on 3 April 1906, 'I lay great stress on Cavalry regiments being in Egypt and South Africa because the training ground is so good.'[475]

The King kept close tabs on Haldane through Esher, maintaining via that conduit a steady flow of wishes upon which he expected Haldane to act. Their relations remained broadly good, though towards the end of 1907 Haldane was for a short period out of favour for being, as Esher saw it, 'too progressive'.[476] Such reforms as were implemented were initiated by Esher, and the King came to regard him as *de facto* Secretary of State. Sent a new order for signing in December 1907, the King asked Knollys to put it in front of Esher first – 'the King has become very suspicious of the W.O. and will not sign anything of this sort, emanating from them, unless it is certified by you!'[477]

When Esher himself was briefly out of favour in the spring of 1908 the King despaired, feeling there was no one he could trust on military matters – he wrote to Esher from Biarritz on 11 April that year to warn him, on the subject of the latest plans for reform, that 'you attach too much importance to the opinions of the General Officers who have no alternative but to express agreement with the present scheme'.[478] The King was very susceptible to what opinion in elevated circles in Europe thought of his country, and was angry to keep hearing from such sources of 'England, in its present unprepared state ... and yet His Majesty is assured that the army is in a better state than it has been before. The King says that this thirst for economy has completely overshadowed the real aim which should be efficiency.' At times, the King did not seem to know who was most appropriate to receive such rebukes: Esher or Haldane. Normal constitutional procedures, of a sort, soon returned. When in the autumn of 1908 the War Secretary was pressurised by Churchill and Lloyd George to cut military spending again, he found the King privately urging him to resist them. Haldane, emboldened by the support he received from above, faced them down, and managed to prepare an army that was not to be embarrassed when 1914 came.

NOT BEING BEASTLY TO THE GERMANS

As soon as the Liberal government had been confirmed in power in January 1906, the King took an opportunity to try to resume something approaching cordial relations with the Kaiser, in the interests of Anglo-German harmony. He sent a charming letter to his nephew on the occasion of his forty-seventh birthday that month, and congratulated him on his impending silver wedding anniversary; he added that 'above all, I am desirous that the feeling between our two countries may be on the best footing'.[479] In reply to this, and further assurances that many of the base rumours the Kaiser heard about British intentions towards him were simply untrue, the Kaiser replied that 'the whole letter breathed such an atmosphere of kindness and warm, sympathetic friendship that it constitutes the most cherished gift among my presents'.[480] It seemed desirable – certainly the Kaiser wanted it – for the two men to meet during 1906; but the Algeciras conference was still proceeding, trying to settle the Moroccan question, and the government deemed it too provocative to the sensibilities of the new ally, France, for the King to be seen cosying up to the Kaiser just then. When the Moroccan question was satisfactorily resolved that summer, an arrangement was made for the two to meet on the King's journey to Marienbad. Grey and Hardinge were both cautious about asking the Kaiser to Windsor. When the suggestion was made by the Germans, the King, on their advice, deferred his answer for three months so as to be sure that his nephew 'is springing no new surprise on us'.[481] There was some justification in this attitude, for, even in the wake of the recent unbridled displays of familial affection, the Kaiser had said that 'meetings with Edward have no lasting value, because he is envious'.[482] When the meeting took place, at Cronberg on 15 August 1906, Hardinge, accompanying the King, deemed it 'a great success', and genuinely believed relations were improving between the two countries.[483]

After a few more ups and downs, the Kaiser finally paid his state visit in the autumn of 1907, Grey and Hardinge having given their approval the previous spring.[484] A flurry of attacks on Britain in the German press during April and May for a moment threatened the visit, but it proceeded, the invitation being issued at the end of June after a visit to Germany by the Lord Mayor of London had passed without incident, and after Hardinge and Knollys had endlessly assessed the temperature. Because the King was much more at one with Grey on foreign policy than he ever was with Lansdowne, he had less need to seek to influence the implementation of foreign policy in the second half of his reign than he had in the first. He also had the reassuring presence of Hardinge at the Foreign Office, and Hardinge and Knollys corresponded regularly, thereby keeping the King always *au fait* with developments.

However, he and Grey disagreed on one question concerning the Kaiser's visit. The Kaiser wanted to bring his War Minister as well as his Foreign Minister with him, which Grey saw might alarm the French.[485] The King said he could not interfere in the question of whom his nephew wished to include in his suite, so Grey's protest was fruitless. However, when the King heard that the Kaiser was planning to bring his Chancellor, Bülow, with him, even he drew the line, because of long memories in Britain about the Chancellor's comments in the Boer War. Hardinge, who was an old friend of Bülow's, told Metternich how unfortunate it would be for the Chancellor to come to Britain and be treated less than cordially by some elements, and Metternich agreed to advise Bülow not to come.[486] The Kaiser threatened not to come either, but to send the Crown Prince with the Kaiserin instead, using the diplomatic device of 'a very virulent attack of influenza', because it had been made clear to him how unpopular he was in England.[487]

The King told his nephew of the 'terrible disappointment' a cancellation would cause, and overrode Grey's advice that a postponement might be better.[488] The Kaiser also had a particularly embarrassing problem at home: his best friend, Count Eulenburg, had been exposed in a lurid homosexual scandal. He was threatened with criminal charges, and the Kaiser wanted to keep his head down. As it turned out, however, the Kaiser came, since Bülow endorsed his uncle's protestations that it would be wrong to cancel; and although Grey briefed the King thoroughly on subjects likely to be raised by the Kaiser, the King made a plan to try to avoid political discussions as far as he possibly could. Such matters as did come up – and the Germans were much concerned at this time with the Baghdad railway – he was more than happy to leave to Grey, or to the Germanophile and Germanophone Haldane. So touchy had matters now become between the King and the Kaiser that the King, noting a reference to Anglo-German relations in a draft of the King's Speech the following January, had Knollys write to Vaughan Nash, Campbell-Bannerman's secretary, to say that 'the word "nephew" in connection with the German Emperor had better be omitted and ... no mention of the relationship should be made'.[489]

Lord Cromer, since 1883 agent and consul-general in Egypt, had turned down the foreign secretaryship on the grounds of indifferent health in 1906; and the following year he sent word to the King that he would have to leave Egypt for the same reason. Cromer had won the King's confidence not least for the role he had played in solving marginal problems concerned with Egypt at the time of the *entente cordiale*; and although he found Cromer personally abrasive, he could not bear to think of this superlative public servant leaving his post. He begged Cromer to reconsider, saying that his leaving would be 'a serious calamity', and suggested that a six months' rest cure might do the trick.[490] Cromer's doctors disagreed, so that was that. The King saw him immediately on his return to England and offered him the Garter, but Cromer declined and asked, instead, for a grant of money. The government suggested £50,000, at which the King observed: 'The Government had better settle the matter. They know my views.'[491] The government made no attempt to interfere with the King's wishes.

SOOTHING RUSSIA

Once the Anglo-French entente was concluded, it created for the King a further ambition, the filling in of a missing link in his country's diplomacy: the establishment of formal good relations with France's other main ally, Russia. Charles Hardinge, while ambassador at St Petersburg, had kept the King and Knollys informed regularly about the course of events, and in October 1905 had, at the King's command, expressed 'a desire for the establishment of the most friendly relations between the two countries and settlement of outstanding differences'.[492] Hardinge, on behalf of his royal master, also urged the Tsar on in his liberal reforms. Apart from explaining away British support for Japan, three important policy areas had to be addressed if an understanding were to be reached: conflicts of international policy in Persia, Afghanistan and China. The revolutionary upheavals of the following month put a brake on this activity, but within months pressure was building in St Petersburg for the King to visit Russia, and Count Witte, the Tsar's Prime Minister, held out the possibility of some sort of friendship treaty if the King came. Given the instability in Russia, the King was unlikely to be allowed by his ministers to travel there; but, just as he had met the Kaiser off Kiel, so his government decided he could meet the Tsar on a yacht in the Baltic. Grey and the government were keen, in the interests of international amity, to remove the remaining obstacles to a better Anglo-Russian understanding, and were convinced an entente could be achieved. Grey did, however, warn Knollys that any further sign of the heavy hand of the Tsar's forces being used against the Russian people would stimulate repugnance in Britain, and make an entente impossible, however much the King might want it.

The King too had reservations about going for a private meeting aboard his yacht during the summer of 1906, not just because of how it might play at home, or because of the unrest in Russia, but because it risked causing offence to the Kaiser, a state visit to whom the King had been avoiding, and who would cause trouble if one were paid to the Tsar first. Also Grey, in a letter to Knollys of 28 March 1906, had made clear the government's position about such a royal visit: 'Even if the state of Russia gets no worse, I do not think the King could pay a visit inland. It is not only a question of risk – that might be less for him than for anyone, but still he ought not to go, if there is any risk; apart from that Russia in its disturbed state is not suitable territory in which to hold a social gathering.'[493] To try to show goodwill the government instead offered to send a naval squadron to the Baltic. The Tsar blocked that idea, writing to the King of the 'state of acute unrest' of his country that persisted after the revolutionary events of 1905, and adding that it was unlikely to be improved by the visit of a foreign fleet.[494] The new ambassador in St Petersburg, Sir Arthur Nicolson, kept the King fully informed about the progress of the anarchy there. None of this boded well for the attempt at an entente, which the King in turn thought would help liberalise Russia and reduce its internal stresses.

As the domestic unrest continued in Russia, the chances of an entente between such an unstable country and Britain seemed remote. Also, both Minto (as Viceroy) and Kitchener (as Commander-in-Chief) let it be known that it would be received badly in India to have the King and his government looking for a formal alliance with the country that had been the main force for destabilisation in Asia. However, Morley told both men that the Cabinet wanted the entente, if and when it was possible, and that was final; but the King, wishing to stop any difficulties early on, telegraphed to Hardinge at the Foreign Office on 22 September to tell him that if the 'Foreign Office does not act in unison with Viceroy of India matters might be very serious, as Russian diplomacy never varies'.[495] On the same day, he asked Grey to do what he could to answer the points made by Kitchener and Minto.

The King's next initiative, he hoped, was to be inviting Isvolsky (who had just become the Tsar's Foreign Minister, and whom the King met in Paris) to London to discuss the future of Anglo-Russian relations. The King seemed successfully to have smoothed the way by telling many whom he met in diplomatic circles just what a fine fellow he thought Isvolsky was – which, of course, got back to Isvolsky and caused him great pleasure.[496] This plan did not, though, find immediate favour with either Grey or Hardinge. They felt the move might be interpreted as rushing the Russians. The King, acting less independently than he had with the French at a similar stage, accepted their advice.[497] Also, Sir Arthur Nicolson reported that the Russian people and government had still not warmed to the idea of an entente, but the Tsar showed willingness to move the process along in spite of that.

Treading carefully, it was possible for the two governments to start formal negotiations in February 1907, Isvolsky and Nicolson having been in regular contact for some months beforehand. The King was kept informed throughout, and suggested that the officers and men of a Russian squadron that had visited Portsmouth in March 1907 should come to London; they were enthusiastically welcomed, a practical gesture that helped the diplomatic processes. At the end of August 1907 a draft treaty was signed at the Russian Foreign Office by Nicolson and Isvolsky, and ratifications signed by the King and the Tsar were exchanged three weeks later, bringing the Anglo-Russian entente formally into existence. Persia had been divided into spheres of influence, and in response to a question from the King during the negotiations, it was admitted that Britain had special influence in the Persian Gulf – a matter kept out of the Treaty for fear of offending the

Germans, but which, to the King's satisfaction, Grey had promised to make a supplementary statement upon once the Treaty was ratified. On Afghanistan, both countries guaranteed its neutrality, and the same applied to Tibet. The King met Isvolsky in Marienbad in early September, and one or two further areas of possible conflict, such as India, were discussed amicably, and new understandings reached.

If the King's part in this entente is not seen by historians as so central as his role in the agreement with France of three years earlier, that was not how it was inevitably viewed at the time. Hardinge, who had been by his side for the meeting with Isvolsky at Marienbad, certainly believed the King's diplomacy was still active and necessary – though, of course, he was so much in the King's debt that his analysis may not be considered objective. Nonetheless, Hardinge wrote to the King on 4 September 1907:

> if it will not be presumptuous on my part to say so, I venture to express the opinion that no Sovereign has ever, by peaceful methods, contributed more than Your Majesty to the pursuit of a successful foreign policy and to the predominance of his country in the Councils of Europe – when a comparison is made of the position of England abroad in 1900 and what the country now occupies, Your Majesty has every reason for a feeling of profound satisfaction.[498]

Despite some in the Liberal party feeling that the alliance condoned what they regarded to be the unpalatable nature of parts of the Tsar's regime, the conclusion of the entente was popularly seen, at home and abroad, as another personal victory for the King: as a result of which Britain found itself in a triple alliance with France and Russia of huge, and eventually terrible, consequence.

CONFUSION ABROAD

By the end of 1907 Campbell-Bannerman's health was failing badly, and the King, who had become rather fond of his Prime Minister and near-contemporary, did what he could to help by inviting the ailing man to Balmoral to recuperate. After leaving Deeside the Prime Minister embarked on a short round of speechmaking, which (as if to demonstrate his robustness and vigour) included a threat to call an election if the Lords continued to override the will of the Commons.

During his stay at Balmoral, the King had implored him to remember that the conflict between the two Houses touched on his own constitutional position, but the Prime Minister apparently saw no way to keep the King out of it. A heart attack in November 1907, the first of several, marked the effective end of the Prime Minister's career, though he remained in office for more than another four months. Asquith became *de facto* leader of the party while the Prime Minister convalesced in Biarritz (at the King's recommendation). Arthur Ponsonby, the Prime Minister's secretary, warned Knollys on 29 December 1907 that 'there is no disguising the fact that he has lost ground considerably during the last two years'.[499] This was breathtaking understatement: Sir Henry was almost dead.

On his return to England he presided at a Cabinet meeting on 12 February, but it was to be his last. He was almost immediately felled by influenza and Asquith again filled his place in an acting capacity. Esher warned Knollys on 27 February that Sir Henry 'cannot possibly go on'.[500] The King paid a rare visit to Downing Street in early March, before his own spring sojourn in Biarritz, to see his Prime Minister. It was the last time they would meet. The King told Campbell-Bannerman that it would be most inconvenient for him if the Prime Minister were to resign while he was abroad, and so asked him whether he could postpone that day until early May, when the King would be back from Biarritz. The King's own health was poor after a winter in London, and the Biarritz trip was no mere luxurious indulgence. The bronchial trouble that would eventually kill him was now disturbing his doctors, who had ordered a warm-weather holiday and no return to London until the weather improved there. The Prime Minister said he would delay his resignation to suit the King. He was glad to hear the King's wishes, since he had been battling with his colleagues to stay in office; they seemed to realise better than he did how ill he was.

The next day the King left for France, but before doing so saw Asquith. There had been wide consultation about the constitutional propriety of this meeting, given that Sir Henry had not resigned and Asquith had therefore not kissed hands; but as even Balfour, as Opposition leader, did not object, the King went ahead with the meeting.[501] They talked about the Licensing Bill, and the King observed that he would be happier for there not to be a great reconstruction of the government on Campbell-Bannerman's departure, and he voiced scepticism about Churchill's claims for Cabinet office, a scepticism his next Prime Minister sought to dispel.[502] Asquith, reporting the conversation to his wife, said that 'he said he had quite made up his mind to send for me at once in the event of anything happening to C-B, or of his sending in his resignation'. In fact, the King had recently consulted Rosebery about whether Asquith or Grey should be Sir Henry's successor, so the matter was not so clear-cut in the King's mind as it might otherwise appear.[503] Also, in case Grey did become Prime Minister, Knollys had canvassed Hardinge about who should succeed him at the Foreign Office. Hardinge was in no doubt that the King should press Morley for that post.[504]

The King's reservations about Churchill are notable. Only a year earlier he and Churchill had coincided with each other at Biarritz, and the King appears to have continued the almost fatherly interest that he had displayed in his young minister so often before. On leaving the resort, Churchill had written to the King 'to say that I very deeply feel the great kindness with which you have treated me during my visit here, and what a pleasure and privilege it has been to me to be allowed to talk to Your Majesty about public matters so fully and freely'.[505] In stark contravention of the attitude the King would subsequently credit Churchill with taking, the minister continued: 'Your Majesty's long friendship with my family, of which I can remember so many evidences from my childhood's days, will always make me wish most earnestly to win and to preserve some measure of Your Majesty's approval in my public and private conduct.' The King had replied, 'My one wish is that the great qualities you possess may be turned to good account & that your services to the State may be appreciated.'[506]

While in Biarritz the King – whose own health, aggravated by his heavy smoking and obesity, was so problematical that he had to take a ground-floor suite in his favourite hotel to remove the need to climb the stairs – received bulletins about the deterioration of his Prime Minister. The Campbell-Bannerman papers have several letters and telegrams from Biarritz at this time, purely enquiring after Sir Henry's health: the King's concern was undoubtedly genuine and consistent. In the middle of March he heard that Sir Henry was now so weak and pessimistic about his health that he wished to resign. The King asked that, if possible, this be postponed until after Easter, the earliest the Monarch could return from Biarritz. Knollys kept him almost daily posted with news of Sir Henry's failure to make a recovery. To avoid any appearance of being taken on the hop, the King further requested, on 17 March 1908, that 'in the event of Prime Minister's resignation or fatal crisis in illness, the King would like authoritative announcement made that before he left England it was settled that Mr Asquith should at once come out to see His Majesty at Biarritz'.[507] Knollys told him that this would be 'a very simple affair', and need cause no problems, not least because Asquith had told the King that 'he proposed to make no alterations whatever at first'.[508] This was a rare bout of naivety by Knollys, who in his desire to please the King had not foreseen the controversy this would cause, or the difficulties of the King being abroad when, effectively, the country had no Prime Minister.

Also, Asquith — setting the tone for his premiership — would soon change his mind about needing to reconstruct the government. Knollys assumed that Asquith had not told his colleagues about his intention to avoid a reshuffle, and was worldly enough to realise that when the time came 'Mr Haldane, Mr Harcourt and Mr Churchill will set to work "wire pulling"'. For the moment, in accordance with the King's request, the Prime Minister stayed his hand; but, as Asquith told Knollys in a letter at the end of March, the 'status quo cannot go on' as things were 'very demoralising', and a fresh start had to be made by the government.[509]

By this time, Knollys had already relayed to the King the news that Asquith was keen to reconstruct the government: not just that, but that Asquith had already decided who should move where in this reconstruction.[510] Given that Sir Henry had not yet resigned, the King felt this forwardness to be in dubious taste and 'rather dreadful' — 'it reminds one of a dying animal with the vultures hovering about him'.[511] The King also commented on Asquith's 'drastic intentions' — presumably the elevation of Lloyd George to the Treasury and Churchill to the Cabinet as President of the Board of Trade. Admitting the decline in his prerogative and power, the King said that he could not see why 'in these democratic days' he had to come home to hold a Council for the transmission of seals of office — 'that could all be perfectly accomplished at Paris at my Embassy, which is British ground'. That, though, was a sick man talking: as Knollys realised, such a ceremony would be unthinkable, and would damage the Crown. The King also signalled to Knollys two things he would expect of Asquith: that Reginald McKenna, the President of the Board of Education, should become First Lord of the Admiralty, and that Fisher should remain in his post as First Sea Lord.

Things were getting out of hand. The King, who had he been at home would almost certainly have imposed some sort of restoration of order, was instead in the South of France having a rest. As he had become older and his health had worsened, his interest in politics and his energy for it had declined, particularly since the coming of the Liberal government. Hardinge entertained him with long, frequent and ingratiating dispatches from the Foreign Office, reporting on world events, but the King's appetite for domestic matters was far less keen. The Prime Minister had, by the end of March, been laid up for six weeks and unable to run his ministry, and Asquith as yet had not the formal authority to do so. The King, on medical advice, prolonged his stay in Biarritz. He had Knollys brief Asquith that nothing rash should be done, and that there was no need for immediate action. Facing the realities of severe ill-health, the King had forgotten his own advice to his mother at the time of the 1885 crisis. He was not blind to the realities, though: he wrote to Knollys on 25 March to say that 'the poor Prime Minister still holds on – though I know his days if not his hours are numbered'.[512]

Knollys seemed, from the tone of his correspondence to the King, to realise that what was happening was taking the situation off the edge of any available map. As he relayed Asquith's more and more detailed plans, he ventured, in a tone of unusual uncertainty, that 'I believe I shall be carrying out Your Majesty's views by resisting Sir H. C-Bannerman's resignation being effected until the Easter holidays.'[513] Given that Knollys had already written of his certainty that Sir Henry would be dead by the Easter holidays, this seems to suggest a loss of grip. Nonetheless, Knollys kept the King as well informed as was possible, not least about Asquith's plans for his ministry. 'He thinks that Lord Elgin should retire,' he wrote on 25 March. 'He is of no use either in the Cabinet or in the House of Lords ... that Lord Tweedmouth should be moved to another office – he looks upon him as being quite unequal to the work of his present office – that Lord Ripon and Sir H Fowler should go.'[514]

In the same letter, Knollys confirmed that Asquith wanted Lloyd George to succeed him at the Treasury, which will not have improved the King's health, and that Churchill would enter the Cabinet. Knollys warned Asquith that the King would 'never agree' to Loulou Harcourt, son of the great Liberal statesman Sir William, going to the Admiralty, and wanted McKenna instead, but had no luck in persuading Asquith that Gladstone, the Home Secretary, regarded by the King as 'inefficient', should go. Hoping the King would take the hint and come home, Knollys reported how 'demoralising' Asquith had found the state of affairs, but even the threatened promotions of Lloyd George and Churchill were insufficient to make the King budge, as was Knollys's insistence that Sir Henry's life 'could not be prolonged beyond a number of *days* not *weeks*'.

In fact, the King (at his distant remove) had entirely misjudged the situation, and the need was urgent. There was massive public pressure for the sick Prime Minister to stand down; and, in those days before the 1911 Parliament Act, newly appointed ministers had to resign their seats and offer themselves for approval by their voters at by-elections. If the resignation of the ailing Prime Minister and the reshuffle by his successor were delayed any longer, the ministers who had to seek re-election would not be able to do so in time to be back in the Commons for the start of the new session after the Easter recess. Knollys himself was embarrassed by the King's attitude, and, knowing Asquith would immediately become Prime Minister, wrote to him on 30 March to say that 'when you see him, I hope you will urge upon him as strongly as possible the propriety of his coming back. I am *sure* he ought to return, and I have gone as far, and perhaps further, in what I have said to him than I am entitled to go. But of course he will attach far more weight to your opinion on this subject, speaking as Prime Minister, than to mine.'[515] He also revealed to Asquith that he had told the King 'that it would not look at all well that these ceremonies should take place in Paris'.[516] Asquith replied at once, agreeing entirely: 'I shall not fail to urge this view upon him as strongly as I can.'[517] Davidson, accompanying the King, sent a note of hope to Knollys. Mrs Keppel, out for a drive with the King, had asked him whether Campbell-Bannerman's death would make any difference to the King's plans. 'He said he could not say,' Davidson reported, 'but he meant to do whatever the future Prime Minister suggested – which I take it evidently that he will return home (if asked to do so).'[518]

Knollys telegraphed to the King on 1 April to say that Sir Henry, who was now giving up the ghost, would 'probably resign' by the end of the week; but the King, who feared this would necessitate his immediate return to England, wired back that he was 'most anxious that he should not resign till Easter vacation'.[519] Scarcely had this message been sent, however, than the King received a message from Campbell-Bannerman saying he was resigning. He said:

> the state of doubt and anxiety in which I am is most prejudicial to my health, and this to a large extent because I know how inconvenient and

unpleasant the position must be to your Majesty ... I trust in seeking to be relieved of my position your Majesty will take into consideration my weakness, the great sense of responsibility which weighs upon me, and my anxiety as to the effect upon public affairs of my continued inability to discharge the duties of my office.[520]

The King, who immediately telegraphed his 'sincere regret', admitted he had 'no other alternative but to accept'.[521] Indeed, one of the King's own physicians had examined Campbell-Bannerman that morning, and ordered him to resign.[522] Sir Henry, who would be dead within three weeks, sent another message of gratitude for being relieved of his duties, and advising the King – as the King had expected – to send for Asquith. The King had made up his mind on another matter: he was not coming home. He wrote to Asquith asking him to form a government, adding that he would 'be glad to see him here at any time that he can conveniently come in order to hear from him what proposals he has to make.'[523] This unprecedented arrangement caused much annoyance at home, where politicians felt that they had already been messed about enough by the King; and there were protests in particular that Asquith would, on a trip to the South of France that would take at least four days there and back, miss a vital debate on the Licensing Bill.

A formal protest to this effect was made by Haldane; but he was told by Fritz Ponsonby, obviously at the King's instigation, that if the Bill were that important the debate on it should be postponed until after Asquith had kissed hands. *The Times*, too, took umbrage at the 'inconvenient and dangerous departure from precedent' in which the King had engaged, though the article concerned was written by Colonel Charles À Court Repington, who bore a personal grudge against the King for his having refused to reinstate him as a commissioned officer after his involvement in a divorce case.[524] Indeed, only the previous month, Esher had been asked by Knollys 'to give Mr Haldane a hint that Your Majesty will never consent to the re-instatement of Colonel À Court Repington in the Army.'[525] In an unprecedented piece of news management, Knollys had an item 'inserted' in several newspapers, via Downing Street, on 10 April: 'It is understood that the visit of the King to Biarritz has been undertaken solely in conformity with the strongly expressed opinions of His Majesty's medical advisers owing to the repeated attacks of influenza to which the King has been subjected during the spring of successive years.'[526]

In fact, Asquith himself was quite happy with the arrangement, observing 'that he would be glad to come out as it would be an advantage to be abroad during the difficult time of forming a Cabinet'.[527] Nor was the Opposition vexed. Knollys had thought to raise the prospect of this turn of events with Balfour on 24 February, and the ex-Prime Minister had told him that 'there is I imagine no precedent for a King appointing a ministry by letters written abroad: though this does not seem to me very material.'[528]

Whether it actually mattered where the kissing of hands took place, the King had made a far graver error – whatever the difficulties with his health – of allowing his own convenience to come before constitutional requirements. Since he had insisted on Campbell-Bannerman's delaying his resignation, he should at least have made sure before he did so that he understood the political situation that he was, as a result, creating. It was 8 April by the time Asquith met the King in Biarritz and completed the formalities. The King, for all his earlier sniffiness about certain appointments, approved the suggested new Cabinet without demur. Arranging to return to London on 16 April, he told Asquith he would see his new ministers then. There had been speculation between Knollys and Esher that a ship might have to convey many members of the administration out to Biarritz, and lie off the coast while a kissing-of-hands took place. However, it did not come to that Gilbertian performance.

When they at last met, the King accepted a radical constitutional departure from his new Prime Minister. He told Admiral Fisher in a letter of 14 April that Asquith had convinced him that, in future, it was essential that the ministers in charge of big spending departments should sit in the Commons.[529] The other great change that was to come in under Asquith was for the moment less visible. For all his difficulties with the House of Lords, Campbell-Bannerman had never seriously steeled himself to take them on, despite the preparatory legislative work that had been undertaken on the question of their constitutional rights. The last King's Speech before Sir Henry's resignation had had as its centrepiece the Licensing Bill. Asquith, a much younger and more intellectually supple man, was prepared to have the fight with the Lords. His appointment of Lloyd George to the Treasury was the key action that made such a fight inevitable. Perhaps the ministers themselves did not entirely appreciate the extent of the conflict they were preparing to have. Certainly, to judge by the stunned shock with which he would receive the news from the battlefield up until the end of his reign, the King had no idea how sharply the natural order of things was about to change.

THE GARDEN-PARTY CRISIS

The King was still pressing for a meeting with the Tsar, and firm plans were made for this to happen off Reval in the Baltic on their yachts during the Whitsun holiday of 1908. The King wanted to go to Russia itself, but Hardinge and Knollys between them conspired to insist that considerations of his safety made such a thing impossible.[530] It was decided to make the arrangements public as late as possible, pending any unforeseen changes in Russia, and so Hardinge was furious to hear that Fisher, whom he cordially hated, had been speaking about it to Benckendorff, the Tsar's ambassador to London.[531] Luckily, Benckendorff had the benefits of discretion pressed upon him, and so the visit proceeded. It was the first ever paid to one of the Russias by a British sovereign.

Although a *de facto* triple alliance between Britain, France and Russia had been in place since the entente with Russia had been concluded, it did not exist officially. Grey went so far, in a Commons statement on 27 May 1908, as to spell out that the King's meeting with the Tsar did not portend such a development. The Liberal left and the Labour party were angry that the King was paying the visit to another ruler who refused to dilute the autocracy of his country. Indeed Ramsay MacDonald, a future Prime Minister, wrote an article attacking the meeting in which he described the Tsar as 'a common murderer', and rebuked the King for 'hobnobbing with a bloodstained creature'.[532] The Labour and Liberal MPs who objected to the visit signed a Commons motion deploring it; and, as a direct result of the attack by MacDonald, Grey saw to it that there was a debate on the matter in the Commons the week before the trip was due to take place. The Labour Members who spoke against the visit, including Keir Hardie, drew attention to the political prisoners who had been incarcerated and executed by the Tsar's government. Grey defended the King and his visit, and the government won the vote; but the King's initiative had caused a serious political controversy.

The King, though, took especial offence at the notion that he was condoning 'atrocities' – to use a word of Hardie's – by his kinsman. He protested that his action did nothing of the sort, that he had no connection with what was happening in Russia, and that affairs there were no concern of his. To express his displeasure he rescinded three invitations to politicians to a garden party that summer: one to Hardie, one to an Independent, Victor Grayson, and another to a Liberal, Arthur Ponsonby, who had not long before entered the House having been Campbell-Bannerman's private secretary. Ponsonby's behaviour brought the matter close to home. His father was Sir Henry Ponsonby, who had been Queen Victoria's private secretary; and his brother was Fritz Ponsonby, the King's assistant private secretary. It was Arthur Ponsonby who blew this rare act of pique on the King's part up into a great issue. He said that the withdrawal of the invitation 'was no longer a private affair, but an insult to my constituents and an attempt by the Sovereign to influence votes of members by social pressure'.[533] Inevitably, this resulted in the press taking up the issue, and embroiling the King still further in political controversy.

Hardie, on 23 June, wrote to Knollys to ask why he had been struck off the list. On 9 July the Labour party passed a resolution condemning the disinvitation, and all its MPs asked the Lord Chamberlain to take their names off the official list of royal guests until Keir Hardie was put back on it. Then, coming straight to the point, Keir Hardie said (showing a poor grasp of history) that the Monarch had been outside politics since the days of Charles I, and had better stay there. The next step hardly improved the position: the King, returning to his customary good nature, restored Hardie and Grayson to the list, but refused to restore Ponsonby, on the ground that with his background he should have known better.

Apart from the peculiarly English nature of this discrimination, the King had not, it seemed, quite understood the facts of the matter. In the division at the end of the Commons debate on the question, Ponsonby had voted against his own side because he felt that the Liberal government had poorly advised the King about relations with Russia. Alexander Murray, the Liberal Chief Whip, took up the cause on Ponsonby's behalf with Knollys. He said Ponsonby had had no thought of personally attacking the Sovereign or of behaving disloyally. Knollys showed a submission from Murray to the King who, hearing Ponsonby's defence, said he accepted the explanation and regarded the matter as closed. However, there is no doubt that the King had made a misjudgment in his handling of the matter and that, coming so hard on the heels of his decision to stay on in Biarritz, he seemed to be losing his constitutional touch.

When the meeting between the Tsar and the King took place in June 1908 scarcely anything of political or diplomatic importance occurred. It was mainly a reacquaintance of two branches of the same family after a long estrangement, and provided an opportunity for the King to flatter and boost the morale of his distressed nephew, which in itself greatly improved Anglo-Russian relations. The King did have private conversations with the Tsar's chief minister, Stolypin. However, Sir Arthur Nicolson, the British ambassador to St Petersburg, put near the head of his recollections of the event that 'there was an immense amount of food'.[534] One effect of the meeting, to the prospect of which the King cannot have been blind, was that it was construed as a provocation by the Germans. Nicolson's role was to brief the King extensively before the first meetings took place, not just on matters of local protocol, but on the relations between Isvolsky and Stolypin, and the exact detail of the Anglo-Russian convention and its relations to the *entente cordiale*. Nicolson also briefed the King on the immediate state of Russian politics, finances, the army and navy, education and culture. The King was also keen to know whether the Tsar would mention the Anglo-Japanese alliance and, if so, what his response should be. Even this Monarch, who was wont to take initiatives in foreign policy, knew when he had to abide by the rules.

The King had been asked by his friends the Rothschild brothers to raise with the Tsar the question of the frequent attacks on Jews in Russia.[535] He stalled, noting that this was a matter of some political import, and he could raise it only if Sir Charles Hardinge, accompanying him as head of the Foreign Office, and Nicolson agreed.[536] They told him there was no harm in his bringing up the matter with Stolypin, which he did in the course of a general talk about Russian internal affairs. He won an assurance from Stolypin that legislation would be introduced to relieve the Jews of some of their disabilities, and reported this back to the Rothschilds, advising them to wait, with him, to see whether Stolypin delivered on his promise. The Rothschilds were deeply dissatisfied.[537] Another of the King's Jewish friends, Cassel, had solicited the King to discuss with the Tsar the question of a loan to Russia – a matter Hardinge decreed 'a great abuse by Cassel of the King's friendliness towards him, to ask His Majesty to mix himself up in any way in a financial transaction of which the King and his

Government know nothing'.[538] For once, the King did not listen to Hardinge, but asked the Tsar to receive Cassel if he went to Russia – Cassel being, to Hardinge's apparent distaste, a Privy Councillor.[539] The King's debt to Cassel put the financier, after all, in a higher bracket in his necessary affections even than that occupied by the dutiful Hardinge.

The only quasi-political act in which the King indulged when he met the Tsar did upset his ministers. On the spur of the moment, he made his nephew an Admiral of the Fleet, principally because the Tsar had conferred a similar honour upon him. Back in London his First Lord of the Admiralty, McKenna, was highly put out at not having been consulted. Asquith and Grey concurred, recognising the difficulties they would have had if questions had been asked about the award in the House of Commons. The Prime Minister, alerted by a telegram from Hardinge – whom the King had sounded out on the question, and who had given the King his approval – complained that:

> without, for the moment, giving an opinion as to the wisdom or otherwise of this proposal, I feel bound to point out that it would have been more in accordance with constitutional practice, and with the accepted conditions of ministerial responsibility, if, before His Majesty's departure, some intimation had been given to me and to my colleagues that it was in contemplation. We are now placed face to face with a *fait accompli*, in regard to which we have had no opportunity of consultation or decision.[540]

Asquith, under fire from his left wing, reminded Knollys that the whole endeavour had, from the start, been 'a delicate affair'. Knollys, on the King's return, informed him of the strength of feeling in the Cabinet about what he had done, and told Asquith on 15 June that the King had been 'totally unaware of the constitutional point' and that he 'regretted he had, without knowing it, acted irregularly'.[541] To get his own back, the King had Knollys add this at the end of the letter: 'PS. The King deplores the attitude taken up by Mr Asquith on the Women's Suffrage Bill.'

The King's visit to the Tsar, just one of a series of meetings that year with other European crowned heads, inevitably rankled with the Kaiser. Despite being told by Metternich, his man in London, that the King ardently desired peace, the Kaiser wrote on a dispatch containing this sentiment: 'Untrue. He aims at war. I am to begin it, so that he does not get the odium.'[542] Throughout the King's reign the growth of German seapower had been the main source of friction between the two countries, though one the Liberal government had tried to solve. Soon after coming to office, Campbell-Bannerman had offered to fix the ratio of British to German ships at five to three, generous to the Germans given that Britain was an island and had a vast overseas empire to police. The Kaiser, egged on by Admiral Tirpitz, had rejected this attempt to stop what would later be called an 'arms race', despite advice from Metternich that what was on offer was a good deal for Germany. In a misplaced gesture of goodwill, the British government unilaterally decided to reduce the naval estimates, which was also a helpful measure at a time when taxes were already under an upward pressure. The Conservative press immediately attacked the policy, but the King, assured by Fisher that it was sound – it still left Britain with thirty-nine ships against America's eighteen and Germany's eleven – supported him. Fisher argued that the new Dreadnoughts so far outclassed the ships being built elsewhere that they were worth more than their literal numbers in terms of fighting advantage.

However, the Germans had no intention of stopping building up their fleet. Expenditure was increased to the point where, by 1908, it was estimated they would have thirty-seven ships by 1914, including thirteen Dreadnoughts. Fisher, accepting that this would make the German fleet a serious rival, suggested to the King early in 1908 that the navy should now emulate Gambier at Copenhagen in September 1807, when without a declaration of war he sank much of the Danish fleet, and launch an immediate attack on the Germans. The King would not hear of it (and, even if he would have heard of it, he would have had a job convincing his ministers of the usefulness of the action).

Fisher came under attack from some sections of opinion, who argued that he was not doing enough to counter the threat from Germany. This led to an unprecedented happening: a royal rebuke for the faithful Esher. Esher had been asked to join the Council of the Imperial Maritime League, a pressure group whose aim was to have the government build up naval strength and, as a means to this end, incidentally to get rid of Fisher. Esher sent a copy of his letter refusing this post to the rival Navy League, which supported Fisher. He rather stupidly said they could make the letter public, stupidly because in it he also cast doubt on the claims from some quarters that the German naval building programme was no cause for concern. This was interpreted by the press as a senior adviser of the Sovereign's highlighting a new danger from Germany, and sparked an international furore at the highest levels.

The Kaiser, already increasingly sensitive to British accusations that the expansion of the German fleet was a threat to peace between the two countries, took a bizarre course. He wrote a letter to the First Lord of the Admiralty, Lord Tweedmouth, saying that Esher's sentiments were unfounded. He sent a copy of this letter to the King, who replied to him frostily on 14 February 1908 that 'your writing to my First Lord of the Admiralty is a "new departure", and I do not see how he can prevent the press from calling attention to the great increase in building of German ships of war, which necessitates our increasing our navy also'.[543] The Kaiser, for his part, was convinced that attacks on his country in the British newspapers were inspired and orchestrated directly by his uncle, and the attachment of Esher's name to one such attack seemed to prove his point.[544]

Needless to say, all this was deeply embarrassing to the King, who wanted nothing more than a quiet life where the Kaiser was concerned. Perhaps the worst side-effect of Esher's indiscretion was that Tweedmouth, a man caricatured as a fool but in fact suffering from the brain tumour that would kill him the following year, wrote back to the Kaiser and revealed in detail to him the building plans of the Royal Navy. Fisher took the blame for Esher's initial mistake, telling the King that Esher had only been defending him – which was largely true. Esher had also, however, been defending a man he knew to be one of the King's favourites, so his action is capable of more than one construction. Presumably to vent his wrath, and also to ensure that one seen to be so close to the throne did not enter the habit of doing such things, the King wrote Esher a letter of unprecedented stiffness. In it, he said the remarks about Fisher in the Navy League letter had been 'very unfortunate', as had the remarks about the German navy. He upbraided Esher for his indiscretion, branding it 'injudicious'.[545] Esher was mortified and threw himself on the King's mercy, which he received. Rather naughtily, he claimed the letter sent to the Navy League had never been intended for such widespread publication, which was disingenuous to say the least.

Fisher had the satisfaction of Tweedmouth's successor as First Lord, McKenna, agreeing to build four Dreadnoughts at once, and if necessary six the following year. Lloyd George, the Chancellor, was furious, and so too was another new recruit to the Cabinet, Churchill. For all his later bellicosity, Churchill wanted a reduction in defence spending to pay for projects of social reform. It was only when Grey threatened to leave the government that the Dreadnought building programme, of which the King greatly approved, was saved.

OLD DIPLOMACY

After urging initially from Cassel, and then from Asquith and Grey, the King and the Kaiser met in August 1908 at Cronberg, when the King was *en route* once more to Marienbad. The King for once had a definite purpose in seeing his unruly nephew. Sir Frank Lascelles, the long-serving ambassador at Berlin, was retiring, not least because both the King (who had been on the best terms with Lascelles for years) and the Foreign Office thought he had become too pro-German; he was no longer as adept at complaining on the King's behalf to the Kaiser as he had once been. The Prince of Wales had for some time been of this view too. When in March 1905 the Germans were making a fuss about his not having been to visit one of the regiments in Germany of which he was Colonel-in-Chief, the Prince had told Knollys that 'although I like Lascelles, I fear he has become too German in his ideas for my taste'.[546]

As well as discussing possible replacements, the meeting was also viewed by Grey as an opportunity for the King to discuss arms reductions between the two countries. Grey's enthusiasm for the King conducting foreign policy directly in this way was not matched by the Sovereign's. Whereas in the Lansdowne years he would probably have jumped at the chance to lead so directly, now he told Grey that he felt brokering such a deal went beyond what could be expected of a constitutional monarch. In effect, this expectation was being defined, or redefined, by the King, according to his personal energies and interests at any given time. What perhaps he did not realise was that this extension of his prerogatives, once forfeited, would never be restored.

Nonetheless, the King agreed, without much keenness, to do what he could for Grey, for which purpose the Foreign Secretary drafted him a lengthy memorandum in advance of the meeting, which was to be entirely private and unencumbered by too many officials. Grey was happy to leave things in the King's hands because he accepted that neither he nor any of his colleagues or officials could know as well as the King how best to approach and handle his nephew, which was the true value of King Edward in an age of autocrats. 'The King's own knowledge and judgment', as Grey put it, 'is much superior to that of any of us.'[547] Grey was easy about whether the King showed the Kaiser the memorandum; it contained much pacific sentiment about there being 'nothing in the relations between the two Governments to cause this anxiety' about peace between Britain and Germany.[548] Much of the memorandum was, however, concerned not with the present but with the future – with fears that the naval building programmes of the two countries might endanger peace. Grey made it clear that Britain, as an island nation, needed a bigger navy than other powers, but wrote to Knollys almost immediately expressing his worry that 'the Emperor is so sensitive at anything which may be construed as an attempt to influence German naval expenditure that I cannot feel sure as to how he will take my memorandum'.[549]

As it turned out, when the King raised the question of naval expenditure the Kaiser showed no interest in discussing it, and the King was not prepared to force him. It was probably as well: when Hardinge broached the subject with the Kaiser 'while smoking his cigar after luncheon', the Kaiser flew into an imperial rage. Hardinge then asked that Germany consider British sensibilities, and was told that 'no discussion with a foreign government could be tolerated; such a proposal would be contrary to the national dignity, and would give rise to internal troubles if the Government were to accept it. He would rather go to war than submit to such dictation.' The matter of the ambassador was, though, settled: it was to be Sir Edward Goschen, who had been serving in that capacity at Vienna, and who the Kaiser (according to Hardinge's secret memorandum of the meeting) said 'was just the person whom he himself would have selected'.[550] Goschen did not want the job: he felt that the Germans were intractable, that war was inevitable, and that there would be nothing he could do to stop it. However, the King intervened personally, once in Austria later in August, to tell Goschen it was his express wish that he should take it. Reluctantly, but in practice left with no choice, Goschen accepted. His predictions were to be proved exact, for he left Berlin in August 1914.

Hardinge put great political significance on Grey's urging the King to do this diplomatic work for him. 'For the first time in history,' he recorded, 'the British Government briefed the King to act as their spokesman in an interview with the Head of a Foreign State, and it serves as indisputable proof of the confidence they felt in the wisdom and tact of the Sovereign in dealing with such matters.'[551] For his part, the Kaiser was determined to bind his uncle to him. Within ten days of the meeting, word leaked out from Berlin – much to the Foreign Office's chagrin – that the King and Queen would pay a visit there early in 1909, a matter that had only been floated at the meeting. Commenting on the tactic, Hardinge noted in a letter to Knollys that 'it was what I thought they would probably do so as to make it difficult to draw back'.[552]

TROUBLE IN THE EAST

For a time in 1908 it looked as though European war might not be much longer delayed. A revolution took place in Turkey that some attributed to the meeting of the King and the Tsar at Reval. Ottoman power in Europe had survived only so long because of rivalry between Britain and Russia: united, it seemed to Turkey they might drive the Turk out of Christian lands in the Balkans. On 3 July a revolt began in Macedonia that brought down, within three weeks, the despotism there. Turks and Christians, alike freed from autocracy, started to be friends, and there was optimism about the future of the region. The King, visiting Franz Josef in Vienna, reviewed the situation, but sought to take no initiative in relation to it, even though his country and his host's were co-signatories of the Treaty of Berlin. His main diplomatic purpose was to secure the Emperor's help in persuading Germany to stop its naval building programme. However, the Kaiser had got to the old Emperor first, and had persuaded him that all the King was interested in was isolating Germany; so the Emperor resolved not to become involved. Also, there was the little matter that Austria's foreign policy was nothing without its alliance with Germany. The King also took advantage of his stay in Marienbad to lunch with Clemenceau and Isvolsky, completing a useful round of diplomacy and helping practically to keep Britain's new alliances in good repair. The French Prime Minister Georges Clemenceau, told the King of his 'shock' at the 'ignorance' of Lloyd George on foreign policy, a remark the King mischievously reported back to Hardinge. Lloyd George was in Germany researching state old age pensions, having been warned in no uncertain terms by Grey to keep his mouth shut on matters affecting the Foreign Office, and Hardinge reported back to the King that 'his caperings abroad ... have excited the derision even of his own party'.[553]

While the King was in Vienna, having a highly enjoyable time with Franz Josef despite the diplomatic failure of his mission, the Emperor's slippery chief minister, Baron von Aehrenthal, was designing an intervention in the Balkans that threatened to precipitate war. Unsure of what might happen next in that region, and believing that the 'Young Turk' rebellion that had freed Macedonia could lead to long-term instability, Aehrenthal decided that Austria had better annex Bosnia and Herzegovina, which it had administered on behalf of the Sultan since the Congress of Berlin in 1878. Austria would defend the decision by telling the other powers that it would set up stable, constitutional government in those territories. To complicate matters further, Ferdinand of Bulgaria had decided to proclaim himself tsar of that country, no longer owing allegiance to the Sultan. The King had picked up no inkling of the annexation project from Franz Josef, because Franz Josef simply did not know, and was, when the King was advised of the plan on reaching Marienbad a couple of days later, still being persuaded of the sense of the plan by Aehrenthal.

The King refused to believe a report that such a development might be in the offing, made to him by a friend of his in Marienbad, Henry Wickham Steed of *The Times*. On 18 August, three days after Wickham Steed had given the King his news, the decision was formally taken in Vienna, though not yet announced. The King had, after all, received Aehrenthal while in Austria, and Hardinge had had talks with him too, during which all had agreed that a fresh start had to be, and would be, made in Anglo-Austrian relations.[554] The Austrians had given specific assurances to the King of non-intervention in the Near East. The following month, when Isvolsky (who had seen the King in Marienbad) went to Vienna, he gave Russian support for the annexation, provided that Russian warships were allowed to pass through the Dardanelles: an important point, since the Russian navy had been all but wiped out by the Japanese three years earlier, and most of the ships it had left were those trapped in the Black Sea.

The first confirmation the King had of the annexation plan was on 4 October, when he received a letter from Hardinge warning him of Austria's intention, gleaned from a meeting with Mensdorff, the ambassador to London.[555] The gloss Hardinge put on the move for the King was that it was 'due to the fact that Aehrenthal's policy in the

Near East has been generally recognised to have been a complete failure so far, and that he is now anxious to retrieve his position by some material advantage which he will be able to show to prove that his occupation of the Ministry of Foreign Affairs has not been a complete fiasco'.[556] Thus was a main seed of the Great War sown. The next day a letter came to the King from Franz Josef 'dans l'esprit de l'amitié intime et traditionelle qui nous unit', telling him that, to prevent a threat to the peace on the frontiers of his country, he would be annexing the two territories.[557] The King was brought the news at Balmoral by Mensdorff. The great peacemaker, as he was becoming known after the success of the ententes, was furious. He met Mensdorff with none of the usual diplomatic courtesies. He felt he had been duped, given how recently he had seen Franz Josef, and he now recognised that the Treaty of Berlin was nothing more than 'a scrap of paper'.[558] He had also, though, been carefully briefed by Hardinge, who wrote to Knollys the day before Mensdorff's visit: 'Please ask the King to adopt an attitude of great reserve when the Austrian ambassador presents the Emperor's letter.'[559] The King played the part perfectly.

To complicate the matter further, the declaration of Bulgarian independence, and the proclamation of Ferdinand as tsar, had all been done with Austria's knowledge; yet the Kaiser decided it had been arranged by the King, and that the plans had been hatched during the sojourn at Marienbad. He felt that the King, in encouraging the plot, had been seeking to ruin various German investors who had put up money for a railway to Baghdad, which was to run through Bulgaria. As with much the Kaiser concluded in these years, it was complete rubbish.

Once Franz Josef published the details of the annexation, Serbia issued a formal protest to the other guarantors of the Treaty of Berlin, and the Greeks on Crete demanded immediate union with Greece, throwing off Turkish suzerainty. The Treaty signatories divided according to their new alliances: Germany and Italy behind Austria, Britain, France and Russia against – Russia in that camp despite Isvolsky's earlier dealings with Aehrenthal, which the Russian Foreign Minister was desperate to keep secret. Grey protested to the other powers, but Germany and Austria ignored the protests. They knew that Russia was in no state to prosecute an overseas war, and nor did they expect France and Britain to do so; and they were right. The King, for his part, wrote a letter more in sorrow than in anger to Franz

Josef. There was simply nothing this builder of alliances could do. He did, though, have the consolation of being seen as the upholder of a great international treaty, which made him newly popular with the dispossessed Turks – a group that the Kaiser, to his present frustration, had been trying to conciliate and win over ever since his accession.

Isvolsky came to London in October 1908, the result of an invitation delivered by the King at Marienbad. He was told by the King that another Balkan conference was plainly needed to settle the dispute and to avoid war. Isvolsky agreed with the King, and undertook to pursue the policy on an imminent visit to Berlin. Isvolsky was also keen to win the King's support for his earlier policy of securing the right for Russian ships to travel through the Dardanelles, though he did not confess to the King the deal he had provisionally done with Aehrenthal on this. Asquith, who was keen on the idea of a conference, was more troubled by the notion of allowing the Russians the freedom of these straits. However, the King wrote to his Prime Minister on 13 October that he was:

> afraid that unless some hope is given to Russia that England and the other Powers might grant the national aspirations of Russia on this question, that Monsieur Isvolsky will return to his country a discredited man, and will have to resign, and it is impossible to say who his successor might be. The King feels that after the Russian convention with England of a year ago, we are bound, if we wish to retain her friendship, to give way on this important point. He hopes the Cabinet are looking at this question from a European and International point of view and not from merely a domestic one.[560]

Later that month, the King wrote to the Tsar, the letter drafted by Hardinge, once more extolling Isvolsky's virtues.[561]

Asquith and most of his senior colleagues were persuaded by this argument, even though the context in which the King urged them to look at the problem was, in the words of Asquith's official biographers, 'somewhat in advance of the policy of his Government'.[562] The Prime Minister replied to the King the same day to minute his and the Cabinet's concurrence with the Sovereign, agreeing that 'the existing restrictions on Russia's freedom of egress are of no strategic value to Great Britain'.[563] However, Crewe and Morley both argued that Britain should be given something by Russia in return for this concession; and to try to meet this point of view Grey had established with Isvolsky that a more conditional right of egress from the Black Sea would be sufficient for the Russians. The King pronounced himself pleased, and it was settled between him, Grey and Hardinge that Britain would raise the matter with Turkey at the earliest tactful opportunity.[564]

The King was less willing, in that autumn of great instability, to be dragged into the affairs of Serbia. The Serbs had wanted to form a united country with Bosnia, Herzegovina and Montenegro, neighbouring territories where there were large Serb populations. Such a union would also give them access to the sea, recreating their country in its medieval borders and preventing them from being alone in Europe, apart from Switzerland, in having no ports; but now Austria had put paid to that. The Crown Prince of Serbia asked to be allowed to visit England in November 1908, and at first the King gave his approval. However, when he realised that the turmoil in the Balkans would not quickly subside, he asked for the trip to be put off.[565] The King, on Hardinge's advice, also refused an audience at the end of October for Milanovitch, the Serbian Foreign Minister, who was in London.[566] It was probably as well, because when Milanovitch met Grey and Hardinge it was to tell them that, unless Austria gave Serbia some territorial compensation for the annexation, the Serbs would prepare to declare war on Austria. The King realised the importance of a British display of friendship towards Turkey at this time, and had a familiar means of doing it: inviting Hardinge to send Cassel there to give financial assistance. This Hardinge, and Cassel, loyally did.[567]

Austria, backed by Germany, ridiculed Serbia's pretensions, and there was no prospect of a conference. Russia could not force Austria's hand, because Aehrenthal threatened to release documentary proof of the earlier deal he had done with Isvolsky on the Dardanelles – as the King was later informed by Hardinge. No one with any power was prepared to force the issue; and the King, whatever the Kaiser might have thought of him, was certainly no warmonger. Nonetheless the King was angry with Austria for causing the crisis, and wanted to leave Mensdorff off the list of those diplomats invited to Windsor for a grand formal reception early in 1909. Hardinge, fearing this would simply stoke up anti-British feeling in the Austrian press, and bring criticism directly upon the King, talked the Monarch out of his planned snub. 'I quite understand the King's annoyance about Austria,' Hardinge told Knollys on 19 January 1909, 'but I think it would be very marked if Mensdorff were the only ambassador uninvited.'[568] The King was attacked by the press in any case, following recognition of the immense diplomatic help given by Britain to Serbia, for which the King was held responsible. It was a tribute to the continental perception of how far the King had been his own foreign secretary – partly a misunderstanding of the British way of government, but also partly true.

The crisis restored the King's interest in foreign affairs to the level it had reached earlier in his reign. When on his annual holiday at Biarritz in March 1909 he had Hardinge send him full reports of what was happening in the Balkans, and he read them assiduously. In early 1909 the Serbs and Austrians reached an agreement, and the powers signatory to the Treaty of Berlin unanimously agreed to abrogate the old clause, thus recognising Austria's action. The King was so upset, still, at Austria's behaviour that he threatened to forgo his annual cure at Marienbad, but was persuaded to relent on that point by Sir Fairfax Cartwright, his new ambassador to Vienna, in order to try to improve Anglo-Austrian relations. The King did, however, draw the line at congratulating Aehrenthal on his elevation to count by the Emperor in recognition of his work, and forcefully declined Cartwright's advice that he should do so. His visit to Marienbad that summer did not, despite hints dropped by Aehrenthal that it might be welcome, include a visit to the Emperor, or any interviews with senior Austrians. As far as he was concerned, there was little point in pushing at that door again. Also, as Hardinge pointed out to Knollys, 'I cannot help thinking that Aehrenthal wished to get the King to propose a visit so as to make political capital out of it.'[569]

MIDDLE-CLASS GOVERNMENT

The significance of Asquith's accession to power, as Sir Sidney Lee saw it in a more class-conscious time, was that 'hitherto the Prime Ministers of England had been either connected with the nobility or with the wealthy families of the land. But the new Prime Minister was a forcible representative of the middle class, and the new Chancellor of the Exchequer a Welsh solicitor of extremely humble origin.'[570] The end of aristocratic government meant a new vulnerability for the Lords, of whose excesses Campbell-Bannerman had been relatively tolerant, largely because of his limited energy for a fight. In Asquith and Lloyd George, in particular, the Lords now had a more formidable set of adversaries. The King realised this, and from the start was warning the Unionist leaders – with Asquith's knowledge – of the consequences of truculence by the Upper House in this democratic age. When the Lords had threatened to throw out the Licensing Bill, for example, in October 1908, the King had told Lansdowne that 'if the attitude of the Peers was such as to suggest the idea that they were obstructing an attempt to deal with the evils of intemperance, the House of Lords would suffer seriously in popularity'.[571] The Lords' objection was purely political: the Bill would reduce over a fourteen-year period the number of licensed outlets for drink, much to the gratification of that large section of Liberal support contained in the temperance movement. The licensed trade, with its historic financial backing for the Conservatives, was threatening to withdraw that support if the party did not jump to the brewers' defence. The Bill was duly thrown out, which only increased the Lords' sense of purpose, and the Commons' determination to squash them.

Though he strongly disagreed with some of his ideas, the King was to start with on cordial and courteous terms with his new Prime Minister. Asquith sought to observe the proprieties: when on 28 October 1908 he 'officially' recommended Dr Alfred Wallace, a prominent naturalist, for the Order of Merit – which was, of course, the King's private award – Knollys asked the King whether Asquith should not be told that such a recommendation should only be made unofficially.[572] The King replied 'I quite agree in principle.'[573] Asquith took no offence at this, nor at any other such indications of the approved ways of conducting business. He did suffer from what the King regarded as the usual problem with Prime Ministers, being somewhat reticent and causing the King, as usual, to feel that important information was being kept from him.

This, though, was a minor fault compared with what the King perceived in Lloyd George. It was not just the Welsh philanderer's attachment to Lords reform that upset the King: it was his adherence to the ideas of women's suffrage, something with which even Asquith was not in entire agreement. On 5 December 1908 the Chancellor of the Exchequer addressed the Women's Liberal Association at the Albert Hall, and promised them that the suffrage question would be brought before the Commons. To be fair to him, he did warn the militants that their sometimes violent campaign – whose apotheosis would be reached with Emily Davidson's throwing herself under King George's horse at the 1913 Derby – would be counter-productive.

However, the King (as always a thorough reader of the newspapers) had seen an announcement that Lloyd George would be addressing this meeting, and had written two days before the event to Asquith saying that he was 'rather disgusted' by the prospect.[574] He said that, given his understanding that Asquith was not in favour of votes for women, the Chancellor's presence at the meeting was 'a most improper thing' that showed 'an entire absence of good judgement, good taste and propriety.' He warned Asquith: 'I shall have no more to do with him than is absolutely necessary.' On 7 December Asquith mounted a defence of his colleague, assuring the King that Lloyd George had tried to extricate himself from the engagement, but had been held to it. He had also kept a promise not to commit the government in any way; and the King was reminded that although Asquith himself might have been against women's suffrage, it was an open question in the Cabinet. None of this appeased the King, whose hostility to women's having the vote was unabated. He believed that if Lloyd George had really not wanted to speak at the meeting, he could have got out of it.[575]

Lloyd George had already upset the King that autumn. For a start, he wrote to the King in the third person as 'Mr Lloyd George' and not as 'the Chancellor of the Exchequer', a breach of protocol upon which the King frowned. Worse, while on his German jaunt the previous summer he had made some unfortunate interventions in questions of foreign policy, a problem further exacerbated by some silly and jejune remarks by Churchill – a man whom, a year earlier, the King had described to the Prince of Wales as '*almost more* of a cad in office than he was in opposition'.[576] Churchill, addressing a miners' meeting in Swansea in August 1908, had poured scorn on the notion that war with Germany was inevitable, and had mocked Lord Cromer for issuing warnings of Germany's aggressive intentions. Meanwhile, Lloyd George had spoken of his belief in a closer Anglo-German understanding. The King was furious because he felt that what both men had done undermined Grey's authority as Foreign Secretary, and had Knollys draft a letter of rebuke to Asquith.[577] He then ordered the letter be not sent, and instead communicated directly with Grey and asked him to make his displeasure plain. This Grey gladly did, and included a short instruction to Churchill about what was really happening between Germany and Britain. Knollys complained to Hardinge, asking him to ensure that the appropriate backbone was put into Grey; Hardinge replied that 'nothing could be more mischievous or more likely to lead to anarchy than the incursions of such ignorant people as Churchill and Lloyd George into the domain of foreign politics.'[578] For his part, Esher warned Knollys – for the King's ear – that Haldane believed that 'Lloyd George and Winston have been planning to capture and destroy Asquith.'[579] Knollys's views, which presumably echoed the King's, were that Lloyd George and Churchill 'do much harm as they don't behave like gentlemen, are disloyal to their colleagues and spend most of their time in unprincipled intrigues. It appears to me that Asquith is no more able to keep them in order than his predecessor.'[580]

The winter of 1908–9 heard an echo of the farce with the Shah and his Garter. Grey was keen to propitiate the Turks by awarding the Turkish Grand Vizier, Kiamil Pasha, the GCB. The King would not have it. Knollys wrote to Asquith on 19 January 1909 to say that, as well as the King's being unable to think of any precedent for such a course – the Grand Vizier was not part of the Sultan's suite visiting the country, for example – Britain was not sufficiently closely allied with Turkey to make such an award desirable. Knollys said it appeared to the King to be 'wrong in principle' to give a British decoration to the Grand Vizier just because, as had been the case, he had made a pacific speech about the Eastern Question and sought to mend fences with Austria.[581] In any case, the King felt that, if such an award were to be made to a foreign statesman, Isvolsky had first claim on it, for services rendered.

Asquith replied on 26 January expressing his and Grey's 'regret' at the King's view.[582] He reeled off the oriental Prime Ministers who had in late years been thus favoured, and told the King that 'the situation in Oriental countries differs so much from what exists in Europe that it is often a matter of political importance to bestow a high honour on an Oriental when the grant of a similar honour to a European would not have an equal political result.' Playing what he must have thought would be a trump card, Asquith mentioned that one of the more recent acts in a twenty-year record of friendship between Kiamil Pasha and Britain was the offer to Cassel to establish (on, one presumes, a non-altruistic basis) a National Bank of Turkey. Nonetheless, Asquith agreed not to press the matter further for the moment, but hoped that at a later date the King would change his mind, for the good of Anglo-Turkish relations.

Now, of course, these were familiar lines, and the King had heard them all before. Evoking 1902, Knollys replied:

the Persian Prime Minister was given the GCB when he accompanied
the Shah to England, when it was considered by Lord Lansdowne to be
of such great importance to conciliate the Shah and his minister, that he
urgently pressed the King, who consented with the utmost reluctance to
confer the Garter on the Shah and the Bath on his Minister – an utterly
useless step as it turned out, and as the King foresaw; and which he at
the time, and always since, much regretted.[583]

If that were not enough to silence Asquith, Knollys added: 'The King
is glad to see that you do not propose to press the matter upon him,
and he desires me to say that in his opinion a sound Foreign policy
should be carried on wholly independent of the bestowal of honours.'
'*Requiescat in pace*' was Asquith's only reply.[584]

BERLIN, AT LAST

As a means of defusing the tension between Britain and Germany over
the development of German seapower, the King had been willing,
before the Cronberg meeting of August 1908, to consider making a
state visit to Berlin. The King felt that the Kaiser's relatively pacific
behaviour during the Bosnian crisis in the autumn of 1908 gave him a
reason to make such a visit. The King telegraphed his nephew with a
New Year greeting on 1 January 1909, and asked whether he and the
Queen could go in the second week of February.[585] The Kaiser agreed.
As proof of his good intentions, the Kaiser wrote to the Tsar on 8
January saying that 'we are quite as anxious as you to improve our
relations with England'.[586] The arrangement of the visit provided
another example of Grey's being by-passed by the King's relationship
with Hardinge: Grey knew nothing about the King's telegram until
after the Kaiser had replied to it, a matter Hardinge implored Knollys
to cover up by informing the Foreign Secretary immediately.[587] There
was a flurry of nervousness just before the visit, when the Queen went
down with a bout of influenza of the non-diplomatic variety, which
threatened to stop her going. 'Unfortunately,' Hardinge wrote to
Knollys, 'if she is prevented from doing so nobody will give the credit
of the failure being due to her health.'[588]

When the visit took place no device of hospitality was left unused by
the Kaiser to flatter his uncle; and if the King did not appear to be

enjoying himself it was not because of political problems, but because
of his growing ill-health and the bronchial trouble that made Biarritz a
far more sensible destination at that time of year than the sub-arctic
Prussian heartland. Grey had advised, not for reasons of the King's
health, that the visit be made at Easter, but the King would not want to
interrupt his routine at that time of year of Biarritz with Mrs Keppel.[589]
At some of the dinners and entertainments arranged for him the King
fell asleep, and had such a fit of coughing at the British embassy after a
luncheon that a doctor was sent for. It caused the controller of the
Kaiser's household, Count Zedlitz Trutzschler, to reflect that 'I fancy
that the part he plays in the affairs of his country is smaller than we
have imagined' – which, in terms of the two or three years preceding,
was an astute comment. Although the diplomatic effect of the visit was
broadly good, it was asked why the King had waited until the ninth
year of his reign to visit Berlin, when his favours had been showered so
liberally on so many other European capitals – an unfair criticism,
given the frequency with which uncle and nephew had met elsewhere.
That the King came at a time when the navy and the territorial army
were being greatly strengthened was also not lost on the German
Anglophobes.

The expansion of the Royal Navy, carried out in spite of Lloyd
George's and Churchill's opposition, had been welcomed by the King.
He told Asquith on 20 December 1908 that 'as long as Germany
persists in her present programme of shipbuilding we have no
alternative but to build double' – an insistence on the 'two-power'
standard that dictated that Britain had at least as many ships as the
next two strongest naval powers put together. In the month after the
King's return from Berlin the Cabinet had an internal row about
whether six or eight Dreadnoughts should be built, which became so
heated that McKenna, the First Lord, wished to resign. He introduced
the Naval Estimates in the Commons on 16 March 1909, announcing
increased spending; but the Opposition was still not satisfied that the
navy had the power to take on the Germans, and moved an
unsuccessful vote of censure. The King had been pressing Asquith for
information about the state of naval preparedness ever since his return
from Berlin, and Esher had, via Knollys, supplied him with some
embarrassing questions to ask Asquith about German expansion: 'Is it
a fact that the Germans will have in March 1911: 17 Dreadnoughts
ready for sea, and we shall have 12 plus whatever we lay down this
year? In the long run, how can a two power standard be maintained if

Germany lays down 4 battleships per annum and we only lay down 4?'[590] The King, having read the report of the Commons debate, wrote to Fisher on 22 March to say that it had 'disclosed a state of things which is anything but satisfactory' – though Fisher argued in reply that the Germans were lying about the extent of their seapower. When, later in the year, Bülow and Grey tried to come to some understanding about naval building, the King was deeply pessimistic; and it turned out he was right to be so.

A CATHOLIC APPROACH

The King's high sense of propriety in the way members of either House of Parliament acted, and his constant understanding of religious tensions among some of his less enlightened subjects, was exemplified in a correspondence in 1905 with Lord Denbigh, a Roman Catholic. The peer wrote to Knollys to ask why it was that the King objected to his proposing a toast at a dinner of the Catholic Association to 'Pope and King'. Denbigh said he had been doing this for years and could not understand what the fuss was about. Knollys's reply was magisterial. He said the King 'desires me to say that he thinks that on any public occasion the name of the Sovereign should come first and alone. He looks upon the question not as a matter of faith or of religion but how an Englishman ought to act, especially if he is a Member of either House of Parliament.' Knollys added:

> I find it difficult to believe that Catholics would object to the King being
> of opinion that their own Sovereign should be put first and alone as is
> the universal custom when his health is drunk, and you must remember
> that even if Catholics do 'object', all Protestants of every denomination
> resent very greatly that the name of the Pope should be put first, or
> even that it should be coupled with that of the Sovereign of their
> Country.[591]

The King was, as we have seen, no bigot in these matters. However, his efforts early in his reign to soothe Catholic sensibilities had not removed sources of tension between that minority and the Protestants. Much to his concern, the King found himself being dragged into another inter-denominational conflict in the autumn of 1908, over the holding of a Roman Catholic Eucharistic Congress in London. The climax of the Congress was to be a public procession of the Holy Sacrament, attended by the papal legate and most of the grandest British papists. This was advertised as an act of reparation for the Reformation, and it was from this somewhat provocative statement that the trouble stemmed. Protestant groups contended that the procession was a breach of the 1829 Catholic Emancipation Act. Appeals were made to the Supreme Governor of the Church of England – the King – to stop the event; he referred the petitioners to the Home Office, which as well as being the correct constitutional channel also extricated him from so delicate an issue. However, the King had a telegraph sent to Asquith suggesting he ask the Marquess of Ripon – a prominent Catholic, vice-president of the Congress and the Lord Privy Seal – to use his influence to try to have the procession cancelled. Ripon was annoyed and angry at being put to use in this way, his own feeling being that such Catholic processions should be no more illegal than Protestant ones. Nonetheless, he represented Asquith's – and the King's – views to Francis Bourne, the Archbishop of Westminster.

Meanwhile, as the date of the procession neared and the King continued to be inundated with appeals from aggrieved subjects, he expressed his concern at having heard nothing from Herbert Gladstone, the Home Secretary, about what the government intended doing. On 11 September, two days before the scheduled event, the King could contain himself no longer: not least because many of the letters he was receiving seemed to have been provoked by the belief that the King himself wanted the procession to go ahead. This distressed him because, having noted public opinion and fearing a breach of the peace, he certainly did not want any such thing. He sent another telegram to Asquith saying that 'the King feels very strongly with regard to inability of Home Office to stop procession'.[592] Asquith replied that, under the 1829 Act, the procession could be stopped only if it were proved there would be a breach of the peace – and, despite the King's conviction that there would be trouble, it could not. He told the King that Gladstone would be consulting the Monarch, and would be publishing legal opinion justifying his lack of action. In fact, he was already too well aware of the King's mounting anger on the question, having been tacitly informed of it by Crewe: 'The King has taken this damned procession greatly to heart, and asked me to say that he was "greatly cut up about it" – a rather curious phrase.'[593] Crewe elaborated upon what had put the King in this irate state: 'He has received dozens of letters from enraged Protestants, who compare him disadvantageously with his revered mother, now with God, and hint that his ultimate destination may be directed elsewhere.'

However, Gladstone neither consulted the King nor published legal opinion; so the next day, on the eve of the march, the King telegraphed his Prime Minister again telling him that 'present position is extremely unsatisfactory', that public opinion 'inclines to fasten responsibility on the King who is in complete ignorance of reasons for abstaining from interference', and that he wanted 'the government reasons for no interference ... clearly communicated to press to-day for publication before procession in order to fix responsibility in proper quarter'.[594] The procession went ahead, but (thanks to pressure put on the Archbishop by Ripon) without a public display of the host or any vestments, so it passed without incident. Gladstone, somewhat smugly, sent the King a telegram the next day to report to him that there had been no breach of the peace. Understandably provoked by this, the King telegraphed back that 'it appears to the King that an illegal act is illegal, whether its commission involves a breach of the peace or not'.[595] The King also rebuked Gladstone for not having noted earlier the risk of provocation thrown up by the procession, and for not having acted more swiftly to deal with it. Ripon, livid that he had been used in this way and feeling utterly compromised, resigned – allowing Asquith to give old age (he was eighty-one) and ill-health as the reasons in order not to embarrass the government.

The way in which Gladstone had handled this episode helped turn him into the Arnold-Forster of the Liberal government, thereby filling the vacancy for a ministerial whipping-boy that had existed since the end of the Balfour administration. Although Gladstone seemed to lack the principal Forsterian qualification for the post of problems with 'manner', he more than compensated by having none of his distinguished father's brains and less of his administrative ability. 'You will find HM very bitter about Herbert,' Crewe told Asquith once the crisis had passed, 'and longing to get rid of him.'[596] The King wrote to Gladstone to tell him what a mess he had made of the whole business – a view shared by certain of his senior colleagues – and this prompted Gladstone to muse upon whether or not he should resign. Asquith was keen for him to move, but did not wish to see him utterly humiliated, so offered him the largely decorative post of Lord President of the Council. But this struck Gladstone as particularly humiliating, so he refused, and for the moment stayed at the Home Office.

Gladstone's next gross error was to use the fact that the King no longer objected to women serving on Royal Commissions to appoint two of them, Lady Frances Balfour and Mrs H. J. Tennant, to serve on one looking at divorce reform. The King wrote thunderously to Gladstone on 10 September 1909 that the subject of divorce 'cannot be discussed openly and in all its aspects with any delicacy or even decency before ladies', an opinion that should have carried much weight coming, as it did, from one of society's most prominent adulterers.[597] This was not the limit of the King's objection: when, with disgust, he was forced by Asquith to approve the appointments, he told his Prime Minister that they were 'the thin edge of suffragettism'.[598] A couple of weeks later, Asquith saw an opportunity to get rid of Gladstone by making him the first Governor-General of the new Union of South Africa. The King was horrified, feeling that the new dominion had a right to expect to be governed by someone more competent. Knollys told Asquith's secretary on 21 October 1909 that 'if the Prime Minister cannot find a better Governor-General, he supposes he must approve of the appointment, but ... he thinks it a very bad one'.[599]

By the last year or so of his reign the King's health was so poor that, as a consequence, he reordered his priorities. He interfered with his ministers far less than had earlier been the case, though this may partly have been because in Grey and Haldane he had ministers controlling the two areas in which he was most interested – foreign affairs and the army – who more or less had his complete confidence, unlike some of their predecessors. By early 1909 his ministers could have been forgiven for thinking the King was less interested than previously in what was going on in matters of state. However, he could still be roused to take an interest, and to do so forcibly; and with a querulousness provoked by his bad health he was not always so charming or so rational about it as he once had been.

After his traditional March visit to Biarritz in 1909 the King went on a Mediterranean cruise, and had expected to visit the naval squadron at Malta. On his arrival, though, he found it had been ordered to Lemnos the previous day, because of a request from the Foreign Office provoked by the worsening situation in Macedonia. Nonetheless Ponsonby, travelling with the King, fired off a letter to Asquith, saying that 'the King is much displeased that he should not even have been informed of the dispatch of the Mediterranean Squadron ... the King would wish you to impress on the First Lord of the Admiralty that it is his duty to keep His Majesty informed of such movements, to say nothing of common courtesy, when His Majesty happens to be in the Mediterranean with the intention of seeing the squadron at Malta'.[600] The defence by McKenna that he had not been told the King wanted to visit Malta, that he could not earlier have told the King the ships were leaving as the request to post them had not been made, and that the King had been sent details of the movements as soon as they were known, seemed to make little difference to the King.[601] He had Ponsonby wire back to McKenna that he felt the First Lord should have explained to him personally why the ships were going, rather than leaving the King to find out indirectly what was happening from the Commander-in-Chief at Malta; and the King said the whole point of a cruise was not to determine in advance where the yacht might put in. All in all, it was a testy correspondence that seemed to suggest an unreasonableness and caprice on the part of the King that could hardly be expected to increase the respect in which he was held by his ministers, or the deference they would accord to his views. But he was now a very sick man.

'THE PEOPLE'S BUDGET'

The conflict between the Lords and Commons that built up from the moment the Liberals came to power in December 1905 was to lead to the greatest constitutional crisis of the twentieth century; and, although the denouement came in the next reign, much of the fight was conducted while Edward was king. Although there had been acrimony about the will of the people being flouted in the rejection of measures such as the Education Bill, this was still not a terminal threat to constitutional stability. The Liberals had been over-generous at times in interpreting what their mandate allowed them to do, and Unionist successes in by-elections suggested that the country was not entirely behind the government. However, when in the autumn of 1909 the Lords chose to reject the Finance Bill, matters moved to a far higher level of contentiousness.

The King himself was dismayed by the contents of what became known as the People's Budget, because of the assault it made on landed property. This had been done partly to pay for old age pensions, which needed another £8 million, but also to raise an extra £3 million for the navy. To pay for this, large increases were planned in death duties and income tax. In his Cabinet report of 26 April 1909, Asquith detailed the exact revenue-raising powers of the measures: £2,850,000 from estate duties, £750,000 stamp duty, £500,000 land tax, £3,500,000 income tax, £2,600,000 from liquor licences, and £3,400,000 from tobacco and spirits.[602] Writing from Naples to Asquith on 1 May, two days after the Budget had been introduced, the King raised a curious question about it: 'whether in framing the Budget the Cabinet took into consideration the possible (but the King hopes improbable) event of a European war'.[603] The King had the rather charming view that 'the income tax, which has always been regarded as a war tax, now stands so high for unearned income over a certain amount that any great increase would have a most disastrous effect on land generally, more especially if the war lasted for a considerable time'. Also, despite the great mandate won by the Liberals in 1906, the King knew this programme had far from overwhelming support in the country, or indeed in the Liberal party. In June 1909, having been in office for only eight months, Lord Fitzmaurice, Ripon's successor and a brother of Lansdowne, resigned claiming ill-health. The King was not taken in: 'I suppose it is ill-health and not for political reasons that he resigns.' Indeed, Fitzmaurice would die in his bed more than a quarter of a century later, in his ninetieth year.[604] The Unionists, inevitably, took an even sterner view, warning that the measures in the Budget presaged social revolution and the destruction of the British way of life.

The Cabinet fully expected the Lords to reject the Budget, but this did not lessen their anger. One minister, Lewis 'Loulou' Harcourt, in a speech in Lancashire on 15 July 1909, said that 'the black hand of the peerage, which holds its secret sessions at Lansdowne House, has issued edicts of assassination against too many fair measures desired by the people and passed by overwhelming majorities in the only House in which the people are directly represented'.[605] This was too much for the King, whose distaste at having the peerage termed 'assassins' was redoubled by his having recently accepted Harcourt's hospitality, and he protested to Harcourt. He felt, too, that it ill became anyone in a position of responsibility to start stirring up conflict within the country. But even the Cabinet seemed out of control: Asquith, plainly furious, wrote to Knollys tendering apologies for a speech Churchill had made in which he had spoken of having a dissolution to settle the issue. 'I am very much annoyed,' the Prime Minister wrote, 'and so, I know, are several of my colleagues, and I am awaiting such explanation as he has to offer.'[606] At the Cabinet meeting of 21 July Asquith delivered Churchill an epic rebuke, telling him to keep out of matters of 'high policy'.[607] However, Lloyd George, in a speech at Limehouse that month, noted that 'a fully equipped Duke costs as much to keep up as two dreadnoughts'.[608] This was not to be a polite debate, nor one calculated to engage the King's attention constructively.

Hating as always confrontation between branches of the legislature, the King sent for Asquith and warned him, on the royal yacht at Cowes on 2 August 1909, that acts of provocation such as Lloyd George's Limehouse speech had to stop. He contemplated writing a formal letter to Asquith to be read out in Cabinet; and on 1 August Knollys had written to Lord Crewe that 'the King thinks he ought to protest in the most vigorous terms against one of his Ministers making such a speech'.[609] Knollys said Lloyd George's sentiments were 'full of false statements, of Socialism in its most insidious form and of virulent abuse against one particular class, which can only have the effect of setting "class" against "class", and of stirring up the worst passions of its audience'. With due reference to the proprieties, Knollys continued: 'It is hardly necessary, perhaps, to allude to its gross vulgarity'. He concluded:

> The King cannot understand how Asquith can tacitly allow certain of his colleagues to make speeches that would not have been tolerated by any Prime Minister until within the last few years, which HM regards as being in the highest degree improper, and which he almost looks upon as being an insult to the Sovereign when delivered by one of his confidential servants. I have purposely not marked my letter 'confidential'.

Excuses were offered by both Crewe – who, because of his good relations with the King, was increasingly becoming the Cabinet's link-man with the Sovereign – and Asquith, but these were described by the King as 'pitiful'.[610] Asquith wrote to Lloyd George after his audience of the King to speak of the 'great state of agitation and annoyance' in which he had found him as a consequence of the speech.[611] 'I have never known him more irritated, or more difficult to appease,' Asquith continued, marking out the 'menace to property and a Socialistic spirit' that the King had sensed in the speech. Asquith warned Lloyd George to behave, because 'the King, of course, lives in an atmosphere which is full of hostility to us and to our proposals; but he is not himself unfriendly, and, so far, he has "stood" the Budget very well – far better than I expected. It is important, therefore, to avoid raising his apprehensions and alienating his goodwill.' Knollys, later that year, would make a similar point to the Prime Minister, whom he implored 'not to pretend to the King that he liked Mr Lloyd George's speeches, for the King would not believe it, and it only irritated him'.[612] Asquith's relations with the King were still reasonably civil, but fast diminishing in cordiality. The King was not well enough to take such a political crisis in his stride. It was inevitable that the wrath and impatience generated as a result of it should come to be directed at the head of his government; and Asquith, being a clever man, understood and feared the executive difficulties that would result from making an enemy of the King.

Knollys told Crewe, in another letter of 3 August, that the King was depressed that 'his relations with some of the members of the present Cabinet should be increasingly the reverse of harmonious'. Some of the King's annoyance was, though, removed by the receipt at Cowes on 5 August of an explanatory letter from Lloyd George. The Chancellor said he had been stung by the ferocity of the attacks on the Budget and on himself by his opponents, and would welcome an audience of the King as 'the opportunity for a fuller statement of his position, and for learning direct from Your Majesty what are Your Majesty's views'.[613] However, it was clear to the King and to Knollys, who told Esher that the way some ministers treated the King had become 'hopeless', that the established order had changed, and that the man who could have restored normal practice – Asquith – was, for his own reasons, unprepared to do so.[614] The King replied to Lloyd George on 7 August to say he had 'no opinion' of the Budget – a constitutional nicety – and conceded that the Chancellor had been attacked with 'much violence' by his political opponents, which he regretted: 'but he must remind him that though those gentlemen may have passed the fair limits of attack, they are private members and do not hold high office in the Government as is the case with Mr Lloyd George'.[615] The letter ended, however, on a conciliatory note: 'The King ... must give the Chancellor of the Exchequer every credit for the patience and perfect temper which he has shown, under considerable provocation, during the debates on the Budget.' However, a week later the King was confiding in Esher his belief that 'great harm' was being done because of the lack of discipline by Asquith of the two worst offenders – 'LG and WC'.[616]

Knollys warned the King in early September that 'certain members of the Cabinet are prepared to go to all lengths in order to secure a success over the House of Lords, and to adopt the most unscrupulous measures to achieve that object'.[617] He added that the radicals would not be satisfied with a 'temporary victory', and would follow it with 'a Bill with the purpose of crippling the power of the House of Lords'. Knollys wrote as a peer who had regularly supported the Liberal government in votes in the Lords – something unthinkable in an ennobled royal secretary today – but who was horrified by what he perceived as the real agenda of fanatics like Lloyd George and Churchill. Made as he was for this hour, Esher was invited by the King to give his views. Predictably, he did so with recourse to ancient history, inculcating in the Sovereign a view of the royal prerogative that would have served George III well, let alone Queen Victoria. More usefully, Esher also relayed information gleaned from his regular talks with Balfour and Lansdowne. He disclosed that the Tories would feel justified in rejecting the Budget because the Liberals had had no mandate to implement such socialist measures, and because if the Lords did not challenge such a thing there was little point in its existence.

The King began to be bombarded with conflicting advice from sources other than his private court about the constitutional import of the Budget being rejected. McKenna, who was staying with him at Balmoral as Minister in Attendance, told him on 27 September that a rejection would be so unprecedented that it would require immediate legislation to define and limit the Upper House's powers. 'No two principles are more firmly settled in the constitution', McKenna told him, 'than that the House of Commons is alone responsible for taxation, and that it is only by a vote in that House that the life of the Government of the day can be terminated.'[618] For good measure, he said that, as a Finance Bill had to be enacted every year, the Lords could effectively remove a government annually if this attack were allowed to succeed. His most telling point was that, as the Lords had never rejected a Finance Bill, to do so now would 'start the country on a revolutionary path'; the King had to agree that the Lords were making a tactical error.

Knollys picked up this theme in a letter he wrote the next day to Esher, in which he outlined his fears of the 'socialistic' effects of increasing the number of Liberal peers in the Lords – 'it is inevitable that the influence, prestige and authority of the Sovereign will be gradually decreased'.[619] He argued that if only the Unionists would pass the Budget, 'before very long a dissolution must take place, and I am convinced the Unionists will be then returned by a large majority'. The King, ignoring Esher's reactionary bellicosity, tried to do what he could to make the Conservatives see sense: but they felt he was bound to do whatever the government advised him, and that therefore his advice to them came at a discount. In October 1909 he invited to Balmoral one of the leading Conservative peers, Lord Cawdor, who gave him completely opposite advice to that offered by McKenna. In a memorandum to the King, Cawdor said that 'the object of the second chamber is that it should secure to the electors of the country the opportunity of exercising their wishes as to important legislative proposals before they become law'; and the radical nature of some of the provisions of the Finance Bill were precisely of the sort that merited such a reference to the people.[620] Cawdor's point was, in essence, that for all the accusations by Liberals that the House of Lords was behaving anti-democratically, it was in fact seeking to force a new democratic endorsement of the controversial policy.

LORDS VERSUS COMMONS

Esher, ready as always with the letter of the constitution as enshrined in precedent, sent the King a short memorandum on 8 October. Queen Victoria had intervened in 1869 when the Lords and the Commons were deadlocked over the Irish Church Bill, and again in 1884, that time over the Reform and Redistribution Bills. Gladstone had admitted on both those occasions that the Queen's intervention had helped avoid conflict between the two Houses: but 1909 was different. This was tantamount to class war, being fought between the upper and middle classes, and over a far more serious piece of legislation. Knollys, seeing at once how the King would be exposed by the coming fight, was furious with Lansdowne and Balfour for allowing the Sovereign to be set up in this way. 'They appear', he told Esher on 28 September, 'totally to ignore the effect it will probably have on the Crown, and the position the King will be placed in.'[621] Knollys was in no doubt that, to preserve peace, the will of the elected House had to prevail, even though he was probably more aware than most of what that victory would mean not merely for the aristocracy, but for the power of the

Sovereign. Articulating what would, ironically, become the ruling ethos of the Conservative and Unionist party for most of the twentieth century, Knollys told Esher that 'I fear that in politics, at the present day, even the most high-minded politician must not only consider what is right, but must also take into account what is expedient.' The King agreed with Knollys, going so far as to ask Asquith on 6 October 'whether I thought he was well within constitutional lines in taking upon himself to give advice to and, if necessary, put pressure upon the Tory leaders at this juncture'.[622]

Asquith told the King that what he proposed to do would be 'perfectly correct', and in an Esheresque flourish said that 'the nearest analogy was the situation and action of William IV at the time of the Reform Bill. In both cases the country was threatened with a revolution at the hands of the House of Lords.' In 1832 King William had offered, if necessary, to create eighty Whig peers to get the Bill through: the threat alone made the action unnecessary. King Edward agreed that he would not hesitate, in that case, to see both Lansdowne and Balfour; but Asquith was thrown by the King's subsequent observation: what was he to say to the Unionist leaders if they asked him what they would get in return for good behaviour on the Budget? He told Asquith he thought the answer to that was 'an appeal to the country – such as you say you want – only after, and not before, the final decision on the Budget'. Asquith did not know whether he should approve the King making such an offer; and on reflection told the King he did not think the offer would attract the Unionists. Also, he told the King that the Opposition would be in a poor position to fight an election once the Lords had just climbed down, and that the Liberals would find it hard to justify going to the country with only just over half the 1906 Parliament's term having run. Asquith will also have been aware – as perhaps the King was too – that his party would, when the time eventually came, have no chance of repeating the substantial victory of 1906.

As far as Asquith was concerned, the King would make no trouble unless seriously provoked, and, with a view to limiting the chances of such provocation, wrote from Balmoral to Lloyd George to urge him to act with moderation. 'The King is making, and will continue to make, every effort that is constitutionally open to him to secure the acceptance of the Budget Bill by the Lords,' wrote the Prime Minister. 'He is fairly sanguine of success. In the circumstances, as you are (I see) speaking in the country on Saturday, I venture to suggest that you should proceed throughout on the assumption that the Lords *will* pass the Bill.'[623] Asquith confided in his colleague that the King – who, for the record, it will be remembered, had 'no opinion' of the Budget – took 'serious exception' only to the passage on death duties, 'which he thinks might well be eased down in the case of the more moderate-sized estates. He has nothing to say against the land and mineral taxes, or the licence duties.'

The King had his meeting with Lansdowne and Balfour on 12 October, obeying Asquith's injunction that he should not offer them any incentives to comply. The other big concern before the meeting was what the press would say about it if they got hold of the news that it was happening. However, Knollys told Sandars, Balfour's secretary, that, after reflection, the King was 'quite indifferent, as it is with the Prime Minister's approval that he sees them'.[624] The King found Balfour and Lansdowne unhelpful; they told him no decision had been taken, but they knew full well what tactics they would be following, and what tactics their party would want them to follow. Unsurprisingly, they refused the King's invitation to issue the necessary orders to have the Lords pass the Budget.

Knowing these men of old, the King, in a cynical aside to Esher the next day, said he doubted 'whether any result of importance will accrue from my conversation with them, or that they have decided on any particular policy for the present'.[625] In fact, whatever the two grandees wished to do, they were bound by the two forces that had crippled the Conservative party ever since Salisbury's retirement: the uncontrollable urges of the rank and file (especially, though by no means exclusively, in the Lords, where they were determined to vote down the Budget), and the virtually non-existent leadership quality of Balfour. The King did not know which way to turn, though he was beginning to concede to himself that, given the other electoral changes of the preceding decades, the House of Lords could not go on as it was. Nothing now could avert the deadlock the King had been fearing, and, in what was to be the evening of his reign, he was confronted with more hard evidence of his own constitutional impotence: for there was nothing he could do either. His depression intensified. Discovering, on meeting Haldane at a party at about this time, that his War Minister did not know the Prince of Wales, the King took him across the room to introduce him. He did so with the words: 'Let me present you to the last King of England.'[626]

This depression was partly caused by the King's inability to find out what the Unionists were up to. Cards were being played very close to the Unionists' chests and, not being in government, the party was under no obligation to make a full and frank account of itself to the Sovereign. This made the King feel impotent, and he was reduced to sending out his spies, led by Esher, to try to glean information as best they could. A letter from Vaughan Nash, Asquith's secretary, to Knollys on 30 October makes the point:

> The only news I have as to the Lords comes by a somewhat roundabout road. Mr Asquith tells me that Lloyd George has told him that the Bishop of St Asaph told him that the Archbishop of Canterbury told him that Lord Lansdowne told him that notwithstanding every effort and appeal he found that he would be unable to control the action of (I am not sure of the exact expression) the wild men of the House of Lords. This, however, does not square with a report that Mr Asquith had heard to the effect that all but about thirty or so had agreed that they would take their marching orders from Lord Lansdowne.[627]

Asquith went to see the King on 15 November to discuss the predicament. The King complained to him that he simply did not know what the Lords were planning: 'not a line of any sort have I received as to their intentions', he told his Prime Minister, who reflected that there was no reason why the King should have had such a line.[628] He added, 'I know no more than the man in the street what they are doing,' and told Asquith he thought party politics had never been so bitter. The Prime Minister begged to differ, referring to the Home Rule crises of Gladstone's time. Asquith told his wife that the King had 'said some surprisingly shrewd things to me about Lansdowne and Balfour'. One knows the King's instinct was for the status quo: but he seems, from his old knowledge of the two Conservative leaders, not to have trusted that position to be safe in their hands.

Having been passed by the Commons on 5 November 1909 by 379 votes to 149, the Finance Bill was rejected in the Lords on 30 November by 350 votes to 75, the House instead passing a motion in Lansdowne's name that 'this House is not justified in giving its consent to this Bill until it has been submitted to the judgment of the country'.[629] Knollys himself had been inclined to go and vote with his fellow Liberals, telling Esher beforehand that McKenna had advised him that he 'saw no harm whatever in my voting' and that 'it would not be a bad thing if it were supposed (for it can only be a supposition) that the King is opposed to the rejection of the Budget'.[630] Knollys's motives were 'to do one's best to prevent a disaster happening to the Constitution and, incidentally, to the Monarchy'; but the King would not allow him to enter the arena in this way. 'I have decided not to vote,' he told Esher on 13 November.[631] 'Where there is any doubt about a thing, it is always best to do nothing.' The King was annoyed when word seeped out that he had sought to reconcile the two sides, so it was no surprise he should have taken the view on Knollys's intentions that he did.

Opinion in the country, whether among constitutionalists or on the Clapham omnibus, immediately divided over the rightness of what the Lords had done. Many believed the function of the Lords was, as *The Times*'s leading article put it the next day, to be 'the guardian in a peculiar sense of the great mass of things which the nation desires to conserve'.[632] The argument, which was not solely the preserve of Tory reactionaries, went on: 'When, according to the reasoned conviction of the Second Chamber, the proposed changes trench too deeply into what is permanent and organic, it becomes its duty to submit these changes to the judgment of the country. If the country decides against the proposed innovations the Second Chamber is fully justified. If the country accepts the novel proposals, the House of Lords does not call its decision into question.' That was exactly what Lansdowne had agreed to do: when the election came, and if the Liberals won it, the Lords would not vote down the revolutionary Budget.

The Liberals had been faring poorly in recent by-elections, and there was manifestly not the uncritical support for the forces of democracy in their fight against the landed interest for which the Cabinet might have hoped. Esher had been firm in his view, which the result of the subsequent general election did not entirely discount, that the King's prerogatives 'should not be used by Lords or Commons'.[633] He added, 'I feel sure that this would be the view of loyal subjects all over the Empire.' Asquith had warned the King in advance that he would have to seek a dissolution as soon as possible if the Budget went down; and on 2 December the Commons passed, by 349 votes to 134, a motion stating that the Lords' action was 'a breach of the constitution and a usurpation of the rights of the Commons'.[634] The stakes had been raised: if Asquith and his party now had their way, the Lords would in future be merely a revising chamber, with certain delaying powers. A main election promise was that the days of the peers having a veto would be gone for ever.

Esher meanwhile was having secret conversations with Haldane, which he dutifully reported back to Knollys. What he discovered took the argument into a new and, in the King's eyes, perilous phase. It was learned that the Cabinet was considering asking the King to surrender to the Prime Minister his prerogative to create peers, or alternatively to wrest from the King a guarantee about the creation of sufficient Liberal peers to vote the Budget through – which itself would precede legislation to restrict the powers of the Lords.[635] 'I pointed out to him', Esher reported, 'that the former would be an abdication by the Sovereign of his prerogative, not only on his behalf, but on that of his successors, and to my mind was an outrage.' Although with hindsight the proposal was the inevitable response by a government committed to expressing the will of the people to what the Lords had done, it was seismic in its unprecedentedness.

Knollys replied to Esher immediately that he had not shown the letter to the King, in order to spare him further apoplexy for the moment – 'he is not over fond of the Cabinet collectively as it is, though he likes some members of them individually very much, and I feel sure it would be a mistake to set him against them still more by making him acquainted with the outrageous proposals which they are now discussing'.[636] He branded the proposals 'inadmissible' and 'if submitted to the King not worth a moment's thought'. The first 'would be to take away one of the few remaining prerogatives of the Sovereign, and one of such great importance, and which would tend to weaken the Monarchy so considerably that it would be better the King should abdicate than agree to it'. The second was 'hardly constitutional, for no-one can know which side will obtain a majority'. Knollys added that he had twice told Asquith through Nash that 'if they want to have a hold over the House of Lords [he] should bring forward the Budget as the second measure'. Although one cannot doubt Knollys's sincerity, there are signs from his use of language that Esher was very much doing his preliminary thinking for him. However, this was not a matter on which Knollys, and therefore the King, felt casually enough about to make a change of mind on their part, with the useful flexibility for the situation that would have resulted, at all likely. Moreover, Esher was sure that, if the country were to know of the lengths to which the government was prepared to go in dragging the King into the argument, they would throw the government out.

The King dissolved Parliament on 15 December. By this stage, Knollys had broken the news to the King of what his ministers had planned to ask him to do to break the deadlock. On the day of the dissolution Knollys told Asquith's secretary, Nash, that the King had come to the conclusion that he would not be justified in creating new peers ('say three hundred') until after a second general election, and that Asquith should be told that now.[637] This did not amount to a guarantee, but laid out the conditions under which a guarantee might be given. It also suitably postponed the issue, and signified that another election would have to be held purely on the issue of whether the House of Lords should be changed out of all recognition. In what was to prove the last seizing of the constitutional initiative by the King in his short reign, Knollys told Nash that the King felt this safeguard was essential as the deluge would be 'tantamount to the destruction of the House of Lords'.[638] He added that, in a radical departure, the King would be even happier if the creations could all be life peers. But Nash pointed out, quite correctly, that the legislation needed to effect that would never get through the House of Lords.

Whether or not the Lords should retain their veto became the central issue of the election campaign. As part of the price for removing the veto, the duration of parliaments was to be reduced from seven to five years; the King let Asquith know via their secretaries that he would prefer it to be four years. How the legislation needed to reconstitute the powers of the Upper House in this way would be driven through that very chamber was as yet unbroached, at least in public. Knollys also asked Nash whether it had been considered withholding the writ of summons from those peers known to be hostile to the Finance Bill. This could legally be done, and would remove from those not in receipt of the writ the right to vote in the Lords. But it would involve the King (in whose name the writs were issued) in the political process just as much as the creation of a mass of new peers.

The campaign that followed was especially acrimonious, with Lloyd George at the forefront of providing the acrimony. As it went on, the King became more and more concerned by hints from both sides that he was supporting them. Lloyd George had given rise to one such set of rumours, having spoken of 'guarantees' if the Liberals were returned to office. It was assumed the guarantees had been given by the King about using his prerogative to create peers sufficient in number to defeat the Conservatives in the Lords. The King had given Asquith no such guarantees. Knollys and Esher now brought the question they had discussed privately out before the Monarch, and Esher told him that he could refuse to use his prerogative to swamp the Lords with

Liberal peers. When the Cabinet had discussed in December whether Asquith should advise the King to surrender that part of his prerogative, and allow the Prime Minister to create peers – the discussion Haldane had reported to Esher – it had been clear to them that the King would not want to abandon part of the prerogative not just for himself, but for his successors; but the alternative course would drag the King directly into the political fight, where he had made it clear he did not wish to be. The King, when told of the plan by his advisers, recognised this problem at once, and was plunged into depression. It was not just that the Lords would be devalued: it was that the Crown's place in the constitution would be damaged, and not only temporarily.

The requirement the King had imposed about a second election had to remain secret, but it meant a repudiation by Asquith of an intention he had publicised at the opening rally of his party's campaign, in the Albert Hall, a few days earlier. In his speech there, Asquith had implied that 'safeguards' he needed to govern would have to be in place before he would accept the King's commission to form a government in the event of a Liberal victory at the election. Now, the King had warned his Prime Minister that the imposition of the most important safeguard of all would require another election. Knollys also had Esher sound out Balfour, with whom he was staying at the ex-Prime Minister's estate at Whittinghame, about what he would do if the King refused advice from Asquith to create peers, and Asquith had to resign – 'I should very much like to know whether under certain circumstances, Balfour would consent to form a Govt,' he asked on 29 December.[639] 'If the King understood beforehand he could do so, it would strengthen his hand enormously.' It certainly would have helped the King to know that Balfour was willing to serve, but Balfour, of all people, would not be that stupid: he would face certain and immediate defeat in the Commons in those circumstances. The King, through his closest advisers, was seeking to protect himself from obloquy and thereby the Crown from damage in seeking to pin Balfour down. If neither side would govern, the King would be seen by all sides to have no choice but to consent to radical constitutional innovations. In fact, the country was mostly unmoved by what was going on.

Balfour did make clear to Esher that it would be 'impudence' by the Liberals to suggest that the creation of peers should take place before legislation to limit the powers of the Lords.[640] 'He has no shadow of a doubt', Esher continued in a letter to Knollys of 9 January 1910, 'that the King ought not – under any circumstances – to agree.' Balfour felt Asquith should be told to make a formal written submission to the King about his proposals, for which Esher supplied the possible answers. Given that Lansdowne had promised to pass the Budget if the Liberals won the election, there was no crisis necessitating the creation of peers. Balfour felt that 'it would be a breach of the King's duty, if not of his Coronation Oath, to pledge himself to create Peers to pass a Bill which he has never seen'. Balfour's final advice to the King, while he was, typically, not prepared to volunteer to govern himself, was that 'whatever risk may be run by the Sovereign in refusing such a request as it is assumed Asquith will make next month, there would be greater risk in acceding to it'. Or, as Knollys had said, 'it would look as if the King had delivered himself body and soul into the hands of the extreme left'.[641] Balfour was, however, cagey about his own role. He had Sandars write to Knollys on 14 January to say that, while the Leader of the Opposition was glad to see Knollys at any time, it might be wise 'purely in Mr Balfour's interests' to postpone such a meeting until a crisis should arise, for fear of 'misinterpretation'.[642]

For the January 1910 election, the question was whether the government or the peers were right in their view of the Budget. The Liberals lost their overall majority in the Commons, having 275 of their men returned against 273 for the Unionists. Seeing their majority of 220 over their nearest rivals reduced to just 2 was a catastrophic blow, and should have weakened Asquith's hand severely. However, he was able to continue to govern with the help of the forty Labour members and the eighty-two Irish nationalists. This latter form of support was to give some peers the justification they sought for their campaign against the Finance Bill, since they argued that the government was enabled to govern as it chose only with the help of MPs who wished to leave the United Kingdom. As far as the King was concerned, the election proved that the matter was, in terms of a democratic mandate for what the Liberals wanted to do, far less clear-cut than Asquith and his colleagues might have hoped. In remaining highly cautious and reluctant to set any far-reaching constitutional precedents by the use of his prerogatives, the King was to have the justification of the narrowness of the vote.

Lansdowne kept his promise, and the Budget was voted through, although the King feared militant Unionists would vote it down anyway. As the Tories saw it, the Lords had served their constitutional purpose of having a deeply contentious matter referred back to the people, as outlined by *The Times*'s leader-writer the morning after the Budget's defeat. For the Lords, though, the issue was now about much more than the Budget. The Conservative party's latest incarnation was as the Unionist party, its new *raison d'être* being to resist Home Rule. Home Rule could be stopped only in the Lords. Therefore, a removal of the Lords' veto, such as Asquith had threatened, would allow a Home Rule Bill through. This was to be the new battleground.

ENTER THE KING

This shifting of the fight meant that the King would now, it seemed, be properly dragged into the argument. For all his political sense, he could not grasp the motives of party politics; he could see that certain important differences must remain between parties, for reasons of divergent principle and of human ambition. The ease with which he could make up historic international quarrels was not to be replicated in solving apparently less menacing domestic disputes. Esher reported a lightened mood at Windsor in a letter to Balfour of 24 January, saying that 'the recent elections have caused great relief here.... there can be no question with this lowered majority, dependent upon the Irish, of Asquith trying to "bully" the King'. Asquith, certainly slightly chastened by the result, had indeed no intention of bullying; but it was not to be so simple as that.[643] The next day, having had a long talk with his Sovereign, Esher wrote to his son that the King 'is quite clear that he will not assent to any request to make Peers'.[644] Haldane, as Esher's and the King's leading trusty, was also informed of this, with the rider that the King could change his mind only in the light of a 'much more definite expression of opinion from the country'. By 6 February Esher was even more sanguine about the chances of the Liberals behaving moderately, for interesting reasons: 'I gather that the dominant factor in the radical camp is "fear of social consequences",' he wrote to Knollys. 'Neither Asquith, nor Loulou [Harcourt] want [sic] to be socially ostracised. Bridge parties, Margot's [Mrs Asquith's] friends, Loulou's royal parties are going to influence the political decisions of the Liberal party.'[645]

The King had continued to try to mediate between the two sides – and, indeed, he had had an offer from Randall Davidson, the Archbishop of Canterbury, to help him – but to no effect. Pleading exhaustion, Asquith declined a command from the King to come and discuss the matter with him at Windsor at the end of January, absenting himself in the South of France instead (there was a royal precedent for this, but the King was livid). Acquainted with the King's views on the matter, Asquith wrote to him to protest that he was 'physically unfit for any kind of business'.[646]

The King had a pet scheme he wanted to put to the Prime Minister but, in his absence, put it instead to the Leader of the Lords. At a dinner at Windsor on 30 January he privately told Crewe that he felt something ought to be done to redress the inequality in numbers between the two sides in the Lords, but he was sufficiently conservative in his views to want to make the best of the Lords as they were rather than to start from scratch with a completely new chamber. So the only change he proposed to make was in voting: while all existing peers could sit and speak, only a hundred of them would be allowed to vote. The King told Crewe that he thought the hundred should be chosen by the two party leaders in the Lords, fifty each, and that they should serve for the term of a parliament. Crewe pointed out the difficulties of this to the King – not least that the fifty chosen would inevitably be the fifty most slavishly loyal to their party. Nonetheless, the King asked him to go away and think about how the scheme might be put into operation. But nothing came of it, and it is unlikely anything would have come of it had the King lived any longer.

On his return from his rest cure Asquith made a few changes to his administration, to which the King raised no objections, and he and the King discussed what the government's tactics were to be with regard to the Budget. The Conservative peers were now acquiescent, and Asquith was not seeking any guarantees about Liberal creations from the King. The previous day the Cabinet had agreed not to ask the King to use his prerogative to create sufficient peers to get legislation through – yet. Ministers were waiting for an 'actual necessity', a new provocation by the Lords, before the ultimate deterrent could be tried. However, a new danger now presented itself. On 12 February the King, who was sojourning at Brighton, told Knollys that Asquith, who had been to visit him, had said he found himself in a 'very tight place'. This was because his eighty-two Irish supporters were not proving so reliable as he might have liked.[647] Such was the temper of the times that Esher had urged Knollys to have the King keep a private record of his conversation with Asquith, which Knollys thought a good idea.[648] The previous day Asquith had sent the King a formal Cabinet minute, in response to an enquiry about the Government's intentions, saying that no request about the exercise of the prerogative was intended or would be made until the necessity arose, but that if the Irish voted down the Budget 'Your Majesty's present advisers will be confronted with the alternative of resigning office or advising another dissolution.'[649]

The Irish, meanwhile, wanted an assurance that the removal of the Lords' veto would happen immediately, so that the Lords could not block the Home Rule Bill they wanted. The King, for his part, saw Sandars on 15 February, to try to ascertain what the Conservative strategy was; he was told that they would fight on. This caused him to write to Asquith the same day to say that 'from what I can gather I find that the Opposition will probably vote against the Government on the Budget'.[650]

The King opened the new parliament on 21 February. There was great tension in political life, which the election had increased rather than dissipated. Some, including Asquith, had felt that the King might decline to attend the State Opening, because of his irritation over the crisis, and because his personal relations with many members of the Cabinet were not at their best: but he did, as 'on all previous occasions since my accession to the throne'.[651] One line in his speech, in the section that referred to 'proposals ... to define the relations between the Houses of Parliament, so as to secure the undivided authority of the House of Commons over Finance, and its predominance over legislation' caused immediate controversy.[652] It was when the King said that 'the measures, in the opinion of my advisers, should provide that this House [of Lords] should be so constituted and empowered as to exercise impartially in regard to proposed Legislation the functions of initiation, revision and, subject to proper safeguards, delay' that he raised eyebrows; the reference to his advisers' opinion suggested that he was determined not to associate himself with that part of the legislative programme. It was, however, a phrase inserted by the Prime Minister, on which the King made no comment; and it seems the formula was used to absolve the King of any personal responsibility in a matter on which it was known he had strong views in the opposite direction.

On the day of the State Opening, Asquith made it clear in the Commons that the rumours of his having obtained 'guarantees' from the King of a creation of peers in advance of the House of Commons having seen and approved legislation were entirely unfounded. Indeed, he went further and said that it would have been improper to ask for them. Asquith discovered a new boldness at this time. While the option was considered by the Cabinet of resigning after the Irish threat, and leaving it to the King to see whether Balfour could form a government, Asquith in the end sent word to Redmond, the Nationalists' leader, that he would have to act on his responsibility, as Asquith would on his. However, the echo of these brave words did not last long.

THE DEMISE OF THE CROWN

The King's health was failing: his respiratory problems were chronic, and he was in pain when struggling for breath. Such a condition had lasted for more than the previous year, however, and there was no reason to expect the King's health to be forced to a crisis. His friends and confidants found him tired and deeply depressed by the political situation. He should have gone abroad to a better climate long since, but was determined to stay and do what business he could with Asquith. In the end, Asquith prevailed upon him to start earlier than usual for Biarritz. Before going he gave an audience to Haldane, his favourite Liberal minister, and told him he could not possibly agree to the creation of the peers Asquith wanted given the 'inconclusive' result of the recent election.[653] As the two men parted, the King told Haldane: 'This Government may not last. I say nothing of some of my Ministers but I wish you may be very long my Minister.' Hardinge had reported to Knollys on 22 March that 'Grey of his own initiative told me this morning that all the Cabinet are at sixes and sevens and that he does not see how they can possibly get over the next three weeks without breaking up.'[654]

Once at Biarritz the King could not put the political situation out of his mind. Lee notes that it 'worried and distressed him to an extent which was almost incredible', and he was felled with a terrible attack of bronchitis.[655] He certainly did not get the rest he badly needed. He was further worried by various press articles at home, which reached him in Biarritz, speculating upon his own views of and intentions in the political situation. Worst of all was a report he read of a speech by Churchill that included what he felt to be 'nebulous allusions to the Crown', which had prompted immense press comment and the attribution of 'various opinions' to the King.[656] Once more, he made a plea to Asquith to have his ministers keep his name out of their party political fights. Knollys confided in Esher that some of the more 'moderate' Liberals were distressed by Asquith's behaviour, and wanted the King to 'mediate' – 'I say I will mention the matter to him, but that in my opinion he should not do so until he is asked by the Prime Minister to come forward.'[657]

While in Biarritz, the King approved three resolutions, submitted to him by Asquith, that were to form the germ of the Parliament Bill, subsequently the 1911 Parliament Act. They were that the Lords should lose its veto on and power to amend money Bills; that if a Bill passed in three successive sessions in the Commons it could become law even if the Lords three times rejected it; and the length of a parliament was cut from seven to five years. These resolutions were passed in the Commons on 14 April, but then Asquith had to write to the King that the Irish were threatening to vote down the Budget – 'and your Majesty's present advisers would of necessity next week tender their resignation', and 'a crisis, of an unexampled and most embarrassing kind, would thereupon arise', provoking yet another election.[658] To try and forestall this Lloyd George was in deep consultations with the Irish, mainly over the question of whisky duties, which were the main objection from that quarter. However, the Cabinet decided that the alteration of the whisky duties would reframe the Budget in an unacceptable way, and so the Irish were told their wishes could not prevail.

'Your Majesty's advisers', Asquith told the King, 'are strongly and unanimously of opinion that to purchase the Irish vote by such a concession would be a discreditable transaction which they could not defend.'[659] Much more acceptable, it seemed to Asquith, was to ignore the King's condition about a second election and hint to the Irish, as he did in a speech in the Commons on 14 April, that he would tender advice to the King to bring about the circumstances whereby the constitutional deadlock could be broken 'in this Parliament'. In other words, the question of getting a guarantee before legislation, and before a second election, was back on the agenda. This was enough for the Irish, but the King was horrified. Balfour accused the Prime Minister of betraying the dignity of his office. Asquith had told the King the previous day that he felt it might, if the Lords persisted in their opposition to the government, become his duty to advise that 'the necessary steps – whether by the exercise of the Royal Prerogative, or by a Referendum ad hoc, or otherwise – be taken to ensure that the policy approved by the House of Commons by large majorities be given statutory effect in Parliament'.[660] The 'steps' were in the end accepted by King Edward's son: for King Edward, the battle was almost over.

He was appalled by the turn of events: he asked Knollys, 'why don't the moderate Liberals state that, if the Government continues their socialism and arbitrary ways, they cannot support them?'[661] He also mocked Asquith's promises to keep the Crown out of the controversy, when the advice the Prime Minister was planning to tender to him would drag the Crown straight into a fight. For the moment, though, there was nothing the King could do but ask Asquith to be sure to send him a telegram immediately after the Budget vote, on Monday 18 April 1910, informing him of what had happened. The Budget, thanks to the Irish, passed in the Commons. The Lords passed it the following week. Knollys, meanwhile, wrote to Esher that Asquith was about 'to commit the greatest outrage on the King which has ever been committed since England became a Constitutional Monarchy'.[662] He repeated his earlier point that, if the country continued to support the 'radicals' in another election, the King would be best advised to abdicate.

These strong feelings led Knollys into a constitutionally unwise move: he met with Esher, Balfour and the Archbishop of Canterbury in a secret conclave at Lambeth Palace on 27 April 1910. Balfour agreed at that meeting that 'in view of the weakness of the present mandate' the King would be within his rights to reject advice about the creation of peers.[663] This was an astonishingly bold thesis from a notoriously cautious man; it would have been interesting to see just where Balfour would have been found, had the King taken his advice, in the conflagration that would have ensued. Balfour did, though, offer that in such circumstances he would accept the commission to form a government. It was agreed that to protect the position of the King the advice to accept a large creation of peers would have to be formally rejected in a document worded so as to ensure there was no hint of political bias. Balfour claimed this difficult task could be accomplished, and in a way that 'would add much lustre to the position of the Sovereign'. Given the public lack of interest in what was going on, Balfour could well have been right. Esher, as we know, had long held this view; but Knollys himself, for all his instinctive resistance to change, was not so sure. His later advice to King George V, to agree to the guarantees, suggests he would have prevailed upon King Edward to back down too. However, in a letter to Knollys from Biarritz after Asquith's change of policy in mid-April, the King had said that 'he is going to ask me to swamp the House of Lords by a quantity of Peers. As I told you in my last letter I positively decline doing this. Besides I have previously been given to understand I should not be called upon to agree to this preposterous measure.' He said he found the whole thing 'simply disgusting'.[664] He was especially angry that the government was now 'in the hands of Redmond and Co.'. It was especially galling to see the British constitution being torn up at the behest of a bunch of anti-British home rulers.

The passing of the Budget meant no respite for the King, for, although that crisis was over, the veto crisis that would replace it threatened to be far more unpleasant, and far more likely to drag in the Crown. Needless to say, the King did not want there to be a fight on this question, because of the instability it would cause and the loss of respect for legislative institutions that would entail. He hoped it could be settled amicably, but it could not. Just as they would violently object to the composition of the Lords being radically changed, so the Unionists were determined to fight the Bill designed to alter the Upper House's powers and *raison d'être*.

The King's sense of humour was, though, not eclipsed by stress and illness. Pressured in April 1910 to confer a peerage on the new Governor of New Zealand, Sir John Dickson-Poynder, he acceded despite noting that the recipient was 'practically unknown and [his] only claim to distinction lies in the fact that he was converted to Liberal principles somewhat late in life'. Asquith told him the peerage was necessary because the New Zealanders wished to have a member of the House of Lords as Governor. The King said he was 'amused to think that while the mother country is contemplating abolishing peers altogether, New Zealand, perhaps the most democratic of all his dominions, should set so much store on having a Peer as Governor!'[665]

The King returned to London on 27 April, after seven weeks in Biarritz, and picked up the duties of state immediately, a task made easier by the thick traffic of letters between him and Knollys during his absence. A new Viceroy of India had to be appointed, Minto's term being near its end. Morley, the India Secretary, wanted Sir Charles Hardinge; the King, probably Hardinge's greatest admirer, nonetheless wanted Kitchener, rejecting Hardinge because 'a man should stick to his last.... he was a diplomatist, not an administrator': a direct contradiction of the line he had taken just three and a half years earlier, when trying to have Hardinge sent to Washington.[666] Morley refused to accept Kitchener, because of an objection to a soldier being sent to do a civilian job, but was persuaded by the King that they should both go away and think the matter over. He had, in his recent audience with Haldane, enlisted him on the Kitchener side. Later that day he saw Asquith. 'I had a good talk with the King,' the Prime Minister told his wife, 'and found him most reasonable.'[667]

The King spent the ensuing weekend at Sandringham where, with his customary refusal to listen to medical advice, he went outside and caught a chill. The following Monday, 2 May, he suffered a severe bronchial attack. Nonetheless, he was determined to press on, and was keen as ever for information about events. Hardinge relayed to him, for example, on 2 May that Grey, one of the most moderate members of the Cabinet, 'still professes himself to be opposed to asking for guarantees'.[668] On 3 May a memorandum, aimed at stiffening his resolve, arrived from Esher about the demand for guarantees. It contained no new history, but responded to a claim by Crewe that a request for guarantees was not one 'which the King is at liberty to agree or refuse, but is "advice", which, as a Constitutional Sovereign, the King is bound to accept'.[669] Esher was horrified that this assertion had been accepted as fact by the 'radical press', though Crewe believed that the 'calamity' of the Crown's involvement in party politics would not happen, because the Lords would not let it happen.[670]

Esher, meanwhile, was busily dredging up some more precedents. Earl Grey's speech of 9 May 1832 'throws light', he wrote, on Crewe's claim.

> He answers, as a matter of course, that the King may not receive the advice of his Minister, and he goes on to say: 'We offered to His Majesty the advice which we thought it our duty under the circumstances to offer; the alternative was accepted by His Majesty, and he was graciously pleased to accept our resignation.' There is not a word of exception taken by Earl Grey, nor has any authority ever condemned or criticised the action of William IV on that occasion.

This proved, Esher said, that the King could ignore Asquith, 'provided that he can find another set of ministers to carry on the Government'. Esher might have recalled, but did not, William IV's dismissal of Melbourne in 1834, when (as Asquith noted in a brief for King George the following December) 'the dismissed Ministers found an adequate majority in the House of Commons. The King was compelled to take them back again, and they remained in power for another six years.'[671] No wonder even Queen Victoria, for all her imperiousness, had never used that part of her prerogative. In Biarritz, the King had pondered whether giving peerages to the eldest sons of all Liberal peers might be one solution, since they would all end up in the Lords anyway.[672] However strange the idea might seem, it was at least an acknowledgment of democratic reality, and the need for the Crown to review even its most important prerogatives in that light. Poor Esher: he had not noticed the seventy-eight years, the reform Acts, and all the world that had changed since then. Nor, moreover, was he to have this particular captive audience for very much longer.

The King was well enough to see the American ambassador on 3 May; the Premier of Western Australia on 4 May; and Lord Islington, the previously unknown Sir John Dickson-Poynder, on 5 May, as he set out to govern New Zealand. That afternoon the Queen, who had been at Corfu, returned having heard of the seriousness of her husband's illness, and when he did not meet her at Victoria Station the public had their first intimation of his condition. A bulletin was issued by the King's physicians that evening confirming that he had bronchitis. The next morning, 6 May, he could not even smoke a cigar. He asked for Sir Ernest Cassel to come to see him, which Cassel immediately did, and the King reposed some final confidences in him. The King, by now in great pain, was uplifted in the afternoon by news that a horse of his had won at Kempton Park, but he fainted twice, and it was feared he was slipping into a coma. He became unconscious in the evening, shortly after uttering the words: 'No, I shall not give in; I shall go on; I shall work to the end.' At 11.45 p.m., he died.

AFTERMATH

BALFOUR'S REVENGE

In the autumn of 1912, two and a half years after King Edward's death, the royal family was thrown into some distress. The cause was the publication of the *Dictionary of National Biography*'s article on the late King, and when they read it – or at least the section of it entitled 'His relations with politics' – King George and his widowed mother in particular expressed their outrage that so false a picture could be presented of their father, husband and Sovereign. It said:

> King Edward cannot be credited with the greatness that comes of statesmanship and makes for the moulding of history. Neither the constitutional checks on his power nor his discursive tastes and training left him much opportunity of influencing effectually political affairs. No originating political faculty can be assigned him. For the most part he stood with constitutional correctness aloof from the political scene at home. On questions involving large principles he held no very definite views. He preferred things to remain as they were.... His main aim as a traveller was pleasurable recreation and the exchange of social courtesies.... He was a peacemaker, not through the exercise of any diplomatic initiative or ingenuity, but by force of his faith in the blessing of peace and by virtue of the influence which passively attached to his station and to his temperament.... The external show of personal control which belongs to the Crown at home seemed at times to be obscured by his long sojourns in foreign countries.... in his intercourse with foreign rulers and diplomatists, so far as politics came

within the range of the conversation, he confined himself to general avowals of loyal support of ministerial policy.[1]

This analysis – which might be thought to sound like an expression of the true feelings of someone like Balfour, who had been particularly aggrieved by the King's political activities and was unwilling to let the public know the extent to which he had been compromised by them – was not especially accurate. The author of the article, however, had no axe to grind. He was our old friend Sir Sidney Lee, a scrupulously fair and scholarly man best known, at that time, for his Shakespearean researches and a life of Queen Victoria. He was also the editor of the *DNB*. Apparently, Lee had interviewed several leading men of the time who had worked closely with the King, and from them he had tried to assemble a rounded picture of the late Monarch. The royal family, recognising a less than complete account of King Edward, were determined to make Lee revise his portrait, but a simple fiat would not suffice. Lee, a meticulous man who, if anything, erred on the side of tact and fairness in his biographical writings, had a scholar's unwillingness to rewrite history unless presented with incontrovertible evidence that would cause him to do so. As far as he was concerned, he had written the truth. At least one great man, a Privy Councillor no less, had told him so. Therefore, if the royal family's wish was to be fulfilled, new evidence countering Sir Sidney's defamations had to be put before him.

To this purpose the King's assistant private secretary, Arthur Davidson, wrote to (of all people) Balfour on 23 October 1912. He told the ex-Prime Minister how much the King and his mother regretted the picture that had been painted, in this great work of record, of the late King as:

> an easy-going, pleasure-loving Sovereign, whose good manners and amiable disposition gained for him a credit as a diplomatist which he did not deserve – that he had 'no originating political faculty', 'no broad diplomatic views', 'in home politics was content with the role of onlooker', that he 'cannot be credited with the greatness that comes of statesmanship and makes for the moulding of history', and to put it in the fewest words, that he enjoyed a reputation to which he was not entitled, thus implying that he was practically a cypher in the Government of the country of which he was the Ruler.[2]

Now this will have given some trouble to Balfour, or should have done. After all, in order to retain his own self-regard and not own up to the fact that he was, for all his intellectual brilliance, a moral coward, a vacillator and a compromiser, this was very much how he himself had viewed the King. Moreover, he would continue to do so – we are still more than two years away from his notorious letter to Lansdowne asking him to agree that the King had had but little to do with the *entente cordiale*. However, he was hardly going to tell Davidson that, not least since the King's man continued his letter by observing that the 'evidence' given to Lee by the various great men to whom he had spoken had manifestly not been 'accurate', and that the result had caused 'very great pain to the King, to Queen Alexandra and to a very large number of others who, with a more or less intimate knowledge of King Edward, are unable to reconcile Sir S Lee's opinion with facts as they existed during his reign'. Davidson said he was writing to Balfour at Queen Alexandra's suggestion, since she had wanted him to see 'whether this humiliating estimate of King Edward's character and influence is correct and justified or not'. Balfour was assured that he was not required to supply a 'fictitious' reputation for the late King, merely a 'just' one. To help him along, Davidson quoted back at him the very words he had delivered in the Commons on 11 May 1910 on the King's death: 'He did that which no Ministers, no Cabinet, no Ambassadors, neither treaties nor protocols, nor understandings, which no debates, no banquets, no speeches were able to perform.'

Lansdowne, to whom Davidson also wrote, replied swiftly that the *DNB* article was 'an inadequate and unkindly picture of the late King' which served to 'belittle unduly the part played by him in public affairs, whether at home or abroad'.[3] Balfour's own reply was more studied, and arrived after more than a fortnight's rumination. He lengthily complained that where Lee went wrong was not in his facts, but in presenting his facts without their proper contexts – such as not mentioning that the King was absent in Biarritz during the crises of March/April 1908 and the spring of 1910 not for the sake of enjoyment, but for the sake of his extremely poor health. Balfour did describe the *DNB* article as 'utterly misleading' and added the mandarin judgment: 'King Edward's duty was as a constitutional King. It seems to me he performed that duty' – a statement that positioned him, as usual, in the swamp of ambiguity.[4]

A month later Lee himself, who had been shown Balfour's remarks by Davidson, wrote to him in a greatly wounded fashion. 'I notice discrepancies between your letter and the notes, made by me at the time, of the remarks on the subject which you were kind enough to offer when I saw you on 24 November last year.'[5] So: Balfour had been one of Lee's 'great men', and had offered one of those opinions deemed by the royal family to be 'not accurate'. This greatly put Balfour on the spot, and compelled the enlistment of what might most politely be termed his full dialectical resources in order to deal with the matter. Replying to Lee on 11 December 1912 he says that the biographer was no doubt 'compelled to write with the sound of certain indiscreet and unfounded laudations ringing in your ears'. Having suspected this at the time, Balfour had, he pointed out, simply been performing the kindness of redressing the biased opinions offered up by others on the principle of *de mortuis nil nisi bonum*. However, just in case Lee had missed the message that Balfour had, of course, sought all along to convey, he repeated it: King Edward had been 'a great constitutional king'.[6]

He continued: 'I am sorry that there should be, or seem to be, any "discrepancies" between my letter to Davidson and anything I may have said to you last year. I kept no notes of our conversation, and have but a very shadowy memory of its character: but I am not conscious of having changed my views on any substantial point.' This amnesia was particularly convenient, and made the matter one of Lee's word against Balfour's. In such a contest, given the ex-Prime Minister's record of honesty, it is not hard to know which view to accept. Davidson was enlightened in this respect. The *DNB* entry was not revised, and remains on the record to this day a deeply one-sided account of the King's political activity; and one for which posterity has largely to thank Balfour. Davidson continued to make his own enquiries, which proved beyond question the contempt in which Balfour had held his late Sovereign, and acquitted the diligent and truthful Sir Sidney.

Davidson also corresponded with Jack Sandars, Balfour's old secretary, who replied with a candour he manifestly had not learned from his master. He said that the celebrated obituary address of May 1910 had been not remotely true, but simply what was required for the occasion. He added of Balfour that 'he and Lord Salisbury had a very poor opinion of the King's intellectual capacity'.[7] Certainly, the Commons' tributes to the King in May 1910 had been deeply reverential: Asquith, as his Prime Minister, called the King 'the Peacemaker of the World' whose 'duty to the State always came first'.[8] Asquith was sincere and nicely understated in his tribute; but then,

even in all the difficulties he had inflicted on the King, he had never
sought to make the problems personal, even if, on occasion, the King
had in his sickness inadvertently taken them that way. It is quite clear
that he had liked King Edward. Balfour's tribute, by comparison, was
wordy, grandiloquent, almost theatrical, as if he had been helped in its
composition by the late Lord Beaconsfield. He larded this with his own
inescapable ambiguity: 'Genius keeps its own counsels, and I think no
mere attempt at analysing character, no weighing of merits, no attempt
to catalogue great gifts really touches the root of that great secret which
made King Edward one of the most beloved monarchs that ever ruled
over this great Empire.'[9] It was as well he should have said, later on,
that 'the duties of kingship are not becoming easier as time goes on'.

Yet Balfour could not resist using this most sensitive of speeches, at
the most sensitive of times, to belittle the King and aggrandise himself,
and if Davidson had read one passage in his speech closely, he would
have guessed who had put Sir Sidney 'straight' about King Edward.
'There have been, I think, strange misunderstandings with regard to
the relation of the great King who has just departed with the
administration of our foreign affairs,' noted the Prime Minister who
presided over the *entente cordiale*. 'There are people who suppose he took
upon himself duties commonly left to his servants, and that when the
secrets of diplomacy are revealed to the historian it will be found that
he took a part not known, but half-suspected, in the transactions of his
reign.' As we have seen, that is precisely what the King had done, but
Balfour was not having it. His protestation, in throwing down a false
scent, was typical of his slipperiness. 'That is to belittle the King,' he
continued. 'It is not to pay him the tribute which in this connection he
so greatly and so justly deserves.'[10] Balfour then went into the rhetoric
quoted back to him by Davidson, but was referring in that passage not
to the initiatives taken by the King (for Balfour simply would not admit
that he had taken them), but to the more nebulous quality the late
Monarch had had for merely 'embodying' the 'friendly policy' –
originated by others – of this country. In other words, the King had
been nothing more than a front man, precisely the view Balfour, who
was nothing if not consistent, would advance to Sir Sidney when they
met the following year. In speaking on behalf of his party in the Lords,
Lansdowne dutifully stuck to the Balfour line, but did admit that 'I am
convinced that there is not a *Chancellerie* in Europe which does not
recognise that with the death of King Edward VII a great international
force has been removed.'[11]

Balfour was a politician who, for all his superficial refinement and pose of intellectual disinterest, liked power and would do almost anything to retain it. He felt its possession and exercise was the prerogative of professional politicians, in whose number he did not include the King. To have to accept and endure so much interference from a monarch must have been depressing and offensive to one of this philosophical disposition. To have to accept and endure it from a man he regarded as so greatly his intellectual inferior must have been especially distasteful. Enduring it in private was one thing, but realising the public also suspected the truth about the King's influence must, for a man of Balfour's vanity, have been unbearable. No wonder, even so soon after his death, Balfour was determined to have the King's role in the politics of his reign written off, if only to make himself feel better.

CONSEQUENCES

'He died for his country,' Queen Alexandra told Austen Chamberlain on 12 May 1910, when she took the King's former servant to pay his last respects to the Monarch, who lay in an open coffin in his field marshal's uniform in his room at Buckingham Palace.[12] 'All this trouble the last year worried him,' she continued. 'And perhaps he could have calmed it. Perhaps some word from him would have made them wiser.' Now, the question of Lords against Commons had to find a resolution without him. In August 1911 the Lords, after one of the most dramatic debates in British parliamentary history, narrowly gave their assent to the Parliament Bill that removed their veto. The Unionists, in the end, voted to preserve as much of the old ways as they could; there was, in return for their acquiescence, no swamping by Liberal peers. King George, advised by Knollys, agreed to the 'guarantees' his father had found so repugnant. Knowledge of this forced the Unionists' hands, save for a group who fought in the last ditch and whom history has designated the 'ditchers'. Therefore, this particular constitutional issue was not to be the most significant part of King Edward's legacy.

The ultimate political consequences of Edward VII are not, of course, those itemised day to day in his intercourse with ministers. They are seen in the role his monarchy and his kingship played in the evolution of the British constitution, and in particular in the relative powers of the Sovereign, his ministers and Parliament. Care must be taken even in making a comparison between King Edward's reign and the conduct of the monarchy by his son, King George V. King Edward's was the last reign before universal suffrage; and it was the award of the vote to women over thirty in 1918, and to all adults in 1928, that had as its concomitant the greatest, inevitable shift of direct power from the Monarch. The prerogatives – notably the reserve powers to summon and dissolve Parliament, and to appoint or dismiss a Prime Minister – ostensibly remained unchanged by the full democratisation of the electorate. However, the transmission of power 'to the people' inevitably circumscribed the freedom with which a monarch could use those powers and, at the same time, altered the balance of power between Monarch and minister in favour of the minister. The new Sovereign, being both far less experienced than his late father and at that stage less interested in politics and statecraft than King Edward, presented his ministers with an ideal opportunity to exercise their own control.

King George, and not his father, was the first properly constitutional monarch; his father, and not Queen Victoria, was the last monarch to try to retain some of the more ancient, pre-democratic customs and practices of the Crown. 'It was not', Lee wrote in his reflections on the reign, 'until the reign of King Edward that the aristocratic fortress was undermined and a really democratic regime inaugurated.'[13] Certainly, the coming of the Liberal government after 1905 – or, more pointedly, after Asquith took charge in 1908 – shifted the balance away from the aristocratic or landed interest towards the middle classes. How King Edward would have resolved the House of Lords crisis one cannot know, but he might well have taken the course his son did – of accepting Asquith's advice to create the peers if necessary. The essential question would have been whether Knollys had told him of Balfour's willingness to form a government in the event of Asquith's resigning over a refusal to grant guarantees. Scarcely less essential, though, is whether the King, apprised of that likelihood, would have believed that the notoriously slippery Balfour would really do it.

Though modern would-be reformers of the House of Lords contend that there is no link between imperilling the hereditary basis of the peerage and imperilling the hereditary basis of the monarchy, this is not so. This part of history seems to prove it. George V's power was inevitably reduced because he had to allow the hereditary principle to be humbled in August 1911. He acted partly on the advice of Knollys, who became his joint private secretary. Perhaps identical advice would have been tendered to his first master, had he lived; or perhaps it was tendered to King George only because Knollys recognised that, for all his undeniable good qualities, the new King had none of the authority, personality, experience or drive in political matters that would have been required to face down such a constitutional challenge as was presenting itself. Certainly, Knollys held back that most important of details from the new King: the claim at the Lambeth Palace meeting of April 1910 by Balfour that he would be prepared to form a government in the event of Asquith's resigning after being refused guarantees. King George, as his official biographer notes, was not told of this until 1913; and in January 1914 dictated a minute in which he said that this knowledge, had he had it at the time, 'would, undoubtedly, have had an important bearing and influence with regard to Mr Asquith's request for guarantees on November 16 1910'.[14] As it turned out, the mere threat that King George would, if necessary, create 500 peers was enough to prevent it having to be carried out.

The climate at the end of King Edward's reign was very different from at the start: he was no longer so interested in political matters, particularly in domestic affairs; he had lost the energy needed to take on his ministers in the way he had taken on Balfour and Lansdowne; he may have appreciated that the electorate of 1910 (not to mention the political power it wielded) was radically different from the electorate at the time he came to adulthood, before the 1867 Reform Act. These social and political changes made inevitable such erosions of the prerogative as he had to contemplate, but those erosions set precedents, and implicitly acknowledged a change in the status quo ante, that his less politically able and interested son was powerless to reverse. When King Edward died, the monarchy changed for ever. His was the last stewardship of an institution designed for a feudal age and which, by some miracle attributable largely to the benign temper of the English people, had retained many of its feudal trappings into an age of democracy.

King George, especially as he grew in his office, was not (as his biographers have related) slow to take offence at certain actions of his ministers, and to call them to account. However, these were often relatively minor matters, either properly within his constitutional role, for example when he warned Lloyd George about the quality of some of the people he was intending to honour, or eccentrically and harmlessly outside it, such as when rebuking Lord Birkenhead for turning up to an emergency Cabinet meeting on a bank holiday dressed in a tweed suit. From very early on in King Edward's reign, the then Prince of Wales had been intimately acquainted with the details and practice of statecraft by his father in exactly the way King Edward would have wished his own mother to have trained him. But King George was first and foremost by training a naval officer, who was twenty-six before he realised he would have to succeed one day. Politics and the political class were simply not an entertainment for him.

Unlike his father, there is no evidence that King George sought to have members of any administration dismissed because he found them uncongenial, or that he conducted foreign policy without reference to his ministers. Indeed, he was interested in foreign policy only in so far as it concerned his own peoples, in his Empire. When, in 1923, he sent for Baldwin rather than Curzon to be his Prime Minister after the resignation of Andrew Bonar Law, it was not his decision that the nature of politics and of the electoral base had changed so that it was impossible for a peer to be Prime Minister; it was Lord Balfour's, whose advice he had sought and willingly, almost deferentially, acted upon. Had his father been spared to the age of eighty-one, and been asked to discharge the same function, it is difficult to believe that even in the identical context he would have acted as his son did, by relying on Balfour – even if, in the end, the results turned out to be the same.

There seemed to be no getting away from the point Balfour had to make to King George. Curzon could not succeed because, after August 1911, the settled principle was that the House of Commons' will must pertain, even if the majority that gave expression to that will were sustained by a group (in that case the Irish Nationalists) who wanted rid of the English constitution as it affected them. Once that blow against feudalism was struck, the prospect of serious interference by an unelected, unaccountable monarch was more remote than ever. Perhaps, though, the most important factor in making King George's conduct of the monarchy so different from his father's was that for the most part he lacked the basic impulse to challenge politicians and their developments of the constitution as his father did. It was not until his part in the formation of Ramsay MacDonald's Coalition in 1931 that King George really showed his mettle in politics.

King Edward never vetoed any legislation, any more than his far more militant mother did; but before matters reached the legislative stage he had the opportunity, in formal audiences, on country-house weekends and in the margins of dinner-parties, to make his views known. His ministers would be well aware, long before making any public proposal, of whether that proposal would entail a protracted fight with the King. The King might well lose the fight, but it might be decided that such fights were not worth the lengthy expenditure of ministerial time and energy at the highest level. King Edward was determined not to be a rubber-stamp, not because he thought he could be his own prime minister, but because the constitutional arrangements established by his predecessors at least dictated that it was his duty not to be a pushover.

The formidable nature of King Edward's experience, his social familiarity with his ministers and his often obsessive interest in matters of governance gave him the personality and the weight to fulfil what he regarded as his proper constitutional function. In turn, this meant that his influence on the activities of the administrations that served him was profound. This can best be seen in the way he handled certain aspects of foreign policy, not least the construction of the *entente cordiale*. Although the constitutional position of the Sovereign did alter between 1901 and 1910, it arguably altered less than the rest of the complexion of British politics. Nonetheless, the King was to an extent a brake on change to the constitution, though his battle with Asquith was unfinished at his death; his son was equipped to be nothing of the kind. With King Edward's death the politicians took control at home, and – the Empire apart – the British monarchy ceased to be much of an influence in affairs abroad.

Moreover, the accelerated way in which Asquith and Lloyd George pursued radical change in the four years between King Edward's death and the Great War – not just forcing through the Parliament Act, but also Irish Home Rule – suggests that the passing of the old King was something of a liberation for them, and they were determined not to allow his son to have a similar effect in hampering and delaying the fulfilment of their intentions. At last, fifty years after he wrote, Bagehot came true. For the first time, Britain had a monarch who recognisably followed the wish-list the supposed modern father of the constitution had drawn up. The consequence of Edward VII in terms of domestic politics, and on the constitution of which he was the dignified pinnacle, was to ensure that, in future, the men elected by the people held sway over a person historically regarded as the elect of God.

Abroad, his influence was profound both before and after his death. The policy of splendid isolation ended, and did so because the King for long periods acted as his own foreign secretary, more while the

Conservatives were in power than under the Liberals. He was known by the end of his reign as 'Edward the Peacemaker', an ironic appellation when one considers the conflagration that ignited in Europe just four years after his death, and into which England was dragged partly as a result of the alliances he had instigated. Certainly the King's intention was the preservation of peace, but alliances brought with them obligations that could embroil Britain in the worst circumstances: and the worst circumstances were precisely what happened. When the Germans talked of 'encirclement', they imputed the sort of scheming and cunning to King Edward that was more properly the province of their own Kaiser. The King had formed alliances on behalf of his country that incidentally encircled Germany, but the Germans by their own hysterical double-dealing and lack of perspective failed to present themselves as suitable partners for Britain in such a scheme.

It is hard to blame the King for having disliked the Kaiser. His nephew all too often cut the figure of one who seems, to a later generation, to have been urgently in need of extensive psychiatric help. The sheer arrogance and childlike desire for status and recognition that the Kaiser had would always make him a difficult man to deal with. However, the King also allowed himself to be swayed by two other considerations. First, there was the matter of his wife's nationality, and the instinctive dislike he took towards Prussia after the events of 1864. Second, he allowed himself to be seduced by the French, whose application of flattery to him in return for the sincere delight he took in that country's more relaxed way of life made him a soft target. The King and his ministers cannot be faulted for the lengths to which they went, in diplomatic terms, to propitiate the Kaiser, and the Kaiser all too frequently responded to such initiatives with a suspicion and ill-grace that made attempts at friendship impossible. Nonetheless, the result of this cocktail of vanities and prejudices was that England made alliances that ensured they could not merely spectate on the events of August 1914; and King Edward was the prime mover in them.

It would be too easy to record the reign of King Edward VII as the last roar of the monarchical lion before it was finally tamed by democracy, and to downplay, in Balfourian fashion, the King's achievements. That would be to overlook a more subtle political effect that he had, and which still, albeit diluted, has force today. The King fully restored the popularity of the monarchy in Britain. He even seemed to manage to restore it to a large extent in Ireland, where its subsequent decline was entirely the fault of his son's ministers. The fact that revolution was avoided in Britain at a time when the three great European empires crumbled in 1917–18 was mainly, but not entirely, due to those countries' defeat and Britain's victory. The ten years after the war, leading up to the depression, were rife with civil tensions and political agitation in Britain. The monarchy remained above this; that was, of course, due to the statecraft of King George, most particularly in his constructive attitude to the Labour administrations of Ramsay MacDonald.

However, the instinctive trust in and respect for the monarchy held among those classes who, in other lands, comprised the mob was largely a tribute to the good work done in laying the foundations for this sentiment by King Edward. Until his mother's golden jubilee in 1887 public feeling about the monarchy had been ambivalent, though had slowly recovered from the nadir reached in the republican agitation of the early 1870s. The Queen's appearances at the diamond jubilee in 1897 helped convey to the people her example of duty and devotion, and helped remind them how grateful and blessed they should feel as a result. The Prince of Wales had, though, throughout the years of his mother's widowhood, taken her place at the head of society, and had often provided the focal point for public affection that she, by her absence, could not. His efforts on behalf of the working classes had been sincere and, fortunately, much publicised. He came to his own reign with an aura of popularity, and did nothing in his nine years on the throne to forfeit it. Indeed, he was perceived to have risen above the political tumult of those years, and to have won Britain great credit and power abroad. His son, helped by the fact that he was an impeccably decent man, capitalised on this goodwill faultlessly. Although Esher remained a friend of King George and offered him advice, the King did not use this courtier in anything like the way his father had. Instead, King George completed the idea of the modern constitutional monarchy in which a king relies on the advice of his elected ministers. However, someone had had to start the final push that provided this result, and King George's father had done just that. Those social and political foundations, laid between 1901 and 1910, still exist in Britain; and it is well that King Edward helped lay them so strongly, for they are not always kept in good repair.

BIBLIOGRAPHY

I. PRIMARY SOURCES

RA: Papers in the Royal Archives, Windsor Castle. These include the as yet uncatalogued papers of the 1st Viscount Knollys, shown in the notes as 'RA Add 7'.

BL: Papers in the general manuscript collection of the British Library.

BP: Papers of the 1st Earl of Balfour, in the British Library.

CBP: Papers of Sir Henry Campbell-Bannerman, in the British Library.

EP: Papers of the 2nd Viscount Esher, at Churchill College, Cambridge.

HP: Papers of the 1st Baron Hardinge of Penshurst, in the University of Cambridge Library.

SP: Papers of the 3rd Marquess of Salisbury, at Hatfield House.

II. SECONDARY SOURCES

Amery: *The Leo Amery Diaries*, vol. I (1896–1929), ed. John Barnes and David Nicholson (Hutchinson, 1980).

Asquith M: *The Autobiography of Margot Asquith*, 2 vols (Thornton Butterworth, 1920–2).

Asquith S: *H. H. Asquith: Letters to Venetia Stanley*, ed. Michael and Eleanor Brock (Oxford University Press, 1982).

Bagehot: *The English Constitution*, by Walter Bagehot (Oxford University Press, World's Classics, 1928).

Brook-Shepherd: *Uncle of Europe*, by Gordon Brook-Shepherd (Collins, 1975).

Butler and Freeman: *British Political Facts, 1900–1960*, by David Butler and Jennie Freeman (Macmillan, 1963).

Chamberlain: *Politics from the Inside*, by Sir Austen Chamberlain (Cassell, 1936).

Churchill: *Winston S. Churchill*, by Randolph S. Churchill, 2 vols (Heinemann, 1966–7).

DNB: *The Dictionary of National Biography*, January 1901–December 1911, ed. Sir Sidney Lee, 3 vols (Oxford University Press, 1912 – all references to vol. 1).

Dugdale: *Arthur James Balfour*, by Blanche Dugdale, 2 vols (Hutchinson, 1939).

Esher: *Journals and Letters of Reginald, Viscount Esher*, ed. Maurice V. Brett, 2 vols (Ivor Nicholson & Watson, 1934).

Gardiner: *The Life of Sir William Harcourt*, by A. G. Gardiner, 2 vols (Constable, 1923).

Gilmour: *Curzon*, by David Gilmour (John Murray, 1994).

Gladstone: *The Gladstone Diaries*, ed. M. R. D. Foot and H. C. G. Matthew, 14 vols (Oxford University Press, 1968–94).

Grigg: *Lloyd George: The People's Champion, 1902–1911*, by John Grigg (Eyre Methuen, 1978).

Haldane: *Richard Burdon Haldane: An Autobiography* (Hodder & Stoughton, 1929).

Hardie: *The Political Influence of the British Monarchy*, by Frank Hardie (Batsford, 1970).

Hardinge: *Old Diplomacy*, by Lord Hardinge of Penshurst (John Murray, 1947).

Jenkins I: *Asquith*, by Roy Jenkins (Collins, 1964).

Jenkins II: *Mr Balfour's Poodle*, by Roy Jenkins (Collins, 1968).

Lee: *King Edward VII: A Biography*, by Sir Sidney Lee, 2 vols (Macmillan, 1925–7).

Lees-Milne: *The Enigmatic Edwardian: The Life of Reginald 2nd Viscount Esher*, by James Lees-Milne (Sidgwick & Jackson, 1986).

M&B: *The Life of Benjamin Disraeli, Earl of Beaconsfield*, by W. F. Monypenny and G. E. Buckle, 6 vols (John Murray, 1912–20).

Magnus: *King Edward VII*, by Sir Philip Magnus (John Murray, 1964).

Morley: *Recollections*, by John Viscount Morley, 2 vols (Macmillan, 1917).

Nicolson I: *Lord Carnock: A Study in the Old Diplomacy*, by Harold Nicolson (Constable, 1930).

Nicolson II: *King George V: His Life and Reign*, by Harold Nicolson (Constable, 1952).

Ponsonby: *Recollections of Three Reigns*, by Sir Frederick Ponsonby (Eyre & Spottiswoode, 1951).

Pope-Hennessy: *Lord Crewe: The Likeness of a Liberal*, by James Pope-Hennessy (Constable, 1955).

Rhodes James I: *Lord Randolph Churchill*, by Robert Rhodes James (Weidenfeld & Nicolson, 1959).

Rhodes James II: *Rosebery*, by Robert Rhodes James (Weidenfeld & Nicolson, 1963).

Rose: *King George V*, by Kenneth Rose (Weidenfeld & Nicolson, 1984).

R&P: *The Letters of Arthur Balfour and Lady Elcho, 1885–1917*, ed. Jane Ridley and Clayre Percy (Hamish Hamilton, 1992).

St Aubyn: *Edward VII, Prince and King*, by Giles St Aubyn (Collins, 1979).

Simon: *Retrospect: The Memoirs of the Rt Hon. Viscount Simon* (Hutchinson, 1952).

Sommer: *Haldane of Cloan*, by Dudley Sommer (George Allen & Unwin, 1960).

Spender and Asquith: *Life of Herbert Henry Asquith, Lord Oxford and Asquith*, by J. A. Spender and Cyril Asquith, 2 vols (Hutchinson, 1932).

Trevelyan I: *The Life of John Bright*, by G. M. Trevelyan (Constable, 1913).

Trevelyan II: *Grey of Fallodon*, by G. M. Trevelyan (Longmans, 1937).

Wilson: *CB: The Life of Sir Henry Campbell-Bannerman*, by John Wilson (St Martin's Press, 1973).

Young: *Arthur James Balfour*, by Kenneth Young (Bell, 1963).

NOTES

PRINCE

1 Lee, i:81.
2 Ibid, ii:273.
3 Ibid, i:127.
4 Ibid, 128.
5 Ibid, 129.
6 St Aubyn, 201.
7 Lee, i:199.
8 Ibid, 199–200.
9 Ibid, 200.
10 RA T6/124.
11 Lee, i:201.
12 Ibid, 202.
13 Rhodes James II, 57.
14 Lee, i:203.
15 Morley, ii:499.
16 Lee, i:208.
17 DNB, 565.
18 Lee, i:251.
19 Ibid.
20 Ibid, 252.

21 Gladstone vi:288.
22 Lee, i.266.
23 Ibid, 269.
24 Ibid, 303.
25 RA A40/39.
26 Lee, i:367.
27 RA T7/34.
28 SP: Letter from AE to Salisbury, 24 July 1878.
29 Lee, i:364.
30 Magnus, 81.
31 RA Z459/32.
32 Hardie, 92.
33 Magnus, 126.
34 Lee: i:222.
35 RA T5/85.
36 Gladstone, vii:516.
37 Ibid, viii:96.
38 Ibid, 123.
39 RA Z459/30.

40 RA Z459/31.
41 RA Z459/33.
42 RA L1/38.
43 RA Add Mss A12/32.
44 RA T5/104.
45 RA Z459/40.
46 RA Z459/53.
47 RA Add A36/447.
48 Gladstone, viii:203.
49 RA A44/72.
50 Lee, i:333.
51 M&B, v:431.
52 RA T6/64.
53 RA T6/93.
54 RA T6/83.
55 Lee i:399.
56 Ibid.
57 Ibid, 403.
58 SP: Knollys to

Salisbury, 15
October 1875.
59 M&B, v:463.
60 Ibid, 476.
61 RA T6/96.
62 RA T6/97.
63 RA T6/102.
64 RA T6/103.
65 RA T6/121.
66 RA T6/114.
67 Lee, i:422.
68 Ibid, 423.
69 RA Add A36/
    1148.
70 RA T6/115.
71 RA H10/27.
72 Lee, i:434.
73 Ibid.
74 RA T7/31.
75 RA T7/32.
76 St Aubyn, 202.
77 RA T6/20.
78 SP: Letter from
    AE to Salisbury,
    July 1876.
79 See, for example,
    SP: AE to
    Salisbury, 31 May
    1880.
80 SP: Letter from
    Knollys to
    Salisbury, 13
    October 1876.
81 SP: Letter from
    AE to Salisbury,
    13 May 1879.
82 SP: Letter from
    AE to Salisbury,
    1 May 1879.
83 Enclosure in ibid.

84 SP: Letter from
    AE to Salisbury,
    4 February 1879.
85 SP: Letter from
    AE to Salisbury,
    14 January 1879.
86 Lee, i:455.
87 Ibid, 456.
88 RA E61/104.
89 Lee, i:479.
90 Ibid, 482.
91 Ibid, 486.
92 RA T7/38.
93 Magnus, 165.
94 Lee, i:514.
95 RA T8/6.
96 Magnus, 166.
97 Gladstone, ix:508.
98 Ibid, xi:202.
99 Lee, i:519.
100 RA Vic Add Mss
    J/1482.
101 RA Vic Add Mss
    J/1483.
102 RA Vic Add Mss
    J/1485.
103 Magnus, 169.
104 St Aubyn, 223.
105 Ibid.
106 Ibid, 203.
107 RA H10/27.
108 BL: Add Mss
    56087/5.
109 RA T9/43.
110 Hardie, 92.
111 BL: Add Mss
    56087/5.
112 RA Z455/26.
113 BL: Add Mss
    56087/5.

114 RA T9/47.
115 Ibid.
116 RA T9/48.
117 Lee: i:216.
118 RA T9/69.
119 RA A69/17.
120 RA L16/78.
121 RA L16/82.
122 Ponsonby, 62.
123 RA T9/10.
124 RA T9/28.
125 CBP: Add Mss
    41207/1.
126 Gladstone, xi:331.
127 Lee, i:223.
128 Trevelyan, I, 387.
129 Lee, i:241.
130 Wilson, 192–3.
131 Hansard (Lords),
    6 May 1879, col
    1789.
132 RA T8/138.
133 RA T8/139.
134 RA T8/140.
135 Hansard (Lords),
    22 February 1884,
    col 1694.
136 Lee, i:550.
137 SP: Letter from
    Knollys to
    McDonnell, 21
    March 1891.
138 Gladstone,
    xiii:157.
139 Lee, i:553.
140 Magnus, 193.
141 RA T9/68.
142 SP: Letter from
    AE to Salisbury,
    27 July 1886.

143 Ibid.
144 RA T9/70.
145 SP: Letter from AE to Salisbury, 30 July 1886.
146 Magnus, 197.
147 Rhodes James I, 327.
148 SP: Letter from Kilmorey to AE, 21 March 1888.
149 SP: Letter from Drummond Jervois to AE, 20 February 1891.
150 SP: Letter from Knollys to Salisbury, 1 January 1890.
151 SP: Letter from Knollys to McDonnell, 10 March 1892.
152 Rose, 275.
153 Lee, i:642.
154 SP: Letter from AE to Salisbury, 16 October 1888.
155 Magnus, 209.
156 Ibid, 210.
157 Ibid, 211.
158 Ibid, 213.
159 SP: Letter from AE to Salisbury, 9 April 1889.
160 SP: Letter from AE to Salisbury, 11 April 1889.
161 SP: Letter from AE to Salisbury, 16 April 1889.
162 Lee, i:653.
163 Magnus, 213.
164 SP: Cypher from Knollys to Ponsonby, 19 December 1891.
165 SP: Letter from Knollys to Salisbury, 8 August 1891.
166 RA T10/35.
167 Lee, i:692.
168 RA T10/16.
169 Gladstone, xiii:60.
170 RA T10/17.
171 St Aubyn, 238.
172 Nicolson I, 125.
173 SP: Letter from Knollys to Salisbury, 7 August 1898.
174 SP: Memo from McDonnell to Salisbury, 26 October 1897.
175 SP: Memo from Sidney Greville to Salisbury, 9 May 1898.
176 Lee, i:715.
177 SP: Memo from Sidney Greville to Salisbury, 26 April 1900.
178 Lee, i:750.
179 SP: Memo from Sidney Greville to Salisbury, 9 September 1899.
180 Lee, i:759.
181 Ibid, 792.
182 Ibid, 795.
183 SP: Letter from Knollys to McDonnell, 30 December 1900.

INTERLUDE: THE BAGEHOT PROBLEM

1 Bagehot, 30.
2 Ibid, 34.
3 Ibid, 35.
4 Ibid, 40.
5 Ibid, 42.
6 Ibid, 48.
7 Ibid, 51.
8 Ibid, 52.
9 Ibid, 53.
10 Ibid, 59.
11 Ibid, 62.
12 Ibid, 67.
13 Ibid, 66.
14 Ibid, 70.

KING

1 Lee, ii:8.
2 EP: 2/10, Journal, 22 January 1901.
3 EP: 2/10, Journal, 23 February 1901.
4 SP: Memo from Salisbury to ERI, 24 January 1901.
5 BP: Add Mss 49683/55.
6 BP: Add Mss

49683/60.
7 DNB, 589.
8 Lee, ii:50.
9 Magnus, 277.
10 SP: Letter from Knollys to Salisbury, 23 February 1901.
11 Wilson, 346.
12 Lee, ii:12.
13 Ibid, 14.
14 SP: Letter from Knollys to McDonnell, 14 March 1901.
15 RA R22/14.
16 Dugdale, i:252.
17 Ponsonby, 128.
18 Lee, ii:22.
19 BP: Add Mss 49683/62.
20 RA R23/40.
21 RA R22/16.
22 SP: Letter from ERI to Salisbury, 17 February 1901.
23 RA R22/40.
24 RA R22/35.
25 RA R22/37a.
26 RA R22/36.
27 SP: Letter from McDonnell to Knollys, 9 July 1901.
28 SP: Memo from McDonnell to Salisbury, 16 July 1901.
29 Lee, ii:26.
30 SP: Letter from

McDonnell to Knollys, 26 March 1901.
31 Lee, ii:39.
32 Gardiner, i:407–8.
33 Lee, ii:41.
34 Ibid, 42–3.
35 Ibid, 43.
36 Dugdale, i:239.
37 SP: Memo from McDonnell to Knollys, 18 July 1901.
38 Lee, ii:29.
39 Ibid, 30.
40 RA W42/11.
41 SP: Letter from Knollys to Salisbury, 9 June 1901.
42 RA R22/29.
43 RA W42/16.
44 Rhodes James II, 425.
45 Lee, ii:79.
46 Ibid.
47 SP: Letter from ERI to Salisbury, 20 November 1901.
48 Lee, ii:81.
49 SP: Letter from Knollys to McDonnell, 6 November 1901.
50 SP: Letter from ERI to Brodrick, 20 February 1902.
51 Gilmour, 291.

52 Ponsonby, 127.
53 EP: Letter from Knollys to Esher, 8 September 1905.
54 RA R22/94.
55 SP: Memo from Salisbury to ERI, 14 June 1902.
56 SP: Memo from McDonnell to Salisbury, 4 March 1901.
57 RA R22/9.
58 SP: Memo from Salisbury to McDonnell, 21 February 1901.
59 SP: Letter from Knollys to McDonnell, 8 October 1901.
60 SP: Letter from Knollys to McDonnell, 20 October 1901.
61 SP: Memo from McDonnell to Salisbury, 13 February 1902.
62 SP: Memo from Salisbury to McDonnell, undated.
63 SP: Letter from Knollys to McDonnell, 8 July 1902.
64 SP: Letter from McDonnell to

Knollys, 6 March
1902.

65 SP: Memo from
McDonnell to
Salisbury, 7
March 1902.

66 SP: Letter from
Knollys to
McDonnell, 10
May 1902.

67 SP: Letter from
Knollys to
McDonnell, 15
May 1902.

68 RA R22/103.

69 RA W38/1.

70 RA R22/82.

71 Ibid.

72 RA R22/83.

73 RA R22/84.

74 RA R22/32.

75 SP: Letter from
Knollys to
Salisbury, 23
February 1901.

76 SP: Letter from
Knollys to
McDonnell, 31
October 1901.

77 SP: Letter from
Knollys to
Salisbury, 7
January 1902.

78 RA Add C7:
Letter from
McDonnell to
Knollys, 10
January 1902.

79 SP: Letter from
Knollys to

McDonnell, 27
February 1902.

80 SP: Letter from
McDonnell to
Knollys, 24
January 1902.

81 SP: Memo from
McDonnell to
Salisbury, 23
January 1902. Sir
Sidney Lee dates
this memo as
1901, but it is
unequivocally
dated 1902. Also,
the reference to
'The Prince of
Wales' puts it in
1902. There was
no Prince of
Wales on 23
January 1901, as
the Duke of York
was not created
Prince of Wales
until 9 November
that year.

82 RA R22/102.

83 SP: Letter from
Knollys to
Salisbury, 11
March 1902.

84 SP: Statement,
12 March 1902.

85 Lee, ii:115.

86 Ibid, 120.

87 Ibid, 127.

88 Ibid, 128.

89 Ibid, 130.

90 RA W42/49.

91 RA W42/51.

92 RA W42/58.

93 RA W42/59.

94 RA W42/61.

95 RA W42/62.

96 RA W42/63.

97 RA W42/64.

98 RA W42/63.

99 RA W42/65.

100 RA R22/65.

101 RA W42/66.

102 Brook-Shepherd, 113.

103 Lee, ii:153.

104 Ibid, 159.

105 R&P, 177.

106 Lee, ii:160.

107 Young, xvii.

108 RA R22/106.

109 RA R22/108.

110 RA W42/84.

111 RA W42/87.

112 RA W42/90.

113 RA Add C7:
Letter from
Lansdowne to
Knollys, 25 July
1902.

114 RA W42/96.

115 RA W42/101.

116 RA W42/102.

117 RA W42/103a.

118 Ponsonby, 146.

119 Ibid, 147.

120 RA W42/104.

121 RA W42/103.

122 RA W42/1.

123 RA W42/105.

124 RA W42/106.

125 RA W42/106a.

126 RA W42/107.
127 RA W42/110.
128 RA W42/107a.
129 RA W42/107b.
130 RA W42/108.
131 RA W42/109a.
132 RA W42/111a.
133 RA W42/112.
134 RA W42/115.
135 RA R22/125.
136 RA R22/126.
137 RA W42/144.
138 RA W42/145.
139 RA R23/8.
140 RA R23/8a.
141 RA R23/10.
142 Ponsonby, 127.
143 RA W43/6.
144 RA W43/30.
145 RA W43/31.
146 RA R23/45.
147 Ibid.
148 RA W38/70.
149 Esher, i:376.
150 RA R23/52.
151 RA R23/53.
152 RA W43/128.
153 RA W43/3a.
154 RA W43/62.
155 Lee, ii:223.
156 RA W42/83.
157 HP: Vol 3, letter from Knollys to Hardinge, 15 January 1903.
158 Hardinge 1.
159 Ibid, 85.
160 DNB, 594.
161 RA W43/77.
162 RA R23/58.

163 RA R23/60.
164 HP: Vol 4, telegram from Barrington to Hardinge, 8 April 1903.
165 RA W43/75.
166 HP: Vol 4, telegram from Balfour to ERI, 9 April 1903.
167 HP: Vol 4, telegram from Barrington to Hardinge, 10 April 1903.
168 HP: Vol 4, telegram from ERI to Balfour, 10 April 1903.
169 HP: Vol 4, letter from Hardinge to Lansdowne, 12 April 1903.
170 RA W43/75.
171 HP: Vol 4, telegram from Balfour to ERI, 12 April 1903.
172 HP: Vol 4, letter from Knollys to Hardinge, 23 April 1903.
173 Ponsonby, 162-4.
174 RA R23/65.
175 Lee, ii:236.
176 Ibid, 237.
177 Ibid, 237-8.
178 Ibid, 239.
179 Ibid, 245.

180 Hardinge, 96.
181 Ponsonby, 173.
182 Magnus, 315.
183 BP: Add Mss 49683/154.
184 RA W44/8.
185 RA W44/56.
186 BP: Add Mss 49684/35.
187 RA W44/53.
188 RA W44/54.
189 RA W44/86.
190 RA W44/92.
191 RA W44/88.
192 RA R24/83.
193 RA W44/87.
194 RA W44/92.
195 RA W43/190.
196 Lee, ii:257.
197 RA W43/130.
198 RA W43/131.
199 RA W43/132.
200 RA W43/135.
201 RA W43/136-7.
202 Lee, ii:267.
203 Ibid.
204 Ibid.
205 Ibid, 270.
206 Ibid.
207 RA W43/88.
208 Lee, ii:271.
209 Ibid.
210 RA W45/25.
211 RA R24/31.
212 RA R24/32.
213 RA R24/38.
214 RA R24/43.
215 RA W44/34.
216 Lee, ii:285.
217 Ibid, 286.

218 Magnus, 336.

219 Lee, ii:287–8.

220 Ibid, 288.

221 Ibid, 289.

222 Ibid, 293.

223 RA R25/23.

224 RA R45/61.

225 RA W45/53.

226 RA W45/52.

227 RA W45/54.

228 Lee, ii:302.

229 Ibid, 303.

230 Ibid, 310.

231 Hardinge, 124.

232 RA W45/72.

233 Lee, ii:347.

234 Ibid.

235 RA W46/285.

236 Lee, ii:348.

237 Ibid, 358.

238 Young, 214.

239 RA R23/82.

240 RA R24/71.

241 RA R23/84.

242 RA R23/86.

243 RA R23/85.

244 RA R23/88.

245 RA R23/92.

246 Those who wonder whether history repeats itself should compare these events, and the débâcle of the 1906 election in which they culminated, with those of the Conservative party in the 1992–7 parliament.

247 RA R23/89.

248 RA R23/92.

249 Esher, ii:14.

250 Ibid.

251 Ibid, 19.

252 Chamberlain, 157.

253 RA R23/99.

254 RA R23/100.

255 RA R23/101.

256 RA R23/102.

257 RA R23/100.

258 RA R23/103.

259 RA R24/10.

260 Esher, i:390.

261 BP: Add Mss 49684/55.

262 BP: Add Mss 49684/56.

263 RA R23/98.

264 RA R23/100.

265 Ibid.

266 RA R23/102.

267 RA R24/2.

268 RA R24/6.

269 RA R24/25.

270 Amery, 48.

271 Esher, ii:27.

272 RA W38/101.

273 RA R24/13.

274 Lee, ii:195.

275 EP: 10/47, letter from Knollys to Esher, 30 October 1903.

276 BP: Add Mss 49684/11.

277 BP: Add Mss 49684/12, 18.

278 BP: Add Mss 49684/4.

279 BP: Add Mss 49684/51.

280 BP: Add Mss 49684/5.

281 RA W39/39.

282 Lee, ii:200.

283 Ibid, 201.

284 Ibid, 203.

285 BP: Add Mss 49684/80.

286 BP: Add Mss 49684/148.

287 BP: Add Mss 49684/121.

288 BP: Add Mss 49864/129.

289 BP: Add Mss 49864/138.

290 RA W39/52.

291 Lee, ii:205.

292 Ibid, 206.

293 RA R25/37.

294 RA R25/57.

295 RA W39/56.

296 EP:10/47, letter from Knollys to Esher, 28 October 1904.

297 RA R25/68.

298 RA W39/63.

299 EP: 10/48, letter from Knollys to Esher, ? December 1904.

300 RA W39/66.

301 RA R25/69.

302 Lee, ii:211.

303 BP: Add Mss 49685/17.
304 RA W39/85.
305 Lees-Milne, 155.
306 Magnus, 333.
307 RA W39/115.
308 RA R25/10.
309 RA R25/99.
310 RA R25/100.
311 RA R26/97.
312 RA R26/98.
313 Lee, ii:186.
314 RA R26/57.
315 RA R26/77.
316 RA R26/78.
317 EP: 2/10, Journal, 16 November 1905.
318 EP: 2/10, Journal, 20 November 1905.
319 RA R26/95.
320 RA R26/96.
321 EP: 2/10, Journal, 28 November 1905.
322 RA R26/76.
323 Ibid.
324 RA R26/81.
325 RA R26/85.
326 RA W39/115.
327 Gilmour, 348.
328 RA R26/86.
329 BP: Add Mss 49685/42.
330 BP: Add Mss 49685/50.
331 BP: Add Mss 49685/95.
332 RA W64/81.

333 CBP: Add Mss 41207/63.
334 RA W64/88.
335 RA R27/33.
336 CBP: Add Mss 41207/67.
337 EP: 10/49, letter from Knollys to Esher, 25 March 1906.
338 BP: Add Mss 49685/98.
339 RA W71/4.
340 RA W39/123.
341 CBP: Add Mss 41207/6.
342 Wilson, 403.
343 Ibid, 405.
344 Ibid, 426.
345 Morley, ii:247.
346 Haldane, 160.
347 RA Add C7: Letter from Haldane to Knollys, 12 September 1905.
348 RA Add C7: Letter from Knollys to Haldane, 16 September 1905.
349 RA Add C7: Letter from Haldane to Knollys, 19 September 1905.
350 Haldane, 161.
351 Ibid, 162.
352 Wilson, 430.
353 RA Add C7: Letter from Haldane to Knollys, 22 October 1905.
354 RA Add C7: Letter from Knollys to the King, 8 December 1905.
355 Lee, ii:445.
356 RA R27/1.
357 Lee, ii:446.
358 Sommer, 153.
359 RA W20/37.
360 CBP: Add Mss 41207/13.
361 Wilson, 504.
362 Simon, 70.
363 Lee, ii:448.
364 RA W39/127.
365 EP: 2/10, Journal, 13 December 1905.
366 Lees-Milne, 155.
367 EP: 2/10, Journal, 6 December 1905.
368 Magnus, 349.
369 RA W40/78.
370 CBP: Add Mss 41207/12.
371 Churchill, i:420-1.
372 Lee, ii:482.
373 Churchill, ii:94.
374 Ibid, 185.
375 Wilson, 145.
376 RA W39/112.
377 RA R27/36.
378 RA R27/48.
379 EP: 10/49, letter from Knollys to

Esher, 29 November 1907.
380 RA W41/11.
381 Esher, ii:104.
382 RA W41/15.
383 RA W41/11.
384 Magnus, 287.
385 Ibid.
386 Esher, ii:149.
387 Lees-Milne, 161.
388 RA W40/105.
389 RA W40/103.
390 RA W40/104.
391 EP: 10/49, letter from Knollys to Esher, 28 March 1907.
392 RA Add C7: Telegram from Esher to Hardinge, 21 June 1906.
393 RA Add C7: Letter from Hardinge to Esher, 21 June 1906.
394 RA Add C7: Letter from Hardinge to Knollys, 21 June 1906.
395 RA R27/13.
396 RA R27/14.
397 CBP: Add Mss 41207/23.
398 CBP: Add Mss 41207/24.
399 CBP: Add Mss 41207/27.
400 CBP: Add Mss 41207/28.
401 RA R27/78.
402 RA R27/80.
403 RA R27/79.
404 RA R27/81.
405 EP: 6/2, letter from ERI to Esher, 26 April 1906.
406 RA R27/21.
407 RA R27/22.
408 Butler and Freeman, 119.
409 RA R27/65.
410 RA R27/67.
411 Lee, ii:451.
412 Wilson, 579.
413 CBP: Add Mss 52513/98.
414 Lee, ii:330.
415 Ibid, 331.
416 RA R27/100.
417 RA R27/102.
418 CBP: Add Mss 41207/146.
419 RA R27/105.
420 CBP: Add Mss 41207/166.
421 RA W50/89.
422 RA W51/22.
423 RA W51/37.
424 RA W51/79.
425 CBP: Add Mss 41208/1.
426 CBP: Add Mss 52513/67.
427 RA R27/91.
428 CBP: Add Mss 52513/67.
429 Lee, ii:457.
430 RA R27/114.
431 RA R27/116.
432 CBP: Add Mss 41207/154.
433 RA R27/118.
434 CBP: Add Mss 41207/156.
435 EP: 6/2, letter from ERI to Esher, 14 April 1906.
436 Lee, ii:459.
437 CBP: Add Mss 41207/136.
438 CBP: Add Mss 41207/141.
439 CBP: Add Mss 41207/143.
440 RA W39/121.
441 RA R27/108.
442 RA R27/107.
443 Lee, ii:464.
444 RA W40/101.
445 RA W40/102.
446 EP: 10/49, letter from Knollys to Esher, 21 March 1907.
447 RA R27/30.
448 EP: 10/49, letter from Knollys to Esher, 21 March 1907.
449 CBP: Add Mss 41208/50.
450 RA R27/33.
451 CBP: Add Mss 41208/1.
452 RA R27/28.

453 Wilson, 540.
454 Lee, ii:468.
455 Wilson, 511.
456 RA Add C7:
Letter from
Ponsonby to
Gladstone, 13
August 1909.
457 RA Add C7:
Letter from
Davidson to
Knollys, 15
September 1909.
458 CBP Add Mss
41208/74.
459 RA W5/66.
460 RA W5/68.
461 Lee, ii:386–7.
462 Ibid, 387.
463 RA W5/69.
464 RA W5/70.
465 CBP: Add Mss
41208/3.
466 RA R28/7.
467 CBP: Add Mss
41208/61.
468 CBP: Add Mss
41208/11.
469 EP: 2/10, Journal,
10 December
1905.
470 EP: 2/10, Journal,
12 December
1905.
471 RA W20/84.
472 RA W20/85.
473 RA W20/86.
474 RA W48/83.
475 EP: 6/2, letter
from ERI to
Esher, 3 April
1906.
476 EP: 2/10, Journal,
5 December 1907.
477 EP: 10/49, letter
from Knollys to
Esher, 14
December 1907.
478 EP: 6/2, letter
from ERI to
Esher, 11 April
1908.
479 Lee, ii:525.
480 Ibid.
481 RA W49/25.
482 Lee, ii:528.
483 RA W49/93.
484 RA W51/73.
485 RA W52/14.
486 RA W52/38.
487 RA W52/47.
488 RA W52/48.
489 CBP: Add Mss
41208/128.
490 RA W51/69.
491 RA W51/85.
492 RA Add C7:
Letter from
Hardinge to the
King, 24 October
1905.
493 Trevelyan II, 183.
494 RA W49/66.
495 Lee, ii:569.
496 RA W49/20.
497 RA W50/24.
498 HP: Vol 9, letter
from Hardinge to
ERI, 4 September
1907.
499 RA R28/97.
500 RA W41/27.
501 BP: Add Mss
49685/109.
502 Spender and
Asquith, i:195.
503 Rhodes James II,
463–4.
504 RA W52/84.
505 BL: Add Mss
56087/32.
506 Churchill, ii:211.
507 RA Add C7:
Telegram from
Davidson to
Knollys, 17 March
1908.
508 RA Add C7:
Letter from
Knollys to the
King, 17 March
1908.
509 RA R28/126.
510 RA Add C7:
Letter from
Knollys to the
King, 23 March
1908.
511 RA Add C7: Letter
from the King to
Knollys, 25 March
1908.
512 Ibid.
513 RA Add C7:
Letter from
Knollys to the
King, 23 March
1908.
514 RA Add C7:
Letter from

Knollys to the
King, 25 March
1908.
515 Magnus, 403.
516 St Aubyn, 411.
517 RA Add C7: Letter
from Asquith to
Knollys, 31 March
1908.
518 RA Add C7:
Letter from
Davidson to
Knollys, 30 March
1908.
519 RA R28/129.
520 RA R28/130.
521 RA W71/28.
522 RA Add C7:
Letter from
Bertrand Dawson
to Knollys, 1 April
1908.
523 Lee, ii:581.
524 RA R29/1a.
525 RA Add C7:
Letter from
Knollys to the
King, 17 March
1908.
526 RA Add C7: Note
of 10 April 1908.
527 Asquith S, 535.
528 BP: Add Mss
49685/109.
529 Magnus, 375.
530 RA W52/118.
531 RA W53/41.
532 Lee, ii:588.
533 Ibid, 588–9.
534 Nicolson I, 269.

535 RA W53/98.
536 RA W53/99.
537 RA W53/106.
538 RA W53/101.
539 RA W53/104.
540 RA Add C7:
Letter from
Asquith to
Knollys, 10 June
1908.
541 Spender and
Asquith, i:250.
542 Lee, ii:596.
543 Ibid, 606.
544 Ibid, 608.
545 EP: 6/12, letter
from ERI to
Esher, 19
February 1908.
546 RA W45/147.
547 RA W54/5.
548 RA W54/4.
549 RA W54/5.
550 RA W54/6.
551 Magnus, 410.
552 RA W54/11.
553 RA W54/15.
554 RA W54/6.
555 RA W54/71.
556 Ibid.
557 RA W54/70.
558 Lee, ii:633.
559 RA W54/93.
560 RA R29/53.
561 RA X22/53.
562 Spender and
Asquith, i:247.
563 RA R29/54.
564 RA W54/110.
565 RA W54/99.

566 RA W54/116.
567 RA W54/119.
568 RA W54/155.
569 RA Add C7:
Letter from
Hardinge to
Knollys, 20 July
1909.
570 Lee, ii:651.
571 Spender and
Asquith, i:231.
572 RA R29/58.
573 RA R29/58a.
574 RA R29/66.
575 RA R29/68.
576 Wilson, 499.
577 RA R29/44.
578 RA W54/16.
579 RA W41/60.
580 EP: 10/50, letter
from Knollys to
Esher, 29 August
1908.
581 RA R29/76.
582 RA R29/79.
583 RA R29/80.
584 RA R29/82.
585 RA W54/143.
586 Lee, ii:673.
587 RA W54/145.
588 RA W54/162.
589 RA W54/57.
590 RA R29/94.
591 RA X20/51.
592 Lee, ii:661.
593 Jenkins I,190.
594 Lee, ii:661.
595 Ibid, 662.
596 Jenkins I,192.
597 Magnus, 442.

598 RA R30/55.
599 Magnus, 443.
600 Lee, ii:688.
601 RA X5/32.
602 RA R30/4.
603 RA R30/7.
604 RA R30/26a.
605 Lee, ii:665.
606 RA R30/44.
607 RA R30/45.
608 Magnus, 430.
609 Ibid, 430–1.
610 Ibid, 431.
611 Grigg, 208.
612 Jenkins II, 95.
613 Grigg, 210.
614 Magnus, 431.
615 Grigg, 211.
616 EP: 6/2, letter from ERI to Esher, 14 August 1909.
617 St Aubyn, 421–2.
618 RA W66/90.
619 EP: 10/51, letter from Knollys to Esher, 28 September 1909.
620 Lee, ii:667.
621 Magnus, 436.
622 Spender and Asquith, i:257.
623 Grigg, 221.
624 BP: Add Mss 49685/119.
625 EP: 6/2, letter from ERI to Esher, 13 October 1909.
626 Sommer, 231.
627 RA R30/65.
628 Asquith M, ii:126.
629 The Times, 1 December 1909.
630 EP: 10/51, letter from Knollys to Esher, 8 November 1909.
631 EP: 10/51, letter from Knollys to Esher, 13 November 1909.
632 The Times, 1 December 1909.
633 RA W41/101.
634 Lee, ii:669.
635 RA W41/102.
636 EP: 10/51, letter from Knollys to Esher, 2 December 1909.
637 Spender and Asquith, i:261.
638 Ibid.
639 EP: 10/51, letter from Knollys to Esher, 29 December 1909.
640 RA W41/105.
641 EP: 10/51, letter from Knollys to Esher, 29 December 1909.
642 RA Add C7: Letter from Sandars to Knollys, 14 January 1910.
643 Esher, ii:440.
644 Ibid, 442.
645 RA W41/108.
646 RA R30/89.
647 RA R30/93.
648 EP: 10/51, letter from Knollys to Esher, 12 February 1910.
649 RA R30/92.
650 RA R30/101.
651 RA R30/84.
652 Lee, ii:700.
653 Sommer, 230.
654 RA Add C7: Letter from Hardinge to Knollys, 22 March 1910.
655 Lee, ii:703.
656 RA X23/29.
657 EP: 10/51, letter from Knollys to Esher, 3 April 1910.
658 RA XII/28.
659 Ibid.
660 Ibid.
661 St Aubyn, 431.
662 EP: 10/51, letter from Knollys to Esher, 17 April 1910.
663 Magnus, 454.
664 RA Add C7: Letter from the King to Knollys, 16 April 1910.
665 RA X23/29.
666 Lee, ii:711.
667 Jenkins I, 211.
668 RA W55/109.

669 RA W41/112.

670 Pope-Hennessy, 114.

671 RA Add C7: Memorandum from Asquith to King George V, 30 December 1910.

672 Pope-Hennessy, 115.

AFTERMATH

1 DNB, 594.

2 BP: Add Mss 49685/130.

3 BP: Add Mss 49685/142.

4 BP: Add Mss 49685/147.

5 BP: Add Mss 49685/161.

6 BP: Add Mss 49685/163.

7 BP: Add Mss 49685/170.

8 Hansard (Commons), 11 May 1910, cols 794–5.

9 Ibid, col 799.

10 Ibid, col 800.

11 Hansard (Lords), 11 May 1910, col 828.

12 Chamberlain, 269.

13 Lee, ii:725.

14 Nicolson II, 130n.

INDEX

Note: Abbreviations used in the index are – AJB for Arthur Balfour; C-B for Henry Campbell-Bannerman; ERI for King Edward VII (at all stages of his life); FO for Foreign Office; FS for Foreign Secretary; GRI for King George V; WG for William Ewart Gladstone; HoC for House of Commons; HoL for House of Lords; PM for Prime Minister; PoW for Prince of Wales; Sal. for the 3rd Marquis of Salisbury; QRI for Queen Victoria. *Ill.* indicates an illustration.

Arch, Joseph 61

Argentina 171

armaments 232

army: reforms (*1880s* 56–8), (*1900*
83–4), (under ERI 88, 181),
(*1903–5* 185–93), (*1907* 217); *1900*
82–3; in Boer war 121; colonial
garrisons 238; courts–martial
152–3, 237; expenditure 213,
238–9; Guards 189; honours 128;
territorial 236; training 225, 238

Army Council 187, 188

Arnold–Forster, Hugh 182–3, 186,
188–94, 236

Arthur, Prince 22

Asquith, Herbert Henry, 1st Earl of
Oxford and Asquith: in C-B's
administration 204, 205–6, 207–8,
223; during C-B's final illness
245–6, 247–50; on C-B's
resignation 250–1; PM, *1908–9*
222, 233, 255, 263, 265–9, 270–1,
272–8, 281–6; calls election 286–8;
PM, *1910* 288–96, 304, 305;
relations with ERI 278, 301–2;
obituary tribute to ERI 301–2; and
GRI 296–7; *1910–14* 307

Asquith, Margot 289

Australia 82, 101

Austria: and Treaty of Prague 38;
Kaiser in, *1888* 69–70; and
Macedonia 168, 169; and Prussia
15; Austro–Prussian war 70; and
Russia, *1902* 154; *1908* annexations
260–5

Bagehot, Walter: *The English
Constitution* 86–97, 215, 307

Baghdad railway 134, 262

Bagot, Lord 115

Baldwin, Stanley 203

Balfour, Arthur James, 1st Earl of:
character and career 139–40;
relations with ERI 140, 163–4, 165;
on death of QRI 101–2; Leader of
HoC, *1901–2* 101–2, 103, 107, 109;
PM, *1902–5* 94, 95, 102, 103,
113–14, 130, 131, 139–40, 146, 152,
158–61, 163–6, 171, 173, 174–5,
179–95, 213, 214; and Lansdowne
106; and honours system 127,
194–5; and Garter for Shah of
Persia 95, 147–52; Cabinet
resignations 92, 179–81; and army
reform 185–94; *1904* collapse of
government 196–9; resigns 198–9,
203–4; and Curzon 199–203; and
Esher 197–8, 211; *1907* 251; in
1909 crisis 280, 281, 282, 283,
287–8; *1910* 293, 294, 304, 305;
obituary tribute to ERI 302; and
GRI 306; and *DNB* entry for ERI
299–303

Balfour, Lady Frances 274

Balmoral 49–50, 184, 207, 212,
244–5, 279, 280

Baltic fleet 175–6, 177

Baring, Sir Evelyn, Earl Cromer
208, 241, 267

Barrington, Sir Eric 159–60

Beaconsfield, 1st Earl of *see* Disraeli

Beauchamp, Lord 235

Beck, Edmund 60

Belgium 15

Belgrade 169–70

Benckendorff, Alexander, Count 171,
172, 175, 252

Beresford, Charles de la Poer, 1st
Baron 39–40,
64–5, 72

Berlin: *1866* 12; *1880s* 41; *1878*
Congress of 34, 35, 37–8, 40, 43;

prime ministerial office 120;
appointment, kissing hands' 204;
conferring of honours 114, 285;
peer as 306
Privy Council 108, 125; oath 215;
ERI 's membership 23; *1903*
meeting 185
Protestant church 109–10, 158–60,
271–3
Prussia 12–13, 15; war with France
15–17, 18; 200 years celebration
84; *see also* Germany
Pulitzer, Joseph 80

quarantine for dogs 129

radicalism 47, 221
Radolin, Count von 162
railways 78
Rayner, Horace 112–13
Redmond, John 292, 295
Reform Acts 99, 214; *1832* 90, 281;
1867 10, 91, 98; *1884* 48–9, 91, 280
Reid, Sir Robert 221
religious instruction 228
Rennell, Reginald 127
Repington, Col. Charles, à Court
250
republicanism: English 26–7, 47;
French 17–18, 40, 89
rifle shooting 225
Ripon, George Frederick Samuel
Robinson, 1st Marquis of 248, 272,
273
Ritchie, Charles 179, 180
Roberts, Frederick, 1st Earl 84, 128,
152, 187, 192
Roebuck, John 121
Roman Catholic church 108–10,
158–62, 271–3
Rome 158–62

Rosebery, Archibald Primrose, 5th
Earl of: *1873* 9; 1881 46; *1884* 49;
FS, *1886* 53; FS, *1892–5* 63, 75,
76–7; PM 57–8, 77, 99, 179; *1901*
105, 117; and *entente cordiale* 166;
1905 203, 206; *1907* 246
Rothschild, Ferdinand 78, 254
Royal Archives 100
Royal Commissions 9, 59–62; on
aged poor 61–2; on Boer war
120–1; on divorce 274; honours for
188; on housing 59–61; on
industrial relations 61; on tariff
reform, proposed 179; women
serving on 274
Royal Household appointments 9,
114–15, 127, 235
Royal Navy: *1903*, Firth of Forth
naval base; *1907* 223;
Dreadnoughts 223, 256, 257–8,
270; *1908* 256–8, 270; *1909* 270–1
royalty: Bagehot on 92
Rozhdestvensky, Admiral 175
Ruskin, John 89
Russell, John, 1st Earl 95, 96
Russell, Lord Odo (see Ampthill)
Russia: *1866–78* 14, 32–4; *1880s–90s*
42, 73–6; R. Churchill visits 66,
74; ERI visits 75; and Macedonia
168–9, 260; *1901* 105; *1900s*
alliances 132, 135, 141, 146, 151,
153, 154, 162, 170–7; war with
Japan 171, 172–6, 189–90, 261;
North Sea incident 175–6;
revolution 176, 242; relations with
England *1905–7* 241–4; *1908* 252–5,
261–3

Salisbury, Robert Cecil, 3rd Marquis
33; FS *1878–85* 18, 30, 31, 34,
37–8, 43, 50, 60–1; Sec. of State

Turkey: *1876* 32–3; *1877* 14; and
Congress of Berlin 34–5, 37, 43,
167–8; and Crete 43, 262; *1903–5*
167–9, 260, 261; Sultan 141, 142,
146; *1908* 260, 261–4; GCB
proposed for Grand Vizier 268
Tweedmouth, Edward, 2nd Baron
219–20, 248, 257

Unionists 68; *1885* 77; *1909* 275–6,
280, 281, 283; in *1910* election
288–9; subsequently 295, 303; *see
also* Liberal Unionists
United States of America: ERI visits,
1860 6; policy, *1890*s 80–1

Venezuela 80
Victoria, Queen: as mother 4;
attitude to ERI 5, 6, 7, 8–9, 11,
12, 13–14, 19, 20, 21, 22–6, 27–8,
33–4, (and ERI 's tour, *1875*), 36;
40, 50–3, 55, 61, (consults ERI
102); after death of Albert 6–7, 11,
90, 98; as monarch 2, 6–7, 86, 87,
90–1, 92–3, 94, 95–6, 99, 102, 111,
190–1, 214–15, 280; opening
Parliament 107; and Disraeli 9–10,
11, 21, 52; and WG 22–6, 44–5,
46, 49–50, 51–3, 56, 111; Empress
of India 30–1; after *1880* election
44–5, 46; and *1882* government
47–8; and Dilke 47–8; in *1885*
crisis 49–50; and *1885* government
63; and R. Churchill 66; and
Kaiser, *1888–9* 69–71; and
grandson Eddy 73; 173; jubilees
168, 309; death 84–5, 98, 101, 114;
papers archived 100; letters
published 215
Victoria, Princess, 'Vicky', later
Empress Frederick of Germany,

12, 15, 132; on death of husband
68–9; death 134
Victoria, Princess (daughter of ERI)
131
Vienna 69–70, 71–2, 260–1, 265
votes for women 232–3, 255, 266–7,
304

Waldersee, Count 134
Wallace, Alfred 266
War Office: appointments 56–7, 63,
83–4, 181–3, 186, 194, 236, 238;
and army reforms 186–94; courts-
martial 152–3, 237; and monarch
189, 209; name 187
Washington embassy 223–4
water supplies 59
West, Sir Algernon 53, 54
whisky duties 293
Whit Monday holiday 128
William I, Kaiser 68–9
William II, Kaiser: *1864* 13; *1885* 42;
1887 74; *1888*, accession 19, 68–70;
1889 71–2; *1890*s 80; *1895* 78; *1900*
82–3, 84; on death of QRI 84–5,
105; *1901* 132–5; *1902* 136–8; in
England 138; *1903* 162; *1904*, meets
ERI 174; *1905* 177–8; *1906* 239,
242; visits England *1907* 240–1;
1908 255–60, 262, 263; meets ERI
258–60; *1909* 269–70; relations
with ERI 69–72, 308
William IV, King of England 87,
281, 296–7
Windsor Castle 18, 100, 239, 289,
290
Witte, Count 242
Wolseley, Field Marshal Viscount
(General Sir Garnet): and Egypt
40; and army reform 56–7; and
Boer war 82; *1900* 83, 84; envoy
105–6